SHIPS and AIRCRAFT
of the U.S. FLEET

Ninth Edition

Compiled by

John S. Rowe

and

Samuel L. Morison

The SHIPS and AIRCRAFT of the U.S. FLEET

NAVAL INSTITUTE PRESS
Annapolis, Maryland

Library of Congress Catalog Card Number: 65-20822

ISBN: 0-87021-638-4

FOREWORD

Everyone who served in the United States Navy in World War II, and thousands more who loved the Navy, will remember that little paper-bound book which in small compass told the dimensions, armament, and other facts about every ship or small craft in commission, or plane type, with pictures. It was edited by James Fahey, and entitled *The Ships and Aircraft of the U.S. Fleet*. The first edition was published in 1939 and five more followed before the war was crowned with victory. Familiarly, this publication was referred to by sailors as "The Little Black Book." How many disputes it settled and fights it prevented over warships' characteristics I could not guess; but it was always *the* authority that settled such matters.

Here is the ninth edition of that famous compendium which has been compiled and edited by my grandson, Lieutenant (j.g.) Samuel L. Morison, USNR, and John S. Rowe. Navy buffs will find it as useful as the first, with several new features: (1) a more accurate breakdown by classes; (2) more data about individual ships; (3) list of ships disposed of, renamed, and reclassified since the last edition, arranged chronologically; (4) former U.S. Navy ships now in National Defense Reserve Fleet, with the type of each ship noted, and date and place where they are laid up. Don't despise these old buckets! Most of them will be out there "shooting" in the next war.

Here you will find all the World War II and earlier ships that are still in commission, and every new one completed, or building, in 1971. Many things will surprise you. For instance, of those once queens of the sea the "battlewagons," only five remain afloat in the world, and four of these are American. You may also shed a few tears for the gallant cruisers. All that are still using the now old fashioned "fossil fuel" (oil) are scheduled for the scrap heap during this decade.

The remaining World War II destroyers are also on the skids. No fewer than 29 are now being used for naval reserve training; but all are in the book, including that gallant *Allen M. Sumner* class which took the rap of the kamikazes off Okinawa. Here you will find all the new guided-missile frigates. How the meaning of *frigate* has evolved during four centuries from the Spanish *fragata*! Did you know that the old destroyer escorts are now called ocean escorts, or radar picket escort ships? Admiral King said of one of them, which accounted for six Japanese submarines in ten days, "There will always be an *England* in the U.S. Navy" – and there still is one, DLG-22.

Submarines, both nuclear and conventionally powered, take up many very interesting pages; our underwater navy now numbers more than the surface navy did sixty years ago! The authors do not neglect patrol craft, of which no fewer than 1094 of the riverine type were especially built or converted for Vietnam war service. Amphibious warfare assault transports, cargo, and command ships follow, including the new class of fire support ships named after rivers, old LSMRs and an IFS redesignated. The Landing Ship Dock, with a well-deck in its belly for landing craft, is still with us, as is the indispensable LST. The book concludes with miscellaneous auxiliaries and the Coast Guard.

The Navy is ships, and ships are the Navy. This obvious truth needs perhaps to be restated once in a while. To the sailor, his ship is something akin to his family, but different; to be confined with other men between steel walls for weeks – or, in the case of Arctic Submarines, months – creates a special relation of *shipmate* to which there is nothing quite comparable. And for the ship herself, although you may refer to her as "that old bucket," "crate," or whatnot when on board, you entertain an abiding sentiment, even affection. The naval aviators feel the same about their aircraft, although they share their allegiance to the squadron. That is why we all want a book like *Ships and Aircraft of the U.S. Fleet*.

Samuel Eliot Morison
Rear Admiral, USNR (Retired)

PREFACE

It is with deep pride and some apprehension that the editors and compilers of *Ships and Aircraft of the U.S. Fleet*, offer the ninth edition. We realize that no one can surpass the expertise, knowledge, and technique that the former editor, Mr. James C. Fahey, put into the first eight editions.

This edition has been greatly revised and modified for the purpose of making it simpler and easier for the average reader to understand. However, the basic format is unchanged. In the main text is listed the state of the United States Navy and Coast Guard in the spring of 1971. On the last pages of this edition will be found an addenda that updates the main text to September 1971. All facts and statistics are from official unclassified naval records, the editors own libraries, preceding editions of *Ships and Aircraft*, and in some cases the latest editions of *Weyer's Warships of the World* and *Jane's Fighting Ships*. A key to abbreviations and symbols used throughout this edition can be found in the glossary in the back of the book.

To thank everyone who helped in this edition would require several pages in itself, but we feel that a few have to be mentioned by name because of their service "above and beyond the call of duty": Rear Admiral Samuel E. Morison, USNR (Retired) who started us both on our quest for more knowledge about the Navy, for his encouragement and advice; Rear Admiral Ernest M. Eller, USN (Retired), former director, Division of Naval History, for his permission to use the resources of the Naval History Division; Commander Clayton Johnson, USN (Retired), Head of the Ships Histories Section, Division of Naval History, for his patience in putting up with the editor's almost constant queries and for his kind permission to use his files; Mr. John Reilly, naval historian par excellence; Mr. Norman Polmar, editor of the United States Section of the annual *Jane's Fighting Ships*, for his advice in preparation of the final manuscript; Mr. Ed Neurenberg, staff member of the MSC magazine, *Sealift*, for his assistance with MSC ships; Mr. Adrian Van Wyen, former historian for DCNO (Air), for his valuable assistance in assembling the aircraft section; Mr. Christian Bielstein, for his unending supply of illustrations for this edition; Mr. A. D. Baker, for his invaluable comments on portions of the completed manuscript; Captain P. G. Hannon, USN, head of the Ships Inactive Branch of the Navy Department; his secretary, Miss Denise Lariviere; Mr. Sydney Palevitz of the Foreign Military Sales section of the CNO's office; Mr. W. H. McEachern of Naval Air Systems Command; Lieutenant Commander R. E. Black of the Naval Ordnance Command; Mr. John Maffett, Naval Shipbuilding Scheduling Office; Mr. William Davis who relieved us of other commitments so we could concentrate our efforts on this edition; CHINFO for many illustrations; Philadelphia Navy Yard for many photographs of recent ships; commanding officers of countless ships for their interest and comments; numerous aircraft and shipbuilding companies; U.S. Force commanders and their staffs; Navy Department type desk people; and all the many unnamed people who were so very helpful in preparing this edition. To all of these people, we are deeply grateful.

All of the photographs unless otherwise credited are official U.S. Navy, Marine Corps, or Coast Guard photographs.

Comments, corrections, or additions are invited and should be sent to either one of the editors in care of the publishers.

John S. Rowe
Samuel L. Morison

CONTENTS

SHIPS and AIRCRAFT of the U.S. FLEET

1. WARSHIPS

A. Aircraft Carriers

By end-FY 1971 there were 26 aircraft carriers on the Naval Vessel Register; 15 rated as CVA and 11 as CVS. Active: 14 CVA and 3 CVS. In reserve: 1 CVA and 8 CVS (1 of which served as CVA). In addition, 2 CVAN were under construction and 1 was projected. All carriers were originally rated as CV or CVB (41–43, 59, 60) but were reclassified CVA on 10–1–52. See *Essex* class modernization table for reclassification dates to CVS.

Class	Number	No. in Class	Full Load Displ.	Length Overall	Max. Draft	Extreme Beam	Number & Type of Reactors/Boilers & Engines	Screws/ SHP	Max. Speed (Kts)	Accommodations[1] Officers	Enlisted	Guns/Missiles[2]	Planes
Nimitz	CVAN-68	2	91,400	1092′	37′8″	252′	2R/A4W/A1G(G.E.)	4/280,000	30+	569	5,717	3 BPDMS	90+
John F. Kennedy	CVA-67	1	87,000	1047′	35′11″	252′	8B(F&W)/4GT(West.)	4/280,000	30+	505	5,222	3 BPDMS	70+
Enterprise	CVAN-65	1	89,600	1102′	35′9″	252′	8R/A2W(West.)	4/280,000	30+	425	4,475	2 BPDMS	84+
Kitty Hawk	CVA-63	3	80,800	1046′	35′7″	249′	8B(F&W)/4GT(West.)	4/280,000	30+	428	4,154	2 twin TERRIER	70+
Forrestal	CVA-59	4	78,000	1040′	35′5″	252′	8B(B&W)/4GT(West.)	4/260,000	30+	442	4,678	4 5″/54 (CVA-60/62), 1 BPDMS (CVA-59)	70+
Midway	CVA-41	3	64,000	972′	35′5″	238′	12B(B&W)/4GT(West.)	4/212,000	30+	366	4,309	3 5″/54	70+
Antietam	CVS-36	1	38,000	888′	31′	154′	8B(B&W)/4GT(West.)	4/150,000	30+	340	2,887	12 5″/38	[3]
Hancock	CVA-19	3	44,700	899′	31′	192′	8B(B&W)/4GT(West.)	4/150,000	30+	354	3,170	4 5″/38	70+
Intrepid	CVS-11	3	42,000	899′	31′	192′	8B(B&W)/4GT(West.)	4/150,000	25+	340	2,952	4 5″/38	45+
Essex	CVS-9	7	40,600	890′	31′	196′	8B(B&W)/4GT(West.)	4/150,000	30+	340	2,887	4 5″/38	45+

[1] *Includes air wings.* [2] *Conventional armament may vary on individual ships.* [3] *Last employment as a training carrier eliminated this.*

2 NUCLEAR-POWERED ATTACK CARRIERS, *NIMITZ* CLASS

Name	Number	FY/SCB	Builder	Awarded	Keel	Launched	Commissioned	F/S	Homeport/Date/Decommissioned (D)
	CVAN-70	/102	Newport News	Deferred until FY 1973					
Dwight D. Eisenhower	CVAN-69	70/102	Newport News	6–29–70	8–15–70				
Nimitz	CVAN-68	67/102	Newport News	5–16–68	6–22–68				

New nuclear-powered class; heavier but shorter than *Enterprise*. Ships have 2 reactors vice CVAN-65's 8. Fuel core to last 13 years vice CVAN-65's 3.

1 CONVENTIONAL ATTACK CARRIER, *JOHN F. KENNEDY* CLASS

Name	Number	FY/SCB	Builder	Awarded	Keel	Launched	Commissioned	F/S	Homeport/Date/Decommissioned (D)
John F. Kennedy	CVA-67	63/127C	Newport News	4–30–64	10–22–64	5–27–67	9–7–68	AA	Norfolk/9–7–68

Originally requested as CVAN in FY 1960 but deferred because of cost. Equipped with NTDS. Last and largest fossil-fuel carrier built. First CVA to have constant steam pressure catapults. Stack angles to starboard to prevent gases from drifting over flightdeck and blinding landing pilots.

1 NUCLEAR-POWERED ATTACK CARRIER, *ENTERPRISE* CLASS

Enterprise	CVAN-65	58/160	Newport News	11–15–57	2–4–58	9–24–60	11–25–61	PA	Alameda/9–15–70

Largest warship in the world. Block superstructure and no stack provide unmistakable silhouette. Refueled at Newport News 1964–65 and 1969–70; last refueling used *Nimitz* type cores. Were to be 6 in class, but high costs held construction to 1. Two twin TERRIER launchers projected but not installed to hold down cost.

3 CONVENTIONAL ATTACK CARRIERS, *KITTY HAWK* CLASS

America	CVA-66	61/127B	Newport News	11–25–60	1–9–61	2–1–64	1–23–65	AA	Norfolk/1–23–65
Constellation	CVA-64	57/127A	NY Navy	7–23–56	9–14–57	10–8–60	10–27–61	PA	Bremerton/5–20–70
Kitty Hawk	CVA-63	56/127	NY Shipbuilding	10–26–55	12–27–56	5–21–60	4–29–61	PA	San Diego/7–3–70

Improved *Forrestal* class. CVA-63 first carrier armed with missiles. When 91% complete, CVA-64 caught fire in forward hangar deck; 40 died. Defective construction delayed CVA-63 by 22 months. CVA-66 replaced CVAN-65 in Atlantic.

4 CONVENTIONAL ATTACK CARRIERS, *FORRESTAL* CLASS

Independence	CVA-62	55/80	NY Navy	7–31–54	7–1–55	6–6–58	1–10–59	AA	Norfolk/1–10–59
Ranger	CVA-61	54/80	Newport News	2–3–54	8–2–54	9–29–56	8–10–57	PA	Alameda/6–1–67
Saratoga	CVA-60	53/80	NY Navy	7–23–52	12–16–52	10–8–55	4–14–56	AA	Mayport/12–9–68
Forrestal	CVA-59	52/80	Newport News	7–12–51	7–14–52	12–11–54	10–1–55	AA	Norfolk/10–1–55

First class of supercarriers; CVA-59 started with funds from cancelled *United States*. Became CVA 10–1–52; 61/62 authorized as CVAs. Fantails on CVA-59/60 are open; those on 61/62 are enclosed. To increase landing area, 120′ long extension added to port side of flight deck amidships. Forward 5″/54 guns and sponsons have been beached (sponsons retained CVA-61). NTDS installed on all CVAs, 59 on. CVA-59 caught fire 7–29–67 on Yankee Station; 134 died; ship lost all guns, has one BPDMS, forward.

3 CONVENTIONAL ATTACK CARRIERS, *MIDWAY* CLASS

Coral Sea	CVA-43		Newport News	6–14–43	7–10–44	4–2–46	10–1–47	PA	Alameda/1–25–60
Franklin D. Roosevelt	CVA-42		NY Navy	1–21–43	12–1–43	4–29–45	10–27–45	AA	Mayport/6–15–69
Midway	CVA-41		Newport News	8–27–42	10–27–43	3–20–45	9–10–45	PA	Alameda/1–31–70

All initially classified as CVs; to CVB on 7–15–43. First USN carriers with armored flight decks. CVA–42 laid down as *Coral Sea;* renamed 5–8–45. CVA-41 replaced CVA-14 on CVA list. All 3 originally in Atlantic.

MIDWAY CLASS MODERNIZATIONS

Number	Modernized at	FY/SCB	Decommissioned	Started	Recommissioned
CVA-41	PS Navy	55/110	10–14–55	9–1–55	9–30–57
CVA-41	SF Navy	66/101.66	2–15–66	2–15–66	1–31–70
CVA-42	PS Navy	54/110	4–23–54	5–1–54	4–6–56
CVA-43	PS Navy	57/110A	5–24–57	4–16–57	1–25–60

Second modernization caused CVA-41 to look like 43; CVA-41 centerline elevator moved to deck edge. Modernization of CVA-42 cancelled because of excessive cost and time for CVA-41. SCB-110 included angled deck, improved catapults, modified island, and enclosed bow. On CVA-42, a deck-edge elevator was substituted for centerline type in 1968–69 overhaul. Conventional armament reduced with each modernization.

1 CONVENTIONAL ANTISUBMARINE CARRIER, *ANTIETAM* CLASS

Name	Number	FY/SCB	Builder	Awarded	Keel	Launched	Commissioned	F/S	Homeport/Date/Decommissioned (D)
Antietam	CVS-36		Phil. Navy	8–7–42	3–15–43	8–20–44	1–28–45	AR*	Philadelphia/5–8–63 (D)

Originally in *Essex* class. Tested angled deck in early 1950s; first ship so fitted. Received no further modernization. Was training carrier until relieved by CVT-16 on 12–29–62.

3 CONVENTIONAL ATTACK CARRIERS, *HANCOCK* CLASS

Name	Number	FY/SCB	Builder	Awarded	Keel	Launched	Commissioned	F/S	Homeport/Date/Decommissioned (D)
Oriskany	CVA-34		NY Navy	8–8–47	5–1–44	10–13–45	9–25–50	PA	Alameda/11–22–66
Bon Homme Richard	CVA-31		NY Navy	8–7–42	2–1–43	4–29–44	11–26–44	PR*	Bremerton/7–2–71 (D)
Hancock	CVA-19		Beth., Quincy	9–9–40	1–26–43	1–24–44	4–15–44	PA	Alameda/10–1–56

CVA-34 originally ordered 8–7–42; suspended 10–13–45 when 40% complete. Redesigned, reordered, and completed to SCB-27A design. CVA-19/CVS-14 swapped names 5–1–43. CVA-34 has NTDS.

3 ANTISUBMARINE CARRIERS, *INTREPID* CLASS

Name	Number	FY/SCB	Builder	Awarded	Keel	Launched	Commissioned	F/S	Homeport/Date/Decommissioned (D)
Shangri-La	CVS-38		Norfolk Navy	8–7–42	1–15–43	2–24–44	9–15–44	AR*	Boston 7–30–71 (D)
Ticonderoga	CVS-14		Newport News	9–9–40	2–1–43	2–7–44	5–8–44	PA	San Diego/7–1–70
Intrepid	CVS-11		Newport News	7–3–40	12–1–41	4–26–43	8–16–43	AA	Quonset Point/8–1–69

CVS-38 and CVS-14 displaced from CVA list by CVA-67 and CVA-41. During CVA-41 modernization, CVS-11 was re-equipped as light attack carrier and deployed 3 times to Vietnam; resumed CVS role mid-1969. Before decommissioned, CVS-38 operated as light attack carrier, much like CVS-11. Class has steam catapults. CVS-14 was *Hancock*; renamed 5–1–43.

7 ANTISUBMARINE CARRIERS, *ESSEX* CLASS

Name	Number	FY/SCB	Builder	Awarded	Keel	Launched	Commissioned	F/S	Homeport/Date/Decommissioned (D)
Kearsarge	CVS-33		NY Navy	8–7–42	3–1–44	5–5–44	3–2–46	PR*	Long Beach/2–13–70 (D)
Bennington	CVS-20		NY Navy	12–15–41	12–15–42	2–26–44	8–6–44	PR*	Bremerton/1–15–70 (D)
Wasp	CVS-18		Beth., Quincy	9–9–40	3–18–42	8–17–43	11–24–43	AA	Quonset Point/6–15–68
Randolph	CVS-15		Newport News	9–9–40	5–10–43	6–29–44	10–9–44	AR*	Boston/2–13–69 (D)
Hornet	CVS-12		Newport News	9–9–40	8–3–42	8–30–43	11–29–43	PR*	Bremerton/6–26–70 (D)
Yorktown	CVS-10		Newport News	7–3–40	12–1–41	1–21–43	4–15–43	AR*	Boston/6–27–70 (D)
Essex	CVS-9		Newport News	7–3–40	4–28–41	7–31–42	12–31–42	AR*	Boston/6–30–69 (D)

Major difference between CVS-11 and CVS-9 classes: CVS-11 has steam catapults, CVS-9 has hydraulic catapults. CVSs with hydraulic catapults are being phased out. CVS-12 replaced on CVS list by CVS-14.

ESSEX CLASS MODERNIZATIONS

Number	To CVS	Modernization Yards	FY/SCB	Awarded	Completed	Fram II FY
9	3–8–60	PS Navy	49/27A	9–1–48	2–1–51	1962
9	—	PS Navy	55/125	3–1–55	3–1–56	—
10	9–1–57	PS Navy	51/27A	2–15–51	1–2–53	1966
10	—	PS Navy	55/125	7–31–54	10–15–55	—

MODERNIZATION DEFINITIONS

SCB-27A Catapults modified to handle 40,000-lb. (gross) planes, existing H4–1 catapults replaced with H-8 catapults, flight deck strengthened, 4 twin 5″/38 mounts removed from flight deck, elevator capacities and dimensions increased, special provisions for jet aircraft added, 3 ready rooms moved to below flight deck, an escalator installed between ready rooms and flight deck. The last CVs modernized under this program were

11	3–31–62	Newport News	52/27C	9–24–51	6–18–54	1965
11	—	NY Navy	57/125	1–24–56	5–2–57	—
12	6–27–58	NY Navy	52/27A	6–14–51	10–1–53	1965
12	—	PS Navy	56/125	8–24–55	8–15–56	—
14	10–21–69	NY Navy	52/27C	7–17–51	10–1–54	—
14	—	Norfolk Navy	56/125	11–7–55	4–1–57	—
15	3–31–59	Newport News	52/27A	6–22–51	7–1–53	1961
15	—	Norfolk Navy	55/125	3–1–55	2–12–56	—
16[5]	10–1–62	PS Navy	53/27C	7–21–52	9–1–55[1]	—
18	11–1–56	NY Navy	49/27A	9–1–48	9–28–51	1964
18	—	SF Navy	55/125	7–31–54	12–1–55	—
19	—	PS Navy	52/27C	7–17–51	3–1–54	—
19	—	SF Navy	56/125	8–24–55	11–15–56	—
20	6–30–59	NY Navy	51/27A	10–26–50	11–30–52	1963
20	—	NY Navy	55/125	7–31–54	4–15–55	—
31	—	SF Navy	53/27C	7–21–52	11–1–55[1]	—
33	10–1–58	PS Navy	50/27A	1–27–50	3–1–52	1962
33	—	PS Navy	56/125	1–27–56	1–31–57	—
34[2]	—	SF Navy	57/125A	9–8–57	5–29–59[2]	—
36	8–8–53	NY Navy	53/125	9–8–52	12–19–52[3]	—
38	6–30–69	PS Navy	52/27C	7–17–51	2–1–55[1]	—
[39][4]	8–1–57	Newport News	50/27A	8–18–50	9–19–52[4]	—

[1]*Authorization for SCB-27C also included 125 refit; done in 1 yard period.*
[2]*First completed to SCB-27A configuration.*
[3]*Fitted with angled deck (8° 09') to test British-invented concept. Installed in other carriers under SCB-27C/125 (deck angled much deeper).*
[4]*Replaced* Leyte *(CV-32) in 27A program, but did not receive 125 (cancelled 1957). CVS-39 did not receive enclosed bow in her 27A.* [5]*See section 5 (CVT-16).*

Artist's conception of USS *Nimitz* (CVAN-68). Note resemblance to CVA-59 and 63 class. 5–67. **Nimitz** *class.*

given a special weapon capability. Number of CVs modernized under this program limited to 9 because of development of steam catapults and appearance of advanced aircraft in fleet.

SCB-27C CV-11, 14, and 19 received a primitive 27C conversion. C-11 catapults were added, the flight deck was strengthened, #3 centerline elevator was replaced by deck-edge type with greater capacity, blisters were widened by 1' as compared to 27A. After these modifications, CV-11, 14, and 19 returned to the yards for the more advanced 27C conversion. This included an angled deck, hurricane bow, improved MK 7 arresting gear, number of deck pendants decreased by one-half, enlarged forward centerline elevator, air conditioning and sound proofing in island air spaces, enlarged deck lighting. On CV-16, 31, and 38, the blisters were increased 1' over the 27A enlargement. The SCB-27C also included addition of steam catapults in CV-16, 31, and 38, and larger elevators.

SCB-125 Included angled deck and new arresting gear.

SCB-125A Included addition of aluminium flight deck, 2 steam catapults, and heavier arresting gear than SCB-27C/125 ships.

FRAM II Sonar added, CIC remodeled, and other general improvements made.

USS *John F. Kennedy* (CVA-67) during sea trials. Note stack canting to starboard. 8–68. **John F. Kennedy** *class.*

USS *John F. Kennedy* (CVA-67).
John F. Kennedy *class.*

USS *Enterprise* (CVAN-65). Photo gives clear view of area damaged by fire in 1–69. 1–23–69.
Enterprise *class.*

USS *Forrestal* (CVA-59) as she appeared just before she caught fire on "Yankee Station," Gulf of Tonkin. Note two VIGILANTES aft of island and SKYWARRIOR on port catapult. 7–29–67. **Forrestal** *class.*

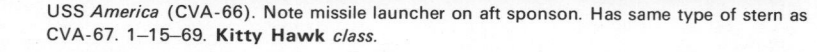

USS *America* (CVA-66). Note missile launcher on aft sponson. Has same type of stern as CVA-67. 1–15–69. **Kitty Hawk** *class.*

USS *Enterprise* (CVAN-65). 7–6–67. **Enterprise** *class.*

USS *Ranger* (CVA-61). 10–67. **Forrestal** *class.*

USS *Coral Sea* (CVA-43) about to commence flight operations. Note helicopter aloft, most planes aft, stack gas going over stern. 9–7–68. **Midway** *class.*

USS *Forrestal* (CVA-59) in early 1969. Two PHANTOMS are on forward catapults, with blast shields immediately aft of them. Note lack of forward sponsons. **Forrestal** *class.*

USS *Franklin D. Roosevelt* (CVA-42). 5–20–65. **Midway** *class.*

USS *Midway* (CVA-41) after modernization 6–16–70. **Midway** *class.*

USS *Wasp* (CVS-18). **Essex** *class.*

USS *Midway* (CVA-41) after modernization. 3–70. **Midway** *class.*

USS *Antietam* (CVS-36), our pioneer angled decker as training carrier with mothballed 5″ guns and empty gun tubs for 40 mm. Note BUCKEYE two-seat trainers and SKYRAIDERS aft. 4–61. **Antietam** *class.*

USS *Intrepid* (CVS-11) as light CVA. Note 17 SKYHAWKS flanked by four CRUSADERS and a lone SKYRAIDER aft 11–15–68. **Intrepid** *class.*

USS *Bennington* (CVS-20) testing the VTOL transport XC-142A. Note island details; typical of CVA-19 and CVS-9, 11 classes. 5–66. **Essex** *class.*

USS *Wasp* (CVS-18), our last active *Essex* class CVS, being replenished underway by *Elokomin* (AO-55). Note SEA KING helicopter aloft to guard against men overboard. 7–30–68. **Essex** *class.*

B. Surface Combatants

Battleships By end-FY 1971 there were 4 battleships on the NVR; all were in reserve. *New Jersey* (BB-62) was the last battleship in the world to see active service.

Class		No. in Class	Full Load Displ.	Length Overall	Max. Draft	Extreme Beam	Number & Type of Boilers/Engines	Screws/ SHP	Max. Speed (Kts)	Accommodations Officers	Enlisted	Armament
Iowa	BB-61	4	57,950	887′3″	38′	108′	8B(B&W)/4GT(G.E.)	4/212,000	33·5	95	2,270	9 16″/50, 10 twin 5″/38

4 BATTLESHIPS, *IOWA* CLASS

Name	Number	Builder	Awarded	Keel	Launched	Commissioned	F/S	Homeport/Date/Decommissioned (D)
Wisconsin	BB-64	Phil. Navy	6–12–40	1–25–41	12–7–43	4–16–44	AR*	Philadelphia/2–24–58 (D)
Missouri	BB-63	NY Navy	6–12–40	1–6–41	1–29–44	6–11–44	PR*	Bremerton/2–26–55 (D)
New Jersey	BB-62	Phil. Navy	7–1–39	9–16–40	12–7–42	5–23–43	PR*	Bremerton/12–17–69 (D)
Iowa	BB-61	NY Navy	7–1–39	6–27–40	8–27–42	2–22–43	AR*	New York/3–8–58 (D)

Last of the great dreadnoughts maintained as potential fighting ships. Until decommissioned in 1955, BB-63 was the only *Iowa* to see continuous service; served as NRT ship between wars. BB-62 recommissioned for Vietnam duty, deployed once, and decommissioned. Picked for recommissioning because BB-63 had speed limitation from grounding in 1950; BB-64 suffered an electrical fire in area of #1 and #2 16″ turrets during last inactivation overhaul and circuitry was not repaired; BB-61's electronic suite was out of date.

continued

BB-61 and 64 were cannibalized to expedite BB-62 recommissioning. Forward control tower of BB-62 remodeled to accommodate sophisticated ECM and ECCM gear. During Vietnam duty, original complement reduced to 70 officers and 1,556 enlisted men; reduction made possible by removal of all guns below 5" and their associated equipment.

Robert de Gast

USS *New Jersey* (BB-62). Note lack of any gun less than 5" and the modified forward gun control tower. **Iowa** *class.*

USS *New Jersey* (BB-62) after recommissioning. **Iowa** *class.*

USS *New Jersey* (BB-62) moving out of mothballs at Philadelphia Navy Yard. *Iowa* (BB-61) is beyond. Bow of *Wisconsin* (BB-64) appears astern of BB-62. **Iowa** *class.*

Cruisers By end-FY 1971, 23 cruisers of all types were on the NVR: 1 nuclear-powered cruiser, 3 guided missile cruisers, 6 guided missile light cruisers, and 13 heavy cruisers. Of the total, 9 were active. By the late 1970s, CGN-9 will be the only cruiser left on the NVR; all fossil-fuel cruisers are scheduled for scrapping by the late 1970s. No more cruisers are scheduled for construction.

Class	Number	No. in Class	Full Load Displ.	Length Overall	Max. Draft	Extreme Beam	Number & Type of Reactors/Boilers & Engines	Screws/ SHP	Max. Speed (Kts)	Accommodations Officers	Accommodations Enlisted	Armament
MISSILE CRUISERS												
Albany	CG-10	3	18,950	674′	33′6″	71′	4B(B&W)/4GT(G.E.)	4/120,000	30·4	86	1,186	2 5″/38, 2 twin TALOS launcher, 2 twin TARTAR launcher, 1 ASROC
Long Beach	CGN-9	1	16,247	721′3″	29′8″	73′3″	2R/C1W	2/80,000	30	79	1,081	2 5″/38, 1 twin TALOS launcher, 2 twin TERRIER launcher, 1 ASROC
Providence	CLG-6	3	15,200	610′	25′5″	66′	4B(B&W)/4GT(G.E.)	4/100,000	32	75	1,045	3 6″/47(CLG-6/7), 6 6″/47(CLG-8), 1 twin 5″/38(CLG-6/7), 3 twin 5″/38(CLG-8), 1 twin TERRIER launcher
Galveston	CLG-3	3	15,142	610′	25′	66′	4B(B&W)/4GT(G.E.)	4/100,000	30·6	125	1,270	6 6″/47(CLG-3), 3 6″/47(CLG-4/5), 1 twin 5″/38(CLG-4/5), 3 twin 5″/38(CLG-3), 1 twin TALOS launcher
HEAVY CRUISERS												
Des Moines	CA-134	3	20,950	716′5″	25′6″	76′4″	4B(B&W)/4GT(G.E.)	4/120,000	31·5	94	1,306	9 8″/55, 6 twin 5″/38, 8 twin 3″/50(CA-134 & 139), 2 twin 3″/50(CA-148)
"Oregon City"	CA-122	1	17,070	673′5″	26′	70′10″	4B(B&W)/4GT(G.E.)	4/120,000	33	129	1,840	9 8″/55, 6 twin 5″/38, 40 40mm(CA-122), 9 twin 3″/50(CA-124)
Boston	CA-69	2	17,820	674′	32′	71′	4B(B&W)/4GT(G.E.)	4/120,000	33	113	1,512	6 8″/55, 5 twin 5″/38, 8 3″/50, 2 twin TERRIER launcher
"Baltimore"	CA-68	7	17,350	674′9″	24′3″	70′8″	4B(B&W)/4GT(G.E.)	4/120,000	31	77	1,106	9 8″/55, 5 twin 5″/38(CA-73), 6 twin 5″/38(remainder), 6 twin 3″/50 (CA-73), 7 twin 3″/50(CA-68, 72, 75, 130, 133, 135), 48 40mm(CA-71 & 131)
LIGHT CRUISERS												
"Cleveland"	CL-55	0	14,400	610′1″	25′	66′4″	4B(B&W)/4GT(G.E.)	4/100,000	33	70	1,286	12 6″/47, 6 twin 5″/38, 28 40mm

3 CONVERTED HEAVY CRUISERS, *ALBANY* CLASS

Name	Number	Builder	Commissioned	Converted at	FY/SCB	Awarded	Started	Completed	Recommissioned	F/S
Columbus	CG-12	Beth., Fore River	6–8–45	PS Navy	59/173	9–23–58	6–1–59	11–30–62	12–1–62	AA
Chicago	CG-11	Phil. Navy	1–10–45	SF Navy	59/173	9–23–58	7–1–59	12–1–63	5–2–64	PA
Albany	CG-10	Beth., Fore River	6–15–46	Boston Navy	58/173	11–26–57	1–2–59	11–2–62	11–3–62	AA

Formerly ships of the *Oregon City* class (CG-10) and *Baltimore* class (CG-11/12) heavy cruisers. CA-123 to CG-10 on 11–1–58; CA-136 to CG-11 on 11–1–58; CA-74 to CG-12 on 9–30–59 vice CA-131. CG-10/11 fitted with NTDS. Under FY 1966, CG-10 given AAW modernization (SCB-002) at Boston Navy Yard. Decommissioned and conversion begun 2–1–67; recommissioned 11–9–68; conversion completed 6–30–69. All conventionally powered cruisers will be discarded in late 1970s.

1 NUCLEAR-POWERED GUIDED MISSILE CRUISER, *LONG BEACH* CLASS

Name	Number	FY/SCB	Builder	Awarded	Keel	Launched	Commissioned	F/S
Long Beach	CGN-9	57/169	Beth., Quincy	10–15–56	12–2–57	7–14–59	9–9–61	PA

Originally authorized as CLGN-160; to CGN-160 in 1957 and then to CGN-9 on 7–1–57. Two 5″/38s installed during first overhaul at Philadelphia to defend against low-flying subsonic aircraft and torpedo boats.

3 GUIDED MISSILE LIGHT CRUISERS, *PROVIDENCE* CLASS

Name	Number	Builder	Commissioned	Converted at	FY/SCB	Awarded	Started	Completed	Recommissioned	F/S
Topeka	CLG-8	Beth., Fore River	12–23–44	NY Navy	57/146	7–23–56	8–19–57	6–12–60	3–26–60	AR*
Springfield	CLG-7	Beth., Fore River	9–9–44	Beth., Quincy	57/146A	1–10–57	8–1–57	8–7–60	7–2–60	AA
Providence	CLG-6	Beth., Fore River	5–15–45	Boston Navy	57/146A	7–23–56	6–1–57	12–31–59	9–17–59	PA

All converted from *Cleveland* class light cruisers. CL-67 to CLG-8, CL-82 to CLG-6 vice CL-65, and CL-66 to CLG-7 on 5–23–57. CLG-6/7 fitted as flagships. CLG-7 conversion begun at Bethlehem, Quincy, but moved 3–22–60 to Boston Navy Yard for completion. Note CLG-8 and CLG-6/7 differences in statistics tables and CLG-3 class notes. CLG-8 decommissioned 6–5–69.

3 GUIDED MISSILE LIGHT CRUISERS, *GALVESTON* CLASS

Name	Number	Builder	Commissioned	Converted at	FY/SCB	Awarded	Started	Completed	Recommissioned	F/S
Oklahoma City	CLG-5	Cramp	12–22–44	Beth., SF	57/140A	1–10–57	5–21–57	8–31–60	9–7–60	PA
Little Rock	CLG-4	Cramp	6–17–45	NY Shipbuilding	57/140A	12–21–56	1–30–57	5–6–60	6–3–60	AA
Galveston	CLG-3	Cramp	—	Phil. Navy	57/140	1–4–56	8–15–56	11–2–60	5–28–58	PR*

All converted from *Cleveland* class. CLG-3 was originally to be CL-93, but never commissioned as such; suspended 6–26–46 when 91·2% complete. Reclassified CLG-93 on 2–4–56; to CLG-3 on 5–23–57 and commissioned. CL-92/91 became CLG-4/5 on 5–23–57; fitted as flagships in same way as CLG-6/7. CLG-3 and 8 are similar conversions as are CLG-4/7. USN officially breaks CLGs into 2 classes because of missile systems, not conversion configurations; see recognition notes with photos. CLG-3 decommissioned 5–25–70. CAG-1/2 now CA-69/70.

3 HEAVY CRUISERS, *DES MOINES* CLASS

Name	Number	Builder	Awarded	Keel	Launched	Commissioned	F/S	Decommissioned
Newport News	CA-148	Newport News	4–8–44	10–1–45	3–6–47	1–29–49	AA	
Salem	CA-139	Beth., Fore River	6–14–43	7–4–45	3–25–47	5–14–49	AR*	1–30–59
Des Moines	CA-134	Beth., Fore River	9–25–43	5–28–45	9–27–46	11–16–48	AR*	7–14–61

Largest, most powerful heavy cruisers. Have fully automatic 8″ guns. CA-148 extensively modified for Second Fleet flagship; deployed several times to Vietnam. CA-148 is last active all-gun cruiser in USN.

1 HEAVY CRUISER, "*OREGON CITY*" CLASS

Name	Number	Builder	Awarded	Keel	Launched	Commissioned	F/S	Decommissioned
Rochester	CA-124	Beth., Fore River	8–7–42	5–29–44	8–28–45	12–20–46	PR*	8–10–61
[Oregon City]	CA-122	Beth., Fore River	8–7–42	4–8–44	6–9–45	2–12–46	Struck	12–15–47

Improved *Baltimore* class. One sister now CG-10, another is CC-1. CA-122 retained original armament.

2 FORMER GUIDED MISSILE CRUISERS, *BOSTON* CLASS

Name	Number	Builder	Commissioned	Converted at	FY/SCB	Awarded	Started	Completed	Recommissioned	F/S	Decommissioned
Canberra	CA-70	Beth., Fore River	10–14–43	NY Shipbuilding	52/48	1–28–52	6–30–52	6–1–56	6–15–56	PR*	2–2–70
Boston	CA-69	Beth., Fore River	6–30–43	NY Shipbuilding	52/48	12–4–51	4–11–52	10–14–55	11–1–55	AR*	5–5–70

Originally of *Baltimore* class. CA-69/70 to CAG-1/2 on 1–4–52; world's first guided missile warships. After 8" turret and one 5" mount removed; two stacks trunked into one. Carry BW-1 TERRIER missile, one of earliest models but now obsolete. Reclassified back to original hull numbers 5–1–68. The 8" guns now considered the main armament.

7 HEAVY CRUISERS, "*BALTIMORE*" CLASS

Name	Number	Builder	Awarded	Keel	Launched	Commissioned	F/S	Decommissioned
Ex-Los Angeles	CA-135	Phil. Navy	8–7–42	7–28–43	8–20–44	7–22–45	PR*	11–15–63
Toledo	CA-133	NY Shipbuilding	8–7–42	9–13–43	5–6–45	10–27–46	PR*	5–21–60
[Fall River]	CA-131	NY Shipbuilding	8–7–42	4–12–43	8–13–44	7–1–45	Struck	10–31–47
Bremerton	CA-130	NY Shipbuilding	8–7–42	2–1–43	7–2–44	4–29–45	PR*	7–29–60
Helena	CA-75	Beth., Fore River	9–9–40	9–9–43	4–28–45	9–4–45	PR*	6–29–63
St. Paul	CA-73	Beth., Fore River	9–9–40	2–3–43	9–16–44	2–17–45	PR*	4–30–71
Pittsburgh	CA-72	Beth., Fore River	9–9–40	2–3–43	2–22–44	10–10–44	PR*	8–28–56
Quincy	CA-71	Beth., Fore River	7–1–40	10–9–41	6–23–43	12–15–43	PR*	7–2–54
[Baltimore]	CA-68	Beth., Fore River	7–1–40	5–26–41	7–28–42	4–15–43	Struck	5–31–56

14 of this class were completed; 2 became CGs and 2 exist as ex-CAGs. CA-71, 131 retain original armament. CA-68 and 71 have 2 cranes on fantail; remainder of class, 1. CA-73 lost 5" gun forward of bridge.

LIGHT CRUISERS, "*CLEVELAND*" CLASS

[Wilkes-Barre]	CL-103	NY Shipbuilding	8–7–42	12–14–42	12–24–43	7–1–44	Struck	6–9–47

This class was to consist of 39 ships, the largest number of cruisers ever completed to one design. Two were cancelled before the war, 9 were completed as CVLs, 1 was cancelled 8–11–45, 1 was completed as a CLG, and 26 were completed as light cruisers. Six additional ships still exist as CLGs. Two additional CL classes, the *Worcester* and *Fargo* classes, were disposed of. *Worcester* (CL-144) and *Roanoke* (CL-145) were largest CLs built for USN; only modern CLs with no 5" armament. The *Fargo* class encompassed 2 ships, which were modified 1-stack *Clevelands*. *Huntington* (CL-107) struck 1962 and *Fargo* (CL-106) struck 1970. *Wilkes Barre* (CL-103) was last light cruiser on NVR.

USS *Albany* (CG-10) in post AAW-modernization configuration. Note 5" guns at base of aft mack. Late 1968. **Albany** *class.*

USS *Newport News* (CA-148). Superstructure amidships, forward of stack, was added when modified for flagship duties. Note crane lying on fantail. 10–11–67.
Des Moines *class.*

USS *Long Beach* (CGN-9). 4–18–68. **Long Beach** *class.*

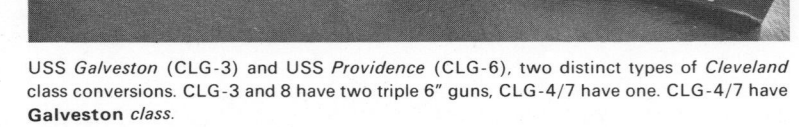

USS *Galveston* (CLG-3) and USS *Providence* (CLG-6), two distinct types of *Cleveland* class conversions. CLG-3 and 8 have two triple 6″ guns, CLG-4/7 have one. CLG-4/7 have
Galveston *class.*

USS *Long Beach* (CGN-9). 6–17–66. **Long Beach** *class.*

enlarged superstructures to provide staff/command spaces. CLG-3/5 have a short radar supporting platform in lieu of third mast, CLG-6/8 have 3 lattice masts.
Providence *class.*

Bethlehem Steel

USS *Oregon City* (CA-122) in her original rig. Note extensive AA batteries, two-tone painted hull, and small pennant number. Ship was laid up after less than 2 years' service. 1946. **"Oregon City"** *class.*

USS *Canberra* (CA-70). Note helicopter deck aft; none on sister CA-69. 8–12–68. **Boston** *class.*

USS *Providence* (CL-82) underway in preconversion rig (see photo of CLG-6 for post-conversion rig). 5–45. **Cleveland** *class.*

USS *St. Paul* (CA-73), last of the active *Baltimores.* Note absence of 5" gun forward of bridge. **Baltimore** *class.*

Destroyers By end-FY 1971 there were 2 DLGNs, 28 DLGs, 3 DLs, 29 DDGs, and 197 DDs on the NVR. Of these, 2 DLGNs, 28 DLGNs, 29 DDGs, and 96 DDs were active (including units under modernization). In addition, 4 DLGNs and 9 DDs were under construction. Construction for the immediate future includes 1 DLGN, 5 DDGs, and 21 DDs. Three DLs and 71 DDs are in reserve, 14 of which have been in reserve since the end of WW II and are virtually unfit for further naval service. 30 DDs serve as NRT ships.

Class	Number	No. in Class	Full Load Displ.	Length Overall	Max. Draft	Extreme Beam	Number & Type of Reactors/Boilers & Engines	Screws/ SHP	Max. Speed (Kts)	Accommodations Officers	Accommodations Enlisted	Armament
FRIGATES												
	DLGN-38	3	10,000	585′	29′6″	61′	2R/D2G(G.E.)	2/				2 5″/54, 2 dual TARTAR "D"/ASROC launcher
California	DLGN-36	2	10,150	596′	29′6″	61′	2R/D2G(G.E.)	2/				2 5″/54, 2 single TARTAR "D" launcher, 1 ASROC
Truxtun	DLGN-35	1	9,000	564′	31′	58′	2R/D2G(G.E.)	2/60,000	29	36	492	1 5″/54, 2 3″/50, 1 twin TERRIER/ASROC launcher
Belknap	DLG-26	9	7,940	547′	29′	55′	4B(B&W)/2GT(G.E.)	2/85,000	32·5	31	387	1 5″/54, 2 3″/50, 1 twin TERRIER/ASROC launcher
Bainbridge	DLGN-25	1	8,590	565′	25′5″	58′	2R/D2G(G.E.)	2/60,000	29	36	464	2 twin 3″/50, 2 twin TERRIER launcher, 1 ASROC
Leahy	DLG-16	9	7,800	547′	24′10″	55′	4B(B&W)/2GT(G.E.)	2/85,000	32·7	31	364	2 twin 3″/50, 2 twin TERRIER launcher, 1 ASROC
Coontz	DLG-9	10	5,800	513′	23′5″	53′	4B(B&W)/2GT(DeLaval)	2/85,000	33	28	347	1 5″/54, 2 twin 3″/50 (DLG-8, 10–13 only), 1 twin TERRIER launcher, 1 ASROC
"Mitscher"	DL-2	2	5,432	493′	26′	50′	4B(F.W.)/2GT(West.)	2/80,000	33·9	34	355	2 5″/54
Norfolk	DL-1	1	7,041	540′	27′	54′3″	4B(B&W)/2GT(G.E.)	2/80,000	32·5	42	498	4 twin 3″/70, 1 ASROC
DESTROYERS												
	DDG	5	8,000	563′	29′	55′	4 Gas Turbines	2/80,000	30+			1 or 2 5″/54, 1 twin TARTAR "D" launcher, 1 ASROC
Mitscher	DDG-35	2	5,155	494′	26′	50′	4B(C.E.)/2GT(G.E.)	2/80,000	32	29	349	2 5″/54, 1 single TARTAR launcher, 1 ASROC
Decatur	DDG-31	4	4,150	418′5″	22′	44′	4B(F.W.)/2GT(G.E.)	2/70,000	31	22	313	1 5″/54, 1 single TARTAR launcher, 1 ASROC
Charles F. Adams	DDG-2	23	4,500	437′	27′3″	47′	4B(B&W)/2GT(G.E.)	2/70,000	30	24	330	2 5″/54, 1 twin or single TARTAR launcher, 1 ASROC
Spruance	DD-963	9	7,100	559′11″	28′	54′	4 Gas Turbines	2/80,000	30+	270 total		2 5″/54, 1 BPDMS, 1 ASROC
Hull	DD-945	5	4,050	418′5″	22′2″	45′1″	4B(B&W)/2GT(G.E.)	2/70,000	32·5	22	306	3 5″/54, 1 twin 3″/50, 2 HEDGEHOG[2]
Forrest Sherman	DD-931	9	4,050	418′	22′	45′	4B(B&W)/2GT(West.)	2/70,000	34	23	315	3 5″/54, 1 twin 3″/50, 2 HEDGEHOG[2]
Carpenter	DD-825	2	3,459	391′	20′11″	41′	4B(B&W)/2GT(West.)	2/60,000	33	21	286	2 5″/38, 1 ASROC
Chevalier	DD-805	4	3,500	391′	21′5″	41′	4B(B&W)/2GT(G.E.)	2/60,000	30	21	275	3 twin 5″/38, 2 HEDGEHOG
Lloyd Thomas	DD-764	5	3,477	391′	21′5″	41′	4B(B&W)/2GT(G.E.)	2/60,000	32·8	23	282	2 twin 5″/38, 1 HEDGEHOG
Kenneth D. Bailey	DD-713	3	3,532	391′	20′	41′	4B(B&W)/2GT(G.E.)	2/60,000	31·5	22	322	3 twin 5″/38, 2 HEDGEHOG
Gearing	DD-710	74	3,512	391′	20′	41′2″	4B(B&W)/2GT(G.E.)	2/60,000	32·2	24	298	2 twin 5″/38, 1 ASROC
"English"	DD-696	9	3,234	376′	18′11″	41′4″	4B(B&W)/2GT(G.E.)	2/60,000	33	20	260	3 twin 5″/38, 1 or 2 twin 3″/50, 2 HEDGEHOG
Allen M. Sumner	DD-692	31	3,300	376′	21′	41′4″	4B(B&W)/2GT(G.E.)	2/60,000	32·5	19	276	3 twin 5″/38, 2 HEDGEHOG
La Vallette	DD-448	55	3,040	376′	20′	40′	4B(B&W)/2GT(G.E.)	2/60,000	35	24	299	4 or 5 single 5″/38, 3 twin 3″/50 (some still have 3–5 twin 40mm; some no 3″ or 40mm). Some, 5 21″ torpedo tubes.
"Radford"	DD-446	0	2,980	376′	19′6″	39′5″	2B(B&W)/2GT(G.E.)	2/60,000	35	21	271	2 5″/38, 1 WEAPON A
"Fletcher"	DD-445	0	2,976	376′	19′11″	39′5″	2B(B&W)/2GT(G.E.)	2/60,000	34·2	22	249	2 5″/38, 2 twin 3″/50, 1 WEAPON A
"Gleaves"	DD-423	0	2,525	348′4″	17′6″	36′1″	4B(B&W)/2GT(G.E.)	2/50,000	34	16	260	4 5″/38, 2 twin 40mm(ex-DMS have only 3 5″), 4–7 20mm, 5 21″ torpedo tubes
"Benson"	DD-421	0	2,575	347′10″	17′6″	36′1″	4B(B&W)/2GT(Beth.)	2/50,000	34	16	260	4 5″/38, 2 twin 40mm, 7 20mm, 5 21″ torpedo tubes

[1] *In addition to the armament listed, nearly all destroyers and frigates in service for the last decade carry, and have carried, two 12·75″ triple torpedo tubes for ASW homing torpedoes.*

[2] *DD-933, 937, 938, 940, 941, 943, 945, 948, 950 with ASW modernization: 2 5″/54, 1 ASROC.*

3 NUCLEAR-POWERED GUIDED MISSILE FRIGATES, *DLGN-38* CLASS

Name	Number	FY	Builder	Awarded	Commissioned	F/S
	DLGN-42					Canc.
	DLGN-41					Canc.
	DLGN-40	72	Newport News			Prod.
	DLGN-39	71	Newport News			Bldg.
	DLGN-38	70	Newport News			Bldg.

Class to be built under total package procurement; originally referred to as DXGN. To have 2 missile launchers for 2 systems vice 3 launchers for 2 systems in DLGN-36 class. DLGN-41/42 were to be authorized in FY 1973, but were cancelled 5–6–71.

2 NUCLEAR-POWERED GUIDED MISSILE FRIGATES, *CALIFORNIA* CLASS

Name	Number	FY	Builder	Awarded	Commissioned	F/S
South Carolina	DLGN-37	68/241.66	Newport News	6–13–68		Bldg.
California	DLGN-36	67/241.66	Newport News	6–13–68		Bldg.

Originally 3 ships projected, but 1 deferred in favor of DXGN. Improved DLGN-35; will have a double-ended missile system (dual TARTAR) as well as 1 gun forward and aft and pylon mast supports.

1 NUCLEAR-POWERED GUIDED MISSILE FRIGATE, *TRUXTUN* CLASS

Name	Number	FY	Builder	Awarded	Commissioned	F/S
Truxtun	DLGN-35	62/222	NY Shipbuilding	6–23–62	5–27–67	PA

Requested as DLG, but Congress authorized as DLGN. Power plant same as DLGN-25; weapon system and major electronic installations similar to DLG-26 class—some features different. Fitted with LAMPS 11–71. Has two fixed homing torpedo tubes.

9 CONVENTIONAL GUIDED MISSILE FRIGATES, *BELKNAP* CLASS

Name	Number	FY	Builder	Awarded	Commissioned	F/S
Biddle	DLG-34	62/212	Bath Iron	1–16–62	1–21–67	AA
Fox	DLG-33	62/212	Todd	1–16–62	5–28–66	PA
William H. Standley	DLG-32	62/212	Bath Iron	1–16–62	7–9–66	AA
Sterett	DLG-31	62/212	PS Navy	9–20–61	4–8–67	PA
Horne	DLG-30	62/212	SF Navy	9–20–61	4–15–67	PA
Jouett	DLG-29	62/212	PS Navy	9–20–61	12–3–66	PA
Wainwright	DLG-28	61/212	Bath Iron	5–18–61	1–8–66	AA
Josephus Daniels	DLG-27	61/212	Bath Iron	5–18–61	5–8–65	AA
Belknap	DLG-26	61/212	Bath Iron	5–18–61	11–7–64	AA

DLGN-35 based on this successful design. DLG-27/28 replaced DLGN-25 in Atlantic. First class to have combined ASROC/missile launchers. Class has NTDS. Fitted with LAMPS 11–71.

1 NUCLEAR-POWERED GUIDED MISSILE FRIGATE, *BAINBRIDGE* CLASS

Name	Number	FY	Builder	Awarded	Commissioned	F/S
Bainbridge	DLGN-25	56/189	Beth, Quincy	9–26–58	10–6–62	PA

Larger than WW II CLAA. First DD type with nuclear power. Has NTDS.

9 CONVENTIONAL GUIDED MISSILE FRIGATES, *LEAHY* CLASS

Name	Number	FY/SCB	Builder	Awarded	Commissioned	F/S
Reeves	DLG-24	59/172	PS Navy	12–8–58	5–15–64	PA
Halsey	DLG-23	59/172	SF Navy	12–5–58	7–20–63	PA
England	DLG-22	59/172	Todd	11–7–58	12–7–63	PA
Gridley	DLG-21	59/172	PS B & DD	11–7–58	5–25–63	PA
Richmond K. Turner	DLG-20	59/172	NY Shipbuilding	11–7–58	6–13–64	AA
Dale	DLG-19	59/172	NY Shipbuilding	11–7–58	11–23–63	PA
Worden	DLG-18	59/172	Bath Iron	11–7–58	8–3–63	PA
Harry E. Yarnell	DLG-17	59/172	Bath Iron	11–7–58	2–2–63	AA
Leahy	DLG-16	59/172	Bath Iron	11–7–58	8–4–62	AA

Specifically designed to serve as AAW screen for carriers, hence the double-ended missile configuration. AAW modifications underway for this class. Modernization program includes installation of NTDS, advanced communications, ECM, and sonar systems, AN/SPS-48 air-search radar (integrates with NTDS), and Mk 76, Mod 5 fire-control systems.

LEAHY CLASS AAW MODERNIZATIONS

Number	Converted at	FY/SCB	Awarded	Started	Recommissioned
24	Bath Iron	67/244	9–12–67	4–10–69	8–29–70
23	Bath Iron	71/244	7–15–70		
22	Bath Iron	67/244	9–12–67	4–10–70	6–26–71
21	Bath Iron	67/244	9–12–67	9–10–68	1–17–70
20	Bath Iron	71/244	7–15–70		
19	Bath Iron	71/244	7–15–70	11–10–70	
18	Bath Iron	67/244	9–12–67	11–10–69	1–16–71
17	Bath Iron	67/244	9–12–67	2–9–68	7–12–69
16	Phil. Navy	66/244	12–29–65	2–15–67	5–4–68

10 CONVENTIONAL GUIDED MISSILE FRIGATES, *COONTZ* CLASS

Name	Number	FY/SCB	Builder	Awarded	Commissioned	F/S
Preble	DLG-15	57/142	Bath Iron	10–26–56	5–9–60	PA
Dewey	DLG-14	57/142	Bath Iron	10–26–56	12–7–59	AA
William V. Pratt	DLG-13	57/142	Phil. Navy	7–23–56	11–4–61	AA
Dahlgren	DLG-12	57/142	Phil. Navy	7–23–56	4–8–61	AA
Mahan	DLG-11	56/142	SF Navy	11–18–55	8–25–60	PA
King	DLG-10	56/142	PS Navy	11–18–55	11–17–60	PA
Coontz	DLG-9	56/142	PS Navy	11–18–55	7–15–60	AA
MacDonough	DLG-8	56/142	Beth., Quincy	1–27–56	11–4–61	AA
Luce (ex-*Dewey*)	DLG-7	56/142	Beth., Quincy	1–27–56	5–20–61	AA
Farragut	DLG-6	56/142	Beth., Quincy	1–27–56	12–10–60	AA

Design based on *Mitscher* class DLs. DLG 6/8 originally authorized as new DL class; to DLG 11–14–56 and completed to *Coontz* design. DLG-10/11 and CVA-34 first ships to have NTDS. This class is only DLG class without "macks." Originally designed to have 5"/54 in ASROC position. Some ships were completed with nothing in "B" position; later backfitted with ASROC launcher when it became operational.

COONTZ CLASS AAW MODERNIZATIONS

Number	Converted at	FY/SCB	Awarded	Started	Recommissioned
15	Phil. Navy	68/243	2–29–68	1–31–69	5–23–70
14	Phil. Navy	69/243	8–22–68	11–24–69	3–13–71
12	Phil. Navy	72/243			
9	Phil. Navy	71/243	7–24–70	2–28–71	
7	Phil. Navy	70/243	11–1–69	2–28–70	5–22–71
6	Phil. Navy	66/243	10–13–66	5–1–68	9–13–69

All ships of this class are to be given AAW modernization similar to that for DLG-16 class. NTDS and updated fire-control radar/computer to be installed in addition to those changes listed in *Leahy* class notes. DLG-6 modernization contract originally awarded to Norfolk 12–29–65. Modernized ships lose their 3"/50 AA.

2 FRIGATES, "*MITSCHER*" CLASS

Name	Number	FY/SCB	Builder	Awarded	Commissioned	F/S	Decommissioned
Wilkinson	DL-5	48/5	Beth., Quincy	8–3–48	8–3–54	AR*	12–19–69
Willis A. Lee	DL-4	48/5	Beth., Quincy	8–3–48	10–5–54	AR*	12–69

Originally 4 ships of class completed. First postwar DDs and largest ever. Both had DASH/ASW refits 1960–62. In 1961 DL-5 received prototype SQS-26 bow-mounted sonar; DL-4 followed in 1966. Both twin 3"/70 and all WEAPON A have been removed. DL-4/5 originally laid down as DD-929/930.

1 FRIGATE, *NORFOLK* CLASS

Name	Number	FY/SCB	Builder	Awarded	Commissioned	F/S	Decommissioned
Norfolk	DL-1	48/1	NY Shipbuilding	11–17–48	3–4–53	AR*	1–15–70

Laid down as CLK-1; became DL-1 on 2–9–51. Hull resembles CLAA. Built to provide a rough-weather, long-range ASW capability. All 4 original WEAPON As removed; after ones replaced by ASROC launcher. Was employed as test ship for new ASW weapons.

5 GUIDED MISSILE DESTROYERS

Name	Number	FY/SCB	Builder	Awarded	Commissioned	F/S
	DDG					Proj.
	DDG					Proj.
	DDG					Proj.
	DDG					Proj.
	DDG					Proj.

Formerly known as DXG. This class and DD-963 class are of same design; DDG is the missile version. Equipment used in construction of DXGN/DXG/DD-963 classes will be standardized for economy, ease of maintenance, and interchangeability. To be built under total package procurement.

2 CONVERTED FRIGATES, *MITSCHER* CLASS

Name	Number	FY/SCB	Builder	Commissioned	FY/SCB	Converted at	Awarded	Started	Recommissioned	F/S
John S. McCain	DDG-36	48/5	Bath Iron	10–12–53	64/241	Phil. Navy	12–22–64	6–14–66	9–6–69	PA
Mitscher	DDG-35	48/5	Bath Iron	5–15–53	64/241	Phil. Navy	12–22–64	3–3–66	6–29–68	AA

Originally awarded as DD-927 (35) and DD-928 (36) on 8–3–48. To DL-2/3 on 2–9–51. Former sisters of DL-4/5. Reclassified from DL-2/3 to DDG-35/36 on 3–15–67. Missile system installed, electronics improved, and habitability upgraded. As DDGs, somewhat resemble DDG-31 class.

4 CONVERTED DESTROYERS, *DECATUR* CLASS

Name	Number	FY/SCB	Builder	Commissioned	FY/SCB	Converted at	Awarded	Started	Recommissioned	F/S
Somers	DDG-34	56/85A	Bath Iron	4–3–59	64/240	SF Navy	12–22–64	3–30–66	2–10–68	PA
Parsons	DDG-33	56/85A	Ingalls	10–29–59	64/240	LB Navy	12–22–64	6–30–65	11–3–67	PA
John Paul Jones	DDG-32	53/85	Bath Iron	4–5–56	64/240	Phil. Navy	12–22–64	12–2–65	9–23–67	PA
Decatur	DDG-31	54/85	Beth., Quincy	12–7–56	64/240	Boston Navy	12–22–64	6–15–65	4–29–67	PA

Originally completed as ships of the *Forrest Sherman* class (DDG-31/32) and *Hull* class (DDG-33/34). DD-936 to DDG-31 on 9-15-66; DD-932, 949, and 947 to DDG-32/34 on 3–15–67. Class is easily identified by massive radar masts and ASROC just aft of #2 stack. DDG-31 became DDG after being damaged in a collision on 5–5–64; was less expensive to convert to DDG than repair as DD.

23 GUIDED MISSILE DESTROYERS, *CHARLES F. ADAMS* CLASS

Name	Number	FY/SCB	Builder	Awarded	Commissioned	F/S
Waddell	DDG-24	61/155	Todd, Seattle	11–3–60	8–28–64	PA
Richard E. Byrd	DDG-23	61/155	Todd, Seattle	11–3–60	3–7–64	AA
Benjamin Stoddert	DDG-22	60/155	PS B & DD	3–25–60	9–12–64	PA
Cochrane	DDG-21	60/155	PS B & DD	3–25–60	3–21–64	PA
Goldsborough	DDG-20	60/155	PS B & DD	3–25–60	11–9–63	PA
Tatnall	DDG-19	59/155	Avondale	7–21–59	4–13–63	AA
Semmes	DDG-18	59/155	Avondale	7–21–59	12–10–62	AA
Conyngham	DDG-17	59/155	NY Shipbuilding	7–21–59	7–13–63	AA
Joseph Strauss	DDG-16	59/155	NY Shipbuilding	7–21–59	4–20–63	PA
Berkeley	DDG-15	59/155	NY Shipbuilding	7–21–59	12–15–62	PA
Buchanan	DDG-14	58/155	Todd, Seattle	1–17–58	2–7–62	PA
Hoel	DDG-13	58/155	Defoe	1–17–58	6–16–62	PA
Robison	DDG-12	58/155	Defoe	1–17–58	12–9–61	PA
Sellers	DDG-11	58/155	Bath Iron	1–17–58	10–28–61	AA
Sampson	DDG-10	58/155	Bath Iron	1–17–58	6–24–61	AA
Towers	DDG-9	57/155	Todd, Seattle	3–28–57	6–6–61	PA
Lynde McCormick	DDG-8	57/155	Defoe	3–28–57	6–3–61	PA
Henry B. Wilson	DDG-7	57/155	Defoe	3–28–57	12–17–60	PA
Barney	DDG-6	57/155	NY Shipbuilding	3–28–57	8–11–62	AA
Claude V. Ricketts	DDG-5	57/155	NY Shipbuilding	3–28–57	5–5–62	AA
Lawrence	DDG-4	57/155	NY Shipbuilding	3–28–57	1–6–62	AA
John King	DDG-3	57/155	Bath Iron	3–28–57	2–4–61	AA
Charles F. Adams	DDG-2	57/155	Bath Iron	3–28–57	9–10–60	AA

DDG-2/9 originally ships of *Hull* class (DD-952/959). Became DDG-2/9 on 7–23–58. DDG-5 originally commissioned as *Biddle*; renamed 7–28–64. The DDG-2/14 group has the MK 11 double-rail missile launching system vice the MK 13 single-rail system of the DDG-15/24 group. DDG-20/24 have bow-mounted sonar and an anchor mounted in the bull nose instead of the port bow. DD-712 (now struck) was DDG-1 from 1956–1962. ILP construction: DDG-25/27 for Australia, DDG-28/30 for West Germany.

9 DESTROYERS, *SPRUANCE* CLASS

	DD-965	70	Ingalls	6–23–70		Bldg.
	DD-964	70	Ingalls	6–23–70		Bldg.
Spruance	DD-963	70	Ingalls	6–23–70		Bldg.

Class, projected at 30, is to replace current fleet DDs; formerly known as DX. Ships to be built under total package procurement. Will be first major USN ships to carry gas turbines, General Electric model LM 2500 (high temperature engine; 20,000 SHP). Contract for DD-966/971 awarded to Ingalls 1–15–71.

5 DESTROYERS, *HULL* CLASS

Turner Joy (ex-*Joy*)	DD-951	56/85A	PS B & DD	1–27–56	8–3–59	PA
Richard S. Edwards	DD-950	56/85A	PS B & DD	1–27–56	2–5–59	PA
Morton	DD-948	56/85A	Ingalls	1–27–56	5–26–59	PA
Edson	DD-946	56/85A	Bath Iron.	1–27–56	11–7–58	PA
Hull	DD-945	56/85A	Bath Iron	1–27–56	7–3–58	PA

9 DESTROYERS, *FORREST SHERMAN* CLASS

Mullinnix	DD-944	55/85	Beth., Quincy	10–23–54	3–7–58	AA
Blandy	DD-943	55/85	Beth., Quincy	10–23–54	11–26–57	AA
Bigelow	DD-942	55/85	Bath Iron	7–30–54	11–8–57	AA
Du Pont	DD-941	55/85	Bath Iron	7–30–54	7–1–57	AA
Manley	DD-940	55/85	Bath Iron	7–30–54	2–1–57	AA
Jonas Ingram	DD-938	54/85	Beth., Quincy	2–3–54	7–19–57	AA
Davis	DD-937	54/85	Beth., Quincy	2–3–54	2–28–57	AA
Barry	DD-933	53/85	Bath Iron	12–15–52	8–31–56	AA
Forrest Sherman	DD-931	53/85	Bath Iron	12–15–52	11–9–55	AA

Two classes with only minor differences; first postwar destroyers designed and built. DD-931 class originally consisted of 11 ships; DD-932 and 936 were converted to DDG-32 and 31 respectively. DD-945 class originally consisted of 7 ships; DD-947 and 949 were converted to DDG-34 and 33. All 18 ships were to be converted to DDG (31–48), but in fact only 4 were so modernized. See the following table. DD-951 renamed 7–26–57.

HULL AND *FORREST SHERMAN* CLASS ASW MODERNIZATIONS

Number	FY/SCB	Converted at	Awarded	Started	Recommissioned
950	68/222	LB Navy	5–2–69	3–2–70	1–15–71
948	68/222	LB Navy	5–2–69	9–30–69	8–17–70
943	67/222	Phil. Navy	5–17–68	1–18–69	5–2–70
942	68/222	Phil. Navy	5–17–68	(Cancelled 4–69)	
941	67/222	Boston Navy	3–27–69	5–26–69	5–9–70
940	68/222	Phil. Navy	5–17–68	2–1–70	4–17–71
938	68/222	Phil. Navy	5–17–68	4–30–69	8–1–70
937	68/222	Boston Navy	5–2–69	11–3–69	10–17–70
933	64/251	Boston Navy	12–22–64	1–5–67	4–19–68

Modernization contracts for DD-937, 941, 945, and 948 originally awarded to Philadelphia 5–17–68. Reawarded as indicated; DD-945 was cancelled (replaced by DD-950). DD-931, 942, 944/46, and 951 will not be modernized. Modernization data: 2 twin 3"/50 removed (forward one replaced by deckhouse), #2 5" gun replaced by ASROC, bridge enclosed, deckhouse added between stacks, forward radar mast's capacity increased, ASW torpedoes added below bridge on either side, and part of main deck enclosed.

2 DESTROYERS, *CARPENTER* CLASS (FRAM I, ex-DDE)

Name	Number	Builder	Awarded	Commissioned	F/S
Robert A. Owens	DD-827	Bath Iron	11–10–44	11–5–49	AA
Carpenter	DD-825	Consol. Steel	11–29–44	12–15–49	PA

Begun as ships of DD-710 class but completed and commissioned as hunter-killer destroyers (DDK). To DDE 3–4–50. To DD 6–30–62 after FRAM 1 completed.

4 DESTROYERS, *CHEVALIER* CLASS (FRAM II, ex-DDR)

Name	Number	Builder	Awarded	Commissioned	F/S
Perkins	DD-877	Consol. Steel	6–14–43	4–4–45	NRT
Everett F. Larson	DD-830	Bath Iron	6–14–43	4–6–45	PA
Benner	DD-807	Bath Iron	8–7–42	2–13–45	PR*
Chevalier	DD-805	Bath Iron	8–7–42	1–9–45	PA

First commissioned as fleet DDs. To DDR 3–18–49; extra mast and extra radar around #2 stack added. To DD in 1962. No trace of DDR configuration left. Had less extensive FRAM II than other ships. *Benner* decommissioned 11–20–70.

5 DESTROYERS, *LLOYD THOMAS* CLASS (FRAM II, ex-DDE)

Name	Number	Builder	Awarded	Commissioned	F/S	Decommissioned
Harwood	DD-861	Beth., San Pedro	6–14–43	9–28–45	NRT	
McCaffery	DD-860	Beth., San Pedro	6–14–43	7–26–45	AR*	late 1970
Norris	DD-859	Beth., San Pedro	6–14–43	6–9–45	AR*	12–4–70
Keppler	DD-765	Beth., SF	8–7–42	5–23–47	PA	
Lloyd Thomas	DD-764	Beth., SF	8–7–42	3–21–47	PA	

All commissioned as DDs; to DDE 3–4–50. Retained trainable HEDGEHOG in #2 position and did not receive ASROC. All reverted to DD on 6–30–62. Class has insufficient ASW capabilities. DD-861 to decommission late 1971.

3 DESTROYERS, *KENNETH D. BAILEY* CLASS (FRAM II, ex-DDR)

Duncan	DD-874	Consol. Steel	6–14–43	2–25–45	PR*	1–15–71
Goodrich	DD-831	Bath Iron	6–14–43	4–24–45	AR*	late 1969
Kenneth D. Bailey	DD-713	Fed., Kearny	8–7–42	7–31–45	AR*	4–2–70

Originally ships of DD-710 class. To DDR between 1949 and 1952. Last DDs to be classified as DDRs. All to DD 1–1–69. Three have been struck. Received FRAM II with VDS; no ASROC, no DASH.

74 DESTROYERS, *GEARING* CLASS (FRAM I)

Name	Number	Builder	Awarded	Commissioned	F/S	Former Designation
Meredith	DD-890	Consol. Steel	6–14–43	12–31–45	AA	
O'Hare	DD-889	Consol. Steel	6–14–43	11–29–45	AA	DDR
Stickell	DD-888	Consol. Steel	6–14–43	10–31–45	AA	DDR
Brinkley Bass	DD-887	Consol. Steel	6–14–43	10–1–45	PA	
Orleck	DD-886	Consol. Steel	6–14–43	9–15–45	PA	
John R. Craig	DD-885	Consol. Steel	6–14–43	8–20–45	PA	
Floyd B. Parks	DD-884	Consol. Steel	6–14–43	7–31–45	PA	
Newman K. Perry	DD-883	Consol. Steel	6–14–43	7–26–45	AA	DDR
Furse	DD-882	Consol. Steel	6–14–43	7–10–45	AA	DDR
Bordelon	DD-881	Consol. Steel	6–14–43	6–5–45	AA	DDR
Dyess	DD-880	Consol. Steel	6–14–43	5–21–45	NRT	DDR
Leary	DD-879	Consol. Steel	6–14–43	5–7–45	AA	DDR

Vesole	DD-878	Consol. Steel	6–14–43	4–23–45	AA	DDR
Rogers	DD-876	Consol. Steel	6–14–43	3–26–45	PA	DDR
Henry W. Tucker	DD-875	Consol. Steel	6–14–43	3–12–45	PA	DDR
Hawkins	DD-873	Consol. Steel	6–14–43	2–10–45	AA	DDR
Damato	DD-871	Beth., Staten Is.	6–14–43	4–27–46	AA	DDE
Arnold J. Isbell	DD-869	Beth., Staten Is.	6–14–43	1–5–46	PA	
Brownson	DD-868	Beth., Staten Is.	6–14–43	11–17–45	AA	
Stribling	DD-867	Beth., Staten Is.	6–14–43	9–29–45	AA	
Cone	DD-866	Beth., Staten Is.	6–14–43	8–18–45	AA	
Charles R. Ware	DD-865	Beth., Staten Is.	6–14–43	7–21–45	AA	
Harold J. Ellison	DD-864	Beth., Staten Is.	6–14–43	6–23–45	AA	
Steinaker	DD-863	Beth., Staten Is.	6–14–43	5–26–45	AA	DDR
Vogelgesang	DD-862	Beth., Staten Is.	6–14–43	4–28–45	AA	
Charles H. Roan	DD-853	Beth., Quincy	6–14–43	9–12–46	AA	
Leonard F. Mason	DD-852	Beth., Quincy	6–14–43	6–28–46	PA	
Rupertus	DD-851	Beth., Quincy	6–14–43	3–8–46	PA	
Joseph P. Kennedy Jr.	DD-850	Beth., Quincy	10–1–43	12–15–45	AA	
Richard E. Kraus	DD-849	Bath Iron	6–14–43	5–23–46	AA	AG-151
Robert L. Wilson	DD-847	Bath Iron	6–14–43	3–28–46	AA	DDE
Ozbourn	DD-846	Bath Iron	6–14–43	3–5–46	PA	
Bausell	DD-845	Bath Iron	6–14–43	2–7–46	PA	
Perry	DD-844	Bath Iron	6–14–43	1–17–46	AA	
Warrington	DD-843	Bath Iron	6–14–43	12–20–45	AA	
Fiske	DD-842	Bath Iron	6–14–43	11–28–45	AA	DDR
Noa	DD-841	Bath Iron	6–14–43	11–2–45	AA	
Glennon	DD-840	Bath Iron	6–14–43	10–4–45	AA	
Power	DD-839	Bath Iron	6–14–43	9–13–45	AA	
Sarsfield	DD-837	Bath Iron	6–14–43	7–31–45	AA	
George K. Mackenzie	DD-836	Bath Iron	6–14–43	7–13–45	PA	
Charles P. Cecil	DD-835	Bath Iron	6–14–43	6–29–45	AA	DDR
Herbert J. Thomas	DD-833	Bath Iron	6–14–43	5–29–45	PR*	DDR
Hanson	DD-832	Bath Iron	6–14–43	5–11–45	PA	DDR
Myles C. Fox	DD-829	Bath Iron	6–14–43	3–20–45	AA	DDR
Agerholm	DD-826	Bath Iron	11–10–44	6–20–46	PA	
Basilone	DD-824	Consol. Steel	11–29–44	7–26–49	AA	DDE
Robert H. McCard	DD-822	Consol. Steel	11–29–44	10–26–46	AA	
Johnston	DD-821	Consol. Steel	11–29–44	10–10–45	AA	
Rich	DD-820	Consol. Steel	11–29–44	7–4–46	AA	DDE
Holder	DD-819	Consol. Steel	11–29–44	5–18–46	AA	DDE
New	DD-818	Consol. Steel	11–29–44	4–5–46	AA	DDE
Corry	DD-817	Consol. Steel	11–29–44	2–26–46	AA	DDR
Dennis J. Buckley	DD-808	Bath Iron	8–7–42	3–2–45	PA	DDR
Higbee	DD-806	Bath Iron	8–7–42	1–27–45	PA	DDR
Shelton	DD-790	Todd, Pacific	8–7–42	6–21–46	PA	
Eversole	DD-789	Todd, Pacific	8–7–42	7–10–46	PA	
Hollister	DD-788	Todd, Pacific	8–7–42	3–26–46	PA	
James E. Kyes	DD-787	Todd, Pacific	8–7–42	2–8–46	PA	
Richard B. Anderson	DD-786	Todd, Pacific	8–7–42	10–26–45	PA	
Henderson	DD-785	Todd, Pacific	8–7–42	8–4–45	PA	
McKean	DD-784	Todd, Pacific	8–7–42	6–9–45	PA	DDR
Gurke	DD-783	Todd, Pacific	8–7–42	5–12–45	PA	

continued

Gearing Class—*continued*

Name	Number	Builder	Awarded	Commissioned	F/S	Former Designation
Rowan	DD-782	Todd, Pacific	8–7–42	3–31–45	PA	
William C. Lawe	DD-763	Beth., SF	8–7–42	12–18–46	AA	
Southerland	DD-743	Bath Iron	8–7–42	12–22–44	PA	DDR
Epperson	DD-719	Federal	8–7–42	3–19–49	PA	DDE
Hamner	DD-718	Federal	8–7–42	7–11–46	PA	
Theodore E. Chandler	DD-717	Federal	8–7–42	3–22–46	PA	
Wiltsie	DD-716	Federal	8–7–42	1–12–46	PA	
William M. Wood	DD-715	Federal	8–7–42	11–24–45	AA	DDR
William R. Rush	DD-714	Federal	8–7–42	9–21–45	AA	DDR
Eugene A. Greene	DD-711	Federal	8–7–42	6–8–45	AA	DDR
Gearing	DD-710	Federal	8–7–42	5–3–45	NRT	

99 *Gearings* were commissioned from 1–27–45 (DD-805) to 7–26–49 (DD-824). Class originally designed as continuation of DD-692 class. To increase fuel capacity and range, 14′ was added amidships between the stacks. Other engineering plant modifications were also made. In addition to the 99 completed ships, 49 were cancelled and 5 were delivered incomplete, cannibalized, and scrapped in mid-1950s. Post-completion conversions: 36 to DDR, 11 to DDE. All except DD-713 class reverted to DD in early 1960s. With minor variations resulting from FRAM overhauls, all *Gearings* are basically the same. DD-844 was first FRAM I. DD-849 is rated as experimental. DD-833 modified to test nuclear-biological-chemical warfare defenses; ship can be sealed off to protect personnel; all topside spaces can be reached from inside. No longer carry DASH. DD-786, 790, 826, 841, 844, 845, 867, 890 have both twin 5″/38 forward; all others one forward, one aft. DD-833 decommissioned 12–4–70.

9 DESTROYERS, "*ENGLISH*" CLASS (non-FRAM)

Name	Number	Builder	Awarded	Commissioned	F/S
Willard Keith	DD-775	Beth., San Pedro	8–7–42	12–27–44	NRT
Henley	DD-762	Beth., SF	8–7–42	10–8–46	NRT
Beatty	DD-756	Beth., Staten Is.	8–7–42	3–31–45	NRT
John R. Pierce	DD-753	Beth., Staten Is.	8–7–42	12–30–44	NRT
Purdy	DD-734	Bath Iron	8–7–42	7–18–44	NRT
Maddox	DD-731	Bath Iron	8–7–42	6–16–44	NRT
Harlan R. Dickson	DD-708	Federal	8–7–42	6–2–44	NRT
Compton	DD-705	Federal	8–7–42	11–4–44	NRT
Hank	DD-702	Federal	8–7–42	8–28–44	NRT

NonFRAMed ships of the *Allen M. Sumner* class. For ships still in NRT, see assignments in section 7. Six sister ships have been struck. DD-734, 756 have no 3″/50.

31 DESTROYERS, *ALLEN M. SUMNER* CLASS (FRAM II)

Name	Number	Builder	Awarded	Commissioned	F/S	Decommissioned
Robert K. Huntington	DD-781	Todd, Pacific	8–7–42	3–3–45	NRT	
Stormes	DD-780	Todd, Pacific	8–7–42	1–27–45	AR*	12–5–70
Douglas H. Fox	DD-779	Todd, Pacific	8–7–42	12–26–44	NRT	
Massey	DD-778	Todd, Pacific	8–7–42	11–24–44	NRT	
[Zellars]	DD-777	Todd, Pacific	8–7–42	10–25–44	Struck	3–19–71
James C. Owens	DD-776	Beth., San Pedro	8–7–42	2–17–45	NRT	
Lowry	DD-770	Beth., San Pedro	8–7–42	7–23–44	NRT	
Buck	DD-761	Beth., SF	8–7–42	6–28–46	NRT	
John W. Thomason	DD-760	Beth., SF	8–7–42	10–11–45	PR*	12–8–70
Lofberg	DD-759	Beth., SF	8–7–42	4–26–45	PR*	1–15–71

Strong	DD-758	Beth., SF	8–7–42	3–8–45	NRT	
Putnam	DD-757	Beth., SF	8–7–42	10–12–44	NRT	
John A. Bole	DD-755	Beth., Staten Is.	8–7–42	3–3–45	PR*	11–6–70
Alfred A. Cunningham	DD-752	Beth., Staten Is.	8–7–42	11–23–44	DPR*	2–24–71
Taussig	DD-746	Beth., Staten Is.	8–7–42	5–20–44	PR*	12–1–70
Blue	DD-744	Beth., Staten Is.	8–7–42	3–20–44	PR*	1–27–71
Collett	DD-730	Beth., Staten Is.	8–7–42	5–16–44	PR*	12–18–70
Lyman K. Swenson	DD-729	Bath Iron	8–7–42	5–2–44	PR*	2–12–71
Mansfield	DD-728	Bath Iron	8–7–42	4–14–44	PR*	2–4–71
De Haven	DD-727	Bath Iron	8–7–42	3–31–44	NRT	1971
O'Brien	DD-725	Bath Iron	8–7–42	2–25–44	PA	
Laffey	DD-724	Bath Iron	8–7–42	2–8–44	AA	
Walke	DD-723	Bath Iron	8–7–42	1–21–44	PR*	11–30–70
Hugh Purvis	DD-709	Federal	8–7–42	3–1–45	AA	
Borie	DD-704	Federal	8–7–42	9–21–44	NRT	
Wallace L. Lind	DD-703	Federal	8–7–42	9–8–44	NRT	
Waldron	DD-699	Federal	8–7–42	6–8–44	NRT	
Ault	DD-698	Federal	8–7–42	5–31–44	NRT	
Charles S. Sperry	DD-697	Federal	8–7–42	5–17–44	NRT	
Ingraham	DD-694	Federal	8–7–42	3–10–44	AA	
Moale	DD-693	Federal	8–7–42	2–26–44	NRT	
Allen M. Sumner	DD-692	Federal	8–7–42	1–26–44	NRT	

As completed, DD-692 and 696 classes comprised one class for a total of 58 ships. An additional 12 ships were completed as DMs (see minecraft section). Of the 58 ships completed, 4 were lost in the war, 1 was scrapped in 1946 after being damaged beyond repair, and 1 was sunk as a target after suffering collision. Two separate classes evolved from FRAM II conversion. All FRAMs done by Navy yards. Conversion included VDS, improved electronics, DASH hangar/flight deck in lieu of aft 3" guns, ASW torpedoes, and new stack caps (some ships had to be backfitted as DD-760).

55 DESTROYERS, *LA VALLETE* CLASS

Name	Number	Builder	Awarded	Commissioned	F/S
Porter	DD-800	Todd, Pacific	8–4–42	6–24–44	AR*
Cassin Young	DD-793	Beth., San Pedro	6–14–42	12–31–43	AR*
Norman Scott	DD-690	Bath Iron	7–15–42	11–5–43	PR
Remey	DD-688	Bath Iron	7–15–42	9–30–43	AR*
Uhlmann	DD-687	Beth., Staten Is.	6–14–42	11–22–43	NRT
Picking	DD-685	Beth., Staten Is.	6–14–42	9–21–43	PR*
Stockham	DD-683	Beth., Staten Is.	6–14–42	2–11–44	AR*
Porterfield	DD-682	Beth., San Pedro	6–14–42	10–30–43	PR*
Melvin	DD-680	Federal	6–14–42	11–24–43	AR*
McNair	DD-679	Federal	6–14–42	12–30–43	AR*
Hunt	DD-674	Federal	6–14–42	9–22–43	AR*
Healy	DD-672	Federal	6–14–42	9–3–43	AR*
Gatling	DD-671	Federal	6–14–42	8–19–43	AR*
Cotten	DD-669	Federal	6–14–42	7–24–43	AR*
Chauncey	DD-667	Federal	6–14–42	5–31–43	AR*
[Bennion]	DD-662	Boston Navy	12–18–41	12–14–43	Struck
Kidd	DD-661	Federal	12–15–41	4–23–43	AR*
Bullard	DD-660	Federal	12–15–41	4–9–43	PR
Dashiell	DD-659	Federal	12–15–41	3–20–43	AR*
Charles J. Badger	DD-657	Beth., Staten Is.	12–15–41	7–23–43	AR*
John Hood	DD-655	Gulf, Chickasaw	12–15–41	6–7–44	AR*
Bearss	DD-654	Gulf, Chickasaw	12–15–41	4–12–44	AR*
Knapp	DD-653	Bath Iron	12–15–41	9–16–43	PR*
Caperton	DD-650	Bath Iron	12–15–41	7–30–43	AR*
[Albert W. Grant]	DD-649	Charleston Navy	12–15–41	11–24–43	Struck
Sigourney	DD-643	Bath Iron	12–16–40	6–29–43	AR*
[Braine]	DD-630	Bath Iron	12–16–40	5–11–43	Struck
Abbot	DD-629	Bath Iron	12–16–40	4–23–43	AR*
Shields	DD-596	PS Navy	9–9–40	2–8–45	NRT
Hart	DD-594	PS Navy	9–9–40	11–4–44	PR
Burns	DD-588	Charleston Navy	9–9–40	4–3–43	PR
Bell	DD-587	Charleston Navy	9–9–40	3–4–43	PR
Haraden	DD-585	Boston Navy	9–9–40	9–16–43	PR
Wickes	DD-578	Consol. Steel	9–9–40	6–16–43	PR

continued

La Vallette Class—*continued*

Name	Number	Builder	Awarded	Commissioned	F/S
McKee	DD-575	Consol. Steel	9–9–40	3–31–43	AR
Wren	DD-568	Seattle-Tacoma	9–9–40	5–22–44	AR*
Watts	DD-567	Seattle-Tacoma	9–9–40	4–29–44	PR*
Stoddard	DD-566	Seattle-Tacoma	9–9–40	4–15–44	PR*
Rowe	DD-564	Seattle-Tacoma	9–9–40	3–13–44	AR*
Ross	DD-563	Seattle-Tacoma	9–9–40	2–21–44	AR*
Robinson	DD-562	Seattle-Tacoma	9–9–40	1–31–44	AR*
Laws	DD-558	Seattle-Tacoma	9–9–40	11–18–43	PR*
Franks	DD-554	Seattle-Tacoma	9–9–40	7–30–43	PR
[Cowell]	DD-547	Beth., San Pedro	9–9–40	8–23–43	Struck
[Twining]	DD-540	Beth., SF	9–9–40	12–1–43	Struck
Stephen Potter	DD-538	Beth., SF	9–9–40	10–21–43	PR*
The Sullivans	DD-537	Beth., SF	9–9–40	9–30–43	AR*
Owen	DD-536	Beth., SF	9–9–40	9–20–43	PR*
Miller	DD-535	Beth., SF	9–9–40	8–31–43	AR*
McCord	DD-534	Beth., SF	9–9–40	8–19–43	AR*
Hazelwood	DD-531	Beth., SF	9–9–40	6–18–43	AR*
Trathen	DD-530	Beth., SF	9–9–40	5–28–43	PR*
[Mullany]	DD-528	Beth., SF	9–9–40	4–23–43	Struck
Daly	DD-519	Beth., Staten Is.	9–9–40	3–10–43	AR*
Terry	DD-513	Bath Iron	9–9–40	1–26–43	PR
Foote	DD-511	Bath Iron	9–9–40	12–22–42	DAR
Sigsbee	DD-502	Federal	9–9–40	1–23–43	AR
Schroeder	DD-501	Federal	9–9–40	1–1–43	AR
Stevens	DD-479	Charleston Navy	6–28–40	2–1–43	PR
Hudson	DD-475	Boston Navy	6–28–40	4–13–43	PR
La Vallette	DD-448	Federal	7–1–40	8–12–42	PR

Originally the bulk of the *Fletcher* class, they became *La Vallettes* when *Fletcher* and 17 sisters received ASW modifications in the early 1950s. In mid-1950s, several now decommissioned DDs of class were modernized. Our standard WW II DD, this class are all of the same design with one exception: repeat *Fletchers* (DD-649 and on) have lower main gun director. *Pritchett* (DD-561), *Ingersoll* (DD-651), and *Hopewell* (DD-681) were the last fully active ships of this class. The only active ships in class are now assigned to NRT duties. DD-566 decommissioned late 1969 at Mare Island. *Hazelwood* (DD-531) served as test ship for DASH. Some reserve units still have 1 quint 21" torpedo tube mount.

DESTROYER, "*RADFORD*" CLASS (FRAM II)

Name	Number	Builder	Awarded	Commissioned	F/S	Decommissioned
[Nicholas]	DD-449	Bath Iron	7–1–40	6–4–42	Struck	1–30–70

DESTROYER, "*FLETCHER*" CLASS

Name	Number	Builder	Awarded	Commissioned	F/S	Decommissioned
[Renshaw]	DD-499	Federal	9–9–40	12–5–42	Struck	2–14–70

Both classes originally totalled 18 ships; were originally part of the *La Vallette* class. All were reclassified DDE on 3–26–49 or 1–2–51. Bridge was modified, WEAPON A replaced #2 5" mount and 2 twin 3"/50s replaced #3 and #4 mounts. All 18 were originally scheduled to be FRAMed, but only DD-446/447, 449 were done. The remainder were cancelled 12–15–61. All reverted to DD on 6–30–62. The struck *Conway* (DD-507), *Cony* (DD-508), and *Eaton* (DD-510) briefly served as NRT ships.

DESTROYERS, "*GLEAVES*" CLASS

Name	Number	Builder	Awarded	Commissioned	F/S	Former Designation
[Thorn]	DD-647	Federal	2–10–41	4–1–43	Struck	
[Stockton]	DD-646	Federal	2–10–41	1–11–43	Struck	
[Tillman]	DD-641	Charleston Navy	12–16–40	6–4–42	Struck	
[Herndon]	DD-638	Norfolk Navy	12–16–40	12–20–42	Struck	
[Gherardi]	DD-637	Phil. Navy	12–16–40	9–15–42	Struck	DMS-30
[Doran]	DD-634	Boston Navy	12–16–40	8–4–42	Struck	DMS-41

[Thompson]	DD-627	Seattle-Tacoma	12–16–40	7–10–43	Struck	DMS-38
[Jeffers]	DD-621	Federal	12–16–40	11–5–42	Struck	DMS-27
[Edwards]	DD-619	Federal	12–16–40	9–18–42	Struck	
[Davison]	DD-618	Federal	12–16–40	9–11–42	Struck	DMS-37
[Frankford]	DD-497	Seattle-Tacoma	9–9–40	3–31–43	Struck	
[McCook]	DD-496	Seattle-Tacoma	9–9–40	3–15–43	Struck	DMS-36
[Doyle]	DD-494	Seattle-Tacoma	9–9–40	1–27–43	Struck	DMS-34
[Carmick]	DD-493	Seattle-Tacoma	9–9–40	12–28–42	Struck	DMS-33
[Quick]	DD-490	Federal	9–9–40	7–3–42	Struck	DMS-32
[Fitch]	DD-462	Boston Navy	6–12–40	2–3–42	Struck	DMS-25
[Hambleton]	DD-455	Federal	7–1–40	12–22–41	Struck	DMS-20
[Swanson]	DD-443	Charleston Navy	7–1–39	5–29–41	Struck	
[ex-Wilkes]	DD-441	Boston Navy	7–1–39	4–22–41	Struck	
[Woolsey]	DD-437	Bath Iron	6–15–39	5–7–41	Struck	
[Grayson]	DD-435	Charleston Navy	10–1–38	2–14–41	Struck	
[Kearney]	DD-432	Federal	8–17–38	9–13–40	Struck	

66 ships were completed; 24 converted to high-speed minesweepers (DMS) before or after commissioning. Reverted to DD late 1954, early 1955. DD-441 lost name 7–16–68 when it was assigned to AGS-33.

DESTROYERS, "*BENSON*" CLASS

Name	Number	Builder	Awarded	Commissioned	F/S
[Ordronaux]	DD-617	Beth., Fore River	12–16–40	2–13–43	Struck
[McLanahan]	DD-615	Beth., San Pedro	12–16–40	12–19–42	Struck
[MacKenzie]	DD-614	Beth., San Pedro	12–16–40	11–21–42	Struck
[Laub]	DD-613	Beth., San Pedro	12–16–40	10–24–42	Struck
[Hobby]	DD-610	Beth., SF	12–16–40	11–18–42	Struck
[Gillespie]	DD-609	Beth., SF	12–16–40	9–18–42	Struck
[Gansevoort]	DD-608	Beth., SF	12–16–40	8–26–42	Struck
[Frazier]	DD-607	Beth., SF	12–16–40	7–30–42	Struck
[Coghlan]	DD-606	Beth., SF	12–16–40	7–10–42	Struck
[Parker]	DD-604	Beth., Staten Is.	12–16–40	8–31–42	Struck
[Meade]	DD-602	Beth., Staten Is.	12–16–40	6–22–42	Struck
[Boyle]	DD-600	Beth., Fore River	12–16–40	8–15–42	Struck
[Bancroft]	DD-598	Beth., Fore River	12–16–40	4–30–43	Struck
[Farenholt]	DD-491	Beth., Fore River	9–9–40	4–2–42	Struck

Survivors of a 30-ship class; decommissioned 1946–47. Many serve foreign navies.

USS *Truxtun* (DLGN-35). Note 5" mount forward and absence of separate ASROC launcher. Missile launcher doubles as ASROC launcher. Note radar masts. **Truxtun** *class.*

USS *Biddle* (DLG-34). Main visual difference between DLG-26 and 16 classes is 5″ gun aft vice missile system on DLG-26 class. 4–30–69. **Belknap** *class.*

USS *Leahy* (DLG-16). Note location of helicopter deck as compared to DLG-34. 6–14–68. **Leahy** *class.*

USS *Bainbridge* (DLGN-25). Note ASROC/missile launcher forward. Compare to DLGN-35. **Bainbridge** *class.*

USS *William V. Pratt* (DLG-13). Note geometric aft mast, location of missile launcher, and ASROC as compared to DDG-2 class. **Coontz** *class.*

USS *Norfolk* (DL-1). Note semi-clipper bow and cruiser stern. Also note absence of WEAPON A forward and aft. 4–16–69. **Norfolk** *class.*

USS *Wilkinson* (DL-5) just before decommissioning. Note centerline anchor and absence of twin 3"/50 from "B" position. **"Mitscher"** *class.*

USS *Mitscher* (DDG-35). Note differences between her and former sister *Wilkinson*. Note missile launcher, helicopter deck, and absence of helicopter hangar. 1969.
Mitscher *class.*

USS *Goldsborough* (DDG-20). Compare position of anchor and type of missile launcher with photo of DDG-7. **Charles F. Adams** *class.*

USS *Henry B. Wilson* (DDG-7), one of our first built-for-purpose DDGs. 8–9–63.
Charles F. Adams *class.*

USS *John Paul Jones* (DDG-32). Note overpowering masts, forward superstructure and ASROC aft of #2 stack. Compare to DDG-35. 9–27–67. **Decatur** *class.*

USS *Barry* (DD-933) in post-ASW-modernization rig. Note clipper bow and stem anchor retained from premodernization rig. 4–30–68. **Forrest Sherman** *class,* as modernized.

USS *Turner Joy* (DD-951). Note differences between her and her sisters in and around the bridge. Lacks 3″ gun forward. Has deckhouse added aft of bridge. 4–12–65. **Hull** *class,* in original rig.

USS *Carpenter* (DD-825). Note single 5″ mount; she and sister are only FRAM. Is to have this. Note after mast; bigger than most FRAM masts. 12–27–65. **Carpenter** *class.*

USS *Chevalier* (DD-805). Note lack of ASROC and retention of pre-FRAM armament layout. 3–66. **Chevalier** *class.*

USS *Glennon* (DD-840). Note ASROC control booth just forward of #2 stack, the practice 5″ loader in the "B" position, and the absence of clutter topside. 9–18–65.
Gearing *class.*

USS *Goodrich* (DD-831). Note radar on after deckhouse and VDS gear on fantail. One of the last DDRs to become DD. A *Mount Hood* class AE is in the background. 9–65.
Kenneth D. Bailey *class.*

USS *Norris* (DD-859). Note HEDGEHOG in "B" position and no ASROC.
Lloyd Thomas *class.*

USS *Frank E. Evans* (DD-754) 18 months before collision. Represents typical FRAM II configuration. Note VDS on fantail and closely spaced stacks. *Gearing* and *Allen M. Sumner* class difference is space between stacks. *Sumner* has shorter space. Other differences are minor (see DD-710 class notes). 12–13–67. **Allen M. Sumner** *class.*

USS *Preston* (DD-795) in her last configuration before being struck. Note torpedo tubes just aft of 2nd stack. Bridge front closely resembles alterations that the German Navy made to *Preston's* sisters they have on loan. **La Vallette** *class.*

USS *English* (DD-696), was leadship of a class made up of unFRAMed *Sumners.* **"English"** *class.*

USS *Ludlow* (DD-438), a typical example of the *Benson* and *Gleaves* classes. Main difference between classes is that *Gleaves* class has round-sided stacks and *Benson* has flat-sided stacks. Otherwise, two classes are basically the same. Note two banks of torpedo tubes and diminutive mast aft of #2 stack. **Gleaves** *class.*

C. Ocean Escorts

By end-FY 1971, 6 DEGS, 154 DEs, and 25 DERs were on the NVR. Active were 6 DEGs, 47 DEs, and 3 DERs. In addition, 24 DEs were under construction and 4 DEs served as NRT vessels. Of 103 DEs and 21 DERs in reserve, all were virtually unfit for service.

Class		No. in Class	Full Load Displ.	Length Overall	Max. Draft	Extreme Beam	Number & Type of Boilers/Engines	Screws/ SHP	Max. Speed (Kts)	Accommodations Officers	Enlisted	Armament (varies within each class)[1]
GUIDED MISSILE ESCORT SHIPS												
Brooke	DEG-1	6	3,426	414′	24′2″	44′	2B(F.W.)/1GT(West.)	1/35,000	27·2	17	281	1 5″/38, 1 single TARTAR launcher, 1 ASROC
ESCORT SHIPS												
Knox	DE-1052	46	4,100	438′	25′	47′	2B(C.E.)/1GT(West.)	1/35,000	27	18	213	1 5″/54, 1 ASROC, 1 BPDMS
Garcia	DE-1040	10	3,403	414′	24′	44′	2B(F.W.)/1GT(West.)	1/35,000	27.5	17	211	2 5″/38, 1 ASROC
Bronstein	DE-1037	2	2,710	372′	23′	41′	2B(F.W.)/1GT(West.)	1/20,000	24	16	184	1 twin 3″/50, 1 single 3″/50, 1 ASROC
Claud Jones	DE-1033	4	1,755	312′	18′	39′	4 Diesel (F.M.)	1/9,200	22	15	160	2 single 3″/50 (DE-1034/1035: 1 3″/50)
Courtney	DE-1021	10	1,900	314′6″	19′6″	36′9″	2B(F.W.)/1GT(DeLaval)	1/20,000	26·5	16	156	1 twin 3″/50, 1 WEAPON A (DE-1025, 1030 excluded)
Dealey	DE-1006	3	1,940	314′6″	18′10″	36′	2B(F.W.)/1GT(DeLaval)	1/20,000	26	16	156	1 twin 3″/50, 2 twin 3″/50 (DE-1006 only), 1 WEAPON A (DE-1015 excluded)
"John C. Butler"	DE-339	40	1,990	306′	14′	37′	2B(C.E.)/2GT(G.E.)	2/12,000	24	15	207	2 5″/38, 2 40 mm
"Rudderow"	DE-224	5	1,990	306′	14′	37′	2B(B&W)/2GT(G.E.)	2/12,000	24	16	200	2 5″/38, 4 40 mm

continued

Ocean Escorts—*continued*

Class		No. in Class	Full Load Displ.	Length Overall	Max. Draft	Extreme Beam	Number & Type of Boilers/Engines	Screws/ SHP	Max. Speed (Kts)	Accommodations Officers	Enlisted	Armament (varies within each class)[1]
"Edsall"	DE-129	24	1,850	306′	11′	36′6″	4 Diesel(F.M.)	2/6,000	21	15	201	3 single 3″/50, 8 40mm
"Cannon"	DE-99	16	1,990	306′	14′	37′	4 Diesel(G.M.)	2/4,800	21	15	201	3 single 3″/50, 2 40mm
"Buckley"	DE-51	18	2,170	306′	14′	37′	2B(F.W.)/2GT(G.E.)	2/12,000	23·5	15	198	3 single 3″/50, 3 twin 40mm
RADAR PICKET ESCORT SHIPS												
Wagner	DER-539	2	2,100	306′	11′	36′6″	2B(B&W)/2GT(G.E.)	2/12,000	24	15	207	2 single 5″/38, 1 HEDGEHOG
Savage	DER-386	19	1,990	306′	14′	36′5″	4 Diesel(F.M.)	2/6,000	21·2	16	185	2 single 3″/50, 1 HEDGEHOG
Harveson	DER-316	3	1,710	306′	14′	36′7″	4 Diesel(F.M.)	2/6,000	21·2	14	201	2 single 3″/50, 1 HEDGEHOG

[1] *In addition to the armament listed, nearly all escort ships in service for the last decade carry, and have carried, two 12·75″ triple torpedo tubes for ASW homing torpedoes.*

6 GUIDED MISSILE ESCORT SHIPS, *BROOKE* CLASS

Name	Number	FY/SCB	Builder	Awarded	Commissioned	F/S
Julius A. Furer (ex-*Furer*)	DEG-6	63/199B	Bath Iron	5–24–63	11–11–67	AA
Richard L. Page	DEG-5	63/199B	Bath Iron	5–24–63	8–5–67	AA
Talbot	DEG-4	63/199B	Bath Iron	5–24–63	4–22–67	AA
Schofield	DEG-3	62/199B	Lockheed	1–4–62	5–11–68	PA
Ramsey	DEG-2	62/199B	Lockheed	1–4–62	6–3–67	PA
Brooke	DEG-1	62/199B	Lockheed	1–4–62	3–12–66	PA

Missile version of *Garcia* class; TARTAR vice #2 5″ gun. Have fin-stabilizers and 1200 psi supercharged diesel burning system. Originally to be 19 ships in class. Were to have 5″/54s. Cost $11 million more than DEs. Despite their size, modern DEs are so rated because of single screw and limited speed.

46 ESCORT SHIPS, *KNOX* CLASS

	DE-1097	67/200.66	Avondale	8–25–66		Bldg.
	DE-1096	67/200.66	Avondale	8–25–66		Bldg.
	DE-1095	67/200.66	Avondale	8–25–66		Bldg.
	DE-1094	67/200.66	Avondale	8–25–66		Bldg.
	DE-1093	67/200.66	Avondale	8–25–66		Bldg.
	DE-1092	67/200.66	Avondale	8–25–66		Bldg.
	DE-1091	67/200.66	Avondale	8–25–66		Bldg.
	DE-1090	67/200.66	Avondale	8–25–66		Bldg.
Jesse L. Brown	DE-1089	67/200.66	Avondale	8–25–66		Bldg.
Barbey	DE-1088	67/200.66	Avondale	8–25–66		Bldg.
Kirk	DE-1087	66/200.66	Avondale	8–25–66		Bldg.
Brewton	DE-1086	66/200.66	Avondale	8–25–66		Bldg.
Donald B. Beary	DE-1085	66/200.66	Avondale	8–25–66		Bldg.
McCandless	DE-1084	66/200.66	Avondale	8–25–66		AA
Cook	DE-1083	66/200.66	Avondale	8–25–66		Bldg.
Elmer Montgomery	DE-1082	66/200.66	Avondale	8–25–66		AA
Aylwin	DE-1081	66/200.66	Avondale	8–25–66		AA
Paul	DE-1080	66/200.66	Avondale	8–25–66		AA

Bowen	DE-1079	66/200.66	Avondale	8–25–66	5–22–71	AA
Joseph Hewes	DE-1078	66/200.66	Avondale	8–25–66	4–24–71	AA
Ouellet	DE-1077	65/200.65	Avondale	7–22–64	12–12–70	PA
Fanning	DE-1076	65/200.65	Todd, San Pedro	7–22–64		PA
Trippe	DE-1075	65/200.65	Avondale	7–22–64	9–19–70	AA
Harold E. Holt	DE-1074	65/200.65	Todd, San Pedro	7–22–64	3–26–71	PA
Robert E. Peary (ex-Conolly)	DE-1073	65/200.65	Lockheed	7–22–64		PA
Blakely	DE-1072	65/200.65	Avondale	7–22–64	7–18–70	AA
Badger	DE-1071	65/200.65	Todd, San Pedro	7–22–64	12–1–70	PA
Downes	DE-1070	65/200.65	Todd, Seattle	7–22–64		AA
Bagley	DE-1069	65/200.65	Lockheed	7–22–64		PA
Vreeland	DE-1068	65/200.65	Avondale	7–22–64	6–13–70	AA
Francis Hammond	DE-1067	65/200.65	Todd, San Pedro	7–22–64	7–25–70	PA
Marvin Shields	DE-1066	65/200.65	Todd, Seattle	7–22–64	4–10–71	PA
Stein	DE-1065	65/200.65	Lockheed	7–22–64		PA
Lockwood	DE-1064	65/200.65	Todd, Seattle	7–22–64	12–5–70	PA
Reasoner	DE-1063	65/200.65	Lockheed	7–22–64		PA
Whipple	DE-1062	65/200.65	Todd, Seattle	7–22–64	8–22–70	PA
Patterson	DE-1061	64/199C	Avondale	7–22–64	3–14–70	AA
Lang	DE-1060	64/199C	Todd, San Pedro	7–22–64	3–28–70	PA
W. S. Sims	DE-1059	64/199C	Avondale	7–22–64	1–3–70	AA
Meyerkord	DE-1058	64/199C	Todd, San Pedro	7–22–64	11–28–69	PA
Rathburne	DE-1057	64/199C	Lockheed	7–22–64	5–16–70	PA
Connole	DE-1056	64/199C	Avondale	7–22–64	8–30–69	AA
Hepburn	DE-1055	64/199C	Todd, Seattle	7–22–64	7–3–69	PA
Gray	DE-1054	64/199C	Todd, Seattle	7–22–64	4–4–70	PA
Roark	DE-1053	64/199C	Todd, Seattle	7–22–64	11–22–69	PA
Knox	DE-1052	64/199C	Todd, Seattle	7–22–64	4–12–69	PA

Improved and enlarged *Garcias*. DE-1078/1097 awarded to one builder to cut costs. Originally known as *Joseph Hewes* class. Space aft is provided for BPDMS installation. Six of the class are already fitted with this weapon: DE-1062, 1064, 1067, 1071, 1072, and 1075. Designed for VDS and DASH, but neither installed. Additional ships of this class, DE-1098/1107, were authorized under FY 1968, but all were cancelled because of DXGN/DXG/DX program and to pay for cost overruns in previous programs. DE-1102/1107 were cancelled mid-1968; DE-1098/1101 were cancelled 2/69. DE-1101 was to have a gas turbine propulsion system. Class was originally scheduled to carry the defunct *Sea Mauler* (RIM-46A) missile. DE-1059 served as test ship for LAMPS system (manned helicopters based on ships).

10 ESCORT SHIPS, *GARCIA* CLASS

O'Callahan	DE-1051	63/199A	Defoe	3–21–63	7–13–68	PA
Albert David	DE-1050	63/199A	Lockheed	3–20–63	10–19–68	PA
Koelsch	DE-1049	63/199A	Defoe	3–21–63	6–10–67	AA
Sample	DE-1048	63/199A	Lockheed	3–20–63	3–23–68	PA
Voge	DE-1047	63/199A	Defoe	3–21–63	11–25–66	AA
Davidson	DE-1045	62/199A	Avondale	1–3–62	12–7–65	PA
Brumby	DE-1044	62/199A	Avondale	1–3–62	8–5–65	AA
Edward McDonnell	DE-1043	62/199A	Avondale	1–3–62	2–15–65	AA
Bradley	DE-1041	61/199A	Beth., S.F.	6–22–61	5–15–65	PA
Garcia	DE-1040	61/199A	Beth., S.F.	6–22–61	12–21–64	AA

Enlarged *Bronsteins*; handy ASW ships. *Brooke* DEGs built to same design. Exceed many DDs in size and capability. Original transom-mounted ASW torpedo tubes (MK 25) suppressed. New type boiler has been troublesome.

2 ESCORT SHIPS, *BRONSTEIN* CLASS

Name	Number	FY/SCB	Builder	Awarded	Commissioned	F/S
McCloy	DE-1038	60/199	Avondale	6–13–60	10–21–63	AA
Bronstein	DE-1037	60/199	Avondale	6–13–60	6–15–63	PA

Pioneer class for new breed of DEs, these ships influenced design of *Knox/Brooke/Garcia* classes. First to have "macks". Fleet DD size with ASW capability. Appearance notes: 3" guns vice 5"; taller mack; helicopter pad is forward of #2 mount vice aft.

4 ESCORT SHIPS, *CLAUD JONES* CLASS

Name	Number	FY/SCB	Builder	Awarded	Commissioned	F/S
McMorris	DE-1036	57/131	American	9–4–56	3–4–60	PA
Charles Berry	DE-1035	57/131	American	9–4–56	11–25–59	PA
John R. Perry	DE-1034	56/131	Avondale	5–4–56	5–5–59	PA
Claud Jones	DE-1033	56/131	Avondale	5–4–56	2–10–59	PA

DE-1035/1036 completed by Avondale under contract awarded 7–31–58. DE-1033/1034 were in Atlantic until 5–1–66 HEDGEHOGs replaced on DE-1035/1036 (1961–64) with Norwegian ASW missile TERNE III for tests. Designed for mass production. Only post-WW II DEs to have diesels. As produced, they could not carry the weapons/sonar needed for modern ASW. Class modernization called for addition of VDS and a deckhouse between forward gun and bridge and removal of after gun and depth-charge rack. Other ASW improvements to be added. To date only DE-1035 has been modernized, and her VDS was later removed.

10 ESCORT SHIPS, *COURTNEY* CLASS

Name	Number	FY/SCB	Builder	Awarded	Commissioned	F/S
Joseph K. Taussig	DE-1030	55/72	NY Shipbuilding	10–28–54	9–10–57	AA
Hartley	DE-1029	55/72	NY Shipbuilding	10–28–54	6–26–57	AA
Van Voorhis	DE-1028	55/72	NY Shipbuilding	10–28–54	4–22–57	AA
John Willis	DE-1027	55/72	NY Shipbuilding	10–28–54	2–21–57	AA
Hooper (ex-*Gatch*)	DE-1026	55/72	Beth., SF	10–22–54	3–18–58	NRT
Bauer	DE-1025	55/72	Beth., SF	10–22–54	11–21–57	NRT
Bridget	DE-1024	55/72	PS B & DD	10–19–54	10–24–57	NRT
Evans	DE-1023	55/72	PS B & DD	10–19–54	6–14–57	NRT
Lester	DE-1022	54/72	Defoe	3–2–54	6–14–57	AA
Courtney	DE-1021	54/72	Defoe	3–2–54	9–24–56	AA

Improved *Dealeys*. One propeller with twin rudders. Easily recognized by low silhouette, low stack, and high bow. Refit included removal of aft gun, K-guns, and depth charge racks. Installed DASH hangar/deck and 2 triple MK 32 ASW torpedo tubes (one each side of stack). WEAPON A being removed from this class and *Dealey* class.

3 ESCORT SHIPS, *DEALEY* CLASS

Name	Number	FY/SCB	Builder	Awarded	Commissioned	F/S
Hammerberg	DE-1015	53/72	Bath Iron	12–15–52	3–2–55	AA
Cromwell	DE-1014	53/72	Bath Iron	12–15–52	11–24–54	AA
Dealey	DE-1006	52/72	Bath Iron	7–12–51	6–3–54	AA

First of the postwar DEs built. DE-1014/1015 have *Courtney* class refit. Recognition feature of both classes is the pole mast mounted on a 4-legged base. For tests *Dealey* briefly carried British ASW weapon SQUID.

40 ESCORT SHIPS, "*JOHN C. BUTLER*" CLASS

Name	Number	Builder	Awarded	Commissioned	F/S
Osberg	DE-538	Boston Navy	8–7–42	12–10–45	AR*
Rizzi	DE-537	Boston Navy	8–7–42	6–26–45	AR*
Silverstein	DE-534	Boston Navy	8–7–42	7–14–44	PR*
Howard F. Clark	DE-533	Boston Navy	8–7–42	5–25–44	PR
Edward H. Allen	DE-531	Boston Navy	8–7–42	12–16–43	AR*
Gilligan	DE-508	Federal	8–7–42	5–12–44	PR*
Hanna	DE-449	Federal	8–7–42	1–27–45	PR*
Goss	DE-444	Federal	8–7–42	8–26–44	PR*
Kendall C. Campbell	DE-443	Federal	8–7–42	7–31–44	PR
William Seiverling	DE-441	Federal	8–7–42	6–1–44	PR*
Corbesier	DE-438	Federal	8–7–42	3–31–44	PR
Dufilho	DE-423	Brown, Houston	8–7–42	7–21–44	PR
Chester T. O'Brien	DE-421	Brown, Houston	8–7–42	7–3–44	AR*
Leland E. Thomas	DE-420	Brown, Houston	8–7–42	6–19–44	PR
Robert F. Keller	DE-419	Brown, Houston	8–7–42	6–17–44	AR*
Tabberer	DE-418	Brown, Houston	8–7–42	5–23–44	AR*
Oliver Mitchell	DE-417	Brown, Houston	8–7–42	6–14–44	PR
Melvin R. Nawman	DE-416	Brown, Houston	8–7–42	5–16–44	AR*
Lawrence C. Taylor	DE-415	Brown, Houston	8–7–42	5–13–44	PR
Leyray Wilson	DE-414	Brown, Houston	8–7–42	5–10–44	PR*
Stafford	DE-411	Brown, Houston	8–7–42	4–19–44	PR
La Prade	DE-409	Brown, Houston	8–7–42	4–20–44	PR
Edmonds	DE-406	Brown, Houston	8–7–42	4–3–44	PR*
Dennis	DE-405	Brown, Houston	8–7–42	3–20–44	PR
French	DE-367	Consol. Steel	8–7–42	10–9–44	PR
Rombach	DE-364	Consol. Steel	8–7–42	9–20–44	PR*
Pratt	DE-363	Consol. Steel	8–7–42	9–18–44	PR
Rolf	DE-362	Consol. Steel	8–7–42	9–7–44	PR
Johnnie Hutchins	DE-360	Consol. Steel	8–7–42	8–28–44	AR*
Mack	DE-358	Consol. Steel	8–7–42	8–16–44	PR
George E. Davis	DE-357	Consol. Steel	8–7–42	8–11–44	AR
Lloyd E. Acree	DE-356	Consol. Steel	8–7–42	8–1–44	PR
Kenneth M. Willett	DE-354	Consol. Steel	8–7–42	7–19–44	AR*
Doyle C. Barnes	DE-353	Consol. Steel	8–7–42	7–13–44	PR
Gentry	DE-349	Consol. Steel	8–7–42	6–14–44	PR
Key	DE-348	Consol. Steel	8–7–42	6–5–44	PR
Edwin A. Howard	DE-346	Consol. Steel	8–7–42	5–25–44	PR*
Richard W. Suesens	DE-342	Consol. Steel	8–7–42	4–26–44	PR
Raymond	DE-341	Consol. Steel	8–7–42	4–15–44	AR*
O'Flaherty	DE-340	Consol. Steel	8–7–42	4–8–44	PR
[John C. Butler]	DE-339	Consol. Steel	8–7–42	3–31–44	Struck

Formerly known as WGT (geared turbine drive) class. Armament varies in this class. All originally had two 5"/38, one quad 40 mm, and three twin 40 mm. Four ships were war losses. Two ships, suspended after WW II, were completed as DERs (see *Wagner* class).

5 ESCORT SHIPS, "*RUDDEROW*" CLASS

Name	Number	Builder	Awarded	Commissioned	F/S
Tinsman	DE-589	Beth., Hingham	8–7–42	6–26–44	PR
Thomas F. Nickel	DE-587	Beth., Hingham	8–7–42	6–9–44	PR*
McNulty	DE-581	Beth., Hingham	8–7–42	3–31–44	PR
Leslie L. B. Knox	DE-580	Beth., Hingham	8–7–42	3–22–44	PR
Hodges	DE-231	Charleston Navy	8–7–42	5–27–44	PR

Formerly known as TEV (turbine electric drive, 5" guns) class. 68 ships of this class were built; 47 were converted to APDs. Similar to *Buckley* class except for armament and bridge configuration. Until decommissioned 7–1–70, *Parle* (DE-708) was last active WW II DE.

24 ESCORT SHIPS, "*EDSALL*" CLASS

Name	Number	Builder	Awarded	Commissioned	F/S
Stockdale	DE-399	Brown, Houston	8–7–42	12–31–43	AR
Cockrill	DE-398	Brown, Houston	8–7–42	12–24–43	AR
Janssen	DE-396	Brown, Houston	8–7–42	12–18–43	AR
Willis	DE-395	Brown, Houston	8–7–42	12–10–43	AR
Swenning	DE-394	Brown, Houston	8–7–42	12–1–43	AR
[Merrill]	DE-392	Brown, Houston	8–7–42	11–27–43	Struck
Ricketts	DE-254	Brown, Houston	1–18–42	10–5–43	AR
Pettit	DE-253	Brown, Houston	1–18–42	9–23–43	AR
Hurst	DE-250	Brown, Houston	1–18–42	8–30–43	AR
Swasey	DE-248	Brown, Houston	1–18–42	8–31–43	AR
[J. Richard Ward]	DE-243	Brown, Houston	1–18–42	7–5–43	Struck
Tomich	DE-242	Brown, Houston	1–18–42	7–27–43	AR
Keith	DE-241	Brown, Houston	1–18–42	7–19–43	AR
Moore	DE-240	Brown, Houston	1–18–42	7–1–43	AR
Stewart	DE-238	Brown, Houston	1–18–42	5–31–43	AR
Peterson	DE-152	Consol. Steel	1–18–42	9–29–43	AR*
Poole	DE-151	Consol. Steel	1–18–42	9–29–43	AR
Neunzer	DE-150	Consol. Steel	1–18–42	9–27–43	AR
Chatelain	DE-149	Consol. Steel	1–18–42	9–22–43	AR
Inch	DE-146	Consol. Steel	1–18–42	9–8–43	AR
Huse	DE-145	Consol. Steel	1–18–42	8–30–43	AR*
Hill	DE-141	Consol. Steel	1–18–42	8–16–43	AR
Farquhar	DE-139	Consol. Steel	1–18–42	8–5–43	AR
Douglas L. Howard	DE-138	Consol. Steel	1–18–42	7–29–43	AR
Herbert C. Jones	DE-137	Consol. Steel	1–18–42	7–21–43	AR
Hammann (ex-*Langley*)	DE-131	Consol. Steel	1–18–42	5–17–43	AR

Formerly known as FMR (diesel reverse gear drive) class. Of 85 completed, 3 became APDs, 34 were converted to DERs, 4 lost in war. Only 2 listed here saw post-WW II service. Towards the end of the war, class was to rearm with 5" guns, but only 1 was re-armed (now DER-251). *Peterson* ASW modified 1951–52 viz: trainable HEDGEHOGs added to "B" position vice 3" gun; short pole mainmast, extra sonar added; and deck houses added amidships. *Huse* was designated EDE.

16 ESCORT SHIPS, *"CANNON"* CLASS

Name	Number	Builder	Awarded	Commissioned	F/S
Oswald	DE-767	Tampa	11–9–42	6–12–44	AR
Earl K. Olsen	DE-765	Tampa	11–9–42	4–10–44	AR*
McClelland	DE-750	Western	11–9–42	9–19–44	AR*
Snyder	DE-745	Western	11–9–42	5–5–44	AR*
Kyne	DE-744	Western	11–9–42	4–4–44	AR*
Lamons	DE-743	Western	11–9–42	2–29–44	AR
Hilbert	DE-742	Western	11–9–42	2–4–44	AR
Coffman	DE-191	Federal, Kearny	1–18–42	12–27–43	AR
Straub	DE-181	Federal, Kearny	1–18–42	10–25–43	AR
Trumpeter	DE-180	Federal, Kearny	1–18–42	10–16–43	AR
Cooner	DE-172	Federal, Kearny	1–18–42	8–21–43	AR
Acree	DE-167	Federal, Kearny	1–18–42	7–19–43	AR
Parks	DE-165	Federal, Kearny	1–18–42	6–23–43	AR
Osterhaus	DE-164	Federal, Kearny	1–18–42	6–12–43	AR
McConnell	DE-163	Federal, Kearny	1–18–42	5–28–43	AR
Levy	DE-162	Federal, Kearny	1–18–42	5–13–43	AR

Formerly known as DET (diesel electric tandem motor drive) class. 72 ships completed. 49 were loaned to our allies under ILP or sold; 2 were expended as targets. At beginning of Korean War, 23 ships on the disposal list were upgraded to reserve fleet.

18 ESCORT SHIPS, *"BUCKLEY"* CLASS

Name	Number	Builder	Awarded	Commissioned	F/S
Jack W. Wilke	DE-800	Consol. Steel	11–11–42	3–7–44	AR*
Varian	DE-798	Consol. Steel	11–11–42	2–29–44	AR
Major	DE-796	Consol. Steel	11–11–42	2–12–44	PR
Gunason	DE-795	Consol. Steel	11–11–42	2–1–44	PR*
Frybarger	DE-705	Defoe, Bay City	10–9–42	5–18–44	PR*
Holton	DE-703	Defoe, Bay City	10–9–42	5–1–44	AR
Osmus	DE-701	Defoe, Bay City	10–9–42	2–23–44	PR
Marsh	DE-699	Defoe, Bay City	10–9–42	1–12–44	PR*
Spangler	DE-696	Defoe, Bay City	10–9–42	10–31–43	PR*
Gillette	DE-681	Beth., Quincy	10–29–42	5–12–44	PR
Wiseman	DE-667	Dravo, Neville Is.	11–2–42	4–4–44	PR*
Damon M. Cummings	DE-643	Beth., SF	8–7–42	6–29–44	PR
William C. Cole	DE-641	Beth., SF	8–7–42	5–12–44	PR
Fieberling	DE-640	Beth., SF	8–7–42	4–11–44	PR
Gendreau	DE-639	Beth., SF	8–7–42	5–17–44	PR
Francis M. Robinson	DE-220	Phil. Navy	6–8–42	1–15–44	AR*
Coolbaugh	DE-217	Phil. Navy	6–8–42	10–15–43	AR*
Eichenberger	DE-202	Charleston Navy	6–8–42	11–17–43	AR

Formerly known as TE (turbine electric drive, 3" guns) class. Of 154 ships completed, 46 were converted to APDs. War losses: 3 DEs and 1 APD. 46 ships were leased to England, 6 were war losses, 40 were returned after the war. DE-667, 699 formerly NRT. *Solar* (DE-121) destroyed by internal explosion 4–30–46. Seven early DE/DER conversions of

2 RADAR PICKET ESCORT SHIPS, *WAGNER* CLASS

Name	Number	Builder	Awarded	Commissioned	F/S
Vandivier	DER-540	Boston Navy	8–7–42	10–11–55	AR*
Wagner	DER-539	Boston Navy	8–7–42	11–22–55	AR*

Originally begun as *John C. Butler* class ships; construction suspended 2–17–47. Construction resumed in 1954 for completion as DERs. Only 5" DERs on NVR.

19 RADAR PICKET ESCORT SHIPS, *SAVAGE* CLASS

Name	Number	Builder	Awarded	Commissioned	F/S
Hissem	DER-400	Brown, Houston	8–7–42	1–13–44	PR*
Chambers	DER-391	Brown, Houston	8–7–42	11–22–43	AR*
Calcaterra	DER-390	Brown, Houston	8–7–42	11–17–43	AA
Durant	DER-389	Brown, Houston	8–7–42	11–16–43	PR*
Lansing	DER-388	Brown, Houston	8–7–42	11–10–43	PR*
Vance	DER-387	Brown, Houston	8–7–42	11–1–43	PR*
Savage	DER-386	Brown, Houston	8–7–42	10–29–43	PR*
Rhodes	DER-384	Brown, Houston	8–7–42	10–25–43	AR*
Mills	DER-383	Brown, Houston	8–7–42	10–12–43	AR*
Ramsden	DER-382	Brown, Houston	8–7–42	10–19–43	PR*
Roy O. Hale	DER-336	Consol. Steel	8–7–42	2–3–44	AR*
[Forster]	DER-334	Consol. Steel	8–7–42	1–25–44	ILP
Price	DER-332	Consol. Steel	8–7–42	1–12–44	AR*
Kretchmer	DER-329	Consol. Steel	8–7–42	12–13–43	AR*
Finch	DER-328	Consol. Steel	8–7–42	12–13–43	PR*
Thomas J. Gary	DER-326	Consol. Steel	8–7–42	11–27–43	AA
Falgout	DER-324	Consol. Steel	8–7–42	11–15–43	PR*
[Camp]	DER-251	Brown, Houston	1–18–42	9–16–43	ILP
Otterstetter	DER-244	Brown, Houston	1–18–42	8–6–43	AR*
Sturtevant	DER-239	Brown, Houston	1–18–42	1–16–43	PR*
Blair	DER-147	Consol. Steel	1–18–42	9–13–43	PR*

Originally built as *Edsall* class ships. 28 were converted to DERs under SCB-46B in 1951–58. Superstructure was rebuilt with aluminum, a tripod mast added to support ECM and TACAN, SPS-8 height-finder added on after deckhouse, midships main deck area enclosed, CIC enlarged and moved down to two decks below bridge, mess compartments moved to starboard side amidships, trainable *Hedgehog* added to #2 3" position, and general hability improvements were made. Before conversion, DE-324, 328, 334, 382, 387/389, and 391 served with the Coast Guard. DERs served as seaward extension of DEW line until 1965 when the seaward extension was disestablished. Many were decommissioned. About a dozen were retained for Vietnam service. These had SPS-8 radar removed along with TACAN and some communications gear. Between 1965 and 1969 those DERs still active alternated between stationship Hong Kong, Operation "Market Time," and Taiwan Patrol. DER-400 decommissioned 5–15–70, DER-383 decommissioned 10–27–70, DER-251 decommissioned 7–20–70 for transfer to Vietnam.

the late 1960s have been struck. DE-705 converted to amphibious control ship (DEC) after WW II; mothballed in mid-50s and reverted to DE on 12–27–57. DE-800 was rated as EDE.

Lockheed

USS *Schofield* (DEG-3). Note former DASH helicopter pad aft. 4–2–68. **Brooke** *class.*

3 RADAR PICKET ESCORT SHIPS, *HARVESON* CLASS

Strickland	DER-333	Consol. Steel	8–7–42	1–10–44	PR*
Kirkpatrick	DER-318	Consol. Steel	8–7–42	10–23–43	AR*
Joyce	DER-317	Consol. Steel	8–7–42	9–20–43	PR*

Completed as ships of the *Edsall* class. Converted under SCB-46, though not as extensive as *Savage* class. High bridge structure of *Edsall* class retained; less clutter amidships. SPS-8 radar mounted just under forward mast on top of bridge. Two additional sisters were struck.

USS *Hepburn* (DE-1055). For identification purposes, note fat mack and enclosed areas of main deck amidships. 5–26–69. **Knox** *class.*

USS *Brooke* (DEG-1) fires an ASROC missile. Note location of anchors and MK 32 torpedo tubes below TARTAR launcher. 5–15–69. **Brooke** *class.*

Lockheed Shipbuilding and Construction

USS *Sample* (DE-1048). Compare masts and shorter, thinner mack with *Hepburn*. 2–29–68. **Garcia** *class.*

USS *Bronstein* (DE-1037). First DE with a mack. 5–15–64. **Bronstein** *class.*

USS *Charles Berry* (DE-1035), one of four of class that are only two-stack DEs in USN. Note VDS and deckhouse between forward gun and bridge; added as part of class modernization program. **Claude Jones** *class.*

USS *Hartley* (DE-1029). Note side of WEAPON A removed for maintenance. Ship appears in post-FRAM configuration. **Courtney** *class.*

USS *Cromwell* (DE-1014). **Dealey** *class.*

USS *John C. Butler* (DE-339) in basic WW II configuration. 8–15–55. **"John C. Butler"** *class.*

USS *Parle* (DE-708). **"Rudderow"** *class.*

USS *Peterson* (DE-152). **"Edsall"** *class.*

USS *McClelland* (DE-750). **"Cannon"** *class.*

USS *Frybarger* (DE-705) in DEC configuration. 7–7–53. **"Buckley"** *class.*

USS *Vandivier* (DER-540), one of two DERs with 5″ guns. She appears in configuration of DERs used in DEW-line sea extension. 1957. **Wagner** *class.*

USS *Savage* (DER-386) in configuration of DERs used in Vietnam. Note SPS-8 radar, enclosed mount forward, open aft. 1–68. **Savage** *class.*

USS *Joyce* (DER-317). Compare with DER-540 photo. She is in an interim DER rig between immediate post-WW II *Buckley* class conversion and mid-1950s *Edsall* class conversion. 2–28–51. **Harveson** *class.*

D. Command Ships

By end-FY 1971, there were 2 command ships on the NVR. Both were inactive and were assigned to the Atlantic Reserve Fleet. These ships are unique. The conversion of *Saipan* to a command ship (CC-3) was cancelled and she became *Arlington* (AGMR-2).

Class	Number	No. in Class	Full Load Displ.	Length Overall	Max. Draft	Extreme Beam	Number & Type of Boilers/Engines	Screws/ SHP	Max. Speed (Kts)	Accommodations Officers	Accommodations Enlisted	Flag Officers	Flag Enlisted	Armament
Wright	CC-2	1	19,570	684′	28′	110′	4B(B&W)/4GT(G.E.)	4/120,000	30.8	222	1,498			4 twin 40mm
Northampton	CC-1	1	17,204	676′	26′6″	71′	4B(B&W)/4GT(G.E.)	4/120,000	32	227	1,448	165	275	1 5″/54

LIGHT CARRIER, "*SAIPAN*" CLASS

Name	Number	Builder	Awarded	Keel	Launched	Commissioned	Decommissioned	To AVT
Wright	CVL-49	NY Shipbuilding	9–8–43	8–21–44	9–1–45	2–9–47	3–15–56	5–15–59

Sister to *Arlington* (AGMR-2), formerly *Saipan* (CVL-48). Has hull and machinery of *Baltimore* class CA. Originally classified CV-49; to CVL 7–15–43. Spent most of CVL career as experimental ship for new jets and as training ship. CC statistics follow.

1 CONVERTED LIGHT CARRIER, *WRIGHT* CLASS

Name	Number	FY/SCB	Converted at	Started	Completed	Recommissioned	F/S	Homeport	Date decommissioned (D)
Wright	CC-2	62/228	PS Navy	3–20–63	5–11–63	5–11–63	AR*	Norfolk	5–27–70(D)

Converted to highly successful primary command ship. Forward two-thirds of hangar deck now carry command spaces, which are more sophisticated than in CC-1; after third used to store and repair helicopters. Flight deck forward supports most powerful radio antennas installed on a ship; tallest is 83′. Differs from AGMR-2 by lack of guns at forward corners of flight deck and the presence of pylon radar mast between #1 and #2 stacks.

1 CONVERTED HEAVY CRUISER, *NORTHAMPTON* CLASS

Name	No.	Builder	Awarded	Keel	Cancelled	Reordered	Launched	Commissioned	F/S	Homeport	Date decommissioned (D)
Northampton	CC-1	Beth., Quincy	8–7–42	8–31–44	8–11–45	7–1–48	1–27–51	3–7–53	AR*	Norfolk	4–8–70(D)

Laid down as CA-125 of the *Oregon City* class; cancelled when 56.1% complete. Reordered as tactical command ship and reclassified CLC-1 on 7–1–48. To CC-1 on 4–15–61. Hull one deck higher than CAs to accommodate extra staff. In addition to 5″ guns, also mounted eight 3″/70s; removed in 1962 because of maintenance problems. Can operate but not stow helicopters. Considered to be virtually obsolete because cannot accomodate latest electronic gear now required. Carried the largest radar antenna afloat; removed in 1963. Has tallest unsupported antenna afloat (125′).

USS *Wright* (CC-2). Note cruiser-type hull and radar mast between #1 and #2 stacks. 8–13–63. **"Saipan"** *class.*

Stern view of USS *Wright* (CC-2). Note cruiser stern, masts, and helicopter landing area, 9–25–63. **"Saipan"** *class.*

USS *Alstede* (AF-48) replenishing USS *Northampton* (CC-1). Note 5″ guns on *Northampton* installed off centerline and helicopter deck aft. **Northampton** *class.*

E. Submarines

As of end-FY 1971, 41 SSBNs, 52 SSNs, and 44 SSs were on the NVR. Except for 1 SSN and 2 diesel-powered SS, all were active. In addition 21 SSNs were under construction, including a new class of SSN. Eight of the active SSNs are second rate or experimental, being of limited attack value. The USN *Nomenclature Directive* of 14 August 1968 classified auxiliary submarines (AGSS) as "Auxiliaries," while target, training, and midget submarines (X-craft) were classified as "Service Craft". These types will be found in their appropriate sections.

Class	Number	No. in Class	Standard Displ. Surf.	Standard Displ. Subm.	Length Overall	Max. Draft	Extreme Beam	Number of Reactors/ Engines/Motors	Screws/ SHP	Max. Speed (Kts) Surf.	Max. Speed (Kts) Subm.	Accommodations Officers	Accommodations Enlisted	Armament
FLEET BALLISTIC MISSILE														
Benjamin Franklin	SSBN-640	12	7,320	8,250	425′	31′4″	33′	1R/S5W(West.)	1		20+	20	148	16 A-3 POLARIS, 4 21″ TT fwd.
Lafayette	SSBN-616	19	7,250	8,250	425′	31′4″	33′	1R/S5W(West.)	1		20+	14	126	16 A-2 POLARIS (616, 617, 619, 620, 623 & 625), 16 POSEIDON (remainder), 4 21″ TT fwd.
Ethan Allen	SSBN-608	5	6,955	7,880	410′	30′9″	33′	1R/S5W(West.)	1		20+	15	127	16 A-2 POLARIS, 4 21″ TT fwd.
George Washington	SSBN-598	5	6,019	6,688	382′	30′	33′	1R/S5W(West.)	1		20+	12	127	16 A-3 POLARIS, 6 21″ TT fwd.
NUCLEAR-POWERED ATTACK														
Los Angeles	SSN-688	7	6,900		360′	32′	33′	1R/						4 21″ TT midships, SUBROC
Glenard P. Lipscomb	SSN-685	1						1R/S5Wa(West.)						4 21″ TT midships, SUBROC
Narwhal	SSN-671	1	4,450	5,350	303′	29′	38′	1R/S5G(G.E.)	1		20+	12	95	4 21″ TT midships, SUBROC
Sturgeon	SSN-637	37	3,640	4,640	292′3″	28′9″	31′8″	1R/S5W(West.)	1		20+	12	95	4 21″ TT midships, SUBROC
Tullibee	SSN-597	1	2,317	2,640	273′	21′	23′7″	1R/S2C(C.E.)	1		15+	6	50	4 21″ TT midships
"Thresher"	SSN-593	13	3,700	4,300	278′	28′5″	31′7″	1R/S5W(West.)	1		20+	12	91	4 21″ TT midships, SUBROC
Halibut	SSN-587	1	3,850	5,000	350′	21′5″	29′7″	1R/S3W(West.)	2		15+	10	88	4 21″ TT fwd., 2 21″ TT aft
Triton	SSN-586	1	5,939	6,670	447′	24′	37′	2R/S4G(G.E.)	2		20+	14	156	4 21″ TT fwd., 2 21″ TT aft
Skipjack	SSN-585	5	3,075	3,513	252′	29′5″	31′7″	1R/S5W(West.)	1		20+	8	85	6 21″ TT fwd.
Skate	SSN-578	4	2,570	2,861	267′7″	22′5″	25′	1R/S3W or 1R/S4W(West.)	2		20+	8	87	6 21″ TT fwd., 2 21″ TT aft
Seawolf	SSN-575	1	3,765	4,200	338′	23′1″	28′	1R/S2WA(West.)	2		20+	10	95	6 21″ TT fwd.
Nautilus	SSN-571	1	3,764	4,040	319′5″	25′5″	28′	1R/S2W(West.)	2		20+	10	95	6 21″ TT fwd.
CONVENTIONALLY POWERED ATTACK														
Barbel	SS-580	3	2,145	2,894	219′1″	28′	29′	3D(F.M.)/2EM(G.E.)	1/3,150	14·5	20.7	9	69	6 21″ TT fwd.
"Grayback"	SSG-574	1	2,540	3,515	318′	19′	27′	3D(F.M.)/2EM(Ell.)	2/5,500	20	17	10	78	4 21″ TT fwd., 2 21″ TT aft
Darter	SS-576	1	1,720	2,388	284′6″	19′	27′2″	3D(F.M.)/2EM(Ell.)	2/6,000	19·5	14.3	8	75	6 21″ TT fwd., 2 21″ TT aft
Sailfish	SS-572	2	2,455	3,160	350′5″	18′5″	28′5″	4D(F.M.)/2EM(West.)	2/6,000	19·5	14.3	12	79	6 21″ TT fwd.
Tang	SS-563	6	2,122	2,700	278′	19′	27′1″	3D(F.M.)/2EM(Ell.)	2/3,200	15·5	16	8	75	6 21″ TT fwd., 2 21″ TT aft
"Guppy III"	SS-343	9	2,320	2,870	320′	17′	27′3″	4D(G.M.)/2EM(G.E.)	2/4,610	17·2	14.5	10	74	6 21″ TT fwd., 4 21″ TT aft
"Guppy IIA"	SS-340	10	2,075	2,410	307′	17′	27′	3D(G.M.)/2EM(G.E.)	2/3,430	17	14.1	10	75	6 21″ TT fwd., 4 21″ TT aft
"Guppy II"	SS-339	10	2,040	2,400	307′	17′	27′	3D(G.M.)/2EM(G.E.)	2/4,610	18	16	10	75	6 21″ TT fwd., 4 21″ TT aft
"Guppy IA"	SS-322	2	1,800	2,400	307′	17′	27′	4D(G.M.)/2EM(G.E.)	2/4,610	17·3	15	10	75	6 21″ TT fwd., 4 21″ TT aft
"Fleet Snorkels"	SS-302	0	2,040	2,410	312′	17′	27′	4D(F.M.)/2EM(Ell.)	2/4,610	18·5	9	8	73	6 21″ TT fwd., 4 21″ TT aft

12 FLEET BALLISTIC MISSILE SUBMARINES, *BENJAMIN FRANKLIN* CLASS

Name	Number	FY/SCB	Builder	Awarded	Commissioned	F/S
Will Rogers	SSBN-659	64/216	Gen. Dyn., Groton	7–29–63	4–1–67	AA
Mariano G. Vallejo	SSBN-658	64/216	Mare Island	8–8–63	12–16–66	AA
Francis Scott Key	SSBN-657	64/216	Gen. Dyn., Groton	7–29–63	12–3–66	AA
George Washington Carver	SSBN-656	64/216	Newport News	7–29–63	6–15–66	AA
Henry L. Stimson	SSBN-655	64/216	Gen. Dyn., Groton	7–29–63	8–20–66	AA
George C. Marshall	SSBN-654	64/216	Newport News	7–29–63	4–29–66	PA
James K. Polk	SSBN-645	63/216	Gen. Dyn., Groton	11–1–62	4–16–66	AA
Lewis and Clark	SSBN-644	63/216	Newport News	11–1–62	12–22–65	AA
George Bancroft	SSBN-643	63/216	Gen. Dyn., Groton	11–1–62	1–22–66	AA
Kamehameha	SSBN-642	63/216	Mare Island	8–31–62	12–10–65	AA
Simon Bolivar	SSBN-641	63/216	Newport News	11–1–62	10–29–65	AA
Benjamin Franklin	SSBN-640	63/216	Gen. Dyn., Groton	11–1–62	10–22–65	AA

Modified *Lafayette* class; has quieter machinery and larger crew. Both classes to receive POSEIDON retrofits. All SSBNs have diesel/battery standby power and snorkels for emergency use. (SSBN bases are at Rota, Holy Loch, Pearl Harbor, Charleston, and Guam.)

19 FLEET BALLISTIC MISSILE SUBMARINES, *LAFAYETTE* CLASS

Nathanael Greene	SSBN-636	62/216	Portsmouth Navy	7–21–61	12–19–64	AA
Sam Rayburn	SSBN-635	62/216	Newport News	7–20–61	12–2–64	AA
Stonewall Jackson	SSBN-634	62/216	Mare Island	7–21–61	8–26–64	AA
Casimir Pulaski	SSBN-633	62/216	Gen. Dyn., Groton	7–20–61	8–14–64	AA
Von Steuben	SSBN-632	62/216	Newport News	7–20–61	9–30–64	AA
Ulysses S. Grant	SSBN-631	62/216	Gen. Dyn., Groton	7–20–61	7–17–64	AA
John C. Calhoun	SSBN-630	62/216	Newport News	7–20–61	9–15–64	AA
Daniel Boone	SSBN-629	62/216	Mare Island	7–21–61	4–23–64	AA
Tecumseh	SSBN-628	62/216	Gen. Dyn., Groton	7–20–61	5–29–64	AA
James Madison	SSBN-627	62/216	Newport News	7–20–61	7–28–64	AA
Daniel Webster	SSBN-626	61/216	Gen. Dyn., Groton	1–31–61	4–9–64	PA
Henry Clay	SSBN-625	61/216	Newport News	1–31–61	2–20–64	PA
Woodrow Wilson	SSBN-624	61/216	Mare Island	2–9–61	12–27–63	PA
Nathan Hale	SSBN-623	61/216	Gen. Dyn., Groton	1–31–61	11–23–63	PA
James Monroe	SSBN-622	61/216	Newport News	1–31–61	12–7–63	PA
John Adams	SSBN-620	61/216	Portsmouth Navy	7–23–60	5–12–64	PA
Andrew Jackson	SSBN-619	61/216	Mare Island	7–23–60	7–3–63	AA
Alexander Hamilton	SSBN-617	61/216	Gen. Dyn., Groton	7–22–60	6–27–63	AA
Lafayette	SSBN-616	61/216	Gen. Dyn., Groton	7–22–60	4–23–63	AA

Class incorporates certain designs tested in *Albacore*. First 8 submarines of this class deployed with POLARIS A-2, the remainder with the A-3. All scheduled for C-3 retrofit. Air-ejection missile launch system of first 6 SSBNs in class was upgraded to gas/steam generator system. SSBN-617 launched first A-3. SSBN-629 first to be assigned to PACFLT. SSBN-626 has diving planes experimentally mounted on a bow protrusion. Proved very successful, but there are no reconfiguration plans for other units of the class. All SSBNs have SINS.

POSEIDON (C-3) CONVERSIONS

Number	FY/SCB	Converted at	Awarded	Started	Completed
SSBN-657	71/353				
SSBN-656	71/353				
SSBN-655	71/353				
SSBN-654	71/353				
SSBN-645	70/353	Newport News			
SSBN-644	71/353.68	PS Navy	1–28–71	4–30–71	
SSBN-643	71/353.68	Portsmouth Navy	1–21–71	4–28–71	
SSBN-642	70/353	Gen. Dyn., Groton			
SSBN-641	71/353.68	Newport News	2–12–71	2–15–71	
SSBN-640	71/353.68	Gen. Dyn., Groton	2–24–71	2–25–71	
SSBN-636	71/353.68	Newport News	7–21–70	7–22–70	
SSBN-635	70/353.68	Portsmouth Navy	2–18–70	1–19–70	
SSBN-634	71/353.68	Gen. Dyn., Groton	7–14–70	7–15–70	
SSBN-633	70/353.68	Gen. Dyn., Groton	1–2–70	1–10–70	
SSBN-632	69/353.68	Gen. Dyn., Groton	7–8–69	7–11–69	11–19–70
SSBN-631	70/353.68	PS Navy	10–6–69	10–3–69	12–16–70
SSBN-630	69/353.68	Mare Island	6–23–69	8–4–69	2–22–71
SSBN-629	68/353.68	Newport News	4–19–68	5–11–69	8–11–70
SSBN-628	70/353.68	Newport News	1–6–69	11–10–69	2–18–71
SSBN-627	68/353.68	Gen. Dyn., Groton	11–17–67	2–3–69	6–28–70

All of *Benjamin Franklin* and *Lafayette* classes will get POSEIDON refits. Basically, conversion entails removal of a liner in launching tubes to accommodate larger circumference of POSEIDON (over POLARIS) and modernization of electronic gear. At the same time, the SSBN will be overhauled and refueled.

5 FLEET BALLISTIC MISSILE SUBMARINES, *ETHAN ALLEN* CLASS

Name	Number	FY/SCB	Builder	Awarded	Commissioned	F/S
Thomas Jefferson	SSBN-618	61/180	Newport News	7–22–60	1–4–63	AA
John Marshall	SSBN-611	59/180	Newport News	7–1–59	5–21–63	AA
Thomas A. Edison	SSBN-610	59/180	Gen. Dyn., Groton	7–1–59	3–10–62	AA
Sam Houston	SSBN-609	59/180	Newport News	7–1–59	3–6–62	AA
Ethan Allen	SSBN-608	59/180	Gen. Dyn., Groton	12–30–58	8–8–61	AA

First true SSBNs. Larger than, but similar to, SSBN-598 class; deeper diving. Neither class will receive POSEIDON refit. This class carries A-3. Entire class homeported at Groton. Most of this class base at Rota or Holy Loch.

5 FLEET BALLISTIC MISSILE SUBMARINES, *GEORGE WASHINGTON* CLASS

Name	Number	FY/SCB	Builder	Awarded	Commissioned	F/S
Abraham Lincoln	SSBN-602	59/180A	Portsmouth Navy	7–30–58	3–11–61	AA
Robert E. Lee	SSBN-601	59/180A	Newport News	7–30–58	9–16–60	PA
Theodore Roosevelt	SSBN-600	58/180A	Mare Island	3–15–58	2–13–61	AA
Patrick Henry	SSBN-599	58/180A	Gen. Dyn., Groton	12–31–57	4–9–60	PA
George Washington	SSBN-598	58/180A	Gen. Dyn., Groton	12–31–57	12–30–59	AA

First generation of SSBN, superceding SSGN. Originally ordered as *Skipjack* class attack submarines. SSBN-598 originally laid down as *Scorpion* (SSN) but as a result of a FY 1958 supplement SSN-598/602 were modified to SSBN by insertion of a 130′ section housing launching tubes just aft of sail. Class had A-1 missiles; retrofitted to A-3.

7 NUCLEAR-POWERED ATTACK SUBMARINES, *LOS ANGELES* CLASS

Name	Number	FY/SCB	Builder	Awarded	Commissioned	F/S
	SSN-694	71/303	Gen. Dyn., Groton	1–31–71		Bldg.
	SSN-693	71/303	Newport News	2–4–71		Bldg.
	SSN-692	71/303	Gen. Dyn., Groton	1–31–71		Bldg.
	SSN-691	71/303	Newport News	2–4–71		Bldg.

continued

Los Angeles Class—*continued*

Name	Number	FY/SCB	Builder	Awarded	Commissioned	F/S
	SSN-690	70/303	Gen. Dyn., Groton	1–8–71		Bldg.
	SSN-689	70/303	Newport News	1–8–71		Bldg.
Los Angeles	SSN-688	70/303	Newport News	1–8–71		Bldg.

A new class to number approximately 25 units. Will go deeper and faster than previous classes. Newport News will build all or most. SSN designs are a technical compromise. To obtain high speeds, the submarine can become too big and noisy, but with very high speeds, detection does not become a real problem.

1 NUCLEAR-POWERED ATTACK SUBMARINE, *GLENARD P. LIPSCOMB* CLASS

Name	Number	FY/SCB	Builder	Awarded	Commissioned	F/S
Glenard P. Lipscomb	SSN-685	68/302	Gen. Dyn., Groton	10–14–70		Bldg.

A 1-unit class. Prototype design with turbine electric drive propulsion to test advanced silencing techniques for superquiet operations as opposed to the noisy geared drive. Will also have full combat capability.

1 NUCLEAR-POWERED ATTACK SUBMARINE, *NARWHAL* CLASS

Name	Number	FY/SCB	Builder	Awarded	Commissioned	F/S
Narwhal (167)	SSN-671	64/245	Gen. Dyn., Groton	7–28–64	7–12–69	AA

Largest built-for-purpose SSN in Navy. Similar to SSN-637 class but has improved propulsion system equipped with natural circulation reactor.

37 NUCLEAR-POWERED ATTACK SUBMARINES, *STURGEON* CLASS

Name	Number	FY/SCB	Builder	Awarded	Commissioned	F/S
Richard B. Russell	SSN-687	69/300	Newport News	7–25–69		Bldg.
L. Mendel Rivers	SSN-686	69/300	Newport News	7–25–69		Bldg.
Cavalla (244)	SSN-684	68/300	Gen. Dyn., Groton	7–24–69		Bldg.
Parche (384)	SSN-683	68/300	Gen. Dyn., Groton	6–25–68		Bldg.
Tunny (282)	SSN-682	67/300	Ingalls	6–25–68		Bldg.
Batfish (310)	SSN-681	67/300	Gen. Dyn., Groton	6–25–68		Bldg.
Redfish (395)	SSN-680	67/300	Ingalls	6–25–68		Bldg.
Silversides (236)	SSN-679	67/300	Gen. Dyn., Groton	6–25–68		AA
Archerfish (311)	SSN-678	67/300	Gen. Dyn., Groton	6–25–68		AA
Drum (228)	SSN-677	66/300.66	Mare Island	3–15–67		PA
Billfish (286)	SSN-676	66/300.66	Gen. Dyn., Groton	7–15–66	3–12–71	AA
Bluefish (222)	SSN-675	66/300.66	Gen. Dyn., Groton	7–15–66	1–8–71	AA
Trepang (412)	SSN-674	66/300.66	Gen. Dyn., Groton	7–15–66	8–14–70	AA
Flying Fish (229)	SSN-673	66/300.66	Gen. Dyn., Groton	7–15–66	4–29–70	AA
Pintado (387)	SSN-672	66/300.66	Mare Island	12–29–65		PA
Finback (230)	SSN-670	65/300.65	Newport News	3–9–65	2–4–70	AA
Seahorse (304)	SSN-669	65/300.65	Gen. Dyn., Groton	3–9–65	9–19–69	AA
Spadefish (411)	SSN-668	65/300.65	Newport News	3–9–65	8–14–69	AA
Bergall (320)	SSN-667	65/300.65	Gen. Dyn., Groton	3–9–65	6–13–69	AA
Hawkbill (366)	SSN-666	65/300.65	Mare Island	12–18–64	2–4–71	PA
Guitarro (363)	SSN-665	65/300.65	Mare Island	12–18–64		PA
Sea Devil (400)	SSN-664	64/188A	Newport News	5–28–64	1–30–69	AA
Hammerhead (364)	SSN-663	64/188A	Newport News	5–28–64	6–28–68	AA

Gurnard (254)	SSN-662	64/188A	Mare Island	10–24–63	12–6–68	PA
Lapon (260)	SSN-661	64/188A	Newport News	5–28–64	12–14–67	AA
Sand Lance (381)	SSN-660	64/188A	Portsmouth Navy	10–24–63		AA
Ray (271)	SSN-653	63/188A	Newport News	3–26–63	4–12–67	AA
Puffer (268)	SSN-652	63/188A	Ingalls	3–26–63	8–9–69	PA
Queenfish (393)	SSN-651	63/188A	Newport News	3–26–63	12–6–66	PA
Pargo (264)	SSN-650	63/188A	Gen. Dyn., Groton	3–26–63	1–5–68	AA
Sunfish (281)	SSN-649	63/188A	Gen. Dyn., Quincy	3–26–63	3–15–69	AA
Aspro (309)	SSN-648	63/188A	Ingalls	3–26–63	2–20–69	PA
Pogy (266)	SSN-647	63/188A	Ingalls	12–7–67	5–15–71	PA
Grayling (209)	SSN-646	63/188A	Portsmouth Navy	9–5–62	10–11–69	AA
Tautog (199)	SSN-639	62/188A	Ingalls	11–30–61	8–17–68	PA
Whale (239)	SSN-638	62/188A	Gen. Dyn., Quincy	11–30–61	10–12–68	AA
Sturgeon (187)	SSN-637	62/188A	Gen. Dyn., Groton	11–30–61	3–3–67	AA

Class built to a modified *Thresher* design with SUBSAFE features; can lay mines. Easily recognized from previous SSNs by taller sails and lower position of diving planes on sails. Numbers in parentheses indicate previous submarine hull numbers that bore the name. SSN-666 and 670 are fitted as DSRV motherships. SSN-660 placed "in service" 1–15–71. On 5–15–69, while being outfitted at Mare Island, *Guitarro* (SSN-665) sank in 35′ of water as a result of negligence. Raised 5–19–69. Electrical/electronic gear heavily damaged. Completion delayed 28 months. *Pogy* (SSN-647) ordered from NY Shipbuilding 3–23–63. Contract cancelled 6–5–67; towed to Ingalls 1–68 for completion.

1 NUCLEAR-POWERED ATTACK SUBMARINE, *TULLIBEE* CLASS

Tullibee (284)	SSN-597	58/178	Gen. Dyn., Groton	11–15–57	11–9–60	AA

Laid down as SSKN; to SSN 8–15–59. Smallest combat nuclear submarine and first designed for ASW. Has reactor plant with turbo-electric drive. Tubes are amidships, angled out from centerline—frees bow area for sonar and other detection devices. No SUBROC. Rated second line.

13 NUCLEAR-POWERED ATTACK SUBMARINES, *"THRESHER"* CLASS

Haddock (231)	SSN-621	61/188	Ingalls, Pascag.	8–24–60	12–22–67	PA
Gato (212)	SSN-615	60/188	Gen. Dyn., Quincy	6–9–60	1–25–68	AA
Greenling (213)	SSN-614	60/188	Gen. Dyn., Quincy	6–9–60	11–3–67	AA
Flasher (249)	SSN-613	60/188	Gen. Dyn., Quincy	6–9–60	7–22–66	PA
Guardfish (217)	SSN-612	60/188	NY Shipbuilding	6–9–60	12–20–66	PA
Dace (247)	SSN-607	59/188	Ingalls, Pascag.	3–3–59	4–4–64	AA
Tinosa (283)	SSN-606	59/188	Portsmouth Navy	12–17–58	10–17–64	AA
Jack (259)	SSN-605	59/188	Portsmouth Navy	3–13–59	3–31–67	AA
Haddo (255)	SSN-604	59/188	NY Shipbuilding	3–3–59	12–16–64	AA
Pollack (180)	SSN-603	59/188	NY Shipbuilding	3–3–59	5–26–64	AA
Barb (220)	SSN-596	58/188	Ingalls, Pascag.	3–3–59	8–24–63	PA
Plunger (179)	SSN-595	58/188	Mare Island	3–23–59	11–21–62	PA
Permit (178)	SSN-594	58/188	Mare Island	1–27–58	5–29–62	PA

Teardrop-hull SSN. Lead-ship, *Thresher* (SSN-593), lost 4–10–63 off New England coast with 129 men; construction on rest of class delayed to incorporate SUBSAFE. SSN-605 is 295′7″ long; SSN-613/615 are 292′2″ and approximately 500 tons heavier. SSN-605 tests different power plant; has 2 propellers on one shaft (sleeve shaft over main, counter-rotating turbine without reduction gear). Propellers are smaller; have 10% more power efficiency with no increase in speed. SSN-594/596 and 607 ordered as *Halibut* SSGNs; to SSN 5–1–62 when REGULUS II cancelled.

1 NUCLEAR-POWERED ATTACK SUBMARINE, *HALIBUT* CLASS

Name	Number	FY/SCB	Builder	Awarded	Commissioned	F/S
Halibut (232)	SSN-587	56/137A	Mare Island	3–9–56	1–4–60	PA

Only SSGN completed and commissioned; 5 originally scheduled. During design stages, converted to nuclear from diesel propulsion. Designed as stable missile platform for REGULUS missiles, she lacks speed and maneuverability. As SSGN was to carry 5 REGULUS I or 2 REGULUS II missiles. To SSN 8–15–65. Missile gear/controls removed and ship used for experiments. Rated second line. Serves as DSRV test ship.

1 NUCLEAR-POWERED ATTACK SUBMARINE, *TRITON* CLASS

Triton (201)	SSN-586	56/132	Gen. Dyn., Groton	10–5–55	11–10–59	AR*

World's longest submarine. Originally completed as SSRN. Only submarine with 2 reactors. Designed for surface operation as high-speed picket; has bulbous bow, no vertical tail fin. Reclassified SSN 3–1–61 when radar picket concept dropped. Still retains huge radar antenna that retracts into sail. Fitted with elaborate CIC. Projected conversion to underwater command ship dropped. Rated second line. Decommissioned 5–3–69.

5 NUCLEAR-POWERED SUBMARINES, *SKIPJACK* CLASS

Snook (279)	SSN-592	57/154	Ingalls	1–18–57	10–24–61	PA
Shark (314)	SSN-591	57/154	Newport News	1–31–57	2–9–61	AA
Sculpin (191)	SSN-590	57/154	Ingalls	1–18–57	6–1–61	PA
Scamp (277)	SSN-588	57/154	Mare Island	7–23–56	6–5–61	PA
Skipjack (184)	SSN-585	56/154	Gen. Dyn., Groton	10–5–55	4–15–59	AA

First teardrop-hull nuclear submarines and first to have single screw. *Scorpion* (SSN-589) overdue 5–7–68 and declared lost 6–6–68 west of Azores; cause of sinking unknown. Class still rated first line.

4 NUCLEAR-POWERED ATTACK SUBMARINES, *SKATE* CLASS

Seadragon (194)	SSN-584	56/121	Portsmouth Navy	9–29–55	12–5–59	PA
Sargo (188)	SSN-583	56/121	Mare Island	9–29–55	10–1–58	PA
Swordfish (193)	SSN-579	55/121	Portsmouth Navy	7–18–55	9–15–58	PA
Skate (305)	SSN-578	55/121	Gen. Dyn., Groton	7–18–55	12–23–57	AA

First class of SSN built for attack purposes. Design similar to SSN-571, but smaller. Rated second line.

1 NUCLEAR-POWERED ATTACK SUBMARINE, *SEAWOLF* CLASS

Seawolf (197)	SSN-575	52/64A	Gen. Dyn., Groton	7–21–52	3–30–57	PA

Intended to be an attack submarine, but used mostly for experiments. Completed with an S2G sodium-cooled reactor, which was later replaced. Rated second line.

1 NUCLEAR-POWERED ATTACK SUBMARINE, *NAUTILUS* CLASS

Nautilus (168)	SSN-571	52/64	Gen. Dyn., Groton	8–20–51	9–30–54	AA

World's first nuclear-powered warship. *Seawolf* and *Nautilus* constructed to compete in design competition and to see which type of reactor was best, SSN-571's water-cooled reactor or SSN-575's sodium-cooled reactor. Water-cooled reactor got honors. Rated second line. Resembles *Guppy IIA* from a distance.

3 CONVENTIONALLY POWERED ATTACK SUBMARINES, *BARBEL* CLASS

Bonefish	SS-582	56/150	NY Shipbuilding	6–29–56	7–9–59	PA
Blueback	SS-581	56/150	Ingalls	6–29–56	10–15–59	PA
Barbel	SS-580	56/150	Portsmouth Navy	8–24–55	1–17–59	PA

Last class of non-nuclear submarines to be built. Hull is based on tests with *Albacore*. Diving planes originally mounted on bow; later moved to sail.

1 CONVENTIONALLY POWERED GUIDED MISSILE SUBMARINE, *"GRAYBACK"* CLASS

Growler	SSG-577	55/161	Portsmouth Navy	7–31–54	8–30–58	PR*

Originally ordered as *Darter* class submarine. To SSG 7–26–56. Converted to carry REGULUS by insertion of a 50′ section amidships and addition of 2 cylindrical hangers, each 11′ high and extending 70′ aft from the bow. Decommissioned 5–25–64 when REGULUS program phased out. Conversion to LPSS deferred because of excessive cost of converting sister *Grayback* to LPSS.

1 CONVENTIONALLY POWERED ATTACK SUBMARINE, *DARTER* CLASS

Darter	SS-576	54/116	Gen. Dyn., Groton	6–30–54	10–20–56	PA

Improved *Tang* class with console controls. Exceptionally quiet. Has higher submerged speed than most conventional submarines.

2 CONVENTIONALLY POWERED ATTACK SUBMARINES, *SAILFISH* CLASS

Salmon	SS-573	52/84	Portsmouth Navy	2–27–52	8–25–56	PA
Sailfish	SS-572	52/84	Portsmouth Navy	2–27–52	4–14–56	PA

Originally radar picket submarines (SSR). To SS 3–1–65; radar gear removed. Both had FRAM II. SS-573 reclassified AGSS 6–29–68 and fitted as DSRV test ship. Project delayed and submarine reconverted to SS and reclassified as such 6–30–69.

6 CONVENTIONALLY POWERED ATTACK SUBMARINES, *TANG* CLASS

Harder	SS-568	49/2A	Electric Boat	11–5–48	8–19–52	PA
Gudgeon	SS-567	49/2A	Portsmouth Navy	10–12–48	11–21–52	PA
Trout	SS-566	48/2A	Electric Boat	5–14–48	6–27–52	PA
Wahoo	SS-565	48/2A	Portsmouth Navy	2–1–48	5–30–52	PA
Trigger	SS-564	47/2A	Electric Boat	8–19–47	3–31–52	PA
Tang	SS-563	47/2A	Portsmouth Navy	8–12–47	10–25–51	PA

First postwar attack submarines completed. *Gudgeon* first SS to circumnavigate world. Original length of submarines 269′2″. Have undergone radical reconstruction at various periods. All had FRAM II.

9 CONVENTIONALLY POWERED ATTACK SUBMARINES, *"GUPPY III"* CLASS

Name	Number	Builder	Awarded	Commissioned	F/S
Pickerel	SS-524	Boston Navy	6–17–43	4–4–49	AA
Volador	SS-490	Portsmouth Navy	6–17–43	1–10–48	AA
Remora	SS-487	Portsmouth Navy	6–17–43	1–3–46	AA
Trumpetfish	SS-425	Cramp	6–6–42	1–29–46	AA
Tiru	SS-416	Mare Island	6–8–42	9–1–48	AA
Greenfish	SS-351	Electric Boat	6–6–42	6–7–46	AA
Corporal	SS-346	Electric Boat	6–6–42	11–9–45	AA
Cobbler	SS-344	Electric Boat	6–6–42	8–8–45	AA
Clamagore	SS-343	Electric Boat	6–6–42	6–28–45	AA

All except SS-416 completed as units of *Balao* or *Tench* classes. SS-416 completed to *"Guppy II"* configuration. Remainder converted to *"Guppy II"* 1948–50 and all to *"Guppy III"* 1960–62. SS-416 has 3 diesels, remainder 4. 15 more conversions to *"Guppy III"* dropped. *"Guppy III"* modernization included improved electronics and addition of 19′ section amidships.

10 CONVENTIONALLY POWERED ATTACK SUBMARINES, *"GUPPY IIA"* CLASS

Name	Number	Builder	Awarded	Commissioned	F/S
Quillback	SS-424	Portsmouth Navy	2–22–43	12–29–44	AA
Trutta	SS-421	Portsmouth Navy	2–22–43	11–16–44	AA
Tirante	SS-420	Portsmouth Navy	2–22–43	11–6–44	AA
[Thornback]	SS-418	Portsmouth Navy	2–22–43	10–13–44	ILP
Threadfin	SS-410	Portsmouth Navy	6–8–42	8–30–44	AA
[Ronquil]	SS-396	Portsmouth Navy	6–8–42	4–22–44	Struck
[Pomfret]	SS-391	Portsmouth Navy	6–8–42	2–19–44	ILP
Bang	SS-385	Portsmouth Navy	6–8–42	12–4–43	AA
Picuda	SS-382	Portsmouth Navy	6–8–42	10–16–43	AA
Menhaden	SS-377	Manitowoc	6–6–42	6–22–45	PR*
Jallao	SS-368	Manitowoc	6–6–42	7–8–44	AA
Hardhead	SS-365	Manitowoc	6–6–42	4–18–44	AA
Entemedor	SS-340	Electric Boat	6–6–42	4–6–45	AA

All completed in *Tench* or *Balao* classes. Orginally 16 in class. Converted to *"Guppy IIA"* 1952–54. Resemble *"Guppy IIIs"* except are 19′ shorter. *Stickleback* (SS-415) rammed and sunk by *Silverstein* (DE-534) 5–29–58.

10 CONVENTIONALLY POWERED ATTACK SUBMARINES, *"GUPPY II"* CLASS

Name	Number	Builder	Awarded	Commissioned	F/S
Grenadier	SS-525	Boston Navy	6–17–43	2–10–51	AA
Grampus	SS-523	Boston Navy	6–17–43	10–26–49	AA
Amberjack	SS-522	Boston Navy	6–17–43	3–4–46	AA
Sirago	SS-485	Portsmouth Navy	6–17–43	8–13–45	AA
Odax	SS-484	Portsmouth Navy	6–17–43	7–11–45	AA
Sea Leopard	SS-483	Portsmouth Navy	6–17–43	6–11–45	AA
Cutlass	SS-478	Portsmouth Navy	6–17–43	3–17–45	AA
Tusk	SS-426	Cramp	6–6–42	4–11–46	AA
[Halfbeak]	SS-352	Electric Boat	6–6–42	7–22–46	Struck
Dogfish	SS-350	Electric Boat	6–6–42	4–29–46	AA
Cubera	SS-347	Electric Boat	6–6–42	12–19–45	AA
[Catfish]	SS-339	Electric Boat	6–6–42	3–19–45	Struck

Completed as units of *Tench* or *Balao* class. SS-484 was *"Guppy IA"*. Originally 24 units were converted to *"Guppy II"* 1948–50. Nine of these converted to *"Guppy III"* in early 1960s. *Cochino* (SS-345) was lost off Norway 8–26–49 as a result of battery explosion.

2 CONVENTIONALLY POWERED ATTACK SUBMARINES, *"GUPPY IA"* CLASS

[Chivo]	SS-341	Electric Boat	6–6–42	4–28–45	Struck
Caiman	SS-323	Electric Boat	6–6–42	7–17–44	PA
Blackfin	SS-322	Electric Boat	6–6–42	7–4–44	PA

All completed as units of *Balao* class; originally 12 converted to *"Guppy IA."* Six were reclassified AGSS, and 2 have been scrapped. There are no active submarines below the hull number SS-322. The two remaining *"Guppy IA"* subs are to decommission early to mid-1972.

CONVENTIONALLY POWERED ATTACK SUBMARINE, *"FLEET SNORKEL"* TYPE

[Sabalo]	SS-302	Cramp	12–24–41	6–19–45	Struck

Originally 19 *Balao* and *Tench* class submarines were converted to fleet snorkels. Two were sold or loaned, 12 were reclassified AGSS (listed in section 5), and 4 were scrapped. SS-331, 337, and 480 of this class reclassified AGSS 1967–68 but reverted to SS 10–1–69. SS-302 decommissioned and struck 7–1–71.

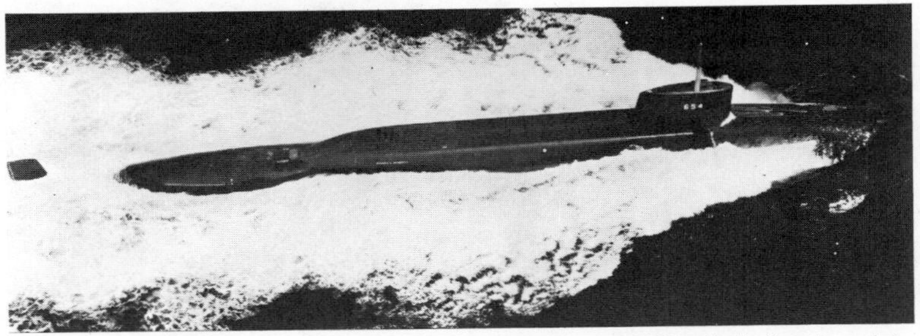

USS *George C. Marshall* (SSBN-654). The darkened area amidships is the location of the missile tubes. There are eight on each side. 3–27–66. **Benjamin Franklin** *class.*

USS *Andrew Jackson* (SSBN-619). 6–4–63. **Lafayette** *class.*

USS *Robert E. Lee* (SSBN-601). **George Washington** *class.*

USS *Daniel Webster* (SSBN-626) assisted by tug as she prepares to get underway for the first deployment of the POLARIS A-3 missile. 9–28–64. **Lafayette** *class.*

USS *Andrew Jackson* (SSBN-619). Note location of diving planes as compared to SSBN-626. 6–4–63. **Lafayette** *class.*

USS *John Marshall* (SSBN-611). **Ethan Allen** *class.*

General Dynamics

USS *Bergall* (SSN-667). Note location of sail as compared to WW II fleet boats. 3–30–69. **Sturgeon** *class.*

USS *Gurnard* (SSN-662). Note clean lines and cigar-shaped hull. 12–12–68. **Sturgeon** *class.*

Glenard P. Lipscomb (SSN-685). An artist's conception of the quiet submarine. 8-68. **Glenard P. Lipscomb** *class.*

General Dynamics

USS *Narwhal* (SSN-671). Her appearance is very similar to SSN-637 class, but slightly longer. 7–69. **Narwhal** *class.*

USS *Tullibee* (SSN-597), our smallest nuclear submarine and first SSN with turboelectric machinery, passing the Portuguese training ship *Sagres*. USS *Jallao* (SS-368) is to the left in background. **Tullibee** *class.*

USS *Haddock* (SSN-621) on sea trials. 12–1–67. **"Thresher"** *class.*

USS *Halibut* (SSN-587) as SSGN-587. Note missile hanger and tracks just aft of it for launching missile; since removed. 2–60. **Halibut** *class.*

USS *Skipjack* (SSN-585). Note tall sail. 4–1–59. **Skipjack** *class.*

USS *Triton* (SSN-586). Note radar nest in middle of top of sail. Radar used in picket days was housed in this compartment. **Triton** *class.*

USS *Swordfish* (SSN-579). 1–25–65. **Skate** *class.*

USS *Seawolf* (SSN-575) participating in an ASW exercise. 2–58. **Seawolf** *class.*

Ingalls Shipbuilding

USS *Blueback* (SS-581). **Barbel** *class.*

USS *Growler* (SSG-577). Compare with photo of *Grayback* (LPSS-574), a former sister, in section 2.11–28–58. **"Grayback"** *class.*

USS *Nautilus* (SSN-571) entering New York Harbor after making voyage under North Pole. Note location of diving planes as compared to later classes. 8–25–58. **Nautilus** *class.*

USS *Darter* (SS-576) in company with USS *Calcaterra* (DER-390) during ASW exercises. Note extended periscope. 6–20–60. **Darter** *class.*

The former picket submarine *Salmon* (SS-573) underway in her present configuration. Note sail; similar to *Triton's*. **Sailfish** *class.*

USS *Trigger* (SS-564). **Tang** *class.*

USS *Trumpetfish* (SS-425), an example of Guppy III. **"Guppy III"** *class.*

USS *Menhaden* (SS-377). Note torpedo tubes at waterline and extended radar atop sail. 7–57. **"Guppy IIA"** *class.*

USS *Cubera* (SS-347). Note starboard anchor and sail as compared to sail on *Grampus*. **"Guppy II"** *class.*

USS *Grampus* (SS-523). Note sail as compared to SS-347, also a Guppy II. **"Guppy II"** *class.*

USS *Caiman* (SS-323), an example of Guppy IA. **"Guppy IA"** *class.*

USS *Sabalo* (SS-302). Last active Fleet Snorkel submarine. Note old fleet boat bow. Fleet Snorkel can be recognized from Guppy by shape of bow. 9–29–53.
"Fleet Snorkel" *type.*

F. Patrol Ships

By end-FY 1971. there were 17 patrol ships on the NVR, all of which were patrol gunboats. The last of the PC/PCE/PCER/PCS family, *Marysville* (PCER-857), was struck on 7–15–70.

Class	Number	No. in Class	Full Load Displ.	Length Overall	Max. Draft	Extreme Beam	Number & Type of Engines/Turbines	Screws/ SHP	Max. Speed (Kts)	Accommodations Officers	Accommodations Enlisted	Armament
PATROL GUNBOATS												
Asheville	PG-84	17	245	165′	9′6″	23′6″	2D(Cummins)/1G(G.E.)	2/13,000	37·5	4	27	1 3″/50, 1 single 40mm, 2.50 cal. mg.
PATROL RESCUE ESCORTS												
"Somersworth"	PCER-849	0	900	185′	9′	33′	2D(G.M.)	2/1,800	15·4	9	90	unarmed

17 PATROL GUNBOATS, *ASHEVILLE* CLASS

Name	Number	FY/SCB	Builder	Awarded	Commissioned	F/S
Green Bay	PG-101	66/600	Peterson	7–26–66	12–5–69	PA
Douglas	PG-100	66/600	Tacoma	7–26–66	2–6–71	PA
Beacon	PG-99	66/600	Peterson	7–26–66	11–21–69	PA
Grand Rapids	PG-98	66/600	Tacoma	7–26–66	9–5–70	PA
Surprise	PG-97	66/600	Peterson	7–26–66	10–17–69	AA
Benicia	PG-96	66/600	Tacoma	7–26–66	4–25–70	PA
Defiance	PG-95	66/600	Peterson	7–26–66	9–24–69	AA
Chehalis	PG-94	66/600	Tacoma	7–26–66	11–8–69	PA
Welch	PG-93	66/600	Peterson	7–26–66	9–8–69	PA
Tacoma	PG-92	66/600	Tacoma	7–26–66	7–14–69	PA
Canon	PG-90	65/600	Tacoma	1–18–65	7–26–68	PA
Marathon	PG-89	65/600	Tacoma	1–18–65	5–11–68	PA
Crockett	PG-88	65/600	Tacoma	1–18–65	6–24–67	PA
Ready	PG-87	64/600	Tacoma	6–20–64	1–6–68	PA
Antelope	PG-86	64/600	Tacoma	6–20–64	11–4–67	PA
Gallup	PG-85	63/600	Tacoma	6–28–63	10–22–66	PA
Asheville	PG-84	63/600	Tacoma	6–28–63	8–6–66	PA

First type of large patrol craft built for USN since WW II, and first class of mass-produced ship with gas-turbine propulsion in USN. Can shift from diesel to turbine power underway without losing speed. Class originally designated PGM, but reclassified PG 4–1–67 to differentiate from the PGMs built under ILP. Hull numbers duplicate British "Flower" class PGs obtained under reverse lend-lease in WW II. At first this class had design problems, but these have been identified and corrected. PG-96 has test-fired STANDARD missile (SSM-mode), and PG-86/87 are converting to carry four missiles each. They will each have a pair of two-missile launchers, one launcher on either side, aft.

1 PATROL RESCUE ESCORT, *"SOMERSWORTH"* CLASS

Name	Number	Builder	Commissioned	F/S
[Marysville]	PCER-857	Pullman	4–26–45	Struck

Originally 13 of this class used as small hospital ships. Hospital rig removed after WW II. PCERs on list 6–5–54 were reclassified EPCER. Reverted to PCER 4–1–68. Used for oceanography research. PCER-857 decommissioned 7–15–70.

A PCE class of 35 ships once existed. The PCEs served as ASW vessels in WW II and later as NRT ships. All existing PCEs/PCERs were named 2–15–56. PCERs were evolution of PCE design.

Tacoma Boatbuilding

USS *Ready* (PG-87). Note flush deck, fat squat stack, size of gun mount, and egg-shaped radome on top of bridge. 12–26–67. **Asheville** *class.*

USS *Surprise* (PG-97). Note vent forward of stack and lack of egg-shaped radome on top of bridge as compared to PG-87. **Asheville** *class.*

2. AMPHIBIOUS WARFARE SHIPS

By end-FY 1971, there were 203 amphibious vessels on the NVR. Of these, 72 were active, 59 were in the USN reserve, 31 were in the MARAD reserve (USN retains title), 1 was assigned to NRT, and 40 LSTs were assigned to MSC. An additional 144 LPA/LKA, APA/AKA were laid up in MARAD, most have been struck (see section 15). 16 amphibious ships were under construction. New amphibious vessels are designed to replace 2 or 3 WW II vintage vessels. A new type of ship, designated LFS, is in the design stages; will replace all-gun cruisers as fire-support ships. It is expected to have a full load displacement of 8,000 tons and a speed of 20 knots.

Class	Number	No. in Class	Full Load Displ.	Length Overall	Max. Draft	Extreme Beam	Number & Type of Boilers/Engines	Screws/ SHP	Max. Speed (Kts)	Accommodations Officers	Accommodations Enlisted	Troops Officers	Troops Enlisted	Armament
Blue Ridge	LCC-19	2	19,000	620′	27′	108′	2B(F.W.)/1GT(G.E.)	1/22,000	20	269	1,169	—	—	2 twin 3″/50
"Adirondack"	AGC-15	2	12,560	459′	24′7″	63′	2B(C.E.)/1GT(G.E.)	1/6,000	16	60	553	—	—	1 5″/38, 2 twin 40mm
Mount McKinley	LCC-7	3	12,667	459′	25′	65′	2B(B&W)/1GT(G.E.)	1/6,000	16	50	616	—	—	1 5″/38, 2 twin 40mm
"Elk River"	LSMR-501	5	1,280	211′	8′8″	34′5″	2D(G.M.)	2/2,880	13·9	7	131	—	—	1 5″/38, 2 twin 40mm, 8 twin 5″ rocket launcher
Big Black River	LFR-401	3	1,276	203′6″	9′	34′5″	2D(G.M.)	2/2,880	12	7	138	—	—	1 5″/38, 2 twin 40mm, 8 twin 5″ rocket launcher
Carronade	LFR-1	1	1,564	245′	9′8″	37′5″	2D(F.M.)	2/3,000	16.1	12	144	—	—	1 5″/38, 2 twin 40mm, 8 twin 5″ rocket launcher
	LHA-1	5	39,201	820′	27′	106′	2B/2GT	2/70,000	24	[2,807 total]		—	—	3 5″/54, 2 BPDMS
Charleston	LKA-113	5	20,700	550′	28′	82′	2B(C.E.)/1GT	1/22,000	20	31	362	15	211	4 twin 3″/50
Tulare	LKA-112	1	16,818	564′	28′	76′	2B(C.E.)/1GT(DeLaval)	1/22,000	23.4	31	362	18	301	6 twin 3″/50
Rankin	LKA-103	5	10,664	459′	26′3″	61′1″	2B(C.E.)/2GT(G.E.)	1/6,000	16.3	25	335	9	129	1 5″/38, 4 twin 40mm
Winston	LKA-94	2	13,700	459′	28′	63′2″	2B(F.W.)/2GT(G.E.)	1/6,000	16.5	28	335	11	88	4 twin 40mm
"Uvalde"	AKA-88	1	13,000	459′	28′	63′	2B(C.E.)/2GT(G.E.)	1/6,000	16	37	335	12	85	4 twin 40mm
Arneb	LKA-56	1	13,907	459′	28′	63′	2B(F.W.)/2GT(G.E.)	1/6,000	16	29	281	6	112	1 5″/38, 4 twin 40mm
Algol	LKA-54	2	10,958	460′	22′4″	63′6″	2B(F.W.)/2GT(G.E.)	1/6,000	16.8	33	333	9	96	4 twin 40mm
"Achernar"	AKA-53	1	14,000	459′	28′	64′	2B(F.W.)/2GT(G.E.)	1/6,000	15.5	31	335	8	76	1 5″/38, 4 twin 40mm
"Andromeda"	AKA-15	1	13,907	459′	28′	63′	2B(C.E.)/2GT(G.E.)	1/6,000	16.5	23	243	12	402	4 single 3″/50
Francis Marion	LPA-249	1	16,838	564′	27′8″	76′	2B(F.W.)/2GT(G.E.)	1/22,000	22.4	64	505	96	1,561	4 twin 3″/50
Paul Revere	LPA-248	1	16,838	564′	27′	76′	2B(F.W.)/2GT(G.E.)	1/19,200	22.5	77	484	96	1,561	4 twin 3″/50
"Haskell"	APA-117	8	10,679	455′	24′	62′	2B(C.E.)/2GT(West.)	1/8,500	18.4	50	459	99	1,534	4 twin 40mm
"Bayfield"	APA-33	3	13,267	492′	31′6″	70′	2B(C.E.)/2GT(G.E.)	1/8,500	18.1	50	421	51	916	2 5″/38, 4 twin 40mm
Austin	LPD-4	12	16,900	569′	21′6″	105′2″	2B(B&W)/2ST(DeLaval)	2/24,000	21	27	446	103	801	4 twin 3″/50
Raleigh	LPD-1	3	14,651	521′9″	22′	104′	2B(B&W)/2ST(DeLaval)	2/24,000	20	27	435	73	996	4 twin 3″/50
Iwo Jima	LPH-2	7	18,000	602′	29′	84′	2B(C.E.)/1GT(West.)	1/22,000	23	47	605	143	1,581	4 twin 3″/50, 1 BPDMS (LPH-3)
Knudson	LPR-101	2	2,130	306′	15′2″	37′	2B(F.W.)/2GT(G.E.)	2/12,000	24	29	225	8	113	1 5″/38, 3 twin 40mm
"Crosley"	APD-87	7	2,130	306′	17′	37′	2B(F.W.)/2GT(G.E.)	2/12,000	23.5	24	282	8	113	1 5″/38, 3 twin 40mm
Laning	LPR-55	2	2,130	306′	13′	37′	2B(F.W.)/2GT(G.E.)	2/12,000	23.6	27	335	8	113	1 5″/38, 3 twin 40mm
Grayback	LPSS-574	1	2,240	334′	17′	27′	3D(F.M.)/2EM(Ell.)	2/5,500	16.7	9	78	7	60	6 21″ TT fwd., 2 21″ TT aft
Perch	LPSS-313	2	1,659	312′	18′	27′	2D(G.M.)/4EM(G.E.)	2/2,305	13.8	6	68	4	68	4.50 cal. mg.
Anchorage	LSD-36	5	13,700	555′	18′	84′	2B(C.E.)/2GT	2/24,000	20	21	376	25	312	4 twin 3″/50
Thomaston	LSD-28	8	11,525	510′	20′	90′	2B(B&W)/2GT(G.E.)	2/24,000	22.5	21	384	29	312	6 twin 3″/50
Fort Marion	LSD-22	1	9,078	458′	17′6″	72′	2B(C.E.)/2GT(West.)	2/9,000	17	28	290	16	217	2 twin 40mm
Cabildo	LSD-16	8	9,078	458′	17′6″	76′	2B(B&W)/2GT(NN SB)	2/7,000	16	21	295	18	150	2 quad 40mm, 2 twin 40mm
Casa Grande	LSD-13	3	9,078	458′	17′6″	72′	2B(B&W)/2GT(NN SB)	2/7,000	16	18	305	18	182	2 quad 40mm
Newport	LST-1179	20	8,400	517′	15′	68′	6D(G.M.)	2/16,000	20	12	174	20	411	2 twin 3″/50
Suffolk County	LST-1173	7	7,804	442′	17′6″	62′	6D(F.M.)	2/13,700	16.5	15	173	30	604	3 twin 3″/50

Terrebonne Parish	LST-1156	15	5,777	384′	16′1″	56′	4D(G.M.)	2/6,000	15.5	16	189	15	376	3 twin 3″/50
Talbot County	LST-1153	1	6,000	382′	17′3″	54′	2B(C.E.)/2GT(West.)	2/6,000	14.3	13	171	15	153	2 5″/38, 2 twin 40mm
	LST-511	49	4,080	328′	12′4″	50′	2D(G.M.)	2/1,700	11.6	9	109	18	116	4 twin 40mm, 2 single 40mm
	LST-1	13	3,640	328′	14′1″	50′	2D(G.M.)	2/1,700	11.5	9	107	14	119	4 twin 40mm, 2 single 40mm

2 AMPHIBIOUS COMMAND SHIPS, *BLUE RIDGE* CLASS

Name	Number	FY/SCB	Builder	Awarded	Commissioned	F/S
Mount Whitney	LCC-20	66/400	Newport News	8–22–66	1–16–71	AA
Blue Ridge	LCC-19	65/400	Phil. Navy	12–31–64	11–14–70	PA

Originally rated as amphibious force flagships (AGC). To LCC 10–1–68 (LCC-19/20) and 1–1–69 (LCC-7, 11/12, 16/17). First of their type ever designed and built from keel up. To replace LCC-7/AGC-15 class ships. Built with flight deck which provides more antenna surface. At a distance resemble AGMR-1; closer they resemble LPH-2 class except that "island" is amidships directly above keel and antennas extend from the "flight deck"

2 AMPHIBIOUS COMMAND SHIPS, *"ADIRONDACK"* CLASS

Name	Number	F/S	Decommissioned
Taconic	LCC-17	MAR*	12–17–69
Pocono	LCC-16	AR*	9–71

Built on a C2-S-AJ1 hull design. Acquired from MARCOMM 1945 as AGCs. Were 3 in class; leader struck 1961.

3 AMPHIBIOUS COMMAND SHIPS, *MOUNT McKINLEY* CLASS

Estes	LCC-12	MPR*	1970
Eldorado	LCC-11	PA	
Mount McKinley	LCC-7	MPR*	3–26–70

Built to C2-S-AJ1 hull design. Acquired from MARCOMM 1943-44 as AGCs. Were 8 in class; 5 struck 1960–61.

5 INSHORE FIRE SUPPORT SHIPS, *"ELK RIVER"* CLASS

Name	Number	F/S
Smoky Hill River	LFR-531	AR
Red River	LFR-522	AR*
Owyhee River	LFR-515	AR*
Laramie River	LFR-513	AR
Lamoille River	LFR-512	AR*

Originally a 36-ship class; leader became IX-501. Twenty-four struck early 1960s. One became *Targeteer* (YV-3, since struck) and 3 transferred overseas. Two struck sisters saw service in Vietnam 1965-70. Formerly typed LSMR.

3 INSHORE FIRE SUPPORT SHIPS, *BIG BLACK RIVER* CLASS

Name	Number	F/S
Des Plaines River	LFR-412	PR*
Broadkill River	LFR-405	AR*
Big Black River	LFR-401	PR*

Originally a 12-ship class. Commissioned in 1945. The struck *Clarion River* (LFR-409) recommissioned 9–18–65 for Vietnam service. Formerly typed LSMR.

1 INSHORE FIRE SUPPORT SHIP, *CARRONADE* CLASS

Name	Number	F/S	Decommissioned
Carronade	LFR-1	PR*	7–24–70

Originally commissioned 5–25–55 as IFS-1. Class was to be mass-production replacement for LSMRs, but only 1 completed. Mothballed 1960, then recommissioned 10–2–65 for Vietnam duty. To LFR on 1–1–69.

5 AMPHIBIOUS ASSAULT SHIPS (GENERAL PURPOSE), *"LHA-1"* CLASS

Name	Number	FY	Builder	Awarded	Commissioned	F/S
	LHA-5	71	Ingalls	11–6–70		Bldg.
	LHA-4	71	Ingalls	11–6–70		Bldg.
	LHA-3	70	Ingalls	11–15–69		Bldg.
	LHA-2	70	Ingalls	11–15–69		Bldg.
	LHA-1	69	Ingalls	5–1–69		Bldg.

Built under concept definition/contract formulation process. Ingalls will build class, originally projected at 9 ships (4 were cancelled). LHAs combine features of LPDs, LSDs, and LPHs. Ships will be highly automated with reduced crews. Will carry new lightweight 5"/54s.

5 AMPHIBIOUS CARGO SHIPS, *CHARLESTON* CLASS

Name	Number	FY	Builder	Awarded	Commissioned	F/S
El Paso	LKA-117	66/403	Newport News	8–22–66	1–17–70	AA
St. Louis	LKA-116	65/403	Newport News	6–11–65	11–22–69	PA
Mobile	LKA-115	65/403	Newport News	6–11–65	9–20–69	PA
Durham	LKA-114	65/403	Newport News	6–11–65	5–24–69	PA
Charleston	LKA-113	65/403	Newport News	6–11–65	12–14–68	AA

Originally rated as AKAs; to LKA late 1968. First of their type built from keel up. *Charleston* is first USN vessel with a fully automated steam plant. As designed, LKA-113 was to be a separate class because of a power-plant difference; during construction, she was converted to the automated power plant of LKA-114/117.

1 AMPHIBIOUS CARGO SHIP, *TULARE* CLASS

Name	Number	F/S
Tulare	LKA-112	PA

Built to C4-S-1B design. Laid down as SS *Evergreen Mariner*. Near sister to LPA-248/249. Commissioned 1–12–56 as AKA; to LKA 1–1–69. Has helicopter deck.

5 AMPHIBIOUS CARGO SHIPS, *RANKIN* CLASS

Name	Number	F/S	Decommissioned
Washburn	LKA-108	MPR*	12–23–70
Vermilion	LKA-107	AR*	4–14–71
Union	LKA-106	MPR*	6–5–70
Seminole	LKA-104	PR*	12–23–70
Rankin	LKA-103	AR*	5–11–71

Built to a C2-S-AJ3 hull design. Acquired by USN from MARCOMM 1944–45. Commissioned 1945. A sixth ship has been struck.

2 AMPHIBIOUS CARGO SHIPS, *WINSTON* CLASS

Name	Number	F/S	Decommissioned
Merrick	LKA-97	MPR*	9–17–69
Winston	LKA-94	MPR*	1969

Built on a C2-S-B1 hull design. Acquired and commissioned 1945.

1 AMPHIBIOUS CARGO SHIP, "*UVALDE*" CLASS

Yancey	LKA-93	MAR*	1–20–70

Built on a C2-S-B1 hull design. Acquired from MARCOMM and commissioned 10–11–44.

1 AMPHIBIOUS CARGO SHIP, *ARNEB* CLASS

Arneb	LKA-56	AR*	10–71

Built on a C2-S-B1 hull; begun as SS *Mischief*. Acquired from MARCOMM and commissioned 11–16–43 as AKA-56; to LKA 1–1–69. Last active WW II AKA-type.

2 AMPHIBIOUS CARGO SHIPS, *ALGOL* CLASS

Capricornus	LKA-57	MAR*	2–10–70
Algol	LKA-54	MAR*	2–20–70

Built on a C2-S-B1 hull design. Acquired from MARCOMM and commissioned 11–43.

1 AMPHIBIOUS CARGO SHIP, "*ACHERNAR*" CLASS

Muliphen	LKA-61	MAR*	8–31–70

Built on a C2-S-B1 hull design. Acquired from MARCOMM and commissioned 10–44. Hull is ice-strengthened. Class leader serves Spanish Navy.

1 AMPHIBIOUS CARGO SHIP, "*ANDROMEDA*" CLASS

Thuban	LKA-19	MAR*	10–31–68

Built on a C2-S-B1 hull design. Acquired from MARCOMM and commissioned 6–43.

1 AMPHIBIOUS TRANSPORT, *FRANCIS MARION* CLASS

Name	Number	F/S
Francis Marion	LPA-249	AA

Completed 5–25–54 as SS *Prairie Mariner* on a C4-S-1 hull design. Acquired from MARAD 5–25–54 and converted to attack transport under FY 1959. Near sister to LPA-248. Commissioned 7–6–61. To LPA 1–1–69. Has helicopter deck.

1 AMPHIBIOUS TRANSPORT, *PAUL REVERE* CLASS

Paul Revere	LPA-248	PA

Completed on a C4-S-1 hull design as SS *Diamond Mariner* on 12–22–53. Acquired 9–14–56. Converted to APA under FY 1957. Commissioned 9–3–58. To LPA 1–1–69. Has helicopter deck.

8 AMPHIBIOUS TRANSPORTS, "*HASKELL*" CLASS

Name	Number	F/S	Decommissioned
Bexar	LPA-237	MPR*	12–69
Pickaway	LPA-222	MPR*	6–25–70
Okanogan	LPA-220	MPR*	2–5–70
Navarro	LPA-215	MPR*	11–69
Mountrail	LPA-213	MAR*	11–5–69
Talladega	LPA-208	MPR*	10–69
Magoffin	LPA-199	MPR*	5–68
Sandoval	LPA-194	MAR*	3–3–70

Built on a VC2-S-AP5 hull design. Acquired and commissioned as APAs 1944–45. To LPA 1–1–69.

3 AMPHIBIOUS TRANSPORTS, "*BAYFIELD*" CLASS

Henrico (ex-SS *Sea Darter*)	LPA-45	MPR*	2–14–68
Fremont (ex-SS *Sea Corsair*)	LPA-44	MAR*	9–2–69
Chilton (ex-SS *Sea Needle*)	LPA-38	AA	

Built on a C3-S-A2 hull design. *Chilton* commissioned 11–10–43.

12 AMPHIBIOUS TRANSPORT DOCKS, *AUSTIN* CLASS

Name	Number	FY/SCB	Builder	Awarded	Commissioned	F/S
Ponce	LPD-15	65/402	Lockheed	5–17–65		AA
Trenton	LPD-14	65/402	Lockheed	5–17–65	3–6–71	AA
Nashville	LPD-13	64/187C	Lockheed	5–15–64	2–14–70	AA
Shreveport	LPD-12	64/187C	Lockheed	5–15–64	12–12–70	AA
Coronado	LPD-11	64/187C	Lockheed	5–15–64	5–23–70	AA
Juneau	LPD-10	63/187B	Lockheed	5–23–63	7–12–69	PA
Denver	LPD-9	63/187B	Lockheed	5–23–63	10–26–68	PA
Dubuque	LPD-8	63/187B	Ingalls	1–25–63	9–1–67	PA
Cleveland	LPD-7	63/187B	Ingalls	1–25–63	4–21–67	PA
Duluth	LPD-6	62/187B	NY Navy	9–21–61	12–18–65	PA
Ogden	LPD-5	62/187B	NY Navy	9–21–61	6–19–65	PA
Austin	LPD-4	62/187B	NY Navy	9–21–61	2–6–65	AA

Duluth (LPD-6) reassigned to Philadelphia Navy Yard 11–24–65 for completion. LPD-7/13 fitted as amphibious flagships. LPD-7/8 served as test ships for a telescopic hangar that can extend from 25′ to 62′ along the helicopter deck. Eventually the entire class will be so fitted. Well deck measures 168′×50′. Landing craft loaded by overhead monorail crane. Ramps connect helicopter platform, well deck, and storage decks. Shipyard strike delayed completion of LPD-9/15.

3 AMPHIBIOUS TRANSPORT DOCKS, *RALEIGH* CLASS

La Salle	LPD-3	61/187A	NY Navy	8–8–60	2–22–64	AA
Vancouver	LPD-2	60/187	NY Navy	12–30–59	5–11–63	PA
Raleigh	LPD-1	59/187	NY Navy	12–19–58	9–8–62	AA

LPDs are an evolution of the LSDs. Originally designed to replace LPAs and in part LSDs/LKAs. LPD flagships, such as LPD-3, carry extra deck level for command spaces. *Austin/Raleigh* classes can carry six UH-34 or CH-46 helicopters (but normally do not).

7 AMPHIBIOUS ASSAULT SHIPS, *IWO JIMA* CLASS

Inchon	LPH-12	66/401.66	Ingalls	6–16–66	6–20–70	AA
New Orleans	LPH-11	65/401.65	Phil. Navy	12–18–64	11–16–68	PA
Tripoli	LPH-10	63/157	Ingalls	12–10–62	8–6–66	PA
Guam	LPH-9	62/157	Phil. Navy	9–21–61	1–16–65	AA
Guadalcanal	LPH-7	60/157	Phil. Navy	12–21–59	7–20–63	AA
Okinawa	LPH-3	59/157	Phil. Navy	10–24–58	4–14–62	PA
Iwo Jima	LPH-2	58/157	PS Navy	1–30–58	8–26–61	PA

LPH-2 was the first built-for-purpose LPH. No more ships of this type will be built because of the capabilities of the LHA. Resemble WW II CVEs in size. LPH-1, 4/6, and 8 were former *Essex, Commencement Bay* and *Casablanca* class carriers reclassified as LPHs.

2 AMPHIBIOUS TRANSPORTS (SMALL), *KNUDSON* CLASS

Name	Number	F/S
Balduck	LPR-132	PR*
Knudson	LPR-101	PR*

Converted from *Rudderow* class DEs and commissioned as high-speed transports (APD). To LPR 1–1–69. Both ships decommissioned in late 1950s. At least 3 dozen of these ships serve other navies in various ways; are exceptionally versatile.

2 AMPHIBIOUS TRANSPORTS (SMALL), *LANING* CLASS

Hollis	LPR-86	AR*
Laning	LPR-55	AR*

Converted from *Buckley* class DEs; both fitted as flagships. Decommissioned late 1950s.

7 AMPHIBIOUS TRANSPORTS (SMALL), "*CROSLEY*" CLASS

Name	Number	F/S	Decommissioned
Weiss	LPR-135	AR*	1–70
Begor	LPR-127	PR*	
Horace A. Bass	LPR-124	AR*	2–9–59
Diachenko	LPR-123	AR*	10–69
Beverly A. Reid	LPR-119	AR*	10–6–69
Ringness	LPR-100	AR	1–47
Kirwin	LPR-90	AR*	12–20–68

Converted from *Rudderow* class DEs and commissioned 1944-45. Originally rated as APD; to LPR 1–1–69. LPR-90 recommissioned 1–15–65 as replacement tor *Earle B. Hall* (APD-107). LPR-119 recommissioned 3–17–67 as replacement for *Liddle* (APD-60) in active fleet. All except 100, 101, and 127 received FRAM II. In addition, LPR-90, 119, 123 and 135 received other modifications including a tripod mast, additional electronics, and an enclosed CIC in place of forward 40 mm. FRAM II ships had ASW torpedoes.

1 AMPHIBIOUS TRANSPORT SUBMARINE, *GRAYBACK* CLASS

Name	Number	FY/SCB	Commissioned	FY/SCB	Converted at	Awarded	Recommissioned	F/S
Grayback	LPSS-574	53/161	3–7–58	65/350.S	Mare Island	12–29–64	5–9–69	PA

Contract awarded 9–17–52 for construction at Mare Island as an attack submarine of the *Darter* class. Changed to SSG 7–26–56; hull lengthened. Carried 4 REGULUS I missiles, but decommissioned 6–1–64 at Mare Island when REGULUS II cancelled and REGULUS I phased out. Converted to troop transport. Hangar space used to carry troops, gear and mini submarines. Except for addition of PUFFS topside and alteration to hangar doors to serve her new role, she retains SSG configuration.

2 AMPHIBIOUS TRANSPORT SUBMARINES, *PERCH* CLASS

Name	Number	F/S
Sealion (ex SS-315)	LPSS-315	AR*
Perch (ex SS-313)	LPSS-313	NRT

Originally commissioned in *Balao* class. SS-313 converted to troop-carrying submarine at San Francisco Navy Yard, SS-315 converted at Mare Island. SS-313 to SSP 1–19–48. SS-315 to SSP 3–31–48. Both to ASSP 1–31–50; to APSS 10–24–56; to LPSS (with SSG-574) on 1–1–69. *Perch* was declared unsafe for further underwater operations in 1967 and now used as a non operating NRT submarine. LPSS-315 decommissioned 2/70. *Tunny* (LPSS-282, ex SSG-282) has been struck.

5 DOCK LANDING SHIPS, *ANCHORAGE* CLASS

Name	Number	FY/SCB	Builder	Awarded	Commissioned	F/S
Fort Fisher	LSD-40	67/404.66	Gen. Dyn., Quincy	5–2–67		Bldg.
Mount Vernon	LSD-39	66/404.66	Gen. Dyn., Quincy	2–25–66		PA
Pensacola	LSD-38	66/404.66	Gen. Dyn., Quincy	2–25–66	3–27–71	AA
Portland	LSD-37	66/404.66	Gen. Dyn., Quincy	2–25–66	10–3–70	AA
Anchorage	LSD-36	65/404.65	Ingalls	6–29–65	3–15–69	PA

Class strongly resembles earlier LSD classes with two exceptions: has tripods vice pole mast and enclosed 3" mounts forward and either side of bridge. Built to replace older and slower LSDs.

8 DOCK LANDING SHIPS, *THOMASTON* CLASS

Name	Number	F/S	Name	Number	F/S
Monticello	LSD-35	PA	*Point Defiance*	LSD-31	PA
Hermitage	LSD-34	AA	*Fort Snelling*	LSD-30	AA
Alamo	LSD-33	PA	*Plymouth Rock*	LSD-29	AA
Spiegel Grove	LSD-32	AA	*Thomaston*	LSD-28	PA

All built by Ingalls. Commissioned between 9–17–54 (LSD-28) and 3–29–57 (LSD-35).

1 DOCK LANDING SHIP, *FORT MARION* CLASS

Fort Marion	LSD-22	PR*

Same basic characteristics as LSD-16 class but has different engineering plant. Built by Gulf Shipbuilding Corp. Commissioned 1–29–46. Received FRAM II. Decommissioned 2/70.

8 DOCK LANDING SHIPS, *CABILDO* CLASS

Name	Number	F/S	Decommissioned
Whetstone	LSD-27	MPR*	1970
Tortuga	LSD-26	MPR*	1–26–70
San Marcos	LSD-25	AA	
Donner	LSD-20	MAR*	12–23–70
Comstock	LSD-19	PR*	1–70
Colonial	LSD-18	MPR*	6–30–70
Catamount	LSD-17	PR*	4–7–70
Cabildo	LSD-16	MPR*	1970

Originally 11 in class; 1 cancelled, 1 ultimately became Navy's first roll-on/roll-off ship, the *Taurus* (AK-273, now struck), and 1 was loaned to Greece. All commissioned 1945–46. Have helicopter decks. LSD-17/18 and 20/21 received FRAM II.

3 DOCK LANDING SHIPS, *CASA GRANDE* CLASS

Shadwell	LSD-15	MAR*	3–9–70
Rushmore	LSD-14	MAR*	9–30–70
Casa Grande	LSD-13	MAR*	2–6–70

Originally a 7-ship class intended for lend-lease transfer to England. Only 4 ships, LSD-9/12, transferred to RN, the remainder retained by USN. LSD-13/15 commissioned in USN 1944. All of the *Ashland* class (LSD-1/8) have been disposed of except *Whitemarsh* (LSD-8), which is on loan to Taiwan.

20 TANK LANDING SHIPS, *NEWPORT* CLASS

Name	Number	FY/SCB	Builder	Awarded	Commissioned	F/S
Bristol County	LST-1198	67/405.67	National Steel	7–15–66		Bldg.
Barnstable County	LST-1197	67/405.67	National Steel	7–15–66		Bldg.
Harlan County	LST-1196	67/405.67	National Steel	7–15–66		Bldg.
Barbour County	LST-1195	67/405.67	National Steel	7–15–66		Bldg.
La Moure County	LST-1194	67/405.67	National Steel	7–15–66		AA

Fairfax County	LST-1193	67/405.67	National Steel	7–15–66		AA
Spartanburg County	LST-1192	67/405.67	National Steel	7–15–66		AA
Racine	LST-1191	67/405.67	National Steel	7–15–66		PA
Boulder	LST-1190	67/405.67	National Steel	7–15–66	6–4–71	AA
San Bernadino	LST-1189	67/405.67	National Steel	7–15–66	3–27–71	PA
Saginaw	LST-1188	66/405.66	National Steel	7–15–66	1–23–71	AA
Tuscaloosa	LST-1187	66/405.66	National Steel	7–15–66	10–24–70	PA
Cayuga	LST-1186	66/405.66	National Steel	7–15–66	8–8–70	PA
Schenectady	LST-1185	66/405.66	National Steel	7–15–66	6–13–70	PA
Frederick	LST-1184	66/405.66	National Steel	7–15–66	4–11–70	PA
Peoria	LST-1183	66/405.66	National Steel	7–15–66	2–21–70	PA
Fresno	LST-1182	66/405.66	National Steel	7–15–66	11–22–69	PA
Sumter	LST-1181	66/405.66	Phil. Navy	12–29–65	6–20–70	PA
Manitowoc	LST-1180	66/404.66	Phil. Navy	12–29–65	1–24–70	PA
Newport	LST-1179	65/404.65	Phil. Navy	12–29–64	6–7–69	AA

Fastest, largest LSTs ever built. New design features clipper bow, bow ramp vice bow doors, and rounded bottom. Tank deck is connected to main deck by a ramp forward of the bridge. Stern doors, similar to AKR-7 and 9, facilitate loading/unloading. First USN combat vessel equipped with a bow thruster (side propulsion unit).

7 TANK LANDING SHIPS, *SUFFOLK COUNTY* CLASS

Name	Number	F/S
Wood County	LST-1178	AA
Lorain County	LST-1177	AA
Graham County	LST-1176	AA
York County	LST-1175	AA
Grant County	LST-1174	AA
Suffolk County	LST-1173	AA
De Soto County	LST-1171	AA

Originally 8 in class; LST-1172 cancelled. Commissioned 1957–59. Fastest LST class with bow door. Ships are highly maneuverable; have controllable-pitch propellers.

15 TANK LANDING SHIPS, *TERREBONNE PARISH* CLASS

Name	Number	F/S	Decommissioned
Windham County	LST-1170	PA	
Whitfield County	LST-1169	PA	
Wexford County	LST-1168	PR*	
Westchester County	LST-1167	PA	
Washtenaw County	LST-1166	PA	
Washoe County	LST-1165	PR*	3–25–71
Walworth County	LST-1164	AR*	
Waldo County	LST-1163	AR*	12–31–70
Wahkiakum County	LST-1162	AR*	10–16–70
Vernon County	LST-1161	PA	
Traverse County	LST-1160	AR*	12–1–70
Tom Green County	LST-1159	PA	
Tioga County	LST-1158	PR*	12–23–70
Terrell County	LST-1157	PR*	3–25–71
Terrebonne Parish	LST-1156	AA	

Modified *Talbot County* class. Ships are highly maneuverable; have controllable-pitch propellers.

1 TANK LANDING SHIP, *TALBOT COUNTY* CLASS

Name	Number	F/S
Talbot County	LST-1153	AR*

Only steam-driven LST in USN. Originally 3 in class; 1 cancelled, 2 completed. LST-1153 decommissioned 4–3–70. *Tallahatchee County* (LST-1154) became AVB-2 (since struck).

49 TANK LANDING SHIPS, "*LST-511*" CLASS

Name	Number	F/S	Decommissioned
Sutter County	LST-1150	PR*	3–12–71
Sumner County	LST-1148	PR*	
Sedgewick County	LST-1123	PR*	
San Joaquin County	LST-1122	PR*	
St. Clair County	LST-1096	PR*	
Pulaski County	LST-1088	MSC	
Polk County	LST-1084	PR*	10–3–69
Plumas County	LST-1083	MSC	
Pitkin County	LST-1082	PR*	9–71
Park County	LST-1077	PR*	12–71
[Page County]	LST-1076	ILP	
unnamed	LST-1072	MSC	
Orleans Parish	LST-1069	MSC	
Nye County	LST-1067	MSC	
New London County	LST-1066	MSC	
Middlesex County	LST-983	AR*	
Meeker County	LST-980	PR*	12–15–70
Litchfield County	LST-901	PR*	9–70
Kemper County	LST-854	PR*	5–28–69
[Holmes County]	LST-836	ILP	8–71
Henry County	LST-824	PR*	
Harris County	LST-822	MSC	
Hampshire County	LST-819	PR*	12–4–70
Floyd County	LST-762	PR*	
Duval County	LST-758	AR*	10–28–69
Dodge County	LST-722	AR*	
De Kalb County	LST-715	MSC	
Daviess County	LST-692	MSC	
unnamed	LST-664	MSC	
unnamed	LST-649	MSC	
unnamed	LST-643	MSC	
unnamed	LST-630	MSC	
unnamed	LST-629	MSC	
unnamed	LST-626	MSC	
unnamed	LST-623	MSC	
unnamed	LST-613	MSC	
unnamed	LST-607	MSC	
Clearwater County	LST-602	MPR*	
unnamed	LST-590	MSC	
unnamed	LST-587	MSC	
Churchill County	LST-583	AR*	12–11–68
unnamed	LST-581	MSC	
unnamed	LST-579	MSC	
unnamed	LST-572	MSC	
unnamed	LST-566	MSC	
unnamed	LST-550	MSC	
unnamed	LST-546	MSC	
Cheboygan County	LST-533	AR*	1969
Chase County	LST-532	MSC	
unnamed	LST-530	MSC	
Caroline County	LST-525	AR*	

LST-1/1170 originally commissioned with numbers only. All LSTs on NVR and not in MSC were named 7–1–55. Commissioned 1944–45. All LSTs in reserve (17) recommissioned 1965–66 for Vietnam duty. Twenty-eight ships serve MSC in noncombat status. LST-602 originally on loan to Air Force; returned to USN 9/69 and transferred to MARAD 10–17–69 for layup. LST-782, 786, 821, and 831 were outfitted as tenders to PBRs and PCFs in Vietnam. LST-836, 1084, 1141 and 1148 have had FRAM II. Many of this class converted to ARLs, ARBs, ARVAs, ARVEs, and APBs. Many serve foreign navies. *Garrett County* (LST-786), *Harnett County* (LST-821), and *Hunterdon County* (LST-838) were reclassified partol craft tenders (AGP) 9–25–70. LST-602 is scheduled for disposal.

13 TANK LANDING SHIPS, *LST-1* CLASS

Name	Number	F/S
unnamed	LST-491	MSC
unnamed	LST-488	MSC
unnamed	LST-456	MSC
unnamed	LST-399	MSC
Blanco County	LST-344	AR*
unnamed	LST-287	MSC
unnamed	LST-277	MSC
unnamed	LST-276	MSC
unnamed	LST-230	MSC
unnamed	LST-222	MSC
unnamed	LST-176	MSC
unnamed	LST-117	MSC
unnamed	LST-47	MSC

Originally commissioned in Navy between 5–12–43 (LST-176) and 12–3–43 (LST-491). LST-1/488 originally designated ATL while in design stages. About two dozen in same group were built by MARCOMM and had MARCOMM hull numbers. LST-334 recommissioned in 1965 for Vietnam duty; decommissioned 10–3–69. Many were converted for auxiliary uses.

USS *Blue Ridge* (LCC-19). 10–15–70. **Blue Ridge** *class.*

USS *Pocono* (LCC-16). Note new method of side identification as compared to old method in *Eldorado* (LCC-11). Compare aft antenna rig with LCC-11's. 1–6–70. **"Adirondack"** *class.*

Artist's conception of the LHA, which will be the first USN ships of carrier-type configuration to carry landing craft in davits as do RN commando carriers HMS *Bulwark* and HMS *Albion.* Note well deck and heavy appearance of the superstructure.

USS *Eldorado* (LCC-11), last WWII LCC left in fleet. Note that TACAN is aft on LCC-11 and radar is forward. On LCC-16 positions are reversed. Note different pattern on helicopter deck as compared to LCC-16. 9–15–65. **Mount McKinley** *class.*

USS *White River* (LFR-536) firing a rocket. 6–66. **Elk River** *class.*

USS *Tulare* (LKA-112), the first LKA to have a helicopter deck. 12–7–55.
Tulare *class.*

USS *Carronade* (LFR-1). With three ex-LSMRs, she formed a fire-support squadron for our forces in Vietnam. Note *White River* trailing in background. 11–67.
Carronade *class.*

Newport News Shipbuilding

USS *Durham* (LKA-114). This new type is fitted with two 70-ton heavy lift cargo systems, two 40-ton heavy lift booms, and carries four LCM-8, five LCM-6, seven LCVPs, and two smaller personnel landing craft. 4–14–69. **Charleston** *class.*

USS *Washburn* (LKA-108). The platform on the stern is used to accept supplies from helicopters during vertical replenishment at sea. 1969. **Rankin** *class.*

USS *Merrick* (LKA-97). Note numerous landing craft, especially after pair with smaller landing craft inside. 10–1–59. **Winston** *class.*

USS *Yancey* (LKA-93). **"Uvalde"** *class.*

USS *Thuban* (LKA-19). Originally all LKAs from AKA-15/20, 53/63, 88/100 were the *Andromeda* class. Modifications through the years split the class up. *Thuban* is the last of the WW II *Andromeda* class. **"Andromeda"** *class.*

USS *Algol* (LKA-54). **Algol** *class.*

USS *Muliphen* (LKA-61). 10–14–68. **"Achernar"** *class.*

USS *Bexar* (LPA-237), one of the last of the *Haskell* class in commission. **"Haskell"** *class.*

USS *Cambria* (LPA-36). 3–27–68. **"Bayfield"** *class.*

USS *Paul Revere* (LPA-248). Note helicopter platform and two quadruple masts carrying both 30- and 60-ton booms. 1–30–69. **Paul Revere** *class.*

USS *Vancouver* (LPD-2). Note starboard stack forward of twin 3″ mount. Stack is closer to crane in LPD-4 class. 2–10–68. **Raleigh** *class.*

USS *Ogden* (LPD-5). Note basic resemblance of this type to LSDs. Note position of forward stack (starboard) and electronic array on mast as compared to LPD-2. 8–31–65.
Austin *class.*

USS *Sealion* (LPSS-315). Note basic fleet boat configuration, which was retained after conversion to troop carrier. As LPSS carries no major armament. 8–2–65.
Perch *class.*

USS *New Orleans* (LPH-11). Note rectangular stack. In broadside view, note covered 3″ mounts. Earlier ships of class have uncovered mounts forward of bridge. 12–10–68.
Iwo Jima *class.*

USS *Balduck* (LPR-132). Along with her surviving sister, she is fitted as a flagship. Note truck, port side, just aft of 01 level. 12–59. **Knudson** *class.*

USS *Kirwin* (LPR-90). Compare this ship with LPR-132; note lack of clutter on fantail. 10–25–65. **"Crosley"** *class.*

USS *Grayback* (LPSS-574), a conventional submarine adapted for unconventional uses. Compare with photo of former sister *Growler* (SSG-577) in section 1. Note after portion of former missile hangar, clean lines, and PUFFS. 7–69. **Grayback** *class.*

USS *Laning* (LPR-55). LPR type is distinguished by short WW II DE bow, 5" gun, and large divits which nearly hide the stack. 12–59. **Laning** *class.*

USS *Anchorage* (LSD-36), the first LSD to have covered 3″ mounts forward. 1–27–69. **Anchorage** *class.*

USS *Thomaston* (LSD-28). LSDs are easily recognizable by their high freeboard, raised deckline forward, and small bridge structure. Note communications antenna on forecastle. 2–4–69. **Thomaston** *class.*

USS *Fort Marion* (LSD-22). Note almost identical appearance to LSD-16 class. 5–14–58. **Fort Marion** *class.*

USS *Cabildo* (LSD-16). The 5" and 20 mm mounts have been removed. The bridge is set farther back than in LSD-28 class. In this class and earlier classes, stacks are abreast. In later classes, they are staggered. Note massive superstructure as compared to LSD-28 class. 7–8–55. **Cabildo** *class.*

USS *Rushmore* (LSD-14). Compare bridge and forward part of ship with LSD-28 and 16 photos; has a blocked appearance. 10–31–63. **Casa Grande** *class.*

USS *Newport* (LST-1179). Note boxlike superstructure and derrick arms similar to ANL type. There is a 112' long retractable ramp forward. Upper portion of bow folds back when ramp is extended. Note odd-couple stacks and raised stern gate in port quarter view. Few comparisons can be made with WW II type LSTs. 8–27–69. **Newport** *class.*

USS *Graham County* (LST-1176), a ship in the last class of LST built to standard LST design. Clean deck amidships enables LSTs to support light helicopters. Note tall stack. 4–9–63. **Suffolk County** *class.*

USS *Talbot County* (LST-1153), the only steam-driven LST on the NVR. Note superstructure, mast, and guns on bow as compared to LST-1176. **Talbot County** *class.*

USS *Washoe County* (LST-1165). Compare armament, superstructure, and kingpost arrangement with other LST illustrations. 10–64. **Terrebonne Parish** *class.*

USS *Washtenaw County* (LST-1166). Note high fire-control *position.* **Terrebonne Parish** *class.*

USS *Holmes County* (LST-836). Last active ship of her class. 6–20–63. **"LST-511"** *class.*

USS *Blanco County* (LST-344), the oldest named LST on the NVR. Note LCU amidships, trucks inside the LCU, and autos up forward. 10–3–66. **LST-1** *class.*

USS *Garrett County* (LST-786, later AGP-786). Note HUEYs on reinforced deck. Several LSTs, among them LST-786, were modified to act as support ships for river patrol craft. Note PBRs moored to boat booms. A heavy crane was added to starboard side on modified LSTs to lift craft aboard for repairs as needed. Compare with other LST illustrations. 8–12–68. Formerly **"LST-511"** *class.*

3. MINE WARFARE SHIPS

By end-FY 1971 there were 103 mine warfare ships on the NVR. Of these, 31 were active, 18 were assigned to NRT (12 MSCs and 6 MSOs), 53 were in reserve, and 1 was in MARAD reserve. Of the reserve ships, 5 were being modernized and 3 were in caretaker status. Not included in this section is the minehunter *Bittern* (MHC-43); she is on commercial loan, but is still carried on the NVR.

Class	Number	No. in Class	Full Load Displ.	Length Overall	Max. Draft	Extreme Beam	Number & Type of Boilers/Engines	Sscrews/ SHP	Max. Speed (Kts)	Accommodations Officers	Accommodations Enlisted	Armament
MINE COUNTERMEASURES SHIPS												
"Catskill"	MCS-1	1	9,000	454′	20′	60′	4B(C.E.)/2GT(G.E.)	2/11,000	19·6	47	539	2 5″/38,
MINELAYERS												
Robert H. Smith	MMD-23	3	3,370	377′	19′	41′	4B(B&W)/2GT(G.E.)	2/60,000	34·2	22	339	3 twin 5″/38, 3 twin 3″/50
Terror	MMF-5	0	8,680	455′	20′	61′	4B(C.E.)/2GT(G.E.)	2/11,000	20·3	33	495	4 5″/38, 6 quad 40mm, 1 twin 40mm, 8 twin 20mm
MINESWEEPERS												
"Redwing"	MSC-200	8	412	145′	12′	28′	2D(G.E.)	2/880	12·8	5	35	1 20mm, 2 .50 cal. mg., 1 81mm mortar
"Falcon"	MSC-190	4	362	144′3″	10′	28′	2D(Packard)	2/1,200	13·6	4	35	1 20mm, 2 .50 cal. mg.
Bluebird	MSC-121	2	360	144′	10′	28′	2D(Packard)	2/1,200	14	4	35	1 20mm
"Admirable"	MSF-136	4	945	184′6″	9′9″	33′	2D(C.B.)	2/1,710	15	11	93	1 3″/50, 2 twin 40mm
"Auk"	MSF-57	25	1,250	221′2″	13′5″	32′2″	2D(G.M.)	2/3,118	16	9	96	1 3″/50, 2 twin 40mm, 2 twin 20mm
"Ability"	MSO-519	2	934	190′	12′	36′	2D(G.M.)	2/2,700	15	8	75	1 40mm, or 2 .50 cal. mg.
Acme	MSO-508	4	750	173′	14′	36′	2D(Packard)	2/2,280	14·9	8	70	1 40mm, or 1 20mm, or 2 .50 cal. mg.
Dash	MSO-428	4	775	172′	14′	36′	2D(G.M.)	2/1,520	14	8	70	1 40mm, or 2 .50 cal. mg.
Aggressive	MSO-422	45	775	172′	13′	35′	4D(Packard)	2/2,280	14	5	69	1 40mm, or 2 .50 cal. mg.
Agile	MSO-421	1	755	172′	13′	35′	4D(Packard)	2/3,040	14	8	70	2 .50 cal. mg.

1 MINE COUNTERMEASURES SHIP, *"CATSKILL"* CLASS

Name	Number	Builder	Commissioned	FY/SCB	Converted at	Awarded	Started	Recommissioned	F/S	Decommissioned
Ozark	MSC-2	Willamette	9–23–44	63/123	Norfolk SB & DD	6–6–63	9–16–63	6–24–66	MAR*	2–6–70
[Catskill]	MCS-1	Willamette	6–30–44	64/123	Boland	4–28–64	7–9–64	10–6–67	Struck	12–1–70

Originally laid down as CM-6/7 of the *Terror* class minelayers. Reclassified AP-106(1) and AP-107(2) on 5–1–43; to LSV-1(1) and LSV-2(2) on 4–21–44 and commissioned as such. Decommissioned after war. Reclassified MCS-1/2 on 10–18–56, but retained LSV configuration. MCS-1 struck 7–1–61; MCS-2 followed 9–1–61. Laid up in MARAD. MCS-2 reinstated on NVR 10–1–63; MCS-1 followed 6–1–64. Converted to MCS; could also lay mines.

3 FAST MINELAYERS, *"ROBERT H. SMITH"* CLASS

Name	Number	Builder	Awarded	Commissioned	F/S
Gwin (ex DD-772)	MMD-33	Beth., San Pedro	8–7–42	9–30–44	PR*
Shea (ex DD-750)	MMD-30	Beth., Staten Is.	8–7–42	9–30–44	PR*
Harry F. Bauer (ex DD-738)	MMD-26	Bath Iron	8–7–42	9–22–44	AR*

continued

"Robert H. Smith" Class—continued

Originally laid down as fleet DDs of the *Allen M. Sumner* class. Rerated as DMs 7–19–44 and as MMDs 1–1–69. Originally 12 ships in class, 2 were scrapped after WW II and 7 were struck 1970–71. MMD-26, 30, and 33 served in Korean War. Carried 80 mines, no torpedo tubes, were used as DDs.

FLEET MINELAYER, "*TERROR*" CLASS

Name	Number	Builder	Awarded	Commissioned	F/S
[Terror]	MMF-5	Phil. Navy	9–1–39	7–15–42	Struck

Only built-for-purpose minelayer in USN. Originally commissioned as minelayer (CM); to MM 2–7–55, then MMF 10–27–55. One sister exists as MCS.

8 COASTAL MINESWEEPERS, "*REDWING*" CLASS

Name	Number	F/S	Name	Number	F/S
Woodpecker	MSC-209	NRT	*Vireo*	MSC-205	NRT
Widgeon	MSC-208	NRT	*Thrush*	MSC-204	NRT
Whippoorwill	MSC-207	NRT	*Thrasher*	MSC-203	NRT
Warbler	MSC-206	NRT	*Shrike*	MSC-201	NRT

Originally 10 ships in class. Leader and MSC-202 transferred to Spain. Until joining NRT, MSC-201 was rated as experimental.

The 2-ship *Albatross* class (MSC-289/290), built to replace the transferred MSC-200 and 202, have been struck and scrapped. All but 22 of the 250+ MSCs built were transferred to ILP-recipient countries. MSCs and the larger MSOs are of nonmagnetic construction; includes wooden hull and hull fittings of aluminium, bronze and stainless steel.

4 COASTAL MINESWEEPERS, "*FALCON*" CLASS

Phoebe	MSC-199	NRT	*Kingbird*	MSC-194	NRT
Peacock	MSC-198	NRT	*[Jacana]*	MSC-193	ILP
Parrot	MSC-197	NRT	*[Humming Bird]*	MSC-192	ILP
[Meadowlark]	MSC-196	ILP	*[Frigate Bird]*	MSC-191	ILP
[Limpkin]	MSC-195	ILP	*[Falcon]*	MSC-190	ILP

Basically same as *Redwing* class; see statistics table. For NRT assignments, see section 7.

2 COASTAL MINESWEEPERS, *BLUEBIRD* CLASS

Cormorant	MSC-122	PR*
Bluebird	MSC-121	AR*

MSCs commissioned into USN to replace struck MSCOs. MSC-122 decommissioned 12–28–70; MSC-121 on 8–5–71.

4 FLEET MINESWEEPERS, "*ADMIRABLE*" CLASS

Name	Number	F/S	Name	Number	F/S
Superior	MSF-311	AR	*Cruise*	MSF-215	AR
Specter	MSF-306	AR	*Counsel*	MSF-165	PR

Survivors of a class of 120 ships. Same basic design as PCEs and PCERs; both one-stack and no-stack configuration used. Built to meet lend-lease commitments. Many still exist in merchant service and foreign navies.

25 FLEET MINESWEEPERS, "*AUK*" CLASS

Wheatear	MSF-390	AR*	*Champion* (ex BAM-1)	MSF-314	PR
Tercel	MSF-386	AR*	*Velocity*	MSF-128	PR
Sprig	MSF-384	AR*	*Threat*	MSF-124	PR
Scoter	MSF-381	PR	*Symbol*	MSF-123	PR*
Roselle	MSF-379	PR	*Swift*	MSF-122	PR*
Ardent(ex BAM-8)	MSF-340	PR	*Sway*	MSF-120	PR
Spear (ex BAM-22)	MSF-322	PR	*Sage*	MSF-111	AR*
Impeccable (ex BAM-7)	MSF-320	PR*	*Pioneer*	MSF-105	PR
Gladiator (ex BAM-6)	MSF-319	PR*	*Pilot*	MSF-104	AR*
Devastator (ex BAM-5)	MSF-318	PR*	*Herald*	MSF-101	AR*
Defense (ex BAM-4)	MSF-317	PR*	*Starling*	MSF-64	PR
Competent (ex BAM-3)	MSF-316	PR	*Broadbill*	MSF-58	AR*
Chief (ex BAM-2)	MSF-315	PR*			

Total of 105 ships completed. Many now serve foreign navies as escorts or minelayers. Class is very versatile; USN adapted 1 as ADG, 1 as AG, and 5 as AGSs. One serves Coast Guard as training ship.

2 OCEAN MINESWEEPERS, "*ABILITY*" CLASS

Assurance	MSO-521	AA
Alacrity	MSO-520	AA
[Ability]	MSO-519	Struck

Fitted as flagships; all MSOs also fitted as minehunters. About 3 dozen were built under ILP for foreign transfer.

4 OCEAN MINESWEEPERS, *DASH* CLASS

Name	Number	F/S	Name	Number	F/S
Dominant	MSO-431	NRT	*Detector*	MSO-429	NRT
Direct	MSO-430	NRT	*Dash*	MSO-428	NRT

Originally all MSFs and MSOs were in one hull-number series and rated as AMs. On 2–7–55 all AMs below 420 were reclassified MSFs and all AMs from 421 were reclassified MSOs.

45 OCEAN MINESWEEPERS, *AGGRESSIVE* CLASS

Name	Number	F/S	Decommissioned
Venture	MSO-496	AR*	8–2–71
Swerve	MSO-495	AR*	7–1–71
Sturdy	MSO-494	AR*	7–71
Pledge	MSO-492	PA	
Persistent	MSO-491	PA	4–26–71
Leader	MSO-490	PR*	11–29–70
Gallant	MSO-489	PA	
Conquest	MSO-488	PR*	10–29–70
Vital	MSO-474	AA	
Vigor	MSO-473	AA	
[Valor]	MSO-472	Struck	
Skill	MSO-471	AR*	12–15–70
[Salute]	MSO-470	Struck	
[Rival]	MSO-468	Struck	
Reaper	MSO-467	NRT	
Prime	MSO-466	PR*	11–6–70
Pluck	MSO-464	PA	
Pivot	MSO-463	PA	6–19–71*
Pinnacle	MSO-462	AR*	11–24–70
Observer	MSO-461	AR*	
[Notable]	MSO-460	Struck	
Nimble	MSO-459	AR*	11–24–70
Lucid	MSO-458	PR*	12–23–70
Loyalty	MSO-457	PA	
Inflict	MSO-456	PA	
Implicit	MSO-455	PA	
Impervious	MSO-449	PA	
Illusive	MSO-448	PR*	11–29–70
Guide	MSO-447	PA	
Fortify	MSO-446	PA	
Force	MSO-445	PA	
Firm	MSO-444	PA	
Fidelity	MSO-443	AA	
Fearless	MSO-442	AA	
Exultant	MSO-441	AA	
Exploit	MSO-440	AA	
Excel	MSO-439	PA	
Esteem	MSO-438	PR*	9–29–70
Enhance	MSO-437	PR*	10–29–70
Energy	MSO-436	PA	
Endurance	MSO-435	PA	
Embattle	MSO-434	NRT	
Engage	MSO-433	PA	
Dynamic	MSO-432	PA	6–1–71*
Constant	MSO-427	PA	
Conflict	MSO-426	PA	
Bulwark	MSO-425	AR*	7–71
Bold	MSO-424	AR*	7–71
Aggressive	MSO-422	AR*	7–71

Largest class of MSOs. Built to replace the steel-hull MSFs, which were useless in sweeping magnetic mines. Except for MSO-424/425, all were built by private yards. MSO-433 originally named *Elusive*. Active ships with asterisk are in caretaker status.

4 OCEAN MINESWEEPERS, *ACME* CLASS

Name	Number	F/S	Decommissioned
Affray	MSO-511	AA	
Advance	MSO-510	PR*	12–23–70
Adroit	MSO-509	AA	
Acme	MSO-508	PR*	11–6–70

Similar to MSO-519 class at distance. Fitted as flagships. Have plywood hulls and stainless steel engines. Missing MSO numbers transferred.

1 OCEAN MINESWEEPER, *AGILE* CLASS

Name	Number	F/S
Agile	MSO-421	AA

A total of 101 MSOs were completed 1953–60; 65 were retained by USN. Nine ships have been stricken over last 15 years, 2 by grounding, 2 by fire, 5 through force cutbacks. 36 MSO types were transferred to foreign countries under ILP.

OCEAN MINESWEEPER MODERNIZATIONS

Number	FY/SCB	Converted at	Awarded	Started	Recommissioned
MSO-490	69/502	Harbor Boat Building	6–30–70	11–30–70	
MSO-488	69/502	Harbor Boat Building	6–30–70	10–30–70	
MSO-456	68/502	Dillingham	5–15–68	11–30–68	2–10–71
MSO-449	68/502	Dillingham	5–15–68	11–30–68	12–4–71
MSO-448	69/502	Harbor Boat Building	6–30–70	11–30–70	
MSO-446	68/502	Dillingham	5–15–68	10–31–68	9–28–70
MSO-445	68/502	Dillingham	5–15–68	12–31–68	4–7–71
MSO-443	68/502	Beth., Baltimore	5–7–68	9–30–68	12–9–70
MSO-442	68/502	Beth., Baltimore	5–7–68	9–30–68	10–19–70
MSO-441	68/502	Beth., Baltimore	5–7–68	8–31–68	6–8–70
MSO-438	69/502	Harbor Boat Building	6–30–70	9–30–70	
MSO-437	69/502	Harbor Boat Building	6–30–70	10–30–70	
MSO-433	68/502	Dillingham	5–15–68	10–31–68	8–14–70
[MSO-423]	68/502	Beth., Baltimore	5–15–68	8–31–68	Struck 2–1–70

MSO-445 replaced MSO-457 in modernization program 1/69. Modernization includes increasing habitability and replacement or refurbishment of all machinery, piping, degaussing, and electrical systems. Engines are to be replaced. Work had begun on MSO-460, 468, 470, 472, and 519 but this was cancelled 10–16–70. MSO-433, 441/43, 45/46, 449, and 456 remained in commission during modernization.

Sikorsky

USS *Ozark* (MCS-2) with crew at quarters. She and sister, *Catskill* (MCS-1), served as mobile support bases for minecraft. They carried 20 MSLs (MK IV) and two RH-3A helicopters. **"Catskill"** *class.*

USS *Affray* (MSO-511). Note sweep vanes on stern. 3–23–60. **Acme** *class.*

USS *Assurance* (MSO-521). Note fat stack and bridge and compare with illustrations of other classes. Note side-by-side acoustic and special device cable reels for dragging sweep vanes. The tripod mast is unusual for a minesweeper. **"Ability"** *class.*

USS *Direct* (MSO-430), a minesweeper in the *Dash* class, which is the same as the *Aggressive* class except for propulsion machinery. Compare this ship with the illustrations of other MSO classes. **Dash** *class.*

USS *Reaper* (MSO-467). Compare bridge with MSO-521. Note two cable reels aft of stack. They are staggered in this class, but side by side in later classes. Device just forward of mast, attached to the rear of the searchlight platform, is an IFF antenna. **Aggressive** *class.*

USS *Shea* (MMD-30) in post-Korean War rig, last of the MMDs to be laid up (4–9–58). Note minelaying tracks and uncluttered appearance topside. Note side-dropping depth-charge racks superimposed over minelaying tracks on starboard side of aftermost 40 mm mount. **''Robert H. Smith''** *class.*

USS *Chief* (MSF-315), one of a few *Auks* still on NVR. Note 20 mm forward of paravanes and 20 mm on either side of flying bridge. Originally laid down as HMS *Alice* for transfer to England. Compare this ship with illustrations of MSOs, the MSF successor. Note secondary conn amidships between stacks. **''Auk''** *class.*

USS *Mainstay* (MSF-261), a typical example of *Admirable* class MSFs, economy-size versions of the *Auk* class. 20 serve in Mexican Navy. The design of these ships was adapted for other uses. *Mainstay* struck 12–1–59.

USS *Peacock* (MSC-198). Note anchor lying on forecastle. Six serve Indonesian Navy. All of this class on the NVR are in NRT. 5–16–55. **"Falcon"** *class.*

USS *Woodpecker* (MSC-209) leaving Sasebo, Japan, where all active MSCs were based. They served as patrol vessels on "Operation Market Time". 10–7–63. **"Redwing"** *class*.

4. COMBATANT CRAFT

By end-FY 1971, there were 17 patrol craft of all types in service in the USN. Of these, there were 1 PCH, 2 PGHs, and 14 PTFs. Until June 1969, there were about 750 riverine/coastal warfare craft in service. They were specifically built and/or converted for Vietnam War service. These craft were augmented by 26 *Point* class Coast Guard cutters, which were under the operational control of the Navy, but manned by the Coast Guard. The primary purpose of riverine/coastal warfare craft is to prevent the enemy from using the waterways. Large numbers of these riverine/coastal warfare craft have been turned over to the South Vietnamese Navy; soon hardly any will be left in the USN.

Class	Number	No. in Class	Full Load Displ.	Length Overall	Max. Draft	Extreme Beam	Number & Type of Engines	Screws/ SHP	Max. Speed (Kts)	Accommodations Officers	Accommodations Enlisted	Armament
PATROL CRAFT												
High Point	PCH-1	1	108	111′	15′4″	34′	2 Gas Turbines (Proteus)	4/6,200	45	1	18	2 .50 cal. mg., 2 twin 12.75″ torpedo launchers
Flagstaff	PGH-1	1	57	74′4″	4′2″	22′	1 Gas Turbine (R.R.)	1/3,000	52	1	12	1 single 40mm, 2 twin .50 cal. mg., 1 81mm mortar
Tucumcari	PGH-2	1	58	71′8″	4′5″	19′5″	1 Gas Turbine (Proteus)	1/3,000	52	1	12	1 single 40mm, 2 twin .50 cal. mg., 1 81mm mortar
"Osprey"	PTF-23	4	105	94′8″	7′	23′2″	2D(N.D.)	2/6,200	38	4	15	1 single 40mm, 2 20mm, 1 .50 cal. mg./81mm mortar
"Nasty"	PTF-17	6	85	80′5″	7′	24′7″	2D(N.D.)	2/6,200	45	3	16	1 single 40mm, 2 20mm, 1 .50 cal. mg./81mm mortar
"Nasty"	PTF-3	4	85	80′4″	6′7″	24′7″	2D(N.D.)	2/6,200	44	3	16	1 single 40mm, 2 20mm, 1 .50 cal. mg./81mm mortar
RIVERINE WARFARE CRAFT												
	ASPB		28	50′2″	5′	15′	2D (Detroit)	2/—	15	—	6	1 20mm, 1–3 .50 cal. mg., 1 81mm mortar, 1 7.62 mm
	ATC		66	56′	4′6″	17′5″	2D (Grey)	2/—	8·5	—	7	1 20mm, 2 .50 cal. mg., 4 .30 cal. mg.
	CCB		75	60′5″	4′6″	17′5″	2D (Grey)	2/—	8	—	11	2 20mm
	MON		75	60′5″	4′6″	17′5″	2D (Grey)	2/—	8	—	11	2 20mm, 4 .30 cal. mg., 1 105mm howitzer
	PACV		9.2	38′9″	—	23′	1 Gas Turbine (G.E.)	1 prop.	50	1	5	2 .50 cal. mg., 2 single 7.62 mg.
Mark II	PBR		8	31′9″	2′	11′5″	2D(G.M.)	2 jets	25	—	5	1 twin .50 cal. mg., 1 single .50 cal. mg.
Mark I	PBR		7	31′	2′2″	10′7″	2D(G.M.)	2 jets	25	—	4	1 twin .50 cal. mg., 1 single .50 cal. mg.
Mark II	PCF		19	51′4″	—	13′7″	2D(G.M.)	2/960	25	1	5	3 .50 cal. mg., 1 81mm mortar
Mark I	PCF		22	50′1″	5′	13′6″	2D(G.M.)	2/960	25	1	5	3 .50 cal. mg., 1 81mm mortar
Point	WPB		65	82′10″	5′9″	17′3″	2D(G.M.)	2/1,200	18	2	8	4 single .50 cal. mg., 1 .50 cal. mg./81mm mortar

A. Patrol Craft

1 PATROL CRAFT (HYDROFOIL), *HIGH POINT* CLASS

Name	Number	FY/SCB	Builder	Awarded	In Service	F/S
High Point	PCH-1	60/202	Boeing, Seattle	6–14–60	8–15–63	PSA

Rated as experimental. Built entirely of aluminum except for high-yield-steel foils and struts. Hull-borne, she is powered by a 600 SHP diesel that produces a speed of 12 knots. Foils operate fully submerged.

2 PATROL GUNBOATS (HYDROFOIL), *FLAGSTAFF* AND *TUCUMCARI* CLASSES

Tucumcari	PGH-2	66/252	Boeing, Seattle	4–27–66	3–7–68	ASA
Flagstaff	PGH-1	66/252	Grumman	4–28–66	9–14–68	PSA

Two different classes built as competitive design prototypes. Features of both designs will be used in the construction of a projected class of 34 units. Aluminum construction; have diesels for hull-borne operations. Main difference is propulsion PGH-1 has geared propeller with main lifting surface forward; PGH-2 is water-jet propelled with main lifting surface aft. Both ships tested in Vietnam; shipped home 1970. Rerated as "boats" 9–23–70.

4 FAST PATROL CRAFT, *"OSPREY"* CLASS

Number	FY	Builder	Awarded	In Service	F/S
PTF-26	67	Sewart Seacraft	5–19–67	4–8–68	PSA
PTF-25	67	Sewart Seacraft	5–19–67	4–8–68	PSA
PTF-24	67	Sewart Seacraft	5–19–67	3–13–68	PSA
PTF-23	67	Sewart Seacraft	5–19–67	3–13–68	PSA

American built and modified versions of the Norwegian *Nasty* class. Hulls made of aluminum; lack torpedoes. All PTFs reclassified "boats" 9–23–70.

6 FAST PATROL CRAFT, *"NASTY"* CLASS

PTF-22	67	Trumpy	12–20–66	9–23–70	PSA
PTF-21	67	Trumpy	12–20–66	9–23–70	PSA
PTF-20	67	Trumpy	12–20–66	10–5–68	PSA
PTF-19	67	Trumpy	12–20–66	10–5–68	PSA
PTF-18	67	Trumpy	12–20–66	7–1–68	PSA
PTF-17	67	Trumpy	12–20–66	7–1–68	PSA

Class duplicates Norwegian-built PTF-3 class. Boats have double mahogany hulls. PTF-21/22 were in commission from 5–14–69 to 9–23–70. Remainder placed in service upon completion.

4 FAST PATROL CRAFT, *"NASTY"* CLASS

PTF-13	64	Westermoen, Norway	8–27–64	8–31–65	PSA
PTF-12	64	Westermoen, Norway	8–27–64	7–7–65	PSA
PTF-11	64	Westermoen, Norway	8–27–64	7–7–65	PSA
PTF-10	64	Westermoen, Norway	8–27–64	4–22–65	PSA
[PTF-7]	—	Boatservice, Norway	1–1–64	3–1–64	ILP
[PTF-6]	—	Boatservice, Norway	1–1–64	3–1–64	ILP
[PTF-5]	—	Boatservice, Norway	1–1–64	3–1–64	ILP
[PTF-3]	—	Boatservice, Norway	10– –62	1–1–63	ILP

Originally 14 in class. Hulls completed in Norway and shipped to US for installation of guns and electronics. Built to Norwegian *Nasty* class design.

USS *High Point* (PCH-1). Note SEASPRITE helicopter above. This ship can maintain high speed in rough water. Fast hullborne vessels tend to pound themselves to pieces in high seas. 1963. **High Point** *class.*

Grumman

USS *Flagstaff* (PGH-1) riding her foils. Note distance between keel and water and position of foils compared to PGH-2. 1968. **Flagstaff** *class.*

Grumman

USS *Flagstaff* (PGH-1) shown hullborne with foils up. 1968. **Flagstaff** *class.*

USS *Tucumcari* (PGH-2). Note water jet, aft underneath fantail, and lack of guns as compared to PGH-1. She has a solid superstructure as compared to PGH-1's split superstructure 10–25–67. **Tucumcari** *class.*

PTF-3. Except for lack of tubes, she could easily be mistaken for WW II PT. 10–9–62. **"Nasty"** *class.*

B. Landing Craft

Smaller landing craft types now have their own classification category in the Navy's ship-type nomenclature list under the general category of "Combatant Craft". With the exception of the LCUs, these craft have no hull numbers and none of the craft are carried on the NVR. It should be noted that besides the types listed below, the Marines use a variety of landing vehicles, tracked (LVT), descendants of the "Alligators" of WW II.

LCA—Fully tracked landing vehicle with 30-ton capacity, to transfer supplies and equipment from ships to inland points without offloading at beach. Under development.

LCM—56' LCM(6) developed in WW II, still manufactured; versatile, useful craft. Many converted to riverine warfare. 73'8" LCM(8) is further development; hundreds used by Army, Navy. Transportable by LKA, LPD, and LSD.

LCPL—Original designation of "Higgins Boat" of Guadalcanal fame. Current LCPLs are 36' launches used as landing guide and control craft. Many serve as armed river/coastal patrol craft and gunboats in Vietnam.

LCPR—WW II ramped version of the original LCPL; one of earliest landing types still in service. Used by reconnaissance swimmer teams.

LCU—Originally 2 marks of WW II tank landing craft—LCT(5) and LCT(6); these went through several postwar redesignations before becoming LCU. Were classified as service craft until 14 August 1968. Some WW II types survive. Modern versions of these useful haulers still being built for USN and ILP. Sizes, armaments vary; some have experimental propulsion rigs. Used to land tanks and heavy gear on beaches; widely used in Vietnam. Unlike other small landing craft, LCUs have hull numbers. Many, redesignated, serve Naval districts as YFUs.

LCVP—Davit-launched; lands troops, small vehicles. One of the most successful, versatile landing craft types. Built today to original WW II design with slight modifications. Early ones had plated plywood hulls; now reinforced plastic. Some have been armed for Vietnam river operations.

LWT—Designed to salvage stranded landing craft and to beach and tend pontoon causeways and anchors. Early LWTs are pontoon craft fitted with powerful winch and A-frame and 2 outboard diesels. First proved themselves on WW II invasion beaches. New type will have greater speed, pulling capacity, and be deck-transportable by LST.

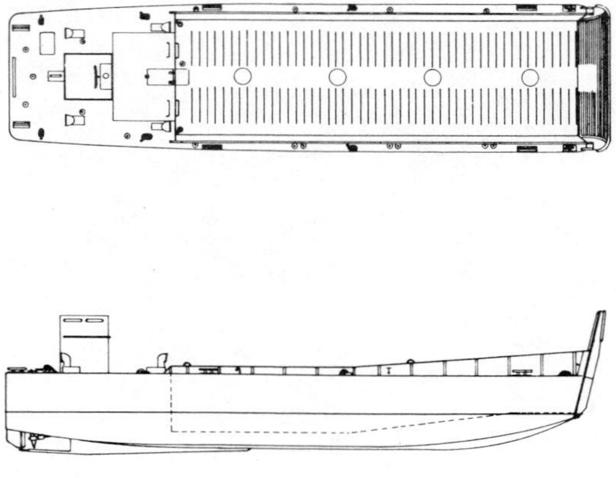

LCM(6).

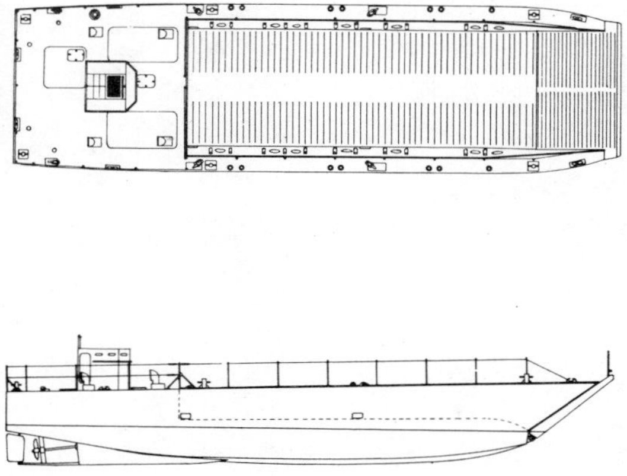

LCM(8).

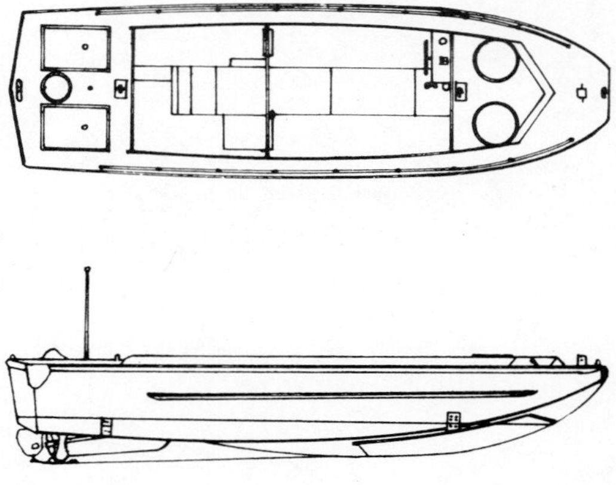

LCP(L) MK I.

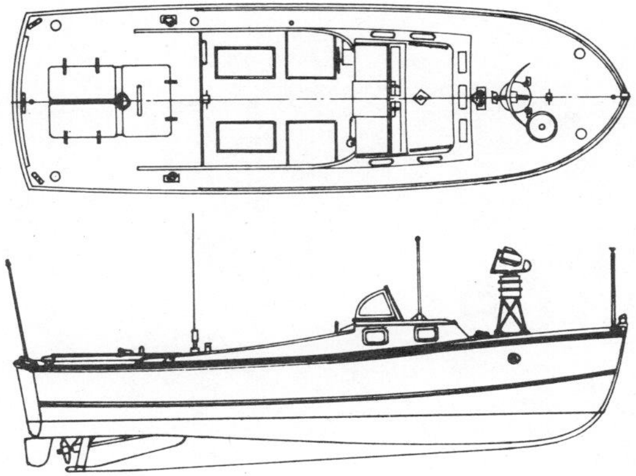

LCP(L) MK II.

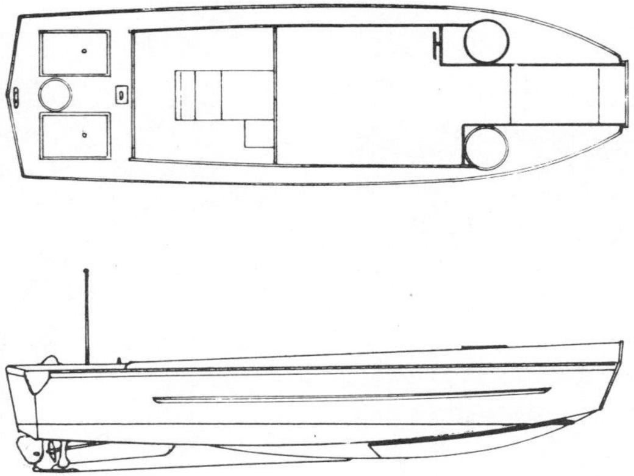

LCP(R).

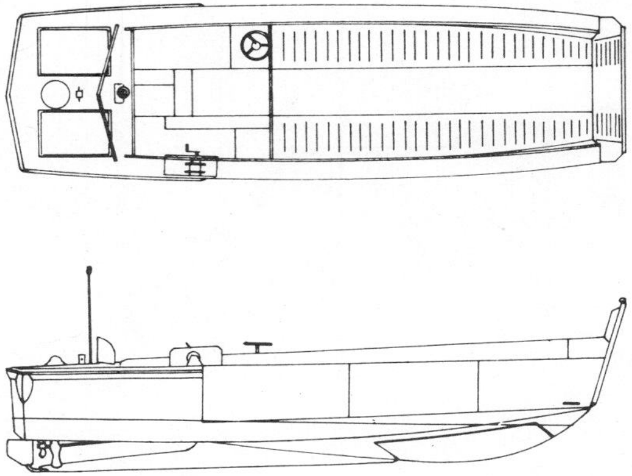

LCVP MK I.

LCP(L) MK IV.

LCU-1622.

C. Mine Countermeasures Craft

Like landing craft, small mine warfare types are now carried under "Combatant Craft" heading. Neglected after WW II, mine warfare came back into its own during the Korean conflict. New craft now in use or under development reflect further impetus given by Vietnam War. None of the types listed below are on the NVR.

MHA—Designation established for ex-civilian craft that may be acquired on mobilization; fitted with minimum sonar capability for emergency use.

MSA—Like MHA, this symbol would apply to mobilized ex-civilian craft equipped with minimum minesweeping capability.

MSB—Originally designed as assault sweepers to be carried on parent ships. As built, too heavy for boom handling; used since in harbors and channels. Many used in Vietnam rivers. At least 6 lost in war. Transportable by large ships, but must be handled at either end of voyage by heavy cranes. Require shore base or MCS support. Earlier MSBs are 57′; newer MSB-29 is larger for better seakeeping. MSBs have hull numbers, were classified as service craft until 8–14–69 when they were rerated.

MSD—Fast riverine minesweeper with 23′ plastic hull and low silhouette. Operates by radio control after sweep gear is streamed.

MSI—111′9″ nonmagnetic type, originally designed as smaller replacement for MSC, a type deemphasized in recent years. Series begun with *Cove* (MSI-1) and *Cape* (MSI-2) of 1958/59; subsequent MSI built for ILP. The later ones have 2 screws, 50% more power, full MSC-sized sweep gear. MSI-1/2 served NRT briefly. MSI-1 was loaned to John Hopkins University on 7–31–70. MSI-2 future unsettled; presently out of service.

MSL—36′ assault sweeping craft, with moored/magnetic/acoustic capability. MCS-1/2 carried 20 of these. Newest Mark MSL has diesel engine, plastic hull.

MSM—Converted LCM(6) for river sweeping. Armed and armored; can simultaneously sweep and fight.

MSR—Combination river minesweeper/armed patrol craft.

MSS—Rated as Minesweeper, Special (Device). Originally completed in 1943 as the liberty ship SS *Harry L. Glucksman* (ex MCE-2445). Built to an EC2-S-C1 hull design. Conversion included removal of all internal machinery, piping, shafting, etc. Hull strengthened. A shock-mounted pilot house was installed forward. Ship will be able to withstand mine explosions and not sink. Converted under FY 1966 (SCB 500) by American Shipbuilding Co., Lorain, Ohio. Contract awarded 8–30–66. Conversion started on the same date. Conversion completed 6–16–69. MSS-1 has the following characteristics: Full Load Displacement: 15,000 tons, Length Overall: 441′, Maximum Draft: 28′, Extreme Beam: 57′, Engines: 5 GM diesels, mounted outboard on either side, Maximum Speed: 10 knots, Accommodations: 1 Officer and 8 Enlisted, no armament.

MSB-49.

MSI-2.

MSL-11.

MSD (with MSR).

MSL-15.

MSR.

MSS-1. The side pods contain propulsion units. Note helicopter deck amidships. 4–25–69.

D. Riverine/Coastal Warfare Craft

All riverine/coastal warfare craft were based in Vietnam and operated under three task forces. PCFs operated under CTF-115 (Coastal Surveillance Force), PBRs operated under CTF-116 (River Patrol Force), and the remaining types operated under CTF-117 (River Assault Force). CTF-117 was later dissolved and its craft transferred to CTF-116. Maintenance and logistic support was provided by shore bases and LST/AGPs, APLs, APBs, and ARLs. On 10–1–69, approximately 190 of the riverine craft listed here were transferred to the Vietnam Navy. By January 1971, the Riverine/Coastal Force ceased to exist as nearly all units had been transferred to Vietnam.

ASPB—New construction craft in 2 Marks having welded steel hulls. Escorts other USN riverine craft and interdicts enemy shipping. Has provisions for minesweeping gear (shallow draft). Faster than the Monitors, but similarly armed.

ATC—Converted from LCM-6 landing craft to carry troops and other equipment for logistic support. Can carry maximum of 40 troops or a 105 mm howitzer and its prime mover. Craft is heavily armored. Those few with helicopter decks are officially designated ATC(H); tiniest aircraft carriers afloat. Some also serve as hospital boats and others as AOs for other riverine craft.

CCB—LCM-6 conversions; heavily armored. Mini-versions of *Northampton* (CC-1) and *Wright* (CC-2). Can carry up to 15 command staff (normally 11). Used mainly by boat group commanders.

MON—Provide direct and indirect fire support. Also serve as security guard for afloat or ashore boat bases. LCM-6 conversion; heavily armored.

PACV—Only air-cushion vehicles in USN. American-built versions of the British SR.N5 hovercraft. USN designation is SK-5. Built at Bell Aerosystems, Buffalo, N.Y. Three additional units are operated by Army. Can carry 20 troops. Rides on 4" air cushion. All transferred to Coast Guard 10/69.

PBR—Divided into 2 types, the MK I and II. First 160 boats are MK I design, the remainder MK II. Both types adapted from commercial design. Especially suited for shallow water operations. All MK I PBRs built by United Boat Builders, Bellingham, Wash. At least a dozen of both MKs have been lost to enemy action. Statistics and armament of both MKs vary. Fitted with water jets vice propellers.

PCF—These are the famous *Swift* boats. Adapted from a commercial, all-metal crew boat. Two types, MK I and II. First 104 boats are MK I, remainder MK II. All of basically same dimensions, but configuration varies. Many are being built under ILP program for Thailand, South Korea, Philippines, and Vietnam. About 2 dozen PCFs have been lost to all causes.

Point—Originally built for the Coast Guard, but placed under operational control of USN for duty in Vietnam. Manned by CG, fly CG colors, but painted dark grey. Welded steel hull, aluminum superstructure. Originally 26 units were placed under control of USN, but now all have been transferred to Vietnam Navy. On units in Vietnam, forward 20 mm replaced by a 81 mm mortar with one ·50 cal. machine gun attached to the top of the mortar. See Coast Guard section for more details.

MK 1 ASPB. Note crank-operated grenade launchers aft of forward 40mm mount, and 81mm mortar aft. Radar is on pole just forward of deckhouse mount. 12–2–67.

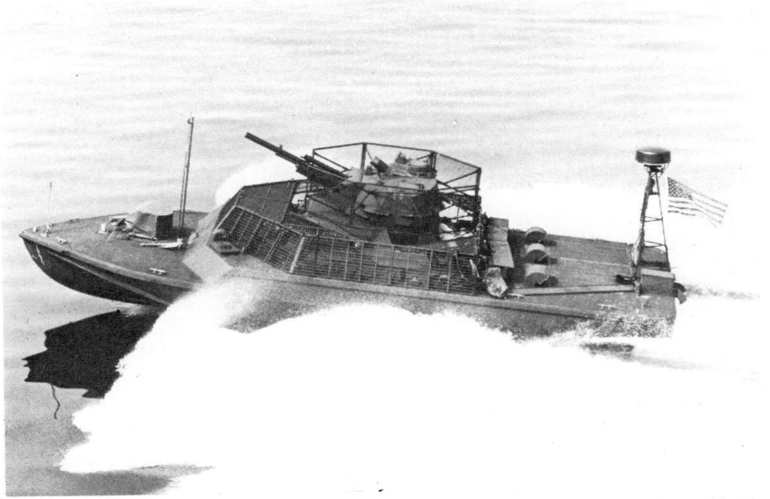

Sikorsky

MK II ASPB. Note difference between MK I and MK II.

ATC. Note blunt bow retained during conversion, sloping well-deck cover for the protection of troops inside, and minesweeping mechanism aft. 5–1–67.

ATC(H) with a HUEY embarked. Except for superimposed helicopter pad over well deck, the ATC and ATC(H) have same configuration. 7–26–67.

U.S. Navy CCB. Note elongated spoon bow vice that of ATC. Resembles *Monitor* except for array of antennas and small shelter aft of forward gun. Flag underneath ensign indicates squadron. Note minesweeping gear aft. 10–67.

USN version of the *Monitor*. Note open turret door, small arms aft of it, and small arms protruding from top works. Note spoon-bill bow.9–26–67.

One of USN's three PACVs. The turbo-shaft engine powers a 7′ centrifugal-lift fan which furnishes the air cushion. Air ports and tail rudders provide directional control. Note space to carry troops on sides. 2–1–68.

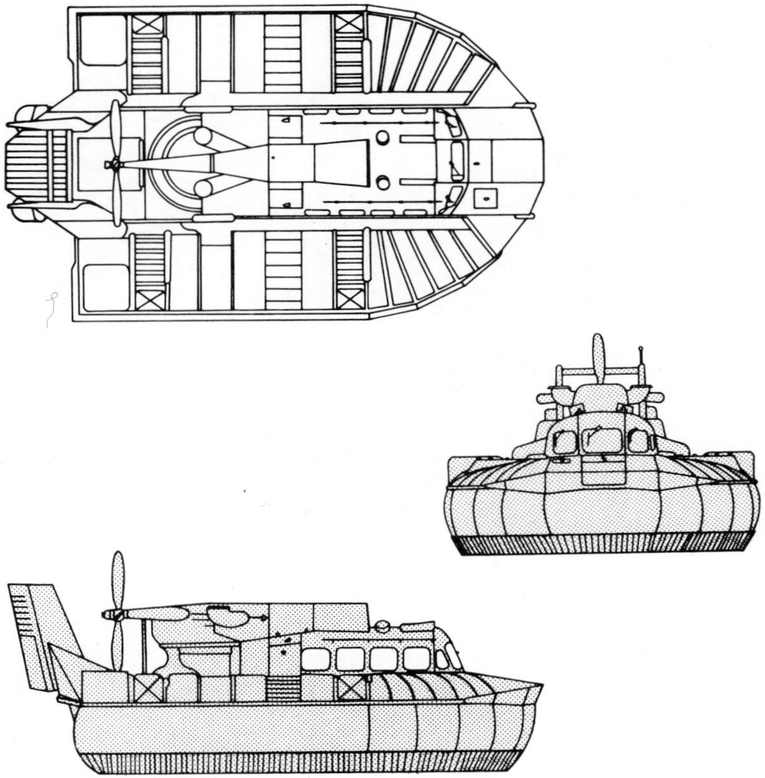

An overhead, broadside, and head-on view of a commercial version of the Navy's PACV. All three transferred to USCG.

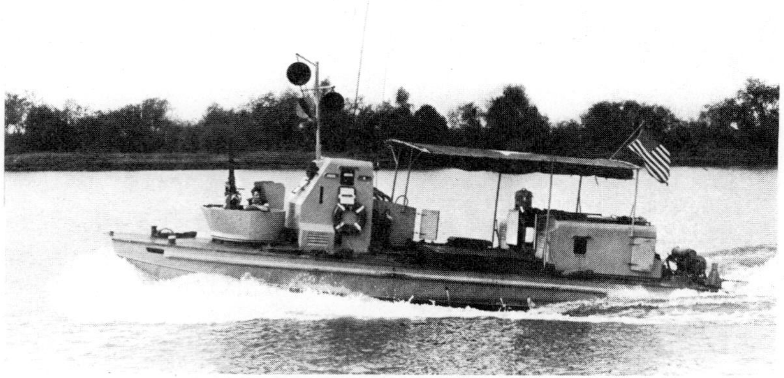

A U.S. Navy RPC used for sweeping mines in shallow rivers. 2–67.

MK I PBR. Hull is fiberglass, lined with plastic foam; immune to marine borers. Craft is propelled and steered by water jets. Note radar pod.

MK I PCF. Compare to photo of MK II PCF. Note machinegun on top of mortar and how far forward pilothouse is as compared to MK II PCF.

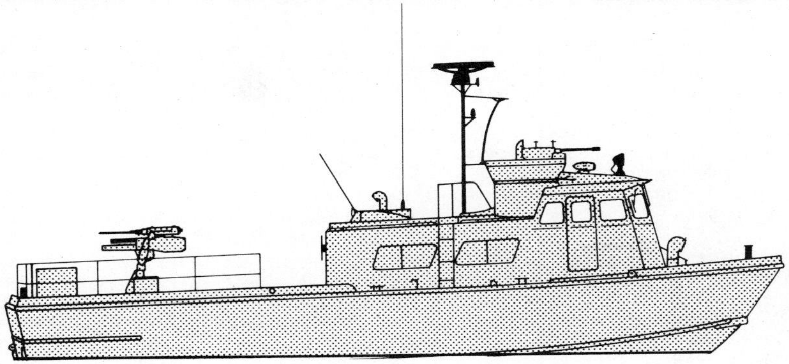

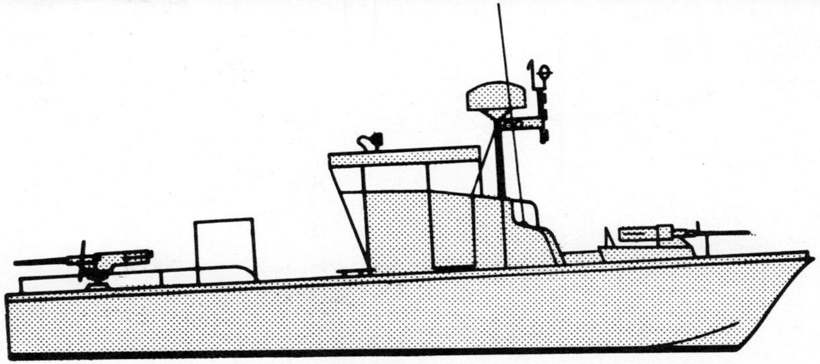

A broadside sketch of a typical MK II PBR. MK II has more powerful engines and enlarged mufflers and is also faster and slightly larger than the MK I.

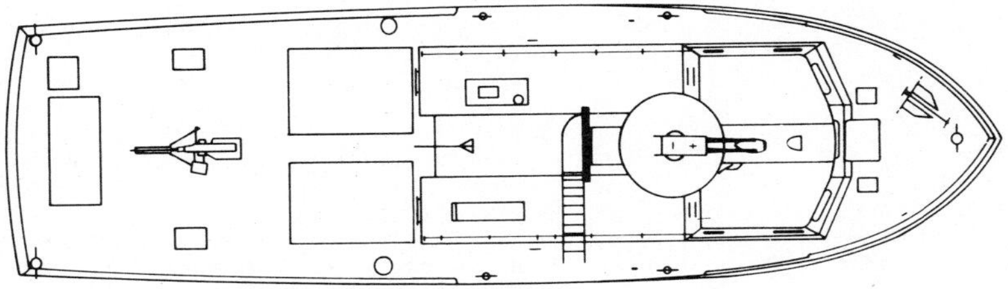

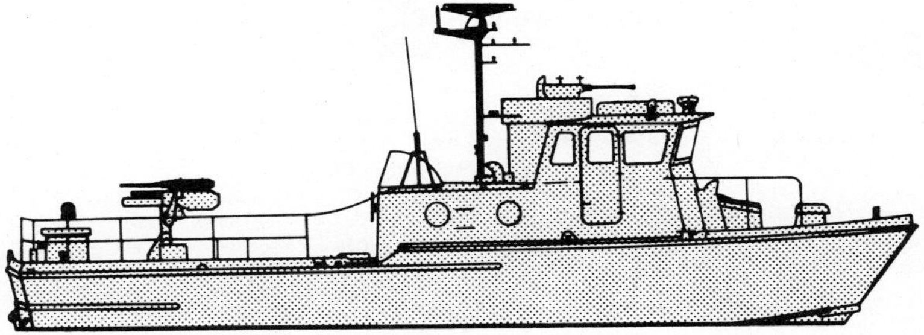

Overhead and broadside view of MK I PCF on left and broadside sketch of MK II PCF on right. Note difference in superstructure and pilothouse. Both have flush decks.

5. AUXILIARY SHIPS

By end-FY 1971, there were 376 auxiliary ships on the NVR. Of these 163 were active, 75 were in the USN reserve, 18 were in the MARAD reserve (still on the NVR), 15 were assigned to NRT, 1 was in special status, 1 was rated as equipment, 93 were assigned to MSC, and 12 were on loan or charter to government or nongovernment agencies. In addition, 13 auxiliaries were under construction and 1 was under conversion.

Class	Number	No. in Class	Full Load Displ.	Length Overall	Max. Draft	Extreme Beam	Number & Type of Boilers/Engines	Screws/ SHP	Max. Speed (Kts)	Accommodations Officers	Accommodations Enlisted	Armament
Samuel Gompers	AD-37	2	20,700	645′	23′	85′	2B(C.E.)/2GT(DeLaval)	1/20,000	18	135	1,668	1 5″/38, 6 .50 cal. mg.
Shenandoah	AD-26	4	14,700	492′	28′	70′	2B(F.W.)/2GT(West.)	1/8,500	18	45	780	1 5″/38
"Klondike"	AD-22	1	15,337	492′	27′	70′	2B(B&W)/2GT(G.E.)	1/8,500	18	80	819	2 3″/50
Cascade	AD-16	1	16,650	492′	27′	70′	2B(F.W.)/2GT(G.E.)	1/8,500	16.8	36	912	1 5″/38
Dixie	AD-14	5	18,000	531′	26′	73′	4B(B&W)/2GT(Parsons)	2/11,000	18.2	60	1,011	1 5″/38
Surfbird	ADG-383	1	1,178	221′	11′	32′	4D(G.M.)	2/3,200	18	9	74	4 .50 cal. mg.
Lodestone	ADG-8	3	900	185′	9′	34′	2D(G.M.)	2/1,900	18	9	59	none
"Virgo"	AE-30	1	11,240	459′	28′	63′	2B(F.W.)/1GT(DeLaval)	1/6,000	17	39	450	4 3″/50
Kilauea	AE-26	8	19,937	564′	28′	81′	3B(F.W.)/2GT(G.E.)	1/22,000	20	38	373	4 twin 3″/50
Nitro	AE-23	3	17,500	512′	29′	72′	2B(C.E.)/2GT(Beth.)	1/16,000	20.6	20	330	2 twin 3″/50
Suribachi	AE-21	2	17,400	512′	29′	72′	2B(C.E.)/2GT(Beth.)	1/16,000	18	16	370	2 twin 3″/50
"Mount Hood"	AE-11	7	15,277	459′	28′	63′	2B(C.E.)/1GT(G.E.)	1/6,000	15	20	270	2 3″/50 (AE-14, 16, & 18), 4 3″/50 (remainder)
"Lassen"	AE-3	1	13,876	459′	26′5″	63′	2D(Nord.)	1/6,000	14.7	22	330	4 3″/50
Asterion	AF-63	2	11,900	459′	27′	63′	2B(B&W)/1GT(West.)	1/8,500	17	16	42	none
Rigel	AF-58	2	15,500	502′	29′	72′	2B(C.E.)/1GT(G.E.)	1/16,000	20	22	330	2 twin 3″/50
Denebola	AF-56	2	11,948	455′	23′9″	62′	2B(C.E.)/1GT(West.)	1/8,500	18.3	18	286	2 twin 3″/50
Aludra	AF-55	1	12,891	459′	26′4″	65′	2B(B&W)/2GT(G.E.)	1/6,000	15.6	20	277	4 twin 3″/50
"Bald Eagle"	AF-50	1	13,860	459′	26′	63′	2B(F.W.)/1GT(G.E.)	1/6,000	16	18	49	2 twin 40mm (AF-52)
"Alstede"	AF-48	3	13,860	459′	28′5	63′	2B(B&W)/1GT(G.E.)	1/6,000	16.5	21	243	2 twin 40mm
"Adria"	AF-30	1	8,365	339′	23′	50′	1D(Nord.)	2/1,700	11	10	73	none
Hyades	AF-28	1	13,900	469′	28′	63′	2B(B&W)/1GT(G.E.)	1/6,000	16	22	297	2 3″/50
Mars	AFS-1	7	16,263	581′	24′	79′	3B(B&W)/2GT(DeLaval)	1/22,000	20	34	441	4 twin 3″/50
S. P. Lee	AG-192	1	1,297	208′	14′	39′	2D	1/1,200	15	9	17	none
Spokane	AG-191	1	8,600	541′	25′11″	53′2″	4B(B&W)/2GT(West.)	2/75,000	31.8	48	753	6 twin 5″/38, 4 quad 40mm, 6 twin 40mm
Flyer	AG-178	1	11,000	459′	26′	63′	2B/1GT	1/6,000	17	14	41	none
Phoenix	AG-172	3	15,199	455′	28′	62′	2B(C.E.)/1GT(G.E.)	1/1,700	16	48	161	none
Kingsport	AG-164	1	11,100	455′	22′	62′	2B(B&W)/1GT(West.)	1/8,500	17	19	108	none
"Mission Capistrano"	AG-162	0	21,880	524′	30′	68′	2B(B&W)/1GT(G.E.)	1/10,000	16	14	71	none
Compass Island	AG-153	2	16,076	563′7″	31′	76′	2B(F.W.)/1GT(G.E.)	1/17,500	20	35	384	none
Sequoia	AG-23	1	120	105′	5′	21′	2D(Winton)	1/400	12	—	—	none
Glover	AGDE-1	1	3,575	415′	24′5″	44′	2B(F.W.)/1GT(West.)	1/35,000	27	17	231	1 5″/38, 1 ASROC, 2 MK 32 torpedo launcher (triple)
Plainview	AGEH-1	1	320	212′	25′	40′	2D(Detroit)2Gas Turb.(G.E.)	2/28,000	50	4	20	2 MK 32 torpedo launcher (triple)
"Banner"	AGER-1	1	700	180′	8′5″	33′	2D(G.M.)	1/1,000	12	7	75	3.50 cal. mg.
Valcour	AGF-1	1	2,800	310′9″	14′	41′	4D(F.M.)	2/6,080	17	30	230	1 quad 40mm, 2 twin 40mm

Range Sentinel	AGM-22	1					2B(C.E.)/1GT(West.)					none
Vanguard	AGM-19	2	24,710	595′	25′	75′	2B(B&W)/1GT	1/8,700	15	21	68	none
Sword Knot	AGM-13	1	8,345	338′	15′	51′	1D(Nord.)	1/1,870	10	12	30	none
Gen. H. H. Arnold	AGM-9	2	14,300	522′11″	25′	72′	2B(B&W)/1GT(West.)	1/9,000	14	88	105	none
Range Recoverer	AGM-2	1	935	177′	11′	32′	2D(G.M.)	1/1,100	10	8	16	none
"Range Tracker"	AGM-1	5	15,200	455′	28′6″	62′	2B(C.E.)/1GT(West.)	1/8,500	17	14	76	none
Arlington	AGMR-2	1	19,800	684′	26′	110′	4B(B&W)/4GT(G.E.)	4/120,000	32.5	50	989	4 twin 3″/50
Annapolis	AGMR-1	1	23,850	557′	30′7″	104′	4B(C.E.)/2GT(A.C.)	2/16,000	19	48	700	4 twin 3″/50
Chain	AGOR-17	1	1,970	214′	15′	41′	2D(C.B.)	2/2,440	14	10	84	none
Hayes	AGOR-16	1	3,080	246′5″	18′8″	75′	2D	2/2,400	15	[44 total]		none
Eltanin	AGOR-8	2	3,886	266′	19′	52′	2D(Alco)	2/2,700	12	14	34	none
Robert D. Conrad	AGOR-3	10	1,370	209′	15′	40′	2D(CTC)	1/10,000	13	9	17	none
Josiah W. Gibbs	AGOR-1	1	2,800	310′9″	14′	41′	4D(F.M.)	2/6,080	18.2	16	41	none
"Garrett County"	AGP-786	0	4,080	328′	12′4″	50′	2D(G.M.)	2/1,700	11.6	9	109	4 twin 40mm, 2 single 40mm
Sgt. George D. Keathley	AGS-35	1	6,090	339′	23′	50′	2D	1/1,870	11.5	11	26	none
Wilkes	AGS-33	2	2,540	285′	15′	48′	2D	1/3,600	15	12	29	none
Chauvenet	AGS-29	2	3,800	393′	15′	54′	2D(West.)	1/3,400	15	24	131	none
Silas Bent	AGS-26	2	2,580	285′	15′	48′	2D(West.)	1/3,000	15	12	32	none
Kellar	AGS-25	1	1,390	209′	14′	39′	2D	1/1,000	12	11	17	none
Bowditch	AGS-21	3	13,050	455′	27′6″	62′	2B(C.E.)/1GT(West.)	1/9,350	17	14	47	none
Albacore	AGSS-569	1	1,500[1]	200′	22′	27′	2D(G.M.)/1EM(West.)	1/15,000	12[4]	5	47	none
Dolphin	AGSS-555	1	846	152′	18′	19′5″	2D(Detroit)/1EM(Ell.)	1/1,650	15	5	15	none
ex-*"Guppy IA"*	AGSS-319	6	2,040	307′	17′	27′	4D(G.M.)/2EM(G.E.)	2/4,610	17.3	10	75	6 21″ TT fwd., 4 21″ TT aft
Torsk	AGSS-423	3	1,900	312′	16′	27′	4D(F.M.)/2EM(Ell.)	2/5,400	20	10	76	6 21″ TT fwd., 4 21″ TT aft
Tigrone	AGSS-419	1	1,990	312′	18′	27′	4D(F.M.)/2EM(G.E.)	2/4,610	20	11	76	6 21″ TT fwd., 4 21″ TT aft
"Sand Lance"	SS-381	1	2,050	312′	17′	27′	4D(F.M.)/4EM(Ell.)	2/4,610	20	10	71	6 21″ TT fwd., 4 21″ TT aft
Charr	AGSS-328	2	2,080	312′	17′	27′	4D(G.M.)/2EM(Ell.)	2/4,610	20	8	74	6 21″ TT fwd., 4 21″ TT aft
Baya	AGSS-318	1	2,220	330′	19′5″	27′3″	3D(G.M.)/2EM(Ell.)	2/4,800	10.5	8	68	4 21″ TT aft
"Balao"	AGSS-285	4	2,040	312′	17′	27′	4D(G.M.)/2EM(G.E.)	2/4,610	20	11	67	6 21″ TT fwd., 4 21″ TT aft
"Pompon"	SSR-267	1	2,340	342′	17′	27′	4D(G.M.)/2EM(Ell.)	2/4,610	20	10	67	6 21″ TT fwd., 4 21″ TT aft
Angler	AGSS-240	2	2,070	312′	17′	27′	3D(G.M.)/2EM(Ell.)	2/3,800	15	8	74	6 21″ TT fwd., 4 21″ TT aft
"Gato"	SS-212	1	2,060	312′	17′	27′	4D(G.E.)/4EM(G.E.)	2/5,400	20	10	70	6 21″ TT fwd., 4 21″ TT aft
"Belmont"	AGTR-4	0	11,114	455′3″	24′2″	62′	2B(C.E.)/1GT(West.)	1/8,500	17.5	26	315	4 .50 cal. mg.
"Haven"	AH-12	3	14,892	520′	26′	72′	2B(B&W)/1GT(G.E.)	1/9,000	18.3	147	1,256	none
Wyandot	AKA-88	1	14,000	459′2″	26′3″	63′	2B(C.E.)/1GT(G.E.)	1/6,000	16.5	38	385	none
Norwalk	AK-279	4	11,300	455′	22′	62′	2B(B&W)/1GT(G.E.)	1/8,500	16.5	18	71	none
Schuyler Otis Bland	AK-277	1	15,910	454′	27′	66′	2B(F.W.)/1GT(G.E.)	1/13,750	18.5			none
Lt. James E. Robinson	AK-274	1	15,199	455′	29′	62′	2B(C.E./1GT(West.)	1/8,500	18	15	40	none
"Eltanin"	AK-270	1	4,942	262′2″	18′7″	51′5″	2D(Alco)	2/3,200	13	14	34	none
Marine Fiddler	AK-267	1	22,094	520′	33′	72′	2B(B&W)/1GT(West.)	1/9,000	15.8	14	43	none
"Antares"	AK-258	3	12,100	456′	26′	65′	2B(C.E.)/1GT(West.)	1/8,500	17	18	204	4 twin 40mm (AK-260), none (remainder)
Pvt. Leonard C. Brostrom	AK-255	1	22,056	520′	32′	72′	2B(B&W)/1GT(G.E.)	1/9,000	17	14	50	none
Lt. George W. G. Boyce	AK-251	7	15,199	455′	29′	62′	2B(C.E.)/1GT(West.)	1/6,000	17	18	42	none
Greenville Victory	AK-237	2	15,200	455′	29′	62′	2B(B&W)/1GT(West.)	1/8,500	18	15	36	none

[1] Displacement is surface displacement for all AGSSs. [2] Speed is surface speed for all AGSSs. [3] Immobilized training hulk; tubes blanked off.

continued

Class	Number	No. in Class	Full Load Displ.	Length Overall	Max. Draft	Extreme Beam	Number & Type of Boilers/Engines	Screws/ SHP	Max. Speed (Kts)	Accommodations Officers	Enlisted	Armament
"Alamosa"	AK-156	6	8,370	335′	23′	50′	1D(Nord.)	1/1,700	11	14	30	none
Point Barrow	AKD-1	1	14,000	492′	22′	78′	2B(F.W.)/2GT(West.)	2/6,000	15	32	186	none
Mark	AKL-12	1	906	179′10″	10′2″	33′	2D(G.M.)	2/1,000	12.2	1	28	1 20mm
"Camano"	AKL-1	1	935	177′	10′	33′	2D(G.M.)	2/1,000	13	5	57	2 20mm
Sea Lift	AKR-9	1	21,700	540′	29′	83′	B/2GT	1/19,400	20	5	49	none
Comet	AKR-7	1	18,286	499′	28′8″	78′	2B(B&W)1GT(G.E.)	1/13,200	18	73 total		none
Altair	AKS-32	1	10,439	455′	23′	62′	2B(C.E.)/2GT(West.)	2/8,500	18	22	228	2 twin 40mm
"Bogue"	AKV-40	2	15,700	495′8″	26′	111′6″	2B(F.W.)/1GT(A.C.)	1/8,500	19	18	246	none
"Commencement Bay"	AKV-37	1	24,130	557′	33′	104′	4B(C.E.)/2GT(A.C.)	2/16,000	17.6	18	647	2 5″/38, 3 quad 40mm, 12 twin 40mm
Cohoes	ANL-78	1	855	169′	15′	34′	2D(B.S.)	2/1,600	12	122	1,048	6 .50 cal. mg.
American Explorer	AO-165	1	31,300	615′	32′	80′	2B(B&W)/1GT(DeLaval)	2/22,000	20	16	37	none
Maumee	AO-149	3	32,953	620′	32′	84′	2B(C.E.)/1GT(West.)	2/20,460	18	17	35	none
Neosho	AO-143	6	38,000	655′	35′	86′	2B(B&W)/2GT(G.E.)	2/28,000	19	29	333	6 twin 3″/50
"Mission"	AO-111	2	21,880	524′	30′	68′	2B(B&W)/1GT(G.E.)	1/10,000	16	14	38	none
Mispillion	AO-105	5	35,091	644′	36′	75′	4B(B&W)/2GT(West.)	2/13,500	16	18	288	4 3″/50
Suamico	AO-49	12	21,880	524′	31′	68′	2B(B&W)/1GT(G.E.)	1/6,000	15	14	38	none
"Mattaponi"	AO-41	1	22,447	520′	30′7″	69′	2B(B&W)/1GT(West.)	1/12,800	16	16	269	4 3″/50
Kennebec	AO-36	1	21,550	501′4″	36′	68′3″	2B(F.W.)/1GT(G.E.)	1/12,000	16.5	19	218	4 3″/50
"Cimarron"	AO-22	18	25,500	553′	33′	75′	4B(F.W.)/2GT(Beth.)	2/13,500	18	20	270	2-4 3″/50
Sacramento	AOE-1	4	52,483	793′	38′5″	107′	4B(C.E.)/2GT(G.E.)	2/100,000	26	33	565	4 twin 3″/50
Alatna	AOG-81	2	7,300	302′	60′11″	19′	2D(Alco)	2/3,400	12	11	40	none
"Tonti"	AOG-76	4	6,000	325′	19′	48′	1D(Ent.)	1/1,400	10	11	30	none
Patapsco	AOG-1	9	4,570	311′	17′	49′	4D(G.M.)	2/3,750	14	9	114	3 3″/50
Wichita	AOR-1	6	38,100	659′	34′	96′	3B(F.W.)/2GT	2/38,000	20	27	362	2 twin 3″/50
Barrett	AP-196	3	19,600	533′	27′	73′	2B(B&W)/1GT(G.E.)	1/13,750	19	426	1,723	none
"Gen. Daniel I. Sultan"	AP-120	0	22,574	609′	29′	76′	4B(C.E.)/2GT(G.E.)	2/18,000	19	491	1,659	none
"Gen. John Pope"	AP-110	0	20,175	623′	26′	76′	4B(F.W.)/2GT(DeLaval)	2/17,000	20	246	4,114	none
"Blackford"	APB-45	3	3,910	328′	14′	50′	2D(G.M.)	2/1,800	10	12	125	2 quad 40mm
"Benewah"	APB-35	4	4,080	328′	14′	50′	2D(G.M.)	2/1,800	12	12	129	2 3″/50, 2 quad 40mm, 8 .50 cal. mg.
"Shenandoah"	AR-28	1	14,700	492′	28′	70′	2B(F.W.)/2GT(West.)	1/8,500	18	45	780	1 5″/38
Markab	AR-23	1	14,383	491′8″	26′6″	72′3″	2B(F.W.)/1GT(G.E.)	1/8,500	18	34	623	4 3″/50
Klondike	AR-22	1	15,460	492′	27′2″	69′5″	2B(B&W)/1GT(G.E.)	1/8,500	18.4	186	1,294	4 3″/50
Amphion	AR-13	2	14,490	492	28′	73′	2B(F.W.)/1GT(West.)	1/8,560	15.5	52	885	1 5″/38
Delta	AR-9	2	13,000	490′	26′	70′	2B(B&W)/1GT(N.N.)	1/8,500	16	46	957	4 3″/50
Vulcan	AR-5	4	16,330	530′	24′5″	73′	4B(B&W)/2GT(N.Y.S.)	2/12,000	18.7	63	1,272	4 5″/38
"Aristaeus"	ARB-1	4	3,640	328′	14′	50′	2D(G.M.)	2/1,800	12	24	248	1 3″/50, 2 quad 40mm
Aeolus	ARC-3	2	7,040	438′	19′3″	58′2″	2B(Wickes)/2GT(West.)	2/6,600	17	23	198	none
Neptune	ARC-2	2	7,444	370′	18′	47′	2B(C.E.)/2RS(Skinner)	2/4,800	14	28	168	2 twin 20 mm (ARC-2 only)
"Luzon"	ARG-2	1	11,450	442′	23′	57′	2B(B&W)/1RS (Elicot Mach.)	1/2,500	11	23	439	3 3″/50, 8 .50 cal. mg.
Achelous	ARL-1	10	3,853	328′	14′	50′	2D(G.M.)	2/1,800	12	18	248	2 quad 40 mm
Bolster	ARS-38	6	2,040	214′	15′	44′	4D(C.B.)	2/2,440	14	10	89	1 40mm, 2 .50 cal. mg.

Escape	ARS-6	8	1,970	214′	15′	44′	4D(C.B.)	2/2,440	14.3	10	91	1 40mm, 2 .50 cal. mg.
Gypsy	ARSD-1	2	1,140	225′	10′	35′	2D(F.M.)	2/2,880	13	6	58	none
Laysan Island	ARST-1	2	4,080	328′	14′	50′	2D(G.M.)	2/1,800	12	41	225	2 quad 40mm
Fabius	ARVA-5	2	4,080	328′	14′	50′	2D(G.M.)	2/1,800	12	23	225	2 quad 40mm
"Aventinus"	ARVE-3	1	4,080	328′	14′	50′	2D(G.M.)	2/1,800	12	20	225	2 quad 40mm
Corpus Christi Bay	ARVH-1	1	15,060	529′	21′	69′	4B(B&W)/2GT(N.Y.S.)	2/13,200	19	22	106	none
L. Y. Spear	AS-36	2	22,640	644′	24′5″	85′	2B(F.W.)/2GT(G.E.)	1/20,000	20	94	1,254	2 single 5″/38, 4 .50 cal. mg.
Simon Lake	AS-33	2	21,000	644′	22′5″	85′	2B(C.E.)/1GT(DeLaval)	1/20,000	18	95	1,326	2 twin 3″/50
Hunley	AS-31	2	18,300	619′	23′4″	83′	16D(F.M.)	1/15,000	18	91	1,312	2 twin 3″/50
"Aegir"	AS-23	0	16,500	492′	26′	70′	2B(F.W.)/1GT(West.)	1/8,500	18.4	95	1,515	1 5″/38, 4 3″/50
Euryale	AS-22	1	15,400	492′	26′	70′	2B(F.W.)/1GT(DeLaval)	1/8,500	16.5	103	1,409	1 5″/38, 4 3″/50
Proteus	AS-19	1	18,500	574′	25′5″	73′	8D(A.C.)	2/11,000	16	85	1,212	1 5″/38
Griffin	AS-13	2	14,500	492′	27′	70′	8D(B.S.)	1/8,500	16.5	87	1,424	4 3″/50
Fulton	AS-11	6	16,050	530′	26′	73′	2D(G.M.)	2/11,200	16	80	1,032	2 5″/38
Pigeon	ASR-21	2	3,411	251′	19′	86′	4D(Alco)	2/6,000	15	16	147	2 3″/50, 4 ·50 cal. mg.
"Penguin"	ASR-12	1	1,740	205′	19′	39′	4D(B.S.)	1/3,000	14	8	91	2 20mm
Chanticleer	ASR-7	7	2,290	251′	16′	44′	4D(Alco)	1/3,000	14	11	109	2 20mm
unnamed	ATA-240	1	820	143′	15′	34′	1D(C.B.)	1/1,500	12	10	26	none
"Sotoyomo"	ATA-121	16	860	143′	14′	34′	2D(G.M.)	1/1,500	12.5	7	41	2 20mm
"Cherokee"	ATF-66	28	1,640	205′	17′	39′	4D(G.M.)	1/3,000	15	5	87	1 3″/50
Edenton	ATS-1	3	3,125	283′	15′	50′	4D(Paxman)	2/6,000	16	9	91	4 .50 cal. mg.
"Chandeleur"	AV-10	0	14,200	492′	24′	70′	2B(F.W.)/1GT(G.E.)	1/8,500	18.4	120	955	1 5″/38, 4 3″/50
"Currituck"	AV-7	0	15,100	541′	22′	72′	4B(B&W)/2GT(N.Y.S.)	2/12,000	19.2	162	1,085	4 5″/38
Norton Sound	AVM-1	1	15,170	543′	23′5″	72′	4B(B&W)/2GT(A.C.)	2/12,000	19.5	142	907	1 5″/54 (experimental), 1 BPDMS (experimental)
Lexington	CVT-16	1	42,000	899′	31′	192′	8B(B&W)/4GT(West.)	4/150,000	28	115	1,500	none

2 DESTROYER TENDERS, *SAMUEL GOMPERS* CLASS

Name	Number	FY/SCB	Builder	Awarded	Commissioned	F/S
Puget Sound	AD-38	65/700	PS Navy	12–29–64	4–27–68	AA
Samuel Gompers	AD-37	64/244	PS Navy	10–31–63	7–1–67	PA

First postwar ADs. Can serve all DD types including DLGNs; can serve 6 DLGs at once. A third ship, approved FY 1969, was cancelled.

4 DESTROYER TENDERS, *SHENANDOAH* CLASS

Name	Number	F/S	Name	Number	F/S
Bryce Canyon	AD-36	PA	*Yellowstone*	AD-27	AA
Isle Royale	AD-29	PR*	*Shenandoah*	AD-26	AA

Ships commissioned between 8–13–45 (AD-26) and 6–9–62 (AD-29). Originally 9 ships in class. AD-30, 33, and 35 cancelled 1945–46. AD-36 was suspended 8–11–45 and laid up incomplete until Korean War when work resumed and she was commissioned. AD-29 completed 3–26–46 and laid up without commissioning. Served as Headquarters Ship, San Diego Reserve Fleet until commissioned as replacement for *Hamul* (AD-20). *Tidewater* (AD-31) leased to Indonesia 2–20–71. AD-29 "in service, in reserve" 1–22–71 as accommodation ship, Long Beach. Decommissioned 6–30–71 and towed to San Diego. *Grand Canyon* (AD-28) now AR-28.

1 DESTROYER TENDER, *"KLONDIKE"* CLASS

Name	Number	F/S
Everglades	AD-24	AR*

Sole survivor of a 4-ship class. Completed 5–23–46, but laid up until commissioned 5–25–51 for Korean War. Now accommodation and depot ship at Philadelphia. Class leader serves as AR-22. AD-23, 25 are in MARAD reserve fleet, permanent custody. AD-24 decommissioned 8–15–70.

1 DESTROYER TENDER, *CASCADE* CLASS

Name	Number	F/S
Cascade	AD-16	AA

Built on a C3-S1-N2 hull. Acquired 9–11–42 and commissioned 3–12–43.

5 DESTROYER TENDERS, *DIXIE* CLASS

Yosemite	AD-19	AA
Sierra	AD-18	AA
Piedmont	AD-17	PA
Prairie	AD-15	PA
Dixie	AD-14	PA

Similar in appearance to *Vulcan* class ARs and *Fulton* class ASs. Commissioned 1940–44. All have had FRAM II. Can serve any type of DD. Have helicopter decks aft. AD-32 cancelled 1945.

1 DEGAUSSING SHIP, *SURFBIRD* CLASS

Surfbird	ADG-383	PR*

First commissioned 11–25–44 as an *Auk* class minesweeper. Reclassified MSF on 2–7–55. Converted and reclassified ADG 5–18–57. Decommissioned 12–18–70.

3 DEGAUSSING SHIPS, "*PCE*" TYPE

Name	Number	F/S
Deperm	ADG-10	PR
Magnet	ADG-9	PR
Lodestone	ADG-8	PR

All began as PCEs; reclassified YDG 1943–44; to ADG 11–1–47; named 2–1–55. All decommissioned 1946–47.

1 AMMUNITION SHIP, "*VIRGO*" CLASS

Chara	AE-31	PA
[Virgo]	AE-30	Struck

Originally of the *Andromeda* class, commissioned 1943–44 as AKAs. Built on C2-S-B1 hull design. Decommissioned late 1950s; struck 1960–61. Laid up in MARAD reserve fleet. Reinstated on NVR 9–1–65. To AE 11–1–65. AE-31 recommissioned 6–25–66; AE-30 on 8–19–66.

8 AMMUNITION SHIPS, *KILAUEA* CLASS

Name	Number	FY/SCB	Builder	Awarded	Commissioned	F/S
Kiska	AE-35	68/703	Ingalls	3–8–68		Bldg.
Mount Baker	AE-34	68/703	Ingalls	3–8–68		Bldg.
Shasta	AE-33	67/703	Ingalls	3–8–68		PA
Flint	AE-32	67/703	Ingalls	3–8–68		PA
Mount Hood	AE-29	66/703	Beth., Sparrows Pt.	1–26–66	5–1–71	PA
Santa Barbara	AE-28	66/703	Beth., Sparrows Pt.	1–26–66	7–11–70	AA
Butte	AE-27	65/703	Gen. Dyn., Quincy	3–30–65	12–14–68	AA
Kilauea	AE-26	65/703	Gen. Dyn., Quincy	3–30–65	8–10–68	PA

A new class of AEs easily recognizable by midships superstructure. Equipped with FAST and built-in helicopter deck aft.

3 AMMUNITION SHIPS, *NITRO* CLASS

Name	Number	F/S	Name	Number	F/S
Haleakala	AE-25	PA			
Pyro	AE-24	PA			
Nitro	AE-23	AA			

Improved *Suribachi* class. FAST retrofitted—provides improved system for transferring missiles. Commissioned 1959.

2 AMMUNITION SHIPS, *SURIBACHI* CLASS

Mauna Kea	AE-22	PA			
Suribachi	AE-21	AA			

First built-for-purpose AEs. Commissioned 1956–57. FAST retrofitted.

7 AMMUNITION SHIPS, "*MOUNT HOOD*" CLASS

Diamond Head	AE-19	AA	*Firedrake* (ex-SS *Winged Racer*)	AE-14	PR*
Paracutin	AE-18	PR*	*Wrangell* (ex-SS *Midnight*)	AE-12	MAR*
Great Sitkin	AE-17	AA			
Mount Katmai	AE-16	PA			
Vesuvius (ex-SS *Gamecock*)	AE-15	PA			

Built on a MARCOMM C2-S-AJ1 hull design. Acquired from MARCOMM and commissioned 1944–45. All built by North Carolina Shipbuilding Co. Will not receive FAST because of age. Class leader lost in WW II.

1 AMMUNITION SHIP, "*LASSEN*" CLASS

[Mazama]	AE-9	Struck			
Mauna Loa	AE-8	AR*			

Built to a C2 hull design. Acquired from MARCOMM and commissioned 1941–44. Three other ships of class, AE-4/6, struck 1968–69 (see disposal section). AE-8 decommissioned 2–26–71.

2 STORE SHIPS, *ASTERION* CLASS

Name	Number	F/S	Name	Number	F/S
Perseus (ex-SS *Union Victory*)	AF-64	MSC	*Asterion* (ex-SS *Arcadia Victory*)	AF-63	MSC

Built to a VC2-S-AP3 hull design. Acquired 1962 for MSC duty; renamed and reclassified 12–4–61.

2 STORE SHIPS, *RIGEL* CLASS

Vega	AF-59	PA			
Rigel	AF-58	AA			

Built to USN specifications on R3-S-4A hull design. AF-58 commissioned 9–2–55; AF-59 on 11–10–55.

2 STORE SHIPS, *DENEBOLA* CLASS

Regulus (ex-SS *Escanaba Victory*)	AF-57	PA	*Denebola* (ex-SS *Hibbing Victory*)	AF-56	AA

Built on a VC2-S-AP3 hull design; completed 1944. Both acquired 1952, commissioned 1954.

1 STORE SHIP, *ALUDRA* CLASS

Aludra (ex-SS *Matchless*)	AF-55	MPR*			

Built to an R2-S-BV1 hull design. Acquired and commissioned 1952. Decommissioned 1969.

1 STORE SHIP, "*BALD EAGLE*" CLASS

Arcturus	AF-52	AA			

Built to a C2-S-B1 hull design. AF-52 originally acquired 3–1–50 as USNS *Golden Eagle* (T-AF-52). Transferred to Fleet, renamed *Arcturus* 9–13–61 and commissioned 11–18–61; armed and equipped for underway replenishment. Three sisters disposed of.

3 STORE SHIPS, "*ALSTEDE*" CLASS

Name	Number	F/S	Decommissioned
Procyon (ex-SS *Flying Scud*)	AF-61	MPR*	12–8–70
Pictor (ex-SS *Great Republic*)	AF-54	MPR*	12–69
Zelima (ex-SS *Golden Rocket*)	AF-49	MPR*	10–69

Built to an R2-S-BV1 hull design 1945–46 as merchantmen. Were 5 in class; AF-48 and 62 disposed of. AF-61 acquired and commissioned 1961.

1 STORE SHIP, "*ADRIA*" CLASS

Name	Number	F/S
Bondia	AF-42	MSC

Built to R1-M-AV3 hull design. Decommissioned after WW II but reacquired from MARAD early 1950s. See MSC section for photo.

1 STORE SHIP, *HYADES* CLASS

Hyades (ex-SS *Iberville*)	AF-28	MAR*

Built to a C2-S-E1 hull design. Acquired from MARCOMM and commissioned 9–30–43. Sister *Graffias* (AF-29) stricken.

7 COMBAT STORE SHIPS, *MARS* CLASS

Name	Number	FY/SCB	Builder	Awarded	Commissioned	F/S
San Jose	AFS-7	67/705	National Steel	7–7–67	10–23–70	PA
San Diego	AFS-6	66/705	National Steel	12–28–65	5–24–69	AA
Concord	AFS-5	65/705	National Steel	12–18–64	11–27–68	AA
White Plains	AFS-4	65/705	National Steel	12–18–64	11–23–68	PA
Niagara Falls	AFS-3	64/208	National Steel	4–1–64	4–29–67	PA
Sylvania	AFS-2	62/208	National Steel	1–19–62	7–11–64	AA
Mars	AFS-1	61/208	National Steel	5–9–61	12–21–63	PA

Designed to replace AF/AKS/AVS. Have built-in helicopter decks aft with capability to maintain and store helicopters.

1 MISCELLANEOUS, *S. P. LEE* CLASS

Name	Number	F/S
S.P. Lee (ex-AGS-31)	AG-192	MSC

Completed 12–2–68 as survey ship; similar to AGOR-3 class. Put in reserve late 1969. Reactivated 9–10–70. To AG-192 on 9–25–70 for service as hydrographic research ship.

1 MISCELLANEOUS, "*ANTIAIRCRAFT CRUISER*" TYPE

Spokane	AG-191	AR

Commissioned 5–17–46 as CL-120 of *Juneau* class light cruisers. To CLAA 3–18–49. Decommissioned 9–49. To AG-191 on 4–1–66. Conversion to sonar test ship for operation by MSC cancelled late 1968.

1 MISCELLANEOUS, *FLYER* CLASS

Name	Number	F/S
Flyer (ex-SS *American Flyer*, SS *Water Witch*)	AG-178	MSC

Built to a C2-S-B1 hull design; completed 1945. Acquired from MARAD 2–9–65. Instated on NVR 3–1–65 under operational control of Navy Electronics Systems Command and manned by MSC.

3 MISCELLANEOUS, *PHOENIX* CLASS

Cheyenne (ex-SS *Middlesex Victory*)	AG-174	MSC
Provo (ex-SS *Drew Victory*)	AG-173	MSC
Phoenix (ex-SS *Capitol Victory*)	AG-172	MSC

Built on a VC2-S-AP3 hull design late WW II. Acquired for use as forward depot ships to test FDL concept. Became cargo carriers 1966. Twelve sisters were to be acquired from MARAD as AG-179/190, but never were.

1 MISCELLANEOUS, *KINGSPORT* CLASS

Kingsport (ex-SS *Kingsport Victory*)	AG-164	MSC

Built to a VC2-S-AP3 hull design in 1944. Acquired for MSC service as the USNS *Kingsport Victory* (T-AK-239). To AG-164 on 11–1–64 and renamed *Kingsport*. Converted into world's first satellite communications ship for "Project Advent". Antenna sphere installed aft of superstructure. With completion of assignment, communications gear and antennas removed. Adapted for hydrophraphic work. Carries 38 scientists.

MISCELLANEOUS, "*TANKER*" TYPE

[Mission Capistrano]	AG-162	MARAD

Built to a T2-SE-A2 hull design in 1944. Acquired for MSC service in 1949 as AO-112 of the *Mission* class. Converted by Todd Shipyards to a sound-testing ship. Carried a 5-story transducer just aft of the forward superstructure that can be raised or lowered as desired.

2 MISCELLANEOUS, "*MARINER*" TYPE

Observation Island (ex YAG-57)	AG-154	PA
Compass Island (ex YAG-56)	AG-153	AA

Built to a C4-S-1A hull design by NY Shipbuilding. Acquired from MARAD and commissioned 1956 (AG-153) and 1958 (AG-154) as EAGs. To AG 4–1–68. AG-154 fitted to test fire POLARIS and POSEIDON. AG-153 tests FBM guidance and navigation systems; played prominent part in development of SINS.

1 MISCELLANEOUS, *SEQUOIA* CLASS

Sequoia	AG-23	Equip.

Commissioned 3–25–33. Used as SecNav's yacht. No longer a commissioned ship.

1 ESCORT RESEARCH SHIP, *GLOVER* CLASS

Glover(ex AG-163)	AGDE-1	AA

Built to *Brooke* class DEG/*Garcia* class DE design; authorized FY 1961 and commissioned 11–13–65. Used to test sonar detection theories, but has full combat capability.

1 HYDROFOIL RESEARCH SHIP, *PLAINVIEW* CLASS

Plainview	AGEH-1	PSA

Authorized FY 1962. Placed in service 3–1–69. Top speed 50 knots; has 80-knot potential. Propulsion plant can be modified to investigate and test other foil types.

1 ENVIRONMENTAL RESEARCH SHIP, "*BANNER*" CLASS

Pueblo	AGER-2	Spec.

Completed late WW II as Army supply ship FS-344. Acquired by USN 4–12–66. Named and classified *Pueblo* (AKL-44). Commissioned 3–13–67. To AGER on 6–1–67. Boarded and captured 1–23–68 by North Korean sea forces. Towed into Wonson, North Korea. Crew released 12–68.

1 MISCELLANEOUS COMMAND SHIP, "*BARNEGAT*" TYPE

Valcour	AGF-1	AA

Commissioned 7–5–46 as AVP-55 in *Barnegat* class. To AGF-1 12–15–65. Several sisters serve Coast Guard.

1 MISSILE RANGE INSTRUMENTATION SHIP, *RANGE SENTINEL* CLASS

Name	Number	FY/SCB	Converted at	Started	Delivered
Range Sentinel	AGM-22	69/731	NW Marine	10–28–69	

Built to a VC2-S-AP5 hull design. Acquired and commissioned as *Sherburne* (APA-205) of *Haskell* class. Decommissioned after WW II, struck 10–1–58 and transferred to MARAD reserve; to AGM-22 4–16–69. Reinstated on NVR 10–22–69. Being converted to FBM missile tracker operated by MSC. Renamed 4–26–71.

2 MISSILE RANGE INSTRUMENTATION SHIPS, *VANGUARD* CLASS

Name	Number	F/S
Redstone (ex AO-114)	AGM-20	MSC
Vanguard (ex AO-122)	AGM-19	MSC

Converted from T2-SE-A2 *Mission* class tanker hulls. Acquired for MSC service. Laid up in MARAD late 1950s and struck. Reinstated on NVR 7–1–64 as AGM-19/20. Third ship of class, *Mercury* (AGM-21) has been struck. Conversion included addition of 72′ midbody. See section 13 for ex-AO, ex-AGM names.

1 RANGE INSTRUMENTATION SHIP, *SWORD KNOT* CLASS

Sword Knot	AGM-13	MPR*

Originally 6 ships in class; converted from C1-M-AV1 merchant ships. Acquired from MARAD. Manned by USAF until 7–1–64 when all 6 were instated on NVR and manned by MSC. Two were scrapped, and two (AGM-14 and 17 are laid up in MARAD, and AGM-16 is now AGS-36.

2 RANGE INSTRUMENTATION SHIPS, *"TRANSPORT"* TYPE

General Hoyt S. Vandenberg	AGM-10	MSC
General H. H. Arnold	AGM-9	MSC

Converted from C4-S-A3 *"General"* class transports. Originally commissioned 1944. Struck and laid up in MARAD late 1950s. Converted to AGMs 1963 and manned by USAF until 7–1–64 when reinstated on NVR.

1 MISSILE RANGE INSTRUMENTATION SHIP, *RANGE RECOVERER* CLASS

Name	Number	F/S	Name	Number	F/S
Range Recoverer	AGM-2	MSC			

Completed 1945 as Army coastal freighter FS-278. Acquired by USN 1960 and converted to AG-161. To AGM on 11–27–60.

5 MISSILE RANGE INSTRUMENTATION SHIPS, *"RANGE TRACKER"* CLASS

Wheeling (ex-SS *Seton Hall Victory*)	AGM-8	MSC	*Sunnyvale* (ex-SS *Dalton Victory*)	AGM-5	MSC
Huntsville (ex-SS *Knox Victory*)	AGM-7	MSC	*Longview* (ex-SS *Haiti Victory*)	AGM-3	MSC
Watertown (ex-SS *Niantic Victory*)	AGM-6	MSC			

Built on a VC2-S-AP3 hull design. All completed 1944–45 under the original names. AGM-3 and 5 acquired early 1950s as AK-238 and AK-256 respectively. Converted to AGMs early 1960s. AGM-6/8 acquired from MARAD and converted to AGM 1960–65.

1 MAJOR COMMUNICATIONS RELAY SHIP, *ARLINGTON* CLASS

Arlington	AGMR-2	PR*

Built on *Baltimore* class heavy cruiser hull and commissioned 7–14–46 as *Saipan* (CVL-48). Decommissioned 10–3–57 and laid up. To AVT-6 on 5–15–59. To CC-3 on 1–1–64 but conversion cancelled when 64% complete. Reauthorized FY 1964 for AGMR conversion. To AGMR-2 on 8–21–64; renamed 4–8–65; converted; recommissioned 8–27–66. Resembles *Wright* (CC-2). Decommissioned 1–14–70.

1 MAJOR COMMUNICATIONS RELAY SHIP, *ANNAPOLIS* CLASS

Annapolis	AGMR-1	AR*

Laid down as *Commencement Bay* class escort carrier *St. Andrews Bay*. Renamed *Gilbert Islands* 4–26–44 and commissioned as CVE-107 on 2–5–45. Decommissioned 1946 but recommissioned for Korean War 9–7–51. Decommissioned at Boston 1–15–55. To AKV-39 on 5–7–59. Struck 6–1–61 but reinstated on NVR 11–1–61 for conversion into AGMR at New York Navy Yard 1962–64. To AGMR on 6–1–63; renamed *Annapolis* 6–22–63. Recommissioned 3–7–64. Hangar deck converted to communications spaces. Has landing area port side amidships for helicopters. Decommissioned 12–20–69.

1 OCEANOGRAPHIC RESEARCH SHIP, *CHAIN* CLASS

[Snatch]	AGOR-18	Struck
Chain	AGOR-17	Loan

Commissioned 1944 in *Escape* class as ARS-27 and 20. Decommissioned after war but converted in mid-1950s to oceanographic research vessels. Both to AGOR 4–1–67. AGOR-17 is operated by a private organization; carries 26 scientists. AGOR-18 operated as *Argo* on loan to Scripps Institute.

1 OCEANOGRAPHIC RESEARCH SHIP, *HAYES* CLASS

Hayes	AGOR-16	Bldg.

Authorized FY 1967 (SCB-726). Building at Todd, Seattle; contract awarded 12–10–68. Has catamaran hull. To be assigned to MSC.

2 OCEANOGRAPHIC RESEARCH SHIPS, *ELTANIN* CLASS

Mizar	AGOR-11	MSC
Eltanin	AGOR-8	MSC

Built on a C1-ME2-13A hull design by Avondale in late 1950s as ice-strengthened AKs. To AGOR 11–15–62 (AGOR-8 from AK-270) and 4–15–64 (AGOR-11 from AK-272). *Eltanin* is run by National Science Foundation but MSC-manned.

10 OCEANOGRAPHIC RESEARCH SHIPS, *ROBERT D. CONRAD* CLASS

Name	Number	FY/SCB	Builder	Awarded	Completed	F/S
Knorr	AGOR-15	66/710	Defoe	9–30–66	1–14–70	Loan
Melville	AGOR-14	66/710	Defoe	9–30–66	8–27–69	Loan
Bartlett	AGOR-13	65/710	NW Marine	7–12–65	3–31–69	MSC
De Steiguer	AGOR-12	65/710	NW Marine	7–12–65	2–28–69	MSC
Thomas Washington	AGOR-10	63/185	Marinette	3–15–63	9–7–65	Loan
Thomas G. Thompson	AGOR-9	63/185	Marinette	3–15–63	8–24–65	Loan
Lynch	AGOR-7	62/185	Marietta	12–13–61	3–27–65	MSC
Sands	AGOR-6	62/185	Marietta	12–13–61	10–1–64	MSC
James M. Gilliss	AGOR-4	60/185	Christy	11–29–60	11–5–62	Loan
Robert D. Conrad	AGOR-3	60/185	Gibbs	5–26–60	11–29–62	Loan

First class of built-for-purpose AGORs. AGOR-3/4, 9/10, 14/15 are under operational control of various universities and institutions. Manned by MSC crew and carry 15 scientists. *Charles H. Davis* (AGOR-5) loaned to New Zealand 8–10–70.

1 OCEANOGRAPHIC RESEARCH SHIP, *JOSIAH WILLARD GIBBS* CLASS

Name	Number	F/S
Josiah Willard Gibbs	AGOR-1	MSC

Commissioned 3–21–44 as *San Carlos* (AVP-51) of *Barnegat* class. Decommissioned after WW II but converted late 1950s to AGOR.

PATROL CRAFT TENDER, "*GARRETT COUNTY*" CLASS

[Hunterdon County]	AGP-838	ILP

Commissioned in LST-511 class 1944. Named 7–1–55. Was in reserve since mid-1940s before recommissioned for Vietnam duty mid-1960s. Reconfigured for service as patrol craft tender; midships deck reinforced to handle light helicopters. To AGP 9–25–70.

1 SURVEY SHIP, *SGT. GEORGE D. KEATHLEY* CLASS

Name	Number	F/S
[Coastal Crusader]	AGS-36	MARAD
Sgt. George D. Keathley	AGS-35	MSC

Built to a C1-M-AV1 hull design. AGS-35 completed late WW II as APC. Acquired early 1950s for MSC; struck and laid up in MARAD 1959. Reacquired and converted to survey ship; to AGS-35 on 12–1–66. AGS-36 acquired early 1960s and converted to AGM-16. Operated by USAF until 7–1–64 when instated on NVR; converted and reclassified AGS-36 on 12–1–69. *Twin Falls* (AGM-11) to become AGS-37.

2 SURVEY SHIPS, *WILKES* CLASS

Name	Number	FY/SCB	Builder	Awarded	Completed	F/S
Wyman	AGS-34	67/728	Defoe, Bay City	9–27–67		Bldg.
Wilkes	AGS-33	67/728	Defoe, Bay City	9–27–67		Bldg.

Improved *Silas Bent* class. To be manned by MSC upon completion in 1971. Resemble AGOR-3 class. Will carry 38 scientists. Fitted with anti-roll devices and small bow propulsion unit to maintain heading when dead in water.

2 SURVEY SHIPS, *CHAUVENET* CLASS

Harkness	AGS-32	66/723	Upper Clyde, Scot.	8–19–66	1–29–71	MSC
Chauvenet	AGS-29	65/723	Upper Clyde, Scot.	8–19–66	11–13–70	MSC

Large surveying ships with helicopter decks aft. Main task will be to survey spots that meet fleet and landing force requirements.

2 SURVEY SHIPS, *SILAS BENT* CLASS

Name	Number	F/S
Kane	AGS-27	MSC
Silas Bent	AGS-26	MSC

AGS-27 completed 5–67; AGS-26 completed 7–65. Both operated for NAVOCEANO.

1 SURVEY SHIP, *KELLAR* CLASS

Name	Number	F/S
Kellar	AGS-25	MSC

First built-for-purpose AGS in USN. Launched 7–30–64 by Marietta Manufacturing Co. Capsized and sunk by hurricane 9–65; completed by Boland Machine Manufacturing Co. 1–31–69.

3 SURVEY SHIPS, *BOWDITCH* CLASS

Michelson (ex-SS *Joliet Victory*)	AGS-23	MSC
Dutton (ex-SS *Tuskegee Victory*)	AGS-22	MSC
Bowditch (ex-SS *South Bend Victory*)	AGS-21	MSC

Built on a VC2-S-AP3 hull design in WW II. Acquired from MARAD and converted to AGSs 1957–58. Chart ocean floor and magnetic fields of gravity.

1 AUXILIARY SUBMARINE, *ALBACORE* CLASS

Albacore	AGSS-569	AA

Commissioned 12–5–53. Highly maneuverable hull form; has no combat capability. SSN-585 class developed from tests performed with this boat. Has undergone 4 major conversions at Portsmouth Navy Yard to test new submarine equipment and theories; has been virtually rebuilt.

1 AUXILIARY SUBMARINE, *DOLPHIN* CLASS

Dolphin	AGSS-555	PA

Built by Portsmouth Navy Yard, capable of deep diving of limited endurance. Commissioned 8–17–68, almost 6 years from date keel laid. Built of aluminum, HY-80 steel, and fiberglass.

6 AUXILIARY SUBMARINES, "*GUPPY IA*" TYPE

Name	Number	F/S	Decommissioned
Tench	AGSS-417	AR*	5–70
Sea Poacher	AGSS-406	AR*	11–69
Atule	AGSS-403	AR*	11–69
Chopper	AGSS-342	NRT	5–70
Blenny	AGSS-324	AR*	11–7–69
Becuna	AGSS-319	AR*	11–7–69

Originally of the *Balao* class (AGSS-417 is a *Tench*). Commissioned 1944. Converted to *Guppy IA* 1951. To AGSS 1969. Two of this type still operate as attack submarines.

3 AUXILIARY SUBMARINES, *TORSK* CLASS

Requin	AGSS-481	NRT
Runner	AGSS-476	NRT
Torsk	AGSS-423	NRT

Originally of the *Tench* class; commissioned 1944–45. All have snorkels. All except AGSS-481 served as attack submarines. AGSS-481 was SSR 1948–59. Was fitted with elaborate air-search radar and control center. Was also lengthened; stern tubes removed. Reverted to SS 8–15–59; to AGSS 6–29–68. 423 to AGSS 5–1–68; 476 to AGSS 2–1–69.

I AUXILIARY SUBMARINE, *TIGRONE* CLASS

Tigrone	AGSS-419	AA

Originally of the *Tench* class; commissioned 10–25–44 as SS. To SSR 3–31–48; to SS 3–1–61; to AGSS 12–1–63. Recommissioned 3–10–62 after 4 years in reserve; serves as sonar research submarine.

1 AUXILIARY SUBMARINE, "*SAND LANCE*" CLASS

Pampanito	AGSS-383	NRT

Originally of the *Balao* class. Commissioned 11–6–43. To AGSS 12–1–62. Class leader in Brazilian Navy.

2 AUXILIARY SUBMARINES, *CHARR* CLASS

Carp	AGSS-338	NRT
Charr	AGSS-328	NRT

Former *Balao* class units. Converted to fleet snorkels. Commissioned SS-328 on 9–23–44 and SS-338 on 2–28–45; to AGSS 7–1–66 and 5–1–68 respectively.

1 AUXILIARY SUBMARINE, *BAYA* CLASS

Baya	AGSS-318	PA

Originally of the *Balao* class. Commissioned 5–20–44. Converted into a floating laboratory for electronic equipment 1958–59; 23′ section added amidships between forward torpedo room and forward battery room. Has a blunt bow which houses electronic gear. Forward tubes removed. Carries 12 scientists. Has a mushroom anchor that is recessed in bottom of submarine. To AGSS 8–12–49.

4 AUXILIARY SUBMARINES, "*BALAO*" CLASS

Name	Number	F/S	Name	Number	F/S
Roncador	AGSS-301	NRT	*Ling*	AGSS-297	NRT
Lionfish	AGSS-298	NRT	*Bowfin*	AGSS-287	NRT

Originally commissioned 1943–45 in *Balao* class. Assigned to NRT since 1960. To AGSS 12–1–62. Like all NRT subs, these are immobile hulks.

1 AUXILIARY SUBMARINE, "*POMPON*" CLASS

Rasher	AGSS-269	NRT

Commissioned 6–8–43 in the *Gato* class. Converted to SSR 1950–52; reclassified SSR 1951. Electronics added in new 31′ amidships section. SSR-269 to AGSS 7–1–60.

2 AUXILIARY SUBMARINES, *ANGLER* CLASS

Angler	AGSS-240	NRT
Croaker	AGSS-246	NRT

Commissioned 1943–44 in the *Gato* class. Converted to SSK 1952–53. Fitted with improved sonar, noise reduction gear, and snorkel. To SSK 1953. Both to SS 8–15–59. To AGSS: 240 on 7–1–63 and 246 on 5–1–67.

1 AUXILIARY SUBMARINE, "*GATO*" CLASS

Cod	AGSS-224	NRT

Commissioned 7–4–43 in the "*Gato*" class. Assigned to NRT since 1959. To AGSS 12–1–62.

TECHNICAL RESEARCH SHIP, "*BELMONT*" CLASS

Name	Number	F/S
[Liberty (ex AG-168) *]*	AGTR-5	Struck

Built on a VC2-S-AP3 hull design during WW II as SS *Simmons Victory*. Acquired from MARAD and converted to AGTR; commissioned 12–30–64. Damaged beyond economical repair 6–8–67 by Israeli attack during Six Day War. Decommissioned 6–28–68.

3 HOSPITAL SHIPS, "*HAVEN*" CLASS

Sanctuary	AH-17	PR*
Repose	AH-16	PR*
Consolation	AH-15	Loan

Built on a C4-S-B2 hull design; commissioned 1945. Originally 6 in class. AH-15 on charter as SS *Hope* since 3–16–60. AH-16/17 reacquired from MARAD and recommissioned late 1965–66 for Vietnam service.

AH-12 struck 1967; AH-13 sunk by collision 1950; AH-14 struck 1961. AH-16 decommissioned 8–15–70, is now annex to Long Beach Naval Hospital.

1 CARGO SHIP, *WYANDOT* CLASS

Wyandot	AK-283	MSC

Built on a C2-S-B1 hull design; commissioned 9-30–44 as AKA-92. Put in reserve late 1950s and struck. Recommissioned for Berlin Crisis service 1962. To MSC, 1963. To AK-283 1–1–69.

4 CARGO SHIPS, *NORWALK* CLASS

Name	Number	FY/SCB	Converted at	Awarded	Delivered	F/S
Marshfield	AK-282	69/715	Boland	8–23–68	5–28–70	MSC
Victoria	AK-281	65/715	Phil. Navy	8–7–64	10–15–65	MSC
Furman	AK-280	64/234	American	9–11–63	10–7–64	MSC
Norwalk	AK-279	63/234	Boland	9–21–62	12–20–63 (completed)	MSC

Built on a VC2-S-AP3 hull design in WW II. Acquired from MARAD for conversion. Carry POLARIS missiles for resupplying FBM tenders (AK-282 will also carry POSEIDON). Under MSC administrative control, but USN operational control. AK-279/280 and 282 dropped *Victory* from present names. AK-281 is ex-SS *Ethiopia Victory*. Photo in MSC section.

1 CARGO SHIP, *SCHUYLER OTIS BLAND* CLASS

Name	Number	F/S
Schuyler Otis Bland	AK-277	MSC

Lone prototype of *Mariner* class built on C3-S-DX2 hull design. Acquired mid-1961 for MSC service. To AK 9–15–61.

1 CARGO SHIP, *LT. JAMES E. ROBINSON* CLASS

Name	Number	F/S
Lt. James E. Robinson	AK-274	MSC

Built on a VC2-S-AP3 hull design in WW II as SS *Czechoslovakia Victory*. Acquired as AKV-3. To AK-274 5–7–59. To AG-170 on 12–1–62 for special duties. To AK on 7–1–64.

1 CARGO SHIP, *"ELTANIN"* CLASS

Name	Number	F/S
Mirfak	AK-271	MSC

Built on a C1-ME2-13a hull design in late 1950s. Two sisters are AGOR-8 and 11. Designed for Arctic service.

1 CARGO SHIP, *MARINE FIDDLER* CLASS

Name	Number	F/S
Marine Fiddler	AK-267	MSC

Built on a C4-S-B5 hull design in WW II. Acquired and converted to carry heavy equipment such as locomotives. Her massive booms have 150-ton lift capability.

3 CARGO SHIPS, *"ANTARES"* CLASS

Name	Number	F/S
Sgt. Jack J. Pendleton	AK-276	MSC
Pvt. Joseph F. Merrell	AK-275	MSC
Betelgeuse	AK-260	AR*

Built on a VC2-S-AP3 hull design. AK-260 completed in 1945; acquired from MARAD and commissioned 4–15–52. Same duties as *Norwalk* class. AK-275/276 completed in WWII; acquired for MSC service early 1950s as AKV-4/5. To AK 5–7–59. AK-260 was SS *Colombia Victory*: AK-275 was SS *Grange Victory*; AK-276 was SS *Mandan Victory*. AK-260 decommissioned 1–15–71.

1 CARGO SHIP, *PVT. LEONARD C. BROSTROM* CLASS

Name	Number	F/S	Name	Number	F/S
Pvt. Leonard C. Brostrom	AK-255	MSC			

Built on a C4-S-B1 hull design in WW II. Was SS *Marine Eagle*. Acquired from Army 1949 for MSC service; converted to heavy lift capability. Has oversized booms and hatches. Near-sister to AK-267.

7 CARGO SHIPS, *LT. GEORGE W. G. BOYCE* CLASS

Name	Number	F/S	Name	Number	F/S
Sgt. Truman Kimbro	AK-254	MSC	*Sgt. Archer T. Gammon*	AK-243	MSC
Lt. Robert Craig	AK-252	MSC	*Sgt. Andrew Miller*	AK-242	MSC
Lt. George W. G. Boyce	AK-251	MSC	*Pvt. Francis X. McGraw*	AK-241	MSC
Sgt. Morris E. Crain	AK-244	MSC			

Built on a VC2-S-AP2 hull design in WW II. An eighth ship of this class became AGM-4. All acquired early 1950s from Army for MSC service. Former merchant names: AK-254, *Hastings Victory*; AK-252, *Bowling Green Victory*; AK-251, *Waterville Victory*; AK-244, *Mills Victory*; AK-243, *Yale Victory*; AK-242, *Radcliffe Victory*; AK-241, *Wabash Victory*.

2 CARGO SHIPS, *GREENVILLE VICTORY* CLASS

Name	Number	F/S	Name	Number	F/S
Pvt. John R. Towle	AK-240	MSC			
Greenville Victory	AK-237	MSC			

Built to a VC2-S-AP3 hull design. Difference between an AP3 and AP2 type is higher SHP in AP3; appearance the same. AK-237 and 240 were acquired from Army for MSC service in early 1950s. Two other ships of this class became AGM-3 and AG-164. AK-240 is ex-SS *Appleton Victory*.

6 CARGO SHIPS, *"ALAMOSA"* CLASS

Name	Number	F/S	Name	Number	F/S
Pvt. Frank J. Petrarca	AK-250	MSC	*Muskingum*	AK-198	MSC
Short Splice	AK-249	MSC	*Herkimer*	AK-188	MSC
Col. William J. O'Brien	AK-246	MSC	*Fentress*	AK-180	MSC

Completed to a C1-M-AV1 hull design. AK-246 and 249 acquired from Army for MSC service. AK-180, 188, and 198 first commissioned 1945; decommissioned after war and transferred to MARCOMM for layup. AK-188 served briefly with Army. AK-180 and 198 acquired directly from MARAD for MSC service. AK-246 is ex-SS *Maiden's Eye*.

1 DOCK CARGO SHIP, *POINT BARROW* CLASS

Name	Number	F/S	Name	Number	F/S
Point Barrow	AKD-1	MSC			

Built to an S2-ST-23a hull design; only such ship ever built. Commissioned in USN 2–28–58 but transferred to MSC 5–29–58. Built for Arctic service. Resembles LSD; can be used for roll-on/roll-off. Hauled SATURN rocket components.

1 LIGHT CARGO SHIP, *MARK* CLASS

Mark	AKL-12	PR*			

Acquired from Army as FS-214 and commissioned 11–47 as AG-143. To AKL-12 on 3–31–49. Decommissioned 10–71.

1 LIGHT CARGO SHIP, "*CAMANO*" CLASS

Brule (ex FS-370)	AKL-28	PR*			

Completed for the Army in WW II. Sisters are AGM-2, AGER-2, IX-306, IX-308.

1 VEHICLE CARGO SHIP, *SEA LIFT* CLASS

Sea Lift	AKR-9	MSC			

Built to a C4-ST-67a hull design in 1967; 6 projected for class. Authorized as AK-278; to LSV-9 in 1964; to AKR-9 on 1–1–69. Resembles AKR-7. Has stern and side ramps for on-loading and off-loading vehicles within the hull. Has stabilizers.

1 VEHICLE CARGO SHIP, *COMET* CLASS

Comet	AKR-7	MSC			

Built on a C3-ST-14a hull design in 1958 as USNS *Comet* (T-AK-269). Resembles AKR-9, but has no stabilizers. To LSV-7 on 6–1–63. To AKR-7 on 1–1–69.

1 STORES ISSUE SHIP, *ALTAIR* CLASS

Altair	AKS-32	MAR*			

Built on a VC2-S-AP3 hull design as SS *Aberdeen Victory*. Acquired by USN 7–7–51 and commissioned 1–31–52 as AK-257. To AKS-32 on 8–12–52. Decommissioned 5–2–69. A second ship of this class, *Antares* (AKS-33), was struck in 1965 after being seriously damaged by fire.

2 CARGO SHIPS AND AIRCRAFT FERRIES, "*BOGUE*" CLASS

Name	Number	F/S	Name	Number	F/S
[*Croatan* (ex CVE-25)]	AKV-43	Scrapped	[*Core* (ex CVE-13)]	AKV-41	Scrapped
Breton (ex CVE-23)	AKV-42	MPR*	*Card* (ex CVE-11)	AKV-40	MPR*

Originally laid down as C3-S-A1 merchant ships; commissioned as *Bogue* class escort carriers 1942–43. Inactivated after WW II. To CVHE on 6–12–55 and CVU on 7–1–58. Reactivated for MSC duty 1958 as *Casablanca* class CVE replacements. To AKV 5–7–59. AKV-40 was mined and sank 5–2–64 dockside, Vietnam; raised 5–19–64 and returned to duty 12–11–64. AKV-43 served with NASA 10–64 to 5–65 as a floating rocket launch pad. See disposal notes for AKV-41, 43.

1 CARGO SHIP AND AIRCRAFT FERRY, "*COMMENCEMENT BAY*" CLASS

[*Commencement Bay* (ex CVE-105)]	AKV-37	Struck	[*Rendova* (ex CVE-114)]	AKV-14	Struck
Rabaul (ex CVE-121)	AKV-21	PR	[*Cape Gloucester* (ex CVE-109)]	AKV-9	Struck
[*Point Cruz* (ex CVE-119)]	AKV-19	Scrapped	[*Kula Gulf* (ex CVE-108)]	AKV-8	Scrapped

Built as *Commencement Bay* class escort carriers; commissioned 1944–46. Were 19 in class. All inactivated mid-1950s. CVE-105 to CVHE 6–12–55. All to AKV 5–7–59. AKV-8 and 19 reactivated for MSC service 1965; forward elevator enlarged and converted into hatch, stacks trunked into one halfway between island and stern on starboard side, slightly inboard. See disposal notes.

1 NET-LAYING SHIP, *COHOES* CLASS

Cohoes	ANL-78	PA			

Originally commissioned 3–23–45 as AN-78. Leader of 15-ship class. Decommissioned late 1947 and placed in reserve. Struck 7–1–63 and transferred to MARAD. Reinstated on NVR 3–67. Converted to river/harbor salvage ship for Vietnam service. Placed in service 6–1–68. To ANL on 1–1–69. Placed in full commission 7–23–69. Another ship of this class, *Shakamaxon* (AN-88), was reacquired and transferred 11–8–68 on loan to the Department of Commerce.

1 TANKER, *AMERICAN EXPLORER* CLASS

American Explorer	AO-165	MSC			

Built to a T5-S-RM2a hull design by Ingalls. Completed 10–59 and transferred to MSC for service. One of the fastest US tankers.

3 TANKERS, *MAUMEE* CLASS

Yukon	AO-152	MSC
Shoshone	AO-151	MSC
Maumee	AO-149	MSC

Built to a T5-S-12a hull design; delivered 1956–57. A fourth ship, *Potomac* (AO-150), exploded and sank 9–61; a new tanker built around the salvaged stern was renamed SS *Shenandoah* and chartered to MSC.

6 OILERS, *NEOSHO* CLASS

Ponchatoula	AO-148	PA	*Hassayampa*	AO-145	PA
Truckee	AO-147	AA	*Mississinewa*	AO-144	AA
Kawishiwi	AO-146	PA	*Neosho*	AO-143	AA

Largest AOs built for USN. Commissioned 1954-56. AO-143/144 and 147 have fantail helicopter decks. Original 5" guns removed. All fitted as flagships.

2 TANKERS, *MISSION* CLASS

Mission Santa Ynez	AO-134	MSC
Mission Buenaventura	AO-111	MSC

Built on a T2-SE-A2 hull design. Survivors of 27-ship class, all of which obtained by MSC 10–1–49. Many of struck ships now active in Merchant Marine as jumboized containerships. One served as AG-162.

5 JUMBOIZED OILERS, *MISPILLION* CLASS

Waccamaw	AO-109	AA	*Navasota*	AO-106	PA
Pawcatuck	AO-108	AA	*Mispillion*	AO-105	PA
Passumpsic	AO-107	PA			

Built to a T3-S2-A3 hull design. Commissioned 1945–46. AO-109 was reclassified AOR-109 on 12–11–50 but conversion cancelled and she reverted to AO on 5–7–51. AO-106 and 109 jumboized under FY 1963, the remainder under FY 1964. During jumboization, new 93' midbody inserted, helicopter deck added forward, propulsion plant renovated, new underway replenishment rig installed, and fuel capacity increased to 50,000 barrels.

12 TANKERS, *SUAMICO* CLASS

Shawnee Trail	AO-142	MSC	*Saugatuck* (ex-*Newton*)	AO-75	MSC
Pioneer Valley	AO-140	MSC	*Millicoma* (ex-*Conastoga*)	AO-73	MSC
Cowanesque (ex-*Fort Duquesne*)	AO-79	MSC	*Cache* (ex-*Stillwater*)	AO-67	MSC
			Pecos (ex-SS *Corsicana*)	AO-65	MSC
Chepachet (ex-*Eutaw Springs*)	AO-78	MSC	*Tallulah* (ex-*Valley Forge*)	AO-50	MSC
Cossatot (ex-*Fort Necessity*)	AO-77	MSC	*Suamico* (ex-*Harlem Heights*)	AO-49	MSC
Schuylkill (ex-*Louisburg*)	AO-76	MSC			

Built to a T2-SE-A1 hull design. All except AO-140 and 142 built for merchant service and acquired and commissioned by USN 1942–43. Decommissioned after war; operated in Naval Transportation Corps and then MSC. AO-140 and 142 returned to MARCOMM from lend-lease; served NOTS and MSC. AO-142 reacquired from MARAD 1–20–65. Some ships can carry dismantled aircraft and helicopters as deck cargo.

1 OILER, *"MATTAPONI"* CLASS

Tappahannock (ex-*Jorkay*)	AO-43	MPR*

Built to a T2-A design and acquired from Merchant Marine after completed; commissioned 1942. Frequently alternated between reserve and active service. Decommissioned 3–6–70.

1 OILER, *KENNEBEC* CLASS

Kennebec (ex-*Corsicana*)	AO-36	MPR*

Built to a T2-A hull design. Shorter version of *"Mattaponi"* class. Acquired from MARCOMM after brief merchant service and commissioned 2–4–42. Decommissioned 1970.

18 OILERS, *"CIMARRON"* CLASS

Chukawan	AO-100	AA	*Marias*	AO-57	AA
Canisteo	AO-99	AA	*Aucilla* (ex-*Escanaba*)	AO-56	AR*
Caloosahatchee	AO-98	AA	*Chikaskia*	AO-54	MAR*
Allagash	AO-97	AR*	*Caliente*	AO-53	PA
Tolovana	AO-64	PA	*Cacapon*	AO-52	PA
Chipola	AO-63	PA	*Ashtabula*	AO-51	PA
Taluga	AO-62	PA	*Guadalupe* (ex-*Esso Raleigh*)	AO-32	PA
Severn	AO-61	AA			
Nantahala	AO-60	AA	*Sabine* (ex-*Esso Albany*)	AO-25	MAR*
Manatee	AO-58	PA			

continued

"Cimarron" Class—continued

Built to a T3-S2-A1 hull design. Acquired from MARCOMM and commissioned 1939–46. Four were converted into the *Sangamon* class escort carriers (since struck). AO-51, 98, and 99 were jumboized, but more extensively than AO-105 class. Extra M frame, 2 gun mounts vice a forward helicopter deck, superstructure extensively rebuilt and stack heightened. Decommissioned: AO-25 on 2–20–69; AO-54 during 12–69; AO-56 on 12–18–70; and AO-97 on 12–21–70.

4 FAST COMBAT SUPPORT SHIPS, *SACRAMENTO* CLASS

Name	Number	FY/SCB	BUILDER	Awarded	Commissioned	F/S
Detroit	AOE-4	66/711	PS Navy	12–29–65	3–28–70	AA
Seattle	AOE-3	65/711	PS Navy	12–19–64	4–5–69	AA
Camden	AOE-2	63/196	NY Shipbuilding	4–25–63	4–1–67	PA
Sacramento	AOE-1	61/207	PS Navy	8–8–60	3–14–64	PA

A new type combining functions of AO, AE, and AK. AOE-1/2 use turbines from scrapped Kentucky (BB-66). AOE-5, authorized FY 1968, cancelled 11–69.

2 GASOLINE TANKERS, *ALATNA* CLASS

Name	Number	F/S	Name	Number	F/S
Chattahoochee	AOG-82	MSC			
Alatna	AOG-81	MSC			

Built to T1-MET-24a hull design for polar service; delivered mid-1957. Have ice-resistant belt. Except for lack of midship mast, resemble *Eltanin* class.

4 GASOLINE TANKERS, *"TONTI"* CLASS

Piscataqua (ex-*Cisne*)	AOG-80	MSC	*Nodaway* (ex-*Belridge*)	AOG-78	MSC
Petaluma (ex-*Raccoon Bend*)	AOG-79	MSC	*Rincon* (ex-*Tarland*)	AOG-77	MSC

Built to a T1-M-BT2 hull design in 1945 for commercial use. Acquired from MARAD by MSC for service in 1950 and renamed. Have been in almost continuous service with MSC ever since. Class leader is on loan to Columbian Navy.

9 GASOLINE TANKERS, *PATAPSCO* CLASS

Name	Number	F/S	Name	Number	F/S
Pinnebog	AOG-58	USAF	*Kishwaukee*	AOG-9	PR*
Noxubee	AOG-56	AA	*Genesee*	AOG-8	PA
Nespelen	AOG-55	AA	*Elkhorn*	AOG-7	PA
Chewaucan	AOG-50	AA	*Patapsco*	AOG-1	PR*
Tombigbee	AOG-11	PA			

Built to a USN design; commissioned 1943–45. AOG-58 never commissioned in USN. AOG-1, 9, 56 reacquired from MARAD 1966. AOG-1 decommissioned 1969; AOG-9 in 1970.

6 REPLENISHMENT FLEET OILERS, *WICHITA* CLASS

Name	Number	FY/SCB	Builder	Awarded	Commissioned	F/S
Kalamazoo	AOR-6	67/707	Gen. Dyn., Quincy	7–19–67		Bldg.
Wabash	AOR-5	67/707	Gen. Dyn., Quincy	7–19–67		PA
Savannah	AOR-4	66/707	Gen. Dyn., Quincy	7–6–66	12–5–70	AA
Kansas City	AOR-3	66/707	Gen. Dyn., Quincy	7–6–66	6–6–70	PA
Milwaukee	AOR-2	65/707	Gen. Dyn., Quincy	6–2–65	11–1–69	AA
Wichita	AOR-1	65/707	Gen. Dyn., Quincy	6–2–65	6–7–69	PA

Built to a USN design. Have built-in helicopter decks. Basically AORs are smaller versions of AOEs.

3 TRANSPORTS, *BARRETT* CLASS

Name	Number	F/S
Upshur (ex-*President Hayes*)	AP-198	MSC
Geiger (ex-*President Adams*)	AP-197	MPR*
Barrett (ex-*President Jackson*)	AP-196	MSC

Built by NY Shipbuilding as liners for the American-President Lines on a MARAD P2-S1-DN3 hull design. Taken over by USN during Korean War for MSC service. Can carry 2,500 men maximum. Photo in MSC section.

TRANSPORT, "*GENERAL DANIEL I. SULTAN*" CLASS

[Gen. William O. Darby]	AP-127	MARAD

Built to a P2-SE2-R1 hull design; commissioned 9–27–45 as *Adm. W. S. Sims.* Name changed 4–28–50. Originally 8 in class. Decommissioned after war and served in AOTS and MSC. Last in class transferred to MARAD reserve permanently. Not struck.

TRANSPORT, "*GENERAL JOHN POPE*" CLASS

[General John Pope]	AP-110	MARAD

Built on a P2-S2-R2 hull design; commissioned 8–5–43. Originally 11 in class. Decommissioned after war. Reacquired from MARAD 1966; last in class to be permanently laid up.

3 SELF-PROPELLED BARRACKS SHIPS, "*BLACKFORD*" CLASS

Vanderburgh (ex LST-1114)	APB-48	PR
Kingman (ex LST-1113)	APB-47	PR
Dorchester (ex LST-1112)	APB-46	PR

All laid down as LST-511 class units. To AKS 12–8–44; to APB 3–6–45. Commissioned 1945. All out of commission since 1947. APB-48 was originally *Presque Isle*; renamed 2–17–45.

4 SELF-PROPELLED BARRACKS SHIPS, "*BENEWAH*" CLASS

Name	Number	F/S	Decommissioned
Nueces	APB-40	PR*	3–2–70
Mercer	APB-39	PR*	
Echols	APB-37	AR	
Colleton	APB-36	PR*	12–69
[Benewah]	APB-35	To IX-311	2–26–71

Built to LST design. Laid down as APLs, but reclassified as APBs during construction. APB-35/36 recommissioned 1–28–67 for Vietnam service. APB-39/40 recommissioned 5–9–68 and 5–3–68 respectively. Served as floating headquarters ships for Riverine Force personnel in Vietnam. APB-39 placed "in service, in reserve" 1–7–70.

1 REPAIR SHIP, "*SHENANDOAH*" CLASS

Name	Number	F/S
Grand Canyon	AR-28	AA

Commissioned 4–5–46 as AD-28 of *Shenandoah* class. To AR-28 on 3–12–71 as *Cadmus* (AR-14) replacement.

1 REPAIR SHIP, *MARKAB* CLASS

Markab (ex-SS *Mormacpenn*)	AR-23	PR*

Built to a C3 hull design; commissioned 6–15–41 as AK-31. To AD-21 on 3–14–42. Decommissioned after war as Orange, Texas, reserve fleet tender. Recommissioned for Korea; decommissioned mid-1950s. To AR-23 on 4–15–60 and recommissioned 7–1–60. Propulsion plant in poor condition. Placed "in service, in reserve" as Mare Island depot ship 12–19–69.

1 REPAIR SHIP, *KLONDIKE* CLASS

Klondike	AR-22	PR*

Was leader of *Klondike* class ADs; commissioned 7–30–45 as AD-22. Decommissioned after war; San Diego reserve fleet tender. Recommissioned 7–15–59 to replace *Hooper Island* (ARG-17). One 5"/38 removed. To AR-22 on 2–20–60. Placed "in service, in reserve" at San Diego as depot ship 12–15–70 (replaced *Aegir*, AS-23).

2 REPAIR SHIPS, *AMPHION* CLASS

Name	Number	F/S
Cadmus	AR-14	AR*
Amphion	AR-13	AR*

AR-14 commissioned 4–23–46; AR-13 on 1–30–46. AR-14 decommissioned 9–14–71.

2 REPAIR SHIPS, *DELTA* CLASS

Name	Number	F/S	Decommissioned
Briareus (ex-*Hawiian Planter*)	AR-12	AR*	9–9–55
Delta (ex-*Hawaiian Packer*)	AR-9	PR*	6–20–70

Built to a C3 hull design as merchant ships. Commissioned: AR-9 on 6–16–41 as AK-29; AR-12 on 11–15–43. AR-9 depot ship at Bremerton. AR-12 was depot ship at Norfolk; replaced by *Bushnell* (AS-15) on 6–30–70.

4 REPAIR SHIPS, *VULCAN* CLASS

Name	Number	F/S	Name	Number	F/S
Jason	AR-8	PA	*Ajax*	AR-6	PA
Hector	AR-7	PA	*Vulcan*	AR-5	AA

Built to similar design as AD-14 and AS-11 classes, but modified for AR mission. AR-5 commissioned 6–16–41; AR-6 on 10–30–42, AR-7 on 2–7–44; AR-8 as ARH-1 on 6–19–44; reclassified AR-8 on 9–9–57.

4 BATTLE DAMAGE REPAIR SHIPS, "*ARISTAEUS*" CLASS

Telamon (ex LST-976)	ARB-8	PR	*Midas* (ex LST-514)	ARB-5	PR
Sarpedon (ex LST-956)	ARB-7	PR	*Zeus* (ex LST-132)	ARB-4	PR

Originally laid down as LSTs. LST-132 and 514 to ARB on 11–3–43; remainder on 8–14–44. Commissioned 1943–45. All decommissioned after war; in reserve since.

2 CABLE REPAIRING SHIPS, *AEOLUS* CLASS

Name	Number	F/S	Name	Number	F/S
Thor	ARC-4	AA			
Aeolus	ARC-3	AA			

Built to a S4-SE2-BE1 hull design as *Artemis* class attack cargo ships. ARC-4 originally commissioned 7–9–45 as *Vanadis* (AKA-49); ARC-3 on 6–18–45 as *Turandot* (AKA-47). Both decommissioned 1946. Both converted to ARCs 1955–56. ARC-3 renamed and reclassified 3–17–55; ARC-4 on 11–14–55. ARC-3 recommissioned 5–14–55; ARC-4 on 1–3–56.

2 CABLE REPAIRING SHIPS, *NEPTUNE* CLASS

Albert J. Meyer	ARC-6	MSC
Neptune	ARC-2	AA

Built to an S3-S2-BP1 hull design as merchant ships; completed 1945–46. ARC-2 acquired from MARAD and commissioned 6–1–53. ARC-6 acquired from Army 1966 for MSC service; used for hydrographic work.

1 INTERNAL COMBUSTION ENGINE REPAIR SHIP, "*LUZON*" CLASS

Tutuila (ex-*Arthur P. Gorman*)	ARG-4	PA

Built to an EC2-S-C1 hull design; commissioned 4–8–44. Last survivor of 12-ship class.

10 LANDING CRAFT REPAIR SHIPS, *ACHELOUS* CLASS

Krishna (ex LST-1149)	ARL-38	PA	*Satyr* (ex LST-852)	ARL-23	PR*
Indra (ex LST-1147)	ARL-37	PR*	*Endymion* (ex LST-513)	ARL-9	PR
Bellerophon (ex LST-1132)	ARL-31	PR	*Egeria* (ex LST-136)	ARL-8	PR
Askari (ex LST-1131)	ARL-30	PR*	*Atlas* (ex LST-231)	ARL-7	PR*
Sphinx (ex LST-963)	ARL-24	PR*	*Achelous* (ex LST-10)	ARL-1	PR

All laid down as LSTs and converted during construction. ARL-1 reclassified from LST on 1–13–43; ARL-7/9 on 11–3–43. Remainder reclassified from LST on 8–14–44. All commissioned 1943–45. ARL-23, 24, 30, 37 recommissioned 1966–67 and ARL-38 transferred from Atlantic on 1–1–66 for Vietnam duty. Tank deck used to house repair shops and supply stores. Used as floating maintenance bases for riverine craft in Vietnam.

6 SALVAGE SHIPS, *BOLSTER* CLASS

Recovery	ARS-43	AA	*Hoist*	ARS-40	AA
Reclaimer	ARS-42	PA	*Conserver*	ARS-39	PA
Opportune	ARS-41	AA	*Bolster*	ARS-38	PA

Commissioned 1945-46. Equipped to salvage all types of ships.

8 SALVAGE SHIPS, *ESCAPE* CLASS

Gear	ARS-34	Loan	*Current*	ARS-22	PA
Safeguard	ARS-25	PA	*Preserver*	ARS-8	AA
Grasp	ARS-24	PA	*Grapple*	ARS-7	PA
Deliver	ARS-23	PA	*Escape*	ARS-6	AA

Commissioned 1943. One sister serves as AGOR-17, 3 are chartered to a civilian salvage firm, and 2 serve the Coast Guard.

2 SALVAGE LIFTING SHIPS, *GYPSY* CLASS

Mender (ex LSM-550)	ARSD-2	PR
Gypsy (ex LSM-549)	ARSD-1	PR

Laid down as LSMs; to ARSD 4–21–45 and commissioned 1946. Can be used as diving tenders. Both decommissioned 11–47. Sisters *Salvager* (ARSD-3) and *Windlass* (ARSD-4) reclassified YMLC-3/4 and are non-self-propelled.

2 SALVAGE CRAFT TENDERS, *LAYSAN ISLAND* CLASS

Palmyra (ex LST-1100)	ARST-3	AR
Laysan Island (ex LST-1098)	ARST-1	AR

Laid down as LSTs; to ARST 12–8–44; commissioned 1945 as ARSTs. Originally 3 in class.

2 AIRCRAFT REPAIR SHIPS (AIRCRAFT), *FABIUS* CLASS

Megara (ex LST-1094)	ARVA-6	AR
Fabius (ex LST-1093)	ARVA-5	PR

Laid down as LSTs; to ARVA 12–8–44; commissioned 1945 as ARVAs.

1 AIRCRAFT REPAIR SHIP (ENGINE), *"AVENTINUS"* CLASS

Chloris (ex LST-1095)	ARVE-4	AR

Laid down as an LST; to ARVE 12–8–44; commissioned 1945 as ARVE. Decommissioned 1947. ARVA/ARVE are in same hull-number series.

1 AIRCRAFT REPAIR SHIP (HELICOPTER), *CORPUS CHRISTI BAY* CLASS

Corpus Christi Bay	ARVH-1	MSC

Commissioned *Albemarle* (AV-5) 12–20–40 in the *Curtiss* class. Modified 1956–57 to handle cancelled SEAMASTER jet seaplane. Decommissioned 1960 and struck 9–1–62. Reacquired 8–64; converted to ARVH. Reclassified and renamed 3–27–65. Transferred to MSC for administrative control and to Army for operational control.

2 SUBMARINE TENDERS, *L. Y. SPEAR* CLASS

Name	Number	FY/SCB	Builder	Awarded	Commissioned	F/S
Dixon	AS-37	66/702	Gen. Dyn., Quincy	4–20–66		PA
L. Y. Spear	AS-36	65/702	Gen. Dyn., Quincy	5–12–65	2–28–70	AA

Designed to handle SSNs/SSs. Can take 4 SSN alongside and provide logistic support for another 12 SSN. Can also repair nuclear power plants. AS-38 authorized FY 1969 but cancelled 3–27–69.

2 SUBMARINE TENDERS, *SIMON LAKE* CLASS

Name	Number	F/S
Canopus	AS-34	AA
Simon Lake	AS-33	AA

Designed to handle and support SSBNs. Can repair SSBN power plants, support and/or replace SSBN missiles. Can take 3 SSBNs alongside at a time and support up to 9 SSBNs. AS-33 commissioned 11–7–64; AS-34 on 11–4–65. AS-35 authorized FY 1965 but never awarded.

SIMON LAKE CLASS POSEIDON (C-3) CONVERSION

Number	FY/SCB	Converted at	Awarded	Started	Completed
AS-34	68/733.68	PS Navy	8–29–67	6–3–69	2–3–70
AS-33	69/733.68	PS Navy	7–1–68	7–7–70	3–9–71

2 SUBMARINE TENDERS, *HUNLEY* CLASS

Name	Number	F/S
Holland	AS-32	AA
Hunley	AS-31	PA

First class of AS to be designed specifically to handle SSBNs. AS-31 commissioned 6–16–62; AS-32 on 9–7–63. Class originally had a hammerhead crane on an amidships turntable; later replaced by two cranes of the type used by AS-11 class.

SUBMARINE TENDER, *"AEGIR"* CLASS

[Aegir]	AS-23	Struck

Built to a C3-S-A2 hull design; acquired 11–20–43; converted to AS and commissioned 9–8–44. Was depot ship at San Diego until replaced 1–25–71.

1 SUBMARINE TENDER, *EURYALE* CLASS

Euryale	AS-22	PR

Built to a C3 hull design as SS *Hawaiian Merchant;* commissioned 12–2–43 as AS. Decommissioned 1947. Was depot ship at Bremerton until replaced 8–28–70.

1 SUBMARINE TENDER, *PROTEUS* CLASS

Name	Number	F/S	Name	Number	F/S
Proteus	AS-19	PA			

Originally *Fulton* class AS; commissioned 1–31–44. Decommissioned 9–26–47. Converted to FBM tender under FY 1959. Alterations included 44′ midbody. Recommissioned 7–8–60. Established SSBN bases at Holy Loch, Rota, and Guam.

2 SUBMARINE TENDERS, *GRIFFIN* CLASS

Pelias (ex-SS *Mormacyork*)	AS-14	PR			
Griffin (ex-SS *Mormacpenn*)	AS-13	PR			

Built to a C3 hull design; acquired 1940 and commissioned 1941. AS-13 serves as depot ship at Stockton. AS-14 was depot ship at Mare Island until replaced 12–19–69.

6 SUBMARINE TENDERS, *FULTON* CLASS

Orion	AS-18	AA	*Bushnell*	AS-15	AR*
Nereus	AS-17	PR*	*Sperry*	AS-12	PA
Howard W. Gilmore (ex-*Neptune*)	AS-16	AA	*Fulton*	AS-11	AA

Built to *Vulcan* class AR and *Dixie* class AD design. Commissioned 1941–45. All have had FRAM II in order to handle SSNs. AS-16 renamed 6–8–43. AS-15 decommissioned 6–30–70; now Norfolk depot ship.

2 SUBMARINE RESCUE SHIPS, *PIGEON* CLASS

Name	Number	FY/SCB	Builder	Awarded	Commissioned	F/S
Ortolan	ASR-22	67/721	Alabama	11–15–67		Bldg.
Pigeon	ASR-21	67/721	Alabama	11–15–67		PA

First built-for-purpose ASRs; 2 more projected. Will be able to serve as DSRV motherships. First USN class with catamaran hull. Each hull is 251′ × 26′. Ships have built-in helicopter decks.

1 SUBMARINE RESCUE SHIP, "*PENGUIN*" CLASS

Name	Number	F/S	Name	Number	F/S
Skylark	ASR-20	AA			

Commissioned *Yustaga* (ATF-165). To ARS 11–13–45. Renamed 12–3–45. Class leader scrapped 1971.

7 SUBMARINE RESCUE SHIPS, *CHANTICLEER* CLASS

Tringa	ASR-16	AA	*Florikan*	ASR-9	PA
Sunbird	ASR-15	AA	*Coucal*	ASR-8	PA
Petrel	ASR-14	AA	*Chanticleer*	ASR-7	PA
Kittiwake	ASR-13	AA			

Based on tug design. Commissioned 1942–47. Armament removed 1957–58. Carry latest rescue equipment but not equipped for deep rescue.

1 AUXILIARY OCEAN TUG, *ATA-240* CLASS

Unnamed (ex-Army LT-455)	ATA-240	PR

Acquired from Army mid-1950s. Decommissioned 4–61. Four sisters struck and transferred to MARAD.

16 AUXILIARY OCEAN TUGS, "*SOTOYOMO*" CLASS

Name	Number	F/S	Decommissioned
Keywadin (ex ATR-140)	ATA-213	MAR*	6–30–70
Catawba (ex ATR-137)	ATA-210	AA	—
Umpqua (ex ATR-136)	ATA-209	AR*	7–1–71
Sagamore (ex ATR-135)	ATA-208	AA	—
Wandank (ex ATR-131)	ATA-204	PR*	7–1–71
Mahopac (ex ATR-123)	ATA-196	PR*	7–1–71
Tatnuck (ex ATR-122)	ATA-195	PR*	7–1–71
Stallion (ex ATR-120)	ATA-193	MAR*	9–20–69

continued in next column

continued from last column

Name	Number	F/S	Decommissioned
Tillamook (ex ATR-119)	ATA-192	PR*	7–25–71
Samoset (ex ATR-117)	ATA-190	MAR*	9–12–69
Penobscot (ex ATR-115)	ATA-188	AR*	7–2–71
Salish (ex ATR-114)	ATA-187	AA	—
Cahokia (ex ATR-113)	ATA-186	USAF	4–22–71
Koka (ex ATR-112)	ATA-185	PR*	9–1–71
Kalmia (ex ATR-111)	ATA-184	PR*	9–1–71
Accokeek (ex ATR-108)	ATA-181	AA	—

Originally classified as rescue tugs (ATR). Reclassified 5–15–44 and commissioned 1944–45 as ATAs. Many of class serve foreign navies, merchant marine and Coast Guard. ATA-181, 187, 208, and 210 to decommission 4–72.

28 FLEET OCEAN TUGS, "*CHEROKEE*" CLASS

Name	Number	F/S	Name	Number	F/S
Utina	ATF-163	AA	*Hitchiti*	ATF-103	PA
Shakori	ATF-162	AA	*Cocopa*	ATF-101	PA
Salinan	ATF-161	AA	*Chowanoc*	ATF-100	PA
Papago	ATF-160	AA	*[Arikara]*	ATF-98	ILP
Paiute	ATF-159	AA	*Abnaki*	ATF-96	PA
Mosopelea	ATF-158	AA	*Tawasa*	ATF-92	PA
Nipmuc	ATF-157	AA	*Seneca*	ATF-91	AR*
Luiseno	ATF-156	AA	*Mataco*	ATF-86	PA
Atakapa	ATF-149	AA	*Lipan*	ATF-85	PA
Tawakoni	ATF-114	PA	*Cree*	ATF-84	PA
Takelma	ATF-113	PA	*Ute*	ATF-76	PA
Quapaw	ATF-110	PA	*Sioux*	ATF-75	PA
Pakana	ATF-108	LOAN	*Kiowa*	ATF-72	AA
Molala	ATF-106	PA	*Apache*	ATF-67	PA
Moctobi	ATF-105	PA			

Originally classified as ATs; commissioned 1942–46. To ATF 5–15–44. Divided into two types—no stack and one stack. One of the more successful designs in USN; basis for design of ASR-7 class. Many serve other navies, others adapted for other missions; 1 became AGS, 2 ASRs, and 2 Coast Guard cutters.

3 SALVAGE AND RESCUE SHIPS, *EDENTON* CLASS

Name	Number	FY/SCB	Builder	Awarded	Commissioned	F/S
Brunswick	ATS-3	67/719	Brooks	9–26–67		PA
Beaufort	ATS-2	67/719	Brooks	9–26–67		PA
Edenton	ATS-1	66/719	Brooks	8–19–66	1–23–71	AA

Capable of lifting as much as 300 tons, fighting fires on other ships, and supporting dives up to depths of 850′. Eventually, ships of this class will replace ATA/ATFs.

SEAPLANE TENDER, "*CHANDELEUR*" CLASS

Name	Number	F/S
[Chandeleur]	AV-10	Struck

Built in a C3-S1-B1 hull design; acquired and commissioned 11–19–42. Was depot ship at Philadelphia; replaced by *Everglades* (AD-24).

SEAPLANE TENDERS, "*CURRITUCK*" CLASS

Name	Number	F/S	Decommissioned
[Salisbury Sound]	AV-13	Struck	4/67
[Pine Island]	AV-12	Struck	6–17–67
[Currituck]	AV-7	Struck	10–31–67

Commissioned 1944–45. A fourth ship of class now AVM-1. AV-13 was *Puget Sound*; renamed 6–5–44.

1 GUIDED MISSILE SHIP, *NORTON SOUND* CLASS

Name	Number	F/S
Norton Sound	AVM-1	PA

Originally commissioned 1–8–45 in *Currituck* class as AV-11. Began service as AVM in 1949; reclassified 8–8–51. Armament removed, missile launcher fitted on former seaplane deck, BPDMS fitted on fantail. Under FY 1963 converted to test TYPHON radar system; since removed. Now has lightweight Mk. 45 5″/54 mount for testing.

1 TRAINING CARRIER, *LEXINGTON* CLASS

Name	Number	Builder	Awarded	Keel Laid	Launched	Commissioned	F/S
Lexington	CVT-16	Beth., Quincy	9–9–40	7–15–41	9–26–42	2–17–43	AT

Originally in *Essex* class. Was *Cabot*; renamed 6–16–42. Decommissioned 4–23–47. Modernized early 1950s (see *Essex* modernization table in section 1). To CVA-16 on 10–1–52; recommissioned 1955. To CVS 10–1–62. Replaced *Antietam* (CVS-36) as training carrier at Pensacola 12–29–62; to CVT 1–1–69. Re-rated auxiliary from warship 9–23–70.

USS *Samuel Gompers* (AD-37). Note the two 30-ton centerline cranes and the two $3\frac{1}{2}$-ton telescopic-boomed traveling cranes, outboard on each side of ship.
Samuel Gompers *class.*

USS *Isle Royale* (AD-29). A second 5″/38 located aft in this class was replaced by a repair shop/landing platform for DASH. **Shenandoah** *class.*

USS *Everglades* (AD-24) with three FRAM I *Gearings* and three NRT *Edsalls* (since struck) moored alongside. Also note *Mitscher* in DL rig on extreme left of photo.
"Klondike" *class.*

USS *Cascade* (AD-16). **Cascade** *class.*

USS *Prairie* (AD-15). **Dixie** *class.*

USS *Virgo* (AE-30). This ship was converted from AKA to AE for Vietnam War service. 7–19–66. **"Virgo"** *class.*

USS *Surfbird* (ADG-383) in MSF configuration. As ADG, sweep gear and armament removed, stern anchors added and superstructure extended aft. **Surfbird** *class.*

USS *Mauna Kea* (AE-22). **Suribachi** *class.*

Captain W. M. Riggs

USS *Butte* (AE-27) on builder's trials. A passive roll-stabilization tank provides a steady platform for ammunition handling under adverse sea conditions. 12–9–68.
Kilauea *class.*

USS *Pyro* (AE-24). **Nitro** *class.*

USS *Paricutin* (AE-18). AE-14, 16, and 18 of this class have helicopter decks aft.
"Mount Hood" *class.*

USS *Mazama* (AE-9). Sister AE-8 has helicopter deck aft. **"Lassen"** *class.*

USS *Aludra* (AF-55). **Aludra** *class.*

USS *Rigel* (AF-58). Note two twin 3"/50s forward and helicopter deck aft. 9–17–66. **Rigel** *class.*

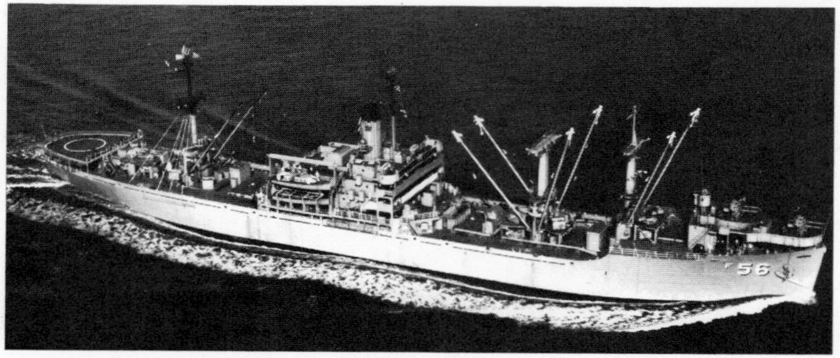

USS *Denebola* (AF-56). 1–27–64. **Denebola** *class.*

USS *Arcturus* (AF-52). **"Bald Eagle"** *class.*

USS *Procyon* (AF-61). 5–17–63. **"Alstede"** *class.*

National Steel and Shipbuilding

USS *White Plains* (AFS-4) on builder's trials. Two UH-46A SEA KNIGHTS provide vertical replenishment. Note "M" frames, the successor to the traditional kingposts. 8–20–68. **Mars** *class.*

USS *Spokane* (AG-191) in CLAA rig. 8–48. **"Antiaircraft Cruiser"** *type.*

USS *Sequoia* (AG-23). **Sequoia** *class.*

Lockheed

USS *Plainview* (AGEH-1), with foils raised and outboard power units lowered. **Plainview** *class.*

Lockheed

USS *Plainview* (AGEH-1), foilborne. **Plainview** *class.*

USS *Compass Island* (AG-153). 11–19–56. **"Mariner"** *type.*

USS *Glover* (AGDE-1). Except for raised stern and absence of #2 5″ gun, could easily be mistaken for a *Garcia* class DE. 1–6–66. **Glover** *class.*

USS *Palm Beach* (AGER-3) when she was active. 9–13–67. **"Banner"** *class.*

USS *Valcour* (AGF-1). Of 30 *Barnegat* class AVPs completed, only this ship and AGOR-1 remain on the NVR. 4–18–66. **"Barnegat"** *type.*

USS *Arlington* (AGMR-2). 1–28–67. **Arlington** *class.*

View of USS *Arlington* (AGMR-2) deck bristling with antennas. Note details of island superstructure and antenna. 2–69. **Arlington** *class.*

USS *Annapolis* (AGMR-1). Note enclosed bow as compared to AGMR-2. Antennas also differ. **Annapolis** *class.*

USS *Albacore* (AGSS-569) in her Phase III configuration. Her stern planes are fitted in an "X" shape for increased ship control and a large auxiliary rudder is in the after part of sail. 10–2–61. **Albacore** *class.*

USS *Dolphin* (AGSS-555). She has a cylindrical pressure hull of constant diameter and is an exceptionally deep-diving submarine. New type of rudder replaces diving planes. Many details are classified. 11–21–68. **Dolphin** *class.*

USS *Tigrone* (AGSS-419), a former fleet submarine and radar picket, now employed as sonar research submarine. Sonar is housed in bow. **Tigrone** *class.*

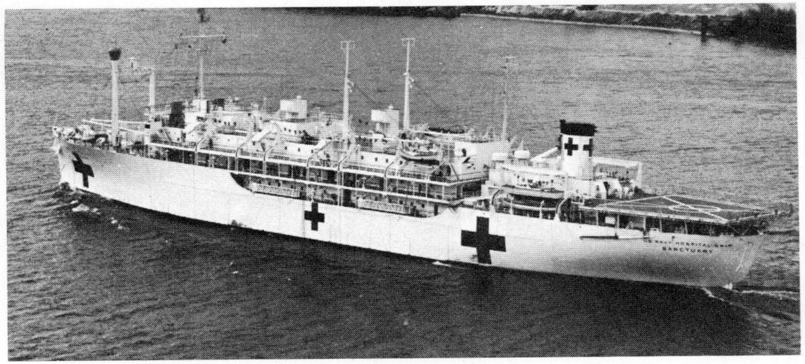

USS *Sanctuary* (AH-17). 11–1–66. **"Haven"** *class.*

USS *Baya* (AGSS-318), a former fleet submarine, now used for electronic research. 3–23–62. **Baya** *class.*

USS *Betelgeuse* (AK-260), was last commissioned AK on NVR. 2–3–59. **"Antares"** *class.*

USS *Cohoes* (ANL-78). **Cohoes** *class.*

USS *Core* (AKV-41). 2–17–66. **"Bogue"** *class.*

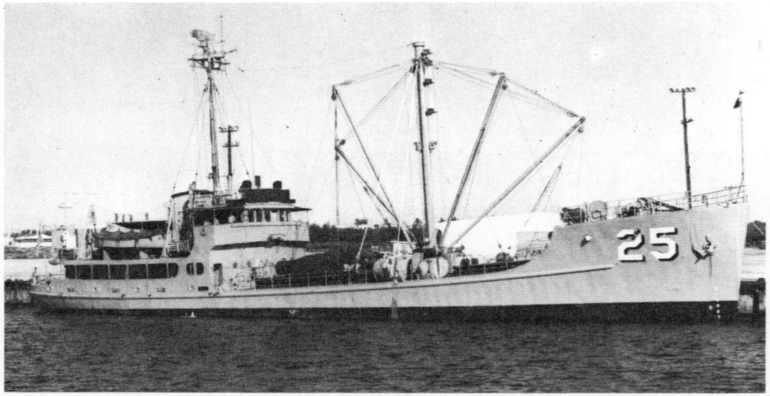

USS *Banner* (AKL-25). Eventually became near sister to *Pueblo* after conversion to AGER-1. Typical example of remaining AKLs on the NVR. **"Camano"** *class.*

USS *Neosho* (AO-143), leader of the largest AO class to be constructed for USN. 1–31–66. **Neosho** *class.*

USS *Mispillion* (AO-105) after conversion. Note staggered kingposts aft and helicopter deck forward. 8–10–66. **Mispillion** *class.*

USS *Kennebec* (AO-36). 12–65. **Kennebec** *class.*

USS *Neches* (AO-47). 3–64. **"Mattaponi"** *class.*

USS *Ashtabula* (AO-51) in post-conversion rig. Note lack of helicopter deck forward as compared with AO-105. 1969. **"Cimarron"** *class.*

USS *Camden* (AOE-2). She carries two UH-46A SEA KNIGHTS, though capable of carrying three. 11–14–66. **Sacramento** *class.*

General Dynamics

USS *Milwaukee* (AOR-2). Compare with photo of AOE-2. Note differences in stack, helicopter deck level, sizes of forward superstructure, and break in hull lines. **Wichita** *class.*

USS *Genesee* (AOG-8). 11–65. **Patapsco** *class.*

USS *Colleton* (APB-36) at anchor in My Tho River, Vietnam, supporting riverine craft. Note helicopter pad. 9–24–67. **''Benewah''** *class.*

USS *Klondike* (AR-22). 8–65. **Klondike** *class.*

USS *Delta* (AR-9) pierside at Subic Bay, Philippines. Alongside, from left to right, are *Mahan* (DLG-11), *King* (DLG-10), *Towers* (DDG-9), and *Hollister* (DD-788). 7–1–62. **Delta** *class.*

USS *Amphion* (AR-13). **Amphion** *class.*

USS *Jason* (AR-8). **Vulcan** *class.*

USS *Diomedes* (ARB-11), a typical ARB in WW II configuration. This ship was transferred to Germany 6–61. 7–1–45. **"Aristaeus"** *class.*

USS *Aeolus* (ARC-3). **Aeolus** *class.*

USS *Tutuila* (ARG-4). The Liberty ship has served in many classifications, but the basic configuration is unmistakable. 1–55. **"Luzon"** *class.*

USS *Indra* (ARL-37). Note "A" frame amidships, lifts heavy gear and small craft. 12–26–67.
Achelous *class.*

USS *Fabius* (ARVA-5). Compare with ARB and ARL. **Fabius** *class.*

USS *Aventinus* (ARVE-3). Now serves Chilian Navy. **"Aventinus"** *class.*

USS *Recovery* (ARS-43). 11–12–63. **Bolster** *class.*

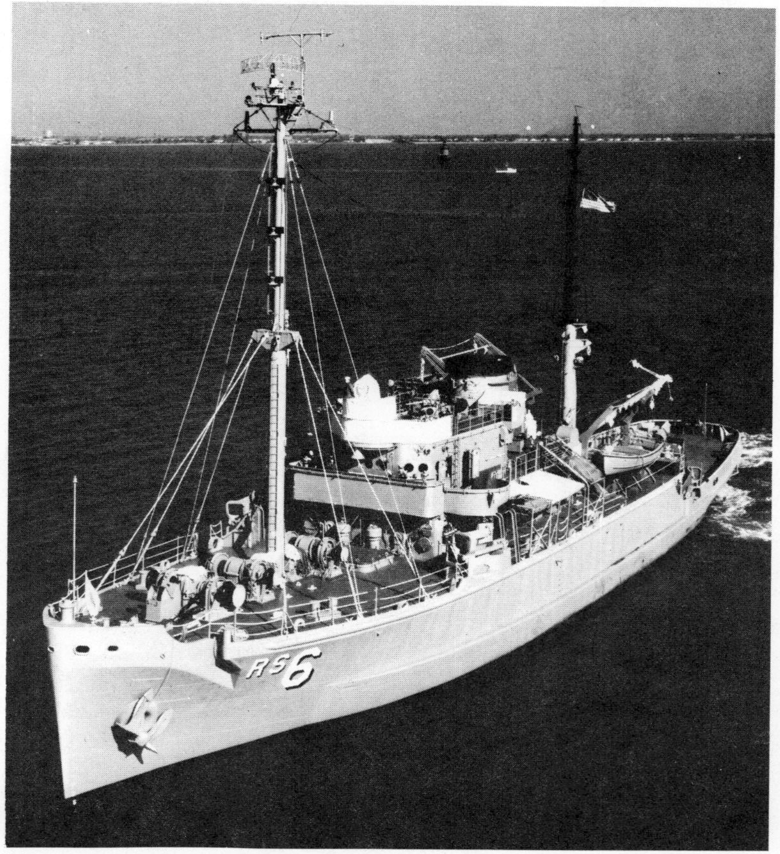

USS *Escape* (ARS-6). 10–2–63. **Escape** *class.*

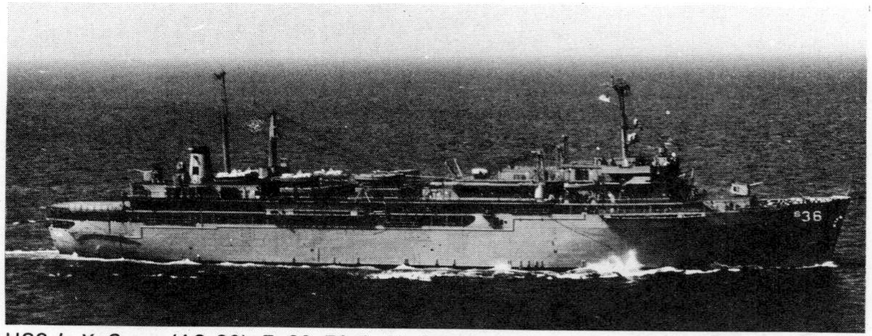

USS *L. Y. Spear* (AS-36). 7–20–70. **L. Y. Spear** *class.*

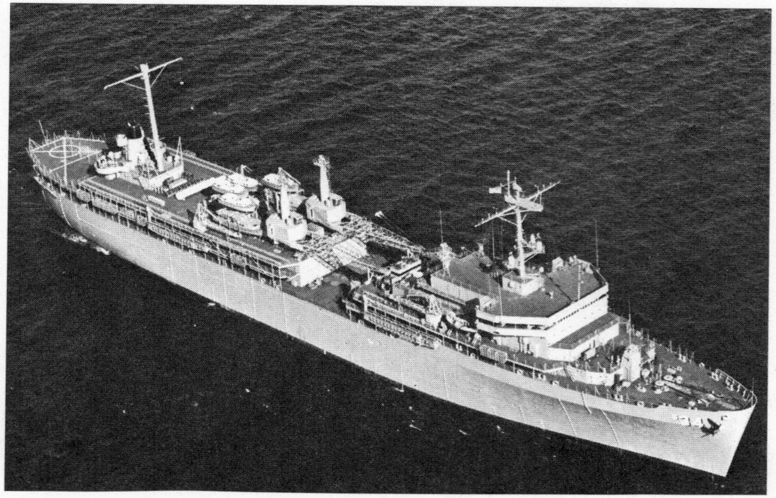

USS *Canopus* (AS-34). Note missile storage tubes amidships at break in superstructure. Note lack of guns as compared with AS-36. 10–13–65. **Simon Lake** *class.*

USS *Hunley* (AS-31). 5–28–62. **Hunley** *class.*

USS *Fulton* (AS-11). **Proteus** *class.*

USS *Proteus* (AS-19) and *Hunley* (AS-31) being resupplied by unidentified MSC AK(FBM). Note SSBNs outboard of both ASs. Compare cranes on AS-31 with other photo of same ship. **Fulton** *class.*

USS *Pelias* (AS-14). **Griffin** *class.*

Artist's conception of ASR-21 class. Note DSRVs and McCann rescue chamber amidships. 9–25–67.

USS *Florikan* (ASR-9). Note tug-like appearance and compare with ASR-21 illustration. 7–28–66. **Chanticleer** *class.*

USS *Wandank* (ATA-204). 8–13–65. **"Sotoyomo"** *class.*

USS *Apache* (ATF-67). 8–31–64. **"Cherokee"** *class.*

USS *Brunswick* (ATS-3) ready for fitting out. 10–14–69. **Edenton** *class.*

Sikorsky Aircraft

USS *Lexington* (CVT-16) engaged in helicopter training operations. Helicopters in photo are Sikorsky SH-34Cs. **Lexington** *class.*

USS *Norton Sound* (AVM-1) in her present configuration. Note BPDMS and missile launchers aft. **Norton Sound** *class.*

6. SERVICE CRAFT

A. Major Service Craft

By end-FY 1971, there were 1,373 service craft on the NVR. Of these, 5 were rated as commissioned ships. This section is divided into 2 parts. The first part covers the commissioned ships and the major service craft. The second part is a summary of the remainder of the service craft.

Name	Number	No. in Class	Full Load Displ.	Length Overall	Max. Draft	Extreme Beam	Number & Type of Reactors/Engines	Screws/ SHP	Max. Speed (Kts)	Accommodations Officers	Accommodations Enlisted	Armament
Unnamed	ARD-12	1	—	489′	5′8″	81′	Non-self-propelled	—	—	6	107	None
Oak Ridge	ARDM-1	3	—	534′	6′4″	81′	Non-self-propelled	—	—	5	157	None
Unnamed	DSRV	2	32[1]	49′2″	—	8′[2]	Elect. Motors (Battery)	1/	5	3	24[3]	None
Unnamed	DSV	1	35[1]	48′3″	—	10′2″	Elect. Motors (Fuel Cells)	1/	5	[4 total]		None
Elk River	IX-501	1	1,785	229′8″	9′4″	50′	1D(G.M.)	2/2,880	11	[25 total]		None
New Bedford	IX-308	1	940	177′	10′	33′	2D(G.M.)	2/1,000	13	5	57	None
Brier	IX-307	1	178	100′	5′	24′	Diesel Reduction Gear	2/600	12	[13 total]		None
Unnamed	IX-306	1	906	179′	10′	33′	2D(G.M.)	2/1,000	12	[18 total]		None
"Atlanta"	IX-304	0		610′		66′4″	4B(B&W)/4GT(G.E.)	4/100,000	31·6	[229 total]		None (as IX)
Constitution	IX-21	1	2,200	175′[4]	20′	45′	Non-self propelled	—	—	1	24	28 24 pdr., 10 12 pdr. (non-op)
Unnamed	NR-1	1	700	136′5″	14′7″	12′5″	1R/Water-Cooled	1/	—	3	9	None
Barracuda	SST-3	1	765	196′	16′	25′	3D(G.M.)/2EM(G.E.)	2/1,050	10	7	49	1 21″ TT fwd.
Mackerel	SST-1	2	303	130′	12′5″	13′5″	2D(G.M.)/2EM(Ell.)	1/380	8·2	2	16	1 21″ TT fwd.
George Eastman	YAG-39	1	11,400	442′	23′	67′	2B(unknown)/RS(F&S)	1/2,380	11	4	45	None
Trieste II	X-2	1	50[1]	78′6″	—	15′3″	Electric Motors	2/	2	[3 total]		None
Unnamed	X-1	1	31	49′6″	7′	8′	1D(Hercules)/1EM	1/30	15	2	6	None

[1] *Displacement in air, out of the water.* [2] *Diameter measurement.* [3] *Maximum number of rescued survivors that can be carried.* [4] *Length between perpendiculars.*

1 AUXILIARY REPAIR DRY DOCK, *"ARD-12"* CLASS

Name	Number	F/S
Arco	ARD-29	PA
[Windsor]	ARD-22	ILP

Completed 1944. ARD-29 commissioned 10–52; ARD-22 in 3–46. Both named 1967. ARD-22 decommissioned 10–9–70 but placed in service same date.

3 MEDIUM AUXILIARY REPAIR DRY DOCKS, *OAK RIDGE* CLASS

Name	Number	F/S
Unnamed (ex ARD-18)	ARDM-3	ASR*
Alamagordo (ex ARD-26)	ARDM-2	AA
Oak Ridge (ex ARD-19)	ARDM-1	AA

Completed 1944 as ARDs. ARD-19 and 26 converted to ARDM 1961–65; ARD-18 1968–69. Commissioned and named: ARDM-1 in 12–63; ARDM-2 in 8–65. ARD-18 to ARDM-3 on 6–17–70.

2 DEEP SUBMERGENCE RESCUE VEHICLES, *DSRV-1* CLASS

Number	Builder	Launched	Completed	F/S
DSRV-2	Lockheed, Sunnyvale	5–1–70		PA
DSRV-1	Lockheed, Sunnyvale	1–24–70		PA

Designed to rescue submariners from sunken submarines. Can operate deeper than the survival depth of any existing US submarine.

1 DEEP SUBMERGENCE VEHICLE, *DSV-1* CLASS

DSV-1	Lockheed, Sunnyvale		FY 1978	

Similar to the DSRV. Unlike DSRV will have a manipulator-like arm to pick up objects outside the hull.

1 UNCLASSIFIED MISCELLANEOUS, *ELK RIVER* CLASS

Name	Number	F/S
Elk River	IX-501	PSA

Commissioned 5–27–45 as LSMR-501. Decommissioned 3–46. Named *Elk River* 10–1–55. Converted to ocean range support ship at Avondale Shipyards for SEALAB III 1967–68. To IX-501 on 4–1–68. Classified as an activity craft. Ship lengthened 21′, center well added for diving, decompression chamber added. IX-310 is a sound testing barge.

1 UNCLASSIFIED MISCELLANEOUS, *NEW BEDFORD* CLASS

New Bedford (ex AKL-17)	IX-308	PSA

Completed in WW II as Army coastal freighter FS-289. Acquired by USN 3–1–50 for MSC service. Named 11–20–61. Classified "equipment" 8–26–63 and name dropped. Serves as torpedo recovery vessel at Keyport, Washington. Rerated 'activity craft," classified IX-308, and name restored 2–69.

1 FORMER COAST GUARD BUOY TENDER, INLAND, *BRIER* CLASS

Brier	IX-307	PSA

Former Coast Guard buoy tender (WLI-299); built 1943. Decommissioned by CG 11–9–67: acquired by USN 3–10–69. To IX-307 8–29–70. Assigned to Naval Ordnance Lab., Solomons Island.

1 UNCLASSIFIED MISCELLANEOUS, *AKL TYPE*

Unnamed	IX-306	ASA

Completed for Army in WW II as FS-221. Acquired by USN on loan from Army 1–69 to test MK 48 torpedo. Has torpedo tubes built into hull as well as deck-mounted tubes.

UNCLASSIFIED MISCELLANEOUS, *"ATLANTA"* CLASS

[Atlanta]	IX-304	Struck

Originally commissioned as CL-104 of *Cleveland* class. Decommissioned 7–1–49. Struck 10–1–62 but reinstated 5–15–64 as IX. Converted to explosives test ship. Placed "out of commission," special 8–31–65. Struck 1970; taken out of mothballs 4–70 for disposal as target.

1 UNCLASSIFIED MISCELLANEOUS, *SAIL FRIGATE* TYPE

Constitution	IX-21	Spec.

Built 1797–98 as a frigate; one of 6 that were first ships built for USN. First put to sea 7–22–1798. Renamed *Old Constitution* 12–1–17; renamed *Constitution* 7–24–25. Restored 1927–30. Now permanently moored in Boston as Flagship, Commandant First Naval District. Rated "in commission, special."

1 SUBMERSIBLE RESEARCH VEHICLE (NUCLEAR PROPULSION), *NR-1* CLASS

Number	FY	Builder	Awarded	Completed	F/S
NR-1	65	Gen. Dyn., Groton	11–18–65	10–27–69	ASA

A highly successful submarine equipped with lights, TV viewers, viewing ports, movie cameras, and a retractable arm for picking objects off ocean bottom. Has "wheels" on bottom of hull so it can drive along ocean floor. Wheel concept first tested on SST-1.

1 TARGET AND TRAINING SUBMARINE, *BARRACUDA* CLASS

Name	Number	F/S
Barracuda	SST-3	ASA

Commissioned 11–10–51 as USS *K-1* (SSK-1), a hunter-killer submarine. Bow housed listening gear. Name changed 12–15–55. To SST-3 on 7–15–59; bow reconfigured to normal SS bow. Serves as mobile target and training submarine. Two sisters *Bass* (SSK-2) and *Bonita* (SSK-3) disposed of as SS-551 and 552 respectively.

2 TARGET AND TRAINING SUBMARINES, *MACKEREL* CLASS

Marlin	SST-2	ASA
Mackerel	SST-1	ASA

SST-1 originally placed "in service" 10–9–53 as USS *T-1*. SST-2 originally placed "in service" 11–20–53 as USS *T-2*. *T-1* renamed *Mackerel* and *T-2* renamed *Marlin* on 5–15–56.

1 MISCELLANEOUS AUXILIARY, *GEORGE EASTMAN* CLASS

[Granville S. Hall]	YAG-40	Struck
George Eastman	YAG-39	PR*

Built on an EC2-S-C1 hull design 1943-44 as merchant ships. Acquired and placed in service 1953. Both placed out of service 1957 but were commissioned 10–20–62. Equipped as experimental ships. YAG-39 participated in nuclear fallout tests mid-1950s. YAG-40 had helicopter fitted forward. YAG-39 decommissioned 9–67.

USS *Alamagordo* (ARDM-2) underway by tow. She and her sister support SSBNs. **Oak Ridge** *class.*

1 SUBMERSIBLE CRAFT, *X-2* CLASS

Name	Number	F/S
Trieste II	X-2	ASA

Purchased from Auguste Picard in 1958 as the *Trieste I*. Rebuilt in early 1960s and renamed *Trieste II*. Designed operating depth is 20,000′, but is limited to 12,000′. Horizontal maneuverability is limited. Has endurance of 5 hours at 2 knots. Has external television cameras and mechanical arm. Classified as X-2, instated on the NVR, and placed "in service" on 9–1–69.

1 SUBMERSIBLE CRAFT, *X-1* CLASS

Unnamed	X-1	ASA

Originally placed "in service" 10–7–55 as *X-1* (SSX-1). Only midget submarine ever built for USN. Hull split into 3 pieces by internal explosion 2–58. Rebuilt at Philadelphia Navy Yard. Completed 12–60.

USS *Windsor* (ARD-22). The hulk of *Frank E. Evans* (DD-754) was drydocked in this ARD for inspection and decommissioning. 5–24–67. **ARD-12** *class.*

USS *Elk River* (IX-501). 11–14–68. **Elk River** *class.*

USS *Constitution* (IX-21) underway in Boston during her annual turn-around cruise. Note tug towing her and tug on port side of ship. 6–5–63. **Sail Frigate** *type.*

USS *Atlanta* (IX-304) in her last configuration. Note superstructure and masts and compare to illustrations in destroyer section. 11–64. **"Atlanta"** *class.*

The unnamed IX-306 underway. Note torpedo resting on deck amidships. 1969. **AKL** *type.*

USS *George Eastman* (YAG-39). 2–17–66. **George Eastman** *class.*

USS *Marlin* (SST-2). Note sonar just forward of sail. **Mackerel** *class.*

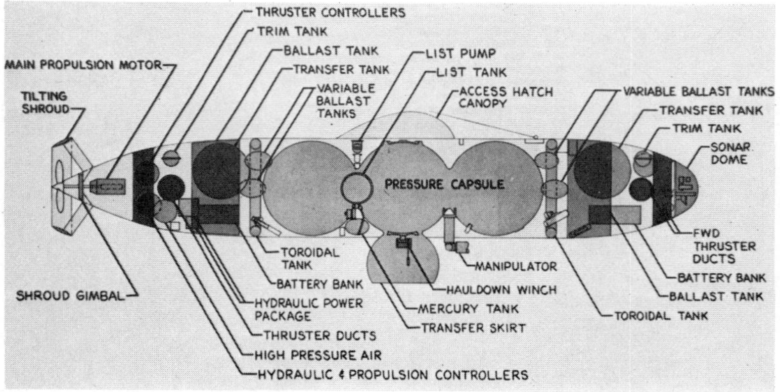

Artist's conception of DSRV. 5–31–67.

General Dynamics

The nuclear-powered research submarine NR-1 during trials. Note unusual bow. 8–20–69. **NR-1** *class.*

USS *Barracuda* (SST-3), formerly an SSK; only survivor of three sisters. **Barracuda** *class.*

The bathyscaph *Trieste II* (X-2), a new addition to the NVR, preparing to dive. Note propulsion units forward and aft. 1–31–69. **X-2** *class.*

The midget submarine X-1. 4–69. **X-1** *class.*

B. Minor Service Craft

By end-FY 1970, there were 1,354 minor service craft on the NVR. This included only service craft that were active or in reserve. With the exception of six service craft covered in Part A, all service craft are noncommissioned. They are rated as "in service" and have officers-in-charge, but do not have the "USS" prefix before their names or hull numbers. Some of the craft listed below have names, as indicated. The variety and number of these craft point up their importance in a modern navy.

Type	No. on List	Remarks
AFDB	7	AFDB-7 named *Los Alamos.*
AFDL	14	
AFDM	3	AFDM-8 named *Richland.*
APL	30	
ARD	14	2 more are commissioned; see section 5. ARD-20 named *White Sands.*
YAG	3	YAG-60 is ex-*Butternut* (ANL-9); YAG-87 is named *Saluda* (ex IX-87); YAG-61 is ex IX-309, YW-87; see section 5 for 2 more.
YC	248	1 more is under construction as YC/YFN.
YCF	3	
YCV	6	
YD	80	
YDT	2	
YF	26	YF-294 named *Phoebus,* YF-328 named *Lynnhaven,* YF-336 is *Suitland,* YF-864 is *Little Compton,* YF-885 is *Keyport,* and YF-886 is named *Kodiak.*
YFB	7	YFB-88/91 are ex LCU-1636, 1638/1640.
YFN	182	2 more under construction.
YFNB	25	2 are in MSC.
YFND	6	
YFNX	14	
YFP	3	
YFR	3	
YFRN	5	
YFRT	9	
YFU	30	Many are ex-LCUs; on loan to Army.
YG	19	
YGN	9	
YHLC	2	YHLC-1 is named *Crilley,* YHLC-2 is named *Crandall;* ex-German commercial salvage craft.
YLLC	4	All converted from LCUs, 1 lost in Vietnam 11/68.
YM	4	1 more is under construction.
YMLC	6	YMLC-3 is named *Salvager* (ex ARSD-3); YMLC-4 is named *Windlass* (ex ARSD-4); 4 other YMLC on loan from Royal Navy are due for return.
YNG	12	
YO	73	YO-47 is named *Casing Head,* YO-48 is named *Crownblock,* YO-49 is named *Whipstock,* and YO-55 is named *Gauger.*
YOG	22	YOG-107 is named *Lt. Thomas W. Fowler.*
YOGN	15	
YON	40	
YOS	15	
YP	23	Used as training craft at Annapolis, Md. and Newport, R.I. 4 more under construction.
YPD	5	
YR	18	
YRB	5	
YRBM	27	
YRDH	5	
YRDM	4	
YRR	14	
YRST	6	YRST-1/3 are ex YDT-11/13; YRST-4 named *Naubec* (ex AN-84); YRST-5/6 are ex-YFNX.
YSD	21	
YSR	28	
YTB	53	7 more are under construction. See next table for YTB names.
YTL	23	
YTM	136	Many are ex-Army tugs and old YTBs. See next table for YTM names.
YV	0	Last unit *Targeteer* (YV-3) (ex LSMR-508) disposed of.
YW	32	1 other unit on NVR as YAG-61.
YWN	13	

Names of Large Harbor Tugs (YTB) and Medium Harbor Tugs (YTM)

Unlike most other service craft, all YTBs and YTMs (with 2 exceptions) are named. Other named service craft are noted in preceding table. Some YTB names honor ships of the "Old Navy."

Number	Name	Number	Name	Number	Name	Number	Name
YTB-752	*Edenshaw*	YTB-799	*Natchitoches*	YTM-272	*Iwana*	YTM-416	*Sonnicant*
YTB-753	*Marin*	YTB-800	*Eufaula*	YTM-273	*Olathe*	YTM-417	*Taconnet*
YTB-756	*Pontiac*	YTB-801	*Palatka*	YTM-359	*Pawtucket*	YTM-418	*Tensaw*
YTB-757	*Oshkosh*	YTB-802	*Cheraw*	YTM-364	*Sassaba*	YTM-419	*Topawa*
YTB-758	*Paducah*	YTB-803	*Nanticoke*	YTM-365	*Segwarusa*	YTM-420	*Wallacut*
YTB-759	*Bogalusa*	YTB-804	*Ahoskie*	YTM-366	*Waubansee*	YTM-421	*Windigo*
YTB-760	*Natick**	YTB-805	*Ocala*	YTM-367	*Wawasee*	YTM-493	*Abinago*
YTB-761	*Ottumwa*	YTB-806	*Tuskegee*	YTM-369	*Shamokin*	YTM-494	*Alnaba*
YTB-762	*Tuscumbia*	YTB-807	*Massapequa*	YTM-371	*Smohalla*	YTM-495	*Barboncito*
YTB-763	*Muskegon*	YTB-808	*Wenatchee*	YTM-372	*Tatarrax*	YTM-518	*Hisada*
YTB-764	*Mishawaka*	YTB-809	*Agawam*	YTM-374	*Vaga*	YTM-519	*Mahoa*
YTB-765	*Okmulgee*	YTB-810	*Anoka*	YTM-380	*Chanagi*	YTM-521	*Nabigwon*
YTB-766	*Wapakoneta*	YTB-811	*Houma*	YTM-381	*Chepanoc*	YTM-522	*Sagawamick*
YTB-767	*Apalachicola*	YTB-812	*Accomac*	YTM-382	*Coatopa*	YTM-523	*Senasqua*
YTB-768	*Arcata*	YTB-813	*Poughkeepsie*	YTM-383	*Cochali*	YTM-524	*Tutahaco*
YTB-769	*Chesaning*	YTB-814	*Waxahachie*	YTM-384	*Waneta*	YTM-525	*Wabanaquot*
YTB-770	*Dahlonega*	YTB-815	*Neodesha*	YTM-386	*Washakie*	YTM-526	*Wahaka*
YTB-771	*Keokuk*	YTM-129	*Osceola*	YTM-387	*Watseka*	YTM-527	*Wahpeton*
YTB-774	*Nashua*	YTM-131	*Massasoit*	YTM-388	*Connewango*	YTM-532	*Ocmulgee*
YTB-775	*Wauwatosa*	YTM-140	*Wahtah*	YTM-390	*Ganadoga*	YTM-533	*Shahaska*
YTB-776	*Weehawken*	YTM-142	*Nokomis*	YTM-391	*Itara*	YTM-534	*Nadli*
YTB-777	*Nogales*	YTM-145	*Montezuma*	YTM-392	*Mecosta*	YTM-535	*Nahasho*
YTB-778	*Apopka*	YTM-148	*Wenonah*	YTM-393	*Nakarna*	YTM-536	*Nahoke*
YTB-779	*Manhattan*	YTM-149	*Toka*	YTM-394	*Winamac*	YTM-537	*Nanigo*
YTB-780	*Saugus*	YTM-151	*Konoka*	YTM-395	*Wingina*	YTM-539	*Sikis*
YTB-781	*Niantic*	YTM-174	*Allaquippa*	YTM-396	*Wovoka*	YTM-540	*Quileute*
YTB-782	*Manistee*	YTM-175	*Chekilli*	YTM-397	*Yanegua*	YTM-541	*Ozette*
YTB-783	*Redwing*	YTM-176	*Junaluska*	YTM-398	*Natahki*	YTM-542	*Chegodega*
YTB-784	*Kalispell*	YTM-177	*Black Fox*	YTM-399	*Numa*	YTM-543	*Etawina*
YTB-785	*Winnemucca*	YTM-178	*Dekaury*	YTM-400	*Otokomi*	YTM-544	*Yatanocas*
YTB-786	*Tonkawa*	YTM-180	*Madokawando*	YTM-401	*Owachomo*	YTM-545	*Accohanoc*
YTB-787	*Kittanning*	YTM-181	*Mazapeta*	YTM-402	*Panameta*	YTM-546	*Takos*
YTB-788	*Wapato*	YTM-182	*Mawkaw*	YTM-403	*Pitamakan*	YTM-547	*Yanaba*
YTB-789	*Tomahawk*	YTM-188	*Negwagon*	YTM-404	*Coshecton*	YTM-548	*Matunak*
YTB-790	*Menominee*	YTM-189	*Nepanet*	YTM-405	*Cusseta*	YTM-549	*Migadan*
YTB-791	*Marinette*	YTM-190	*Orono*	YTM-406	*Kittaton*	YTM-701	*Acoma*
YTB-792	*Antigo*	YTM-195	*Yonaguska*	YTM-407	*Lonoto*	YTM-702	*Arawak*
YTB-793	*Piqua*	YTM-252	*Dekanisora*	YTM-408	*Minniska*	YTM-703	*Canarsee*
YTB-794	*Mandan*	YTM-265	*Hiawatha*	YTM-409	*Anamosa*	YTM-704	*Moratoc*
YTB-795	*Ketchikan*	YTM-266	*Pocahontas*	YTM-412	*Conchardee*	YTM-734	*Mankato*
YTB-796	*Saco*	YTM-268	*Red Cloud*	YTM-413	*Porobago*	YTM-747	*Chicopee*
YTB-797	*Tamaqua*	YTM-269	*Sakarissa*	YTM-414	*Satago*	YTM-748	*Yuma*
YTB-798	*Opelika*	YTM-270	*Satanta*	YTM-415	*Secota*	YTM-750	*Hackensack*

* Class leader

continued

Harbor Tugs—*continued*

Number	Name
YTM-751	*Manteo*
YTM-752	*Kewaunee*
YTM-753	*Naugatuck*
YTM-754	*Woonsocket*
YTM-755	*Waukegan*
YTM-756	*Owatonna*
YTM-757	*Wahpeton*
YTM-758	unnamed
YTM-759	unnamed
YTM-760	*Mascoutah*
YTM-761	*Menasha*
YTM-762	*Pokanoket*
YTM-764	*Cholocco*
YTM-765	*Chiquito*
YTM-766	*Chohonaga*
YTM-767	*Ankachak*
YTM-768	*Apohola*
YTM-770	*Mimac*
YTM-772	*Makah*
YTM-773	*Chilkat*
YTM-774	*Carascan*
YTM-775	*Hastwiana*
YTM-776	*Hiamowee*
YTM-777	*Lelaka*
YTM-779	*Pocasset*
YTM-780/785	Construction cancelled 2/69

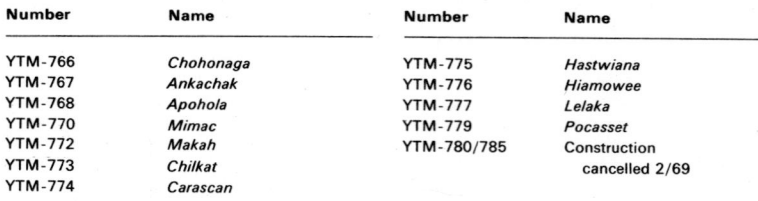

YFRT-520.

YF-880.

YNG-24.

YR-29.

YSD-11.

YTB-795.

YP-668.

7. NAVAL RESERVE TRAINING SHIPS

This section lists 68 ships assigned to Naval Reserve training duty as of 17 August 1971. Data on these ships can be found in sections 1, 2, 3, and 5; in these sections, NRT ships are identified by "NRT" in the fleet status column. The status of NRT ships varies: DDs, DEs, and MSOs are "in commission"; MSCs are "in service, active"; AGSSs/LPSS are "in service, in reserve." NRT submarines are nonoperational. They are immobile dockside trainers rigged to simulate diving and surfacing. All other NRT vessels are seagoing.

Name/Classification	NRT Homeport	Effective Date of Assignment	Remarks
Cod (AGSS-224)	Cleveland, Ohio	5–1–60	Replaced *Gar* (SS-206).
Angler (AGSS-240)	Philadelphia, Pa.	4–1–68	Replaced *Hake* (AGSS-256).
Croaker (AGSS-246)	Portsmouth, N.H.	4–2–68	Replaced *Crevalle* (AGSS-291).
Rasher (AGSS-269)	Portland, Oregon	6–30–67	Replaced *Loggerhead* (AGSS-374).
Bowfin (AGSS-287)	Seattle, Washington	5–1–60	Replaced *Puffer* (SS-268).
Ling (AGSS-297)	New York, N. Y.	5–1–60	Replaced *Hoe* (SS-258).
Lionfish (AGSS-298)	Providence, R. I.	4–15–60	Replaced *Kingfish* (SS-234).
Roncador (AGSS-301)	San Diego, Cal.	5–1–60	To be replaced.
Perch (LPSS-313)	San Diego, Cal.	6–30–67	Replaced *Trepang* (AGSS-412).
Charr (AGSS-328)	Alameda, Cal.	6–30–69	Replaced *Parche* (AGSS-384).
Carp (AGSS-338)	Boston, Mass.	3–18–68	Replaced *Billfish* (AGSS-286).
Chopper (AGSS-342)	New Orleans, La.	8–27–69	Replaced *Batfish* (AGSS-310).
Pampanito (AGSS-383)	Mare Island, Cal.	8–60	Replaced *Sunfish* (SS-281).
Torsk (AGSS-423)	Washington, D.C.	3–4–68	Replaced *Drum* (AGSS-228).
Runner (AGSS-476)	Chicago, Ill.	6–29–70	Replaced *Silversides* (AGSS-236).
Requin (AGSS-481)	St. Petersburg, Fla.	12–3–68	First NRT submarine at this location.
Shields (DD-596)	San Diego, Cal.	11–30–63	Replaced *Tingey* (DD-539).
Uhlmann (DD-687)	Tacoma, Washington	10–1–69	Replaced *Samuel N. Moore* (DD-747)
Allen M. Sumner (DD-692)	Baltimore, Md.	8–18–71	Replaced *Mills* (DER-383).
Moale (DD-693)	Brooklyn, N. Y.	6–1–70	Replaced *J. Douglas Blackwood* (DE-219).
Charles S. Sperry (DD-697)	Philadelphia, Pa.	9–10–69	Replaced *Conway* (DD-507).
Ault (DD-698)	Galveston, Texas	1–1–70	Replaced *Haynsworth* (DD-700).
Waldron (DD-699)	Mayport, Florida	4–1–70	Replaced *English* (DD-696).
Hank (DD-702)	Philadelphia, Pa.	9–1–63	Replaced *McNair* (DD-679).
Wallace L. Lind (DD-703)	Portland, Ore.	8–1–71	Replaced *Braine* (DD-630).
Borie (DD-704)	Alexandria, Va.[1]	10–22–69	Replaced *Gyatt* (DD-712).
Compton (DD-705)	Boston, Mass.	11–1–64	Replaced *Hazelwood* (DD-531).
Harlan R. Dickson (DD-708)	Boston, Mass.	9–1–68	Replaced *The Sullivans* (DD-537).
Gearing (DD-710)	New London, Conn.	8–12–70	Replaced *John W. Weeks* (DD-701).
De Haven (DD-727)	Long Beach, Cal.	10–6–71	Replaced *Mullany* (DD-528).
Maddox (DD-731)	Long Beach, Cal.	6–16–69	Replaced *Vammen* (DE-644).
Purdy (DD-734)	Fall River, Mass.	5–1–66	

John R. Pierce (DD-753)	New York, N.Y.	4–1–65	
Beatty (DD-756)	Tampa, Florida	9–1–68	
Putnam (DD-757)	New Orleans, La.	9–10–69	Replaced *Hyman* (DD-732).
Buck (DD-761)	San Diego, Cal.	7–1–71	
Henley (DD-762)	Norfolk, Va.	10–1–64	
Lowry (DD-770)	Philadelphia, Pa.	11–24–69	Replaced *Cony* (DD-508).
Willard Keith (DD-775)	Norfolk, Va.	10–1–63	Replaced *Bearss* (DD-654).
James C. Owens (DD-776)	San Francisco, Cal.	8–17–71	Replaced *Cowell* (DD-547).
Massey (DD-778)	Brooklyn, N.Y.[2]	11–10–69	Replaced *DeLong* (DE-684).
Douglas H. Fox (DD-779)	Philadelphia, Pa.	11–30–69	Replaced *Eaton* (DD-510).
Robert K. Huntington (DD-781)	Bayonne, N.J.	7–1–69	First FRAMed ship. Replaced *Waller* (DD-466).
Harwood (DD-861)	Charleston, S.C.	1–12–71	Replaced *Gainard* (DD-706).
Perkins (DD-877)	San Francisco, Cal.	7–1–71	Replaced *Twining* (DD-540)
Dyess (DD-880)	Brooklyn, N.Y.	2–16–71	Replaced *Zellars* (DD-777)
Evans (DE-1023)	Seattle, Washington	9–1–68	Replaced *Charles E. Brannon* (DE-446).
Bridget (DE-1024)	Seattle, Washington	9–1–68	Replaced *Whitehurst* (DE-634).
Bauer (DE-1025)	San Diego, Cal.	9–1–68	Replaced *Wiseman* (DE-667).
Hooper (DE-1026)	Long Beach, Cal.	9–1–68	Replaced *Halsey Powell* (DD-686).
Kingbird (MSC-194)	Pensacola, Fla.	9–16–68	Replaced *Fulmar* (MSCO-47).
Parrot (MSC-197)	Atlantic City, N.J.	9–3–68	
Peacock (MSC-198)	Long Beach, Cal.	3–1–71	
Phoebe (MSC-199)	Long Beach, Cal.	12–15–70	
Shrike (MSC-201)	Wilmington, N.C.	9–3–68	Replaced *Plover* (MSCO-33).
Thrasher (MSC-203)	San Francisco, Cal.	12–31–59	
Thrush (MSC-204)	Miami, Fla.	8–8–62	
Vireo (MSC-205)	Seattle, Washington	10–1–70	
Warbler (MSC-206)	Seattle, Washington	10–1–70	
Whippoorwill (MSC-207)	San Francisco, Cal.	12–15–70	
Widgeon (MSC-208)	San Diego, Cal.	10–1–70	
Woodpecker (MSC-209)	Seattle, Washington	12–15–70	Replaced *Cormorant* (MSC-122).
Dash (MSO-428)	Fall River, Mass.	9–1–71	Replaced *Vacana* (MSC-193).
Detector (MSO-429)	Portsmouth, N.H.	9–1–71	Replaced *Frigate Bird* (MSC-194).
Direct (MSO-430)	Perth Amboy, N.J.	9–1–71	Replaced *Limkin* (MSC-195) and *Meadowlark* (MSC-196).
Dominant (MSO-431)	St. Petersburg, Fla.	9–1–71	Replaced *Cove* (MSI-1) and *Cape* (MSI-2).
Embattle (MSO-434)	Long Beach, Cal.	9–1–70	
Reaper (MSO-467)	San Francisco, Cal.	9–1–70	

[1] *Trains Washington, D.C., reservists. Draft is too deep to navigate Potomac River to normal base at Washington Navy Yard.*

[2] *Trains Fort Schuyler, N.Y., reservists. Draft is too deep to navigate channel up to normal berthing place.*

8. MILITARY SEALIFT COMMAND

The Military Sea Transportation Service was established on 1 October 1949 and combined most of the functions that had previously been distributed among such agencies as the Army Transportation Corps and the Naval Transportation Service. On 1 August 1970, MSTS was renamed Military Sealift Command (MSC). As a part of the Navy organization, MSCs nucleus fleet is made up of naval vessels carried on the NVR. All MSC ships are serving in a noncommissioned status and are unarmed. As noncommissioned ships, they have USNS vice USS in front of their names. Also, the letter "T" is placed in front of their classifications to indicate that they are under MSC control ("T" is not a formal part of their nomenclature, however). For example, a regular commissioned Navy ship would be called the USS *General John Pope* (AP-110). A noncommissioned ship under MSC control would be called the USNS *General John Pope* (T-AP-110). Data on the following ships can be found in the Auxiliary or Amphibious sections; MSC ships in these sections are identified by "MSC" in the fleet status column.

Name and Hull Classification	MSC F/S
USNS *Bondia* (T-AF-42)	TAA
USNS *Asterion* (T-AF-63)	TPA
USNS *Perseus* (T-AF-64)	TPA
USNS *Kingsport* (T-AG-164)	TPA
USNS *Phoenix* (T-AG-172)[1]	TFEA
USNS *Provo* (T-AG-173)[1]	TFEA
USNS *Cheyenne* (T-AG-174)[1]	TFEA
USNS *Flyer* (T-AG-178)	TPA
USNS *S. P. Lee* (T-AG-192)	TPA
USNS *Range Recoverer* (T-AGM-2)	TAA
USNS *Longview* (T-AGM-3)	TPA
USNS *Sunnyvale* (T-AGM-5)	TPA
USNS *Watertown* (T-AGM-6)	TPA
USNS *Huntsville* (T-AGM-7)	TPA
USNS *Wheeling* (T-AGM-8)	TPA
USNS *General H. H. Arnold* (T-AGM-9)	TPR
USNS *General Hoyt S. Vandenberg* (T-AGM-10)	TPA
USNS *Vanguard* (T-AGM-19)	TAA
USNS *Redstone* (T-AGM-20)	TAA
USNS *Josiah Willard Gibbs* (T-AGOR-1)	TAA
USNS *Sands* (T-AGOR-6)	TAA
USNS *Lynch* (T-AGOR-7)	TAA
USNS *Eltanin* (T-AGOR-8)	TPA
USNS *Mizar* (T-AGOR-11)	TAA
USNS *De Steiguer* (T-AGOR-12)	TPA
USNS *Bartlett* (T-AGOR-13)	TPA
USNS *Bowditch* (T-AGS-21)	TAA
USNS *Dutton* (T-AGS-22)	TAA
USNS *Michelson* (T-AGS-23)	TPA
USNS *Kellar* (T-AGS-25)	TPA
USNS *Silas Bent* (T-AGS-26)	TPA
USNS *Kane* (T-AGS-27)	TPA
USNS *Chauvenet* (T-AGS-29)	TPA
USNS *Harkness* (T-AGS-32)	TAA
USNS *Sgt. George D. Keathley* (T-AGS-35)	TAA
USNS *Fentress* (T-AK-180)	TPA

Name and Hull Classification	MSC F/S
USNS *Herkimer* (T-AK-188)	TFEA
USNS *Muskingum* (T-AK-198)	TFEA
USNS *Greenville Victory* (T-AK-237)	TAA
USNS *Pvt. John R. Towle* (T-AK-240)	TAA
USNS *Pvt. Francis X. McGraw* (T-AK-241)	TAA
USNS *Sgt. Andrew Miller* (T-AK-242)	TPA
USNS *Sgt. Archer T. Gammon* (T-AK-243)	TAA
USNS *Sgt. Morris E. Crain* (T-AK-244)	TAA
USNS *Col. William J. O'Brien* (T-AK-246)	TAA
USNS *Short Splice* (T-AK-249)	TFEA
USNS *Pvt. Frank J. Petrarca* (T-AK-250)	TPA
USNS *Lt. George W. G. Boyce* (T-AK-251)	TAA
USNS *Lt. Robert Craig* (T-AK-252)	TAA
USNS *Sgt. Truman Kimbro* (T-AK-254)	TPA
USNS *Pvt. Leonard C. Brostrom* (T-AK-255)	TFEA
USNS *Marine Fiddler* (T-AK-267)	TAA
USNS *Mirfak* (T-AK-271)	TAR
USNS *Lt. James E. Robinson* (T-AK-274)	TAA
USNS *Pvt. Joseph F. Merrell* (T-AK-275)	TPA
USNS *Sgt. Jack J. Pendleton* (T-AK-276)	TPA
USNS *Schuyler Otis Bland* (T-AK-277)	TPA
USNS *Norwalk* (T-AK-279) (FBM)	TAA
USNS *Furman* (T-AK-280) (FBM)	TPA
USNS *Victoria* (T-AK-281) (FBM)	TAA
USNS *Marshfield* (T-AK-282) (FBM)	TAA
USNS *Wyandot* (T-AK-283)	TAA
USNS *Point Barrow* (T-AKD-1)	TAR
USNS *Comet* (T-AKR-7)	TAA
USNS *Sea Lift* (T-AKR-9)	TPA
USNS *Suamico* (T-AO-49)[2]	TWWR
USNS *Tallulah* (T-AO-50)[3]	TWWR
USNS *Pecos* (T-AO-65)[2]	TWWR
USNS *Cache* (T-AO-67)[3]	TWWR
USNS *Millicoma* (T-AO-73)[2]	TWWR
USNS *Saugatuck* (T-AO-75)[3]	TWWR
USNS *Schuylkill* (T-AO-76)[3]	TWWR

USNS *Cossatot* (T-AO-77)[3]	TWWR
USNS *Chepachet* (T-AO-78)[3]	TWWR
USNS *Cowanesque* (T-AO-79)[2]	TWWR
USNS *Mission Buenaventura* (T-AO-111)[2]	TWWR
USNS *Mission Santa Ynez* (T-AO-134)[2]	TWWR
USNS *Pioneer Valley* (T-AO-140)[3]	TWWR
USNS *Shawnee Trail* (T-AO-142)[3]	TWWR
USNS *Maumee* (T-AO-149)[3]	TWWR
USNS *Shoshone* (T-AO-151)[2]	TWWR
USNS *Yukon* (T-AO-152)[2]	TWWR
USNS *American Explorer* (T-AO-165)[2]	TWWR
USNS *Rincon* (T-AOG-77)	TFEA
USNS *Nodaway* (T-AOG-78)	TFEA
USNS *Petaluma* (T-AOG-79)	TFEA
USNS *Piscataqua* (T-AOG-80)	TFEA
USNS *Alatna* (T-AOG-81)	TPA
USNS *Chattahoochee* (T-AOG-82)	TFEA
USNS *Barrett* (T-AP-196)	TPA
USNS *Upshur* (T-AP-198)	TPA
USNS *Albert J. Myer* (T-ARC-6)	TPA
USNS *Corpus Christi Bay* (T-ARVH-1)	TFEA
USNS LST-47 (T-LST-47)	TFEA
USNS LST-117 (T-LST-117)	TFEA
USNS LST-176 (T-LST-176)	TFER
USNS LST-222 (T-LST-222)	TFEA
USNS LST-230 (T-LST-230)	TFEA
USNS LST-276 (T-LST-276)	TFEA
USNS LST-277 (T-LST-277)	TFEA
USNS LST-287 (T-LST-287)[1]	TFEA
USNS LST-399 (T-LST-399)	TFEA
USNS LST-456 (T-LST-456)	TFEA
USNS LST-488 (T-LST-488)[1]	TFEA
USNS LST-491 (T-LST-491)	TFEA

USNS LST-530 (T-LST-530)	TFEA
USNS *Chase County* (T-LST-532)[1]	TFEA
USNS LST-546 (T-LST-546)	TFEA
USNS LST-550 (T-LST-550)	TFEA
USNS LST-566 (T-LST-566)	TFEA
USNS LST-572 (T-LST-572)[1]	TFEA
USNS LST-579 (T-LST-579)	TFEA
USNS LST-581 (T-LST-581)	TFER
USNS LST-587 (T-LST-587)	TFER
USNS LST-590 (T-LST-590)[1]	TFEA
USNS LST-607 (T-LST-607)	TFEA
USNS LST-613 (T-LST-613)	TFEA
USNS LST-623 (T-LST-623)	TFEA
USNS LST-626 (T-LST-626)[1]	TFER
USNS LST-629 (T-LST-629)	TFEA
USNS LST-630 (T-LST-630)	TFEA
USNS LST-643 (T-LST-643)[1]	TFER
USNS LST-649 (T-LST-649)	TFEA
USNS LST-664 (T-LST-664)[1]	TFEA
USNS *Davies County* (T-LST-692)[1]	TFEA
USNS *De Kalb County* (T-LST-715)	TFEA
USNS *Harris County* (T-LST-822)[1]	TFEA
USNS *New London County* (T-LST-1066)[1]	TFEA
USNS *Nye County* (T-LST-1067)[1]	TFEA
USNS *Orleans Parish* (T-LST-1069)[1]	TFEA
USNS LST-1072 (T-LST-1072)[1]	TFEA
USNS *Plumas County* (T-LST-1083)	TFER
USNS *Pulaski County* (T-LST-1088)[1]	TFEA
USNS YFNB-6 (T-YFNB-6)[4]	TFEA
USNS YFNB-13 (T-YFNB-13)[4]	TFEA

[1] *Manned by Koreans. Non-Korean LSTs manned by Japanese.*
[2] *Operated under charter by Mathiasen's Tanker Industries, Inc.*
[3] *Operated under charter by Marine Transport Lines. Inc.*
[4] *Assigned to COMMSC, Honolulu.*

USNS *Point Barrow* (T-AKD-1). Ship has since been modified with quonset hut-like covering stretching from aft of stack to stern. Compare configuration with illustration of WW II LSD.

USNS *Kingsport* (T-AG-164). Dome structure has since been removed.

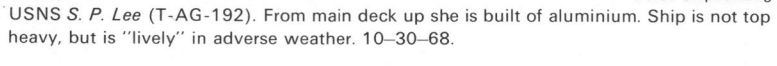

Defoe Shipbuilding

USNS *S. P. Lee* (T-AG-192). From main deck up she is built of aluminium. Ship is not top heavy, but is "lively" in adverse weather. 10–30–68.

USNS *General Hoyt S. Vandenburg* (T-AGM-10), a converted transport, when she was with the Air Force.

MSC

USNS *Longview* (T-AGM-3).

General Dynamics

USNS *Redstone* (T-AGM-20) in postconversion rig. Note horned stack and box-like superstructures. Bears no resemblance to former T-2 configuration. 1–18–67.

USNS *Silas Bent* (T-AGS-26). Compare this with photo of T-AG-192. 9–24–65.

USNS *Josiah Willard Gibbs* (T-AGOR-1). She carries 52 scientific personnel besides crew.

USNS *Mizar* (T-AGOR-11). This ship found remains of *Thresher* (SSN-593) and *Scorpion* (SSN-589).

Northwest Marine Iron Works

USNS *Bartlett* (T-AGOR-13), a ship of the AGOR-3 class. Appearances within the class vary. 3–24–69.

Artist's conception of *Hayes* (AGOR-16). 4–1–68.

USNS *Fentress* (T-AK-180). Compare this with photo of USNS *Bondia*.

USNS *Pvt. John R. Towle* (T-AK-240). 3–29–61.

USNS *Bondia* (T-AF-42), lone survivor of a 17-ship class.

USNS *Victoria* (T-AK-281) (FBM). She carries 16 FBM missiles upright to overseas bases. Note hold just forward of bridge and missile containers. Also note tripod mast.

MSC

USNS AKL-31 (T-AKL-31).

USNS *Comet* (T-AKR-7) transferring cargo to the Army beach discharge lighter *Lieut. Col. John U. D. Page* for transport of heavy equipment to the beach. *Comet* has four sideport loading/landing ramps plus a fifth ramp leading through the stern. 8–25–59.

USNS *Maumee* (T-AO-149). 9–5–68.

NASA

USNS *Croatan* (T-AKV-43) in NASA configuration as seagoing launch platform for sounding rockets. Since struck.

USNS *Mission Buenaventura* (T-AO-111), leadship of a large class of naval tankers. Note austere look as compared to USN AOs.

USNS *Barrett* (T-AP-196). Note thin, side-by-side stacks. Retains luxury liner appearance. Note high superstructure and oval bridge deck.

USNS *General William Weigel* (T-AP-119). This class and AP-120 class have same basic appearance.

USNS *Corpus Christi Bay* (T-ARVH-1). Note MSO, DD, and SS in background. The MSO was lost in an accident 6–66.

USNS LST-607 (T-LST-607) off-loading cargo. Note lack of guns and cargo booms. All MSC LSTs have enlarged cargo hatches just forward of boom for lowering cargo into the tank deck. 5–13–67.

9. AIRCRAFT

The Department of Defense shifted over to a new aircraft identification system on 9–18–62—all hardware already in existence on that date was redesignated. See the last part of this section for an old/new cross-reference list.

Explanation of Aircraft Letters and Numbers

BASIC DESIGNATION—basic-mission letter, a dash, and a design number.
BASIC MISSION SYMBOL—a letter denoting primary function or capability.
DESIGN NUMBER—the sequence number of the same basic mission or type; i.e., a new design.
SERIES SYMBOL—the letter *A* is placed to the right of a new design number. Letters in alphabetical order (except *I* and *O*) denote improvements or modifications on a design.
MODIFIED MISSION SYMBOL—prefix letter indicating the type of mission a design has been modified for.
STATUS SYMBOL—prefix letter that indicates aircraft is being used for special or service test and experimentation.
Example: *Vigilante*, RA-5C
Vigilante is the popular name assigned to the design. *R* is the modified mission (reconnaissance). *A* is the basic mission (attack). *5* is the design number. *C* is the second-design modification or improvement.

Symbols

BASIC MISSION

A. Attack
C. Cargo/transport
E. Airborne early warning
F. Fighter
H. Helicopter
O. Observation
P. Patrol
S. Antisubmarine
T. Trainer
U. Utility
V. VTOL/STOL; vertical or short takeoff or landing
X. Research

MODIFIED MISSION

A. Attack
C. Cargo/transport
D. Direct or controls drone or aircraft or missiles
E. Special electronic installation
H. Search/rescue
K. Tanker; inflight refueling
L. Cold weather; Arctic/Antarctic
M. Missile carrier
Q. Drone aircraft
R. Reconnaissance
S. Antisubmarine
T. Trainer
U. Utility; small payload; tows targets, etc.
V. Staff
W. Weather, meteorology

STATUS PREFIX

G. Permanently grounded
J. Special test; temp.
N. Special test; perm.
X. Experimental
Y. Prototype
Z. Planning

Abbreviations

AEW	Airborne early warning
ASW	Antisubmarine warfare
ATDS	Airborne tactical data system
A/W	All weather
B/N	Bombardier/navigator
C	Carrier-based
COD	Carrier on-board delivery
DIANE	Digital integrated attack navigation equipment
ECM	Electronic countermeasures
F/W	Fair weather
ILP	International Logistics Program
JL	JULIE (active, acoustic)
JL/JZ	JULIE/JEZEBEL
JZ	JEZEBEL (passive, acoustic)
L	Land-based
L-A/W	Limited all weather
LORAN	Long range aid to navigation
MAD	Magnetic anomaly detector
MCM	Mine countermeasures
RAG	Replacement air group
REINS	Radio equipped intertial navigation system
TRIM	Trails, roads, interdiction, multisensor
VERTREPS	Vértical replenishment

Aircraft speeds are in mph.

AIRBORNE EARLY WARNING

Model	Year Ordered/ Delivered	Number Proc.	Crew-Type	Lbs. Gross Weight	Dimensions OAL	Span	OAH	Engine Number	Model	SHP each, or Thrust (#) in Lbs.	Performance Max. Speed/ Range
E-2A	59/60	59	5-C	49,638	56′4″	80′7″	18′4″*	2	T56-A-8	4,050	368/1,654
E-2B	67/69	52	5-C	49,500	56′4″	80′7″	18′4″*	2	T56-A-8	4,050	368/1,654
E-2C	68/71	2	5-C	50,660	57′6″	80′7″	18′4″*	2	T56-A-8	4,050	368/1,654
E-1B	56/58	88	4-C	26,600	45′3½″	72′5″	16′10″	2	R1820-82A	1,525	250/2,000

* Rotor extended.

HAWKEYE, E-2 Series Aerial watchdog; replacing E-1B. ATDS linked with NTDS. E-1C is the projected avionics modification of E-1B. Two E-2As converted to TE-2A for RAG training; ATDS removed. Additional 26 E-2C to be ordered.

TRACER, E-1B Known as Willie Fudd; design based on C-1A TRADER.

ANTISUBMARINE WARFARE

Model	Year Ordered/ Delivered	Number Proc.	Crew-Type	Lbs. Gross Weight	Dimensions OAL	Span	OAH	Engine Number	Model	SHP each, or Thrust (#) in Lbs.	Performance Max. Speed/ Range
S-3A	69/72	6R & D	4-C	41,100	53′4″	68′8″	22′9″	2	TF34-GE-2	9,000#	400+/2,000+
S-2A	50/53	755	4-C	24,500	42′3″	69′8″	16′3½″	2	R1820-82	1,525	237/1,000
S-2B	57/58	64	4-C	24,500	42′3″	69′8″	16′3½″	2	R1820-82	1,525	237/1,000
S-2C	54/54	60	4-C	25,500	42′3″	69′8″	16′3½″	2	R1820-82	1,525	229/1,200
S-2D	57/59	100	4-C	29,150	43′6″	72′7″	16′7½″	2	R1820-82WA	1,525	280/1,200
S-2E	62/62	252	4-C	29,150	43′6″	72′7″	16′7½″	2	R1820-82WA	1,525	265/1,130

S-3A (unnamed) Contract to Lockheed, Burbank for 6 R and D prototypes with option for 193 production models. To replace TRACKER S-2 series. A/W search and destroy capabilities. Ordnance includes homing torpedoes, mines, depth charges, rockets, and missiles. LTV will build the wings, engine mount pods, tail/landing gear assemblies, and all control surfaces.

TRACKER, S-2 Series S-2 series originally designated S2F-1 (Stoofs); present S-2Fs are not to be confused with old designations. S-2A is search/attack. Conversions: 209 a/c to TS-2A in 1957, ASW systems removed; 51 a/c to US-2A; 1 a/c to RS-2C (photo) in 1964; remaining redesignated S-2F. S-2B was given interim JULIE capability. Most (or all) converted to other versions. 66 S-2A/B became US-2B; JULIE removed. In 1966, 48 S-2C became US-2C. A few S-2C (reportedly) converted to RS-2C. S-2D has improved airframe/systems; a few transferred to USAF as AS-2D. S-2E has wider tail, round wing tips. S-2F is S-2A with final JL/JZ systems installed. S-2G is modified S-2E; few details available.

ATTACK

Model	Year Ordered/ Delivered	Number Proc.	Crew-Type	Lbs. Gross Weight	Dimensions OAL	Span	OAH	Engine Number	Model	SHP each, or Thrust (#) in Lbs.	Performance Max. Speed/ Range
A-7A	64/66	199	1-C	38,000	46'1"	38'8"	16'0"	1	TF30-P-6	11,350#	595/4,100
A-7B	67/68	196	1-C	38,000	46'1"	38'8"	16'0"	1	TF30-P-8	12,200#	598/3,800+
A-7E	68/69	317	1-C	42,000	46'1"	38'8"	16'0"	1	TF41-A-2	15,000#	606/2,780
A-6A	58/60	488	2-C	60,626	54'7"	53'0"	15'7"	2	J52-P-8A	9,300#	600/3,225
A-6B	66/67	(mod)	2-C	60,626	54'7"	53'0"	15'7"	2	J52-P-8A	9,300#	600/3,225
A-6C	68/70	12	2-C	60,626	54'7"	53'0"	15'7"	2	J52-P-8A	9,300#	600/3,225
EA-6A	62/65	27	2-C	56,500	55'3"	53'0"	16'4"	2	J52-P-8A	9,300#	620/2,995
EA-6B	66/69	5+	4-C	58,500	59'5"	53'0"	16'4"	2	J52-P-8A	9,300#	620/2,995
KA-6D	69/71	24	2-C	60,626	54'7"	53'0"	15'7"	2	J52-P-8A	9,300#	600/3,225
RA-5C	56/61	107+	2-C	80,000	75'10"	53'0"	19'5"	2	J79-GE-8	17,000#	M.2/2,650
A-4A	52/55	166	1-C	22,500	39'5"	27'6"	15'0"	1	J65-W-16A	7,700#	664/1,700+
A-4B	54/56	542	1-C	22,500	39'5"	27'6"	15'0"	1	J65-W-16A	7,700#	661/1,700+
A-4C	57/59	638	1-C	22,500	40'4"	27'6"	15'0"	1	J65-W-16A	7,700#	649/1,740
A-4E	60/62	500	1-C	24,500	40'3"	27'6"	15'0"	1	J52-P-6A	8,500#	674/1,700+
A-4F	65/66	146	1-C	24,500	40'3"	27'6"	15'0"	1	J52-P-8A	9,300#	661/1,700+
TA-4F	65/66	139	2-C	24,500	42'7"	27'6"	15'2"	1	J52-P-8A	9,300#	661/1,700+
A-4H			1-C	24,500	40'3"	27'6"	15'0"	1	J52-P-8A	9,300#	661/1,700+
TA-4H			2-C	24,500	42'7"	27'6"	15'2"	1	J52-P-8A	9,300#	661/1,700+
TA-4J	67/68	185	2-C	24,500	42'7"	27'6"	15'2"	1	J52-P-8A	9,300#	661/1,700+
A-3A	51/54	45	3-C	78,000	74'8"	72'6"	22'9"	2	J57-P-6B	8,500#	620/2,500
EA-3A	(conv)	5	4-C	78,000	74'8"	72'6"	22'9"	2	J57-P-6B	8,500#	620/2,500
A-3B	55/56	164	3-C	78,000	74'8"	72'6"	23'10"	2	J57-P-10	10,500#	600+/2,200
EA-3B	55/59	25	7-C	78,000	74'8"	72'6"	23'10"	2	J57-P-10	10,500#	600+/2,200
EKA-3B	/67	39	3-C	78,000	74'8"	72'6"	23'10"	2	J57-P-10	10,500#	600+/2,200
KA-3B	/66	50	3-C	78,000	74'8"	72'6"	23'10"	2	J57-P-10	10,500#	600+/2,200
RA-3B	55/59	30	3-C	78,000	74'8"	72'6"	23'10"	2	J57-P-10	10,500#	600+/2,200
TA-3B	/59	12	8-C	78,000	74'8"	72'6"	23'10"	2	J57-P-10	10,500#	600+/2,200

CORSAIR II, A-7 Series A/W tactical strike, close support missions; replaces A-4 SKYHAWK. Design based on F-8E CRUSADER. Weapon delivery avionics include central digital computer. Have 6 wing pods plus 1 pylon each side of fuselage for 7.5 ton payload; 2 SIDEWINDERS. A-7A/B armed with 2/20 mm cannons; A-7E with M61 Gatling gun. Protection includes cockpit armor, 2 back-up power control systems. A-7B has improved engine; A-7C 2-seat version cancelled; A-7D is USAF version. Early A-7Es use A-7B engine. A-7G is ILP version of A-7 series with airframe/equipment changes.

INTRUDER, A-6 Series Primary A/W attack bomber for low-level penetration and close support missions. All-weather capability provided by DIANE. Early A-6s to backfit with EA-6 wing. A-6B is A-6A configured for STANDARD ARM missile. A-6C has TRIM; 12 ordered, some are reconfigured A-6As, some are production models. A-6E with highly improved avionics is projected/pending. EA-6A has tactical ECM with attack capability. 12 additional EA-6Bs are on FY 1970 contract. Four A-6As converted to KA-6Ds in 1969; retain visual attack capability. Long-lead items funded FY 1969 for 20 production tankers.

VIGILANTE, RA-5C A/W tactical reconnaissance a/c with attack capability. First and only carrier-based supersonic bomber; has REINS. Of 59 A-5As ordered 1956, 43 were converted to RA-5C. 46 improved RA-5Cs ordered with first fleet delivery 4–69; have J79-GE-10 engines. The A-5B, an interim aircraft unofficially referred to as A-5CL, was never operational. The few produced were converted almost immediately to RA-5C.

SKYHAWK, A-4 Series By 1971, 2,500 had been produced. Have nonfolding delta wings. A-4C is backfitting with J52-P-8A engine. A-4E has improved engine (27% more range) and 2 extra wing pods. A-4F has avionics hump on top of fuselage, aft of cockpit. A-4H/TA-4H are for Israel; similar to A-4E/F. Many A-4A/B redesignated TA-4A/B (non-combat). TA-4F was formerly TA-4E. TA-4J is light version of TA-4F; air-to-air and air-to-ground launcher systems removed. New versions: A-4M is for USMC (41 in 1970); has J52-P-40B engine. A4G/TA-4G are for Australia; A-4K/TA-4K are for New Zealand. A-4L is the A-4C reconfigured with an uprated engine.

SKYWARRIOR, A-3 Series Largest carrier-based attack bomber. Tail-mounted barbette with 2 20 mm guns removed from later models. One of 2 XA-3As converted to KA-3B. Limited number of A-3A/B remain; no RA-3A and no VA-3B (a conversion). EA-3A/B are ECM versions with bomb capability removed. EKA-3B is for TACOS. TA-3B is B/N trainer. USAF version is B-66 DESTROYER series.

CARGO TRANSPORT

VC-11A		1	16-L	57,500	79'11"	68'10"	24'6"	2	MK511-8	11,400#	590/3,750
VC-4A	/63	2	12-L	36,000	63'9"	78'4"	23'4"	2	MK529-8	2,210	350/2,621
TC-4C	66/68	9	9-L	36,000	67'11"	78'4"	22'9"	2	MK529-8X	2,210	350/2,621
C-2A	62/64	19	3-C	54,830	56'8"	80'7"	15'11"	2	T56-A-8A	4,050	325/1,650
C-1A	53/55	87	2-C	24,600	42'0"	69'8"	16'3½"	2	R1820-82	1,525	280/1,200
EC-1A	55/57	4	5-C	26,000	42'0"	69'8"	16'3½"	2	R1820-82	1,525	290/1,200
C-131F	54/54	33	3-L	47,000	79'2"	105'4"	28'0"	2	R2800-52W	2,500	275/2,000
C-131G	56/57	2	3-L	47,000	79'2"	105'4"	28'0"	2	R2800-52W	2,500	275/2,000
HC-130B	58/60	12	4-L	135,000	97'9"	132'7"	38'3"	4	T56-A-7A	4,050	370/2,300
EC-130E		1+	5-L	155,000	97'9"	132'7"	38'3"	4	T56-A-7A	4,050	384/2,420
KC-130F	58/60	46	7-L	135,000	97'9"	132'7"	38'3"	4	T56-A-7A	4,050	365/4,000
LC-130F	59/60	4	7-L	135,000	97'9"	132'7"	38'3"	4	T56-A-7A	4,050	365/3,600
EC-130G	63/63*	4	11-L	155,000	97'9"	132'7"	38'3"	4	T56-A-7A	4,050	365/3,600
EC-130Q	67/68	(few)	11-L	155,000	97'9"	132'7"	38'3"	4	T56-A-16	4,910	350+/3,400+
LC-130R	67/68	(few)	5-L	155,000	97'9"	132'7"	38'3"	4	T56-A-16	4,910	350+/3,400+
C-123B	tr/62	8	2-L	54,000	76'3"	110'0"	34'6"	2	R2800-99W	2,500	300+/2,500+
C-121J	50/52	50	8-L	140,000	116'2"	123'0"	24'10"	4	R3350-34	3,250	370/3,500
EC-121K	51/53	142	26-L	120,000	116'2"	123'0"	24'10"	4	R3350-34	3,250	300/6,500
WC-121N	53/55	8	16-L	120,000	116'2"	123'0"	24'10"	4	R3350-34	3,250	335/5,000
C-119F	52/53	58	5-L	74,400	86'6"	109'3"	28'6"	2	R3350-36W	3,500	285/2,300
C-118B	50/52	61	6-L	112,000	107'0"	117'6"	28'8"	4	R2800-52W	2,500	269/1,870
VC-118B	50/53	4	5-L	112,000	107'0"	117'6"	28'8"	4	R2800-52W	2,500	269/1,870
C-117D	50/51	(101)	3-L	31,000	67'9"	90'0"	18'3"	2	R1820-80A	1,475	250/2,500
C-54P/Q	43/44	(181)	6-L	68,000	93'10"	117'6"	27'6"	4	R2000-9A	1,450	285/4,300
C-47	42/43		3-L	29,000	64'6"	95'0"	16'11"	2	R1830-90	1,000	230/2,125
C-45	41/41	1294	6-L*	8,730	34'2"	47'8"	9'4"	2	R985AN148	450	218/750

GULFSTREAM II, VC-11A USCG long range staff/administrative sweptwing (25°) turbofan jet. Rolls-Royce engine.

GULFSTREAM I, VC-4A USCG medium range staff/administrative a/c. Rolls-Royce Dart engine.

ACADEME, TC-4C Modified GULFSTREAM I; B/N trainer for A-6. Nose houses INTRUDER avionics. Rolls-Royce Dart engine.

VC-3A (unnamed) Similar to commercial Martin 404. Two transferred from Coast Guard to Navy 1969; redesignated C-3A.

GREYHOUND, C-2A A/W COD transport; design based on E-2A.

TRADER, C-1 Series A/W COD transport/trainer. Similar to S-2A; wide tail as S-2C. Has Wright engine (R1820-8A also used). EC-1A is active/passive ECM version.

SAMARITAN, C-131 Series Cargo/transports.

HERCULES, C-130 Series HC-130B and HC-130H is for USCG SAR. EC-130E is for USCG LORAN calibration. EC-130G has permanent TACAMO. EC-130Q is improved EC-130G. KC-130F is tactical tanker/cargo-personnel/evacuation. C-130F is KC-130F without refueling kit/cargo aerial delivery system. LC-130F has ski/wheel for polar use. LC-130R is improved LC-130F.

PROVIDER, C-123B USCG LORAN logistics supply; transferred from USAF.

C-121 Series C-121J is SUPER CONSTELLATION. WARNING STAR has AEW with radar antennas above and below fuselage. EC-121K also has R3350-42 engines; AEW. EC-121M is EC-121K modified 1959 for ECM. EC-121P is EC-121K improved 1963 with ASW equipment. WC-121N is weather reconnaissance version of EC-121K.

PACKET, C-119F Twin engine/twin boom. USAF version is FLYING BOXCAR.

continued

SKYTRAIN, C-117D Three converted 1961 to LC-117D for polar use. TC-117D is navigation trainer; 8 converted 1960. A few VC-117D acquired 1951.

SKYMASTER, C-54 P/Q Series 30 modified to C-54P. 20 C-54P/Q modified to C-54S 1957. C-54T is modified C-54R. VC-54S is modified VC-54N, P/Q; has C-54S avionics.

SKYTRAIN, C-47 Series 10,000+ built for military. 238 USAF C-47As converted to C-47H; some to polar transport LC-47H; few to SC-47H (ASW trainer). 148 C-47Bs converted to C-47J. TC-47J is navigation trainer. C-47L is C-47H/J equipped for ALUSNA. C-47M is modified for MAAG/MISSION. C-47R is modified C-47M for high altitudes.

NAVIGATOR, C-45J Series Few remain. UC-45J is trainer/utility version. RC-45J is for photo use.

FIGHTER

Model	Year Ordered/ Delivered	Number Proc.	Crew-Type	Lbs. Gross Weight	Dimensions OAL	Span	OAH	Engine Number	Model	SHP each, or Thrust (#) in Lbs.	Performance Max. Speed/ Range
F-111B	62/	7	2-C	70,000	66'9"	70'0"	16'8"	2	TF30-P-12	20,000#	M.2+/3,000
F-14A	69/72	6R & D*	2-C	55,000	61'10"	64'0"	16'0"	2	TF30-P-12	20,000#	M.2+/1,000+
F-8A	54/57	318	1-C	24,416	55'3"	35'8"	15'9"	1	J57-P-12	16,000#	1000+/1,500
F-8B	57/58	130	1-C	24,416	55'3"	35'8"	15'9"	1	J57-P-4A	16,200#	1000+/1,500
F-8C	57/59	187	1-C	25,500	55'3"	35'8"	15'9"	1	J57-P-16A	16,900#	1200+/1,000+
F-8D	59/60	152	1-C	25,500	55'3"	35'8"	15'9"	1	J57-P-20	18,000#	1400+/1,000+
F-8E	61/62	286	1-C	34,000	55'3"	35'8"	15'9"	1	J57-P-20	18,000#	1400+/1,000+
F-8H	cv/68	89	1-C	30,000	55'3"	35'8"	15'9"	1	J57-P-20	18,000#	1400+/1,000+
F-8J	cv/68	136	1-C	31,000	55'3"	35'8"	15'9"	1	J57-P-20	18,000#	1400+/1,000+
F-8K	cv/69	87	1-C	29,000	55'3"	35'8"	15'9"	1	J57-P-16A	16,900#	1200+/1,000+
F-8L	cv/69	63	1-C	27,500	55'3"	35'8"	15'9"	1	J57-P-12	16,000#	1000+/1,500
RF-8A	56/57	144	1-C	24,416	55'3"	35'8"	15'9"	1	J57-P-4A	16,200#	1000+/1,500
RF-8G	cv/65	73	1-C	24,416	55'3"	35'8"	15'9"	1	J57-P-22	16,900#	1200+/1,000+
F-4B	58/61	634	2-C	54,600	58'3"	38'5"	15'10"	2	J79-GE-8	17,000#	1650/2,000+
RF-4B	62/65	46	2-C	44,402	62'11"	34'5"	16'3"	2	J79-GE-8	17,000#	M2.2/1,520
F-4G	cv/	12	2-C	54,600	58'3"	38'5"	16'3"	2	J79-GE-8	17,000#	1650/2,000+
F-4J	65/66	523	2-C	45,950	58'3"	38'5"	15'9"	2	J79-GE-10	17,900#	M2.2/1,590

* To be 463 production models.

F-111B (unnamed) A/W twin-jet tactical fighter/attack. Has variable sweep wing (33'11" swept). Carries nuclear/conventional ordnance and 6 PHOENIX missiles. Of 30 ordered, 7 were produced, 3 lost and 1 flying. Cancelled 1968; main fault was excess weight.

TOMCAT, F-14 Series Long range A/W fighter/attack aircraft to replace F-4 in a phased program. Armed with M61 Gatling, PHOENIX, SPARROW, and SIDEWINDER. First aircraft crashed on second flight, 12–70; hydraulic failure.

CRUSADER, F-8 Series Has 2-position wing. 448 F-8s remanufactured; received new wings, fuselage and arresting gear strengthened, avionics improved, armament retained. Later models of F-8A have J57-P-4A/16 engine. Armament: 2 SIDEWINDERS and retractable rocket pack. 63 F-8B converted to F-8L. 87 F-8C converted to F-8K. F-8D is limited A/W; rocket pack removed. 89 converted to F-8H. F-8E is A/W version. 136 F-8E converted to F-8J. 42 F-8E built for French Navy. RF-8A has 5 cameras, no armament; inactive. 73 RF-8A converted to RF-8G. 40 DF-8F still active. DF-8A inactive; 20 remain. TF-8A was only 2-seat F-8; when remaining F-8As became TF-8A, the single 2-seater became NTF-8A.

PHANTOM, F-4 Series A/W fighter/attack bomber and interceptor. F-4As remaining 1968 became TF-4A. Armament: 6 SPARROW III or 4 SPARROW III and 4 SIDEWINDERS. RF-4B is for photo use. F-4C/D/E are USAF versions. F-4K, M are English versions.

HELICOPTERS

TH-57A	68/68	40	5	2,100	28'8"	* 1–33'	9'6½"	1	250-C18	317	150/400
CH-53A	62/66	263	3	35,000	63'3"	1–72'	24'11"	2	T64-GE-6A/B	3,925	190/227
HH-52A	62/63	50+	3	8,100	44'7"	1–53'	16'0"	1	T58-GE-8B	1,250	109/474
XH-51A	62/63	2	2	3,500	41'0"	1–35'	8'1"	1	T74-P	500#	302/300
QH-50C	60/62	381	0	2.183	7'3½"	2–20'	9'8½"	1	T50-BO-10	275	80/30+
QH-50D	64/64	373	0	2,328	7'3½"	2–20'	9'8½"	1	T50-BO-12	365	92/30+
CH-46A	61/63	160	3	19,431	44'10"	2–50'	16'11"	2	T58-GE-8B	1,250	152/300
UH-46A	64/64	14	3	19,650	44'10"	2–50'	16'11"	2	T58-GE-8B	1,250	166/150
CH-46D	66/66	164	3	23,000	44'10"	2–52'	16'8"	2	T58-GE-10	1,400	166/150
UH-46D	65/66	10	3	23,000	44'10"	2–52'	16'8"	2	T58-GE-10	1,400	166/150
CH-46F	67/68	174	3	23,000	44'10"	2–52'	16'8"	2	T58-GE-10	1,400	166/150
UH-34D	54/57	384	2	13,300	44'2"	1–56'	14'11"	1	R1820-84A	1,525	122/247
UH-34G	53/55	350+	4	12,200	47'2"	1–56'	14'4"	1	R1820-84A	1,525	120/400
SH-3A	57/61	162	4	17,300	54'9"	1–62'	16'8"	2	T58-GE-8B	1,250	210/540
SH-3D	65/66	73	4	18,626	57'0"	1–62'	16'10"	2	T58-GE-10	1,400	166/624
HH-3F	67/69	22	3	21,959	57'3"	1–62'	18'1"	2	T58-GE-5	1,500	156/300
UH-2A	58/62	88	2	10,000	40'6"	1–44'	14'8"	1	T58-GE-8B	1,250	162/671
UH-2B	62/63	96	2	10,000	40'6"	1–44'	14'8"	1	T58-GE-8B	1,250	162/671
HH-2C	68/69	12	4	12,800	52'6"	1–44'	15'5"	2	T58-GE-8B	1,250	157/425
UH-2C	67/68	122	2	11,614	41'0"	1–44'	14'8"	2	T58-GE-8B	1,250	157/425
UH-1B	Loan	33	2	8,500	42'7"	1–44'	12'8½"	1	T53-L-9/11	1,100	138/292
UH-1D	Loan	45	1	8,500	42'7"	1–48'	12'8½"	1	T53-L-9/11	1,100	138/292
UH-1E	62/64	209	2	8,500	42'7"	1–44'	12'8½"	1	T53-L-11	1,100	111/260
AH-1G	69/69	38	2	9,500	44'5"	1–44'	13'5"	1	T53-L-13	1,400	137/194
AH-1J	68/70	49	2	10,000	44'9"	1–44'	13'5"	1	T400CP-400	1,400	140/197
HH-1K	68/70	27	3	9,500	52'11"	1–44'	18'9"	1	T53-L-13	1,400	119/262
TH-1L	68/69	45	3	9,500	52'11"	1–44'	18'9"	1	T53-L-13	1,400	119/262
UH-1L	66/69	8	3	9,500	52'11"	1–44'	18'9"	1	T53-L-13	1,400	119/262

* Numbers 1 and 2 indicate rotors.

SEARANGER, TH-57A Skid gear, trainer with Allison engine. Replaces TH-13M SIOUX.

SEA STALLION, CH-53A USMC A/W assault, twin turbine cargo.

SEAGUARD, HH-52A USCG SAR; high altitudes/sea level for arctic/tropical regions.

XH-51A, (unnamed) Test/evaluate rigid rotor concept; contactor R&D. Has wing with forward thrust propulsion.

DASH, QH-50 Series ASW drone. Approximately 375 remain; most lost operationally. QH-50C/D armed with 2 MK 44 or 1 MK 46 torpedo. QH-50D has no tail section.

SEA KNIGHT, H-46 Series CH-46A,D are USMC A/W troop-cargo, water-landing a/c. CH-46D has a/c recovery, rescue/transfer boom. UH-46A is USN A/W VERTREP for AFS/AOE ships.

SEAHORSE/SEABAT, H-34 Series 221 SEAHORSE UH-34D remain on list. Six converted 1957 to LH-34D. 24 UH-34E built; 7 converted from UH-34D. SEABAT UH-34G is SH-34G without ASW system; most converted from H-34D. 122 SH-34J obtained 1957/58; few remain. 44 converted to UH-34J; ASW removed.

SEA KING, H-3 Series Twin-turbine, amphibious A/W ASW, auto hover. HH-3A has sonar removed, lightweight armor, 7.62mm turret; 12 ordered 1968, delivered 1969. Nine RH-3A converted 1964 to MCM. Eight converted 1961 to VH-3A. HH-3F used for USCG SAR. HH-3G is reconfigured SH-3A for noncombat SAR; sonar removed.

SEASPRITE, H-2 Series UH-2A is A/W rescue, utility; has single engine. UH-2B is F/W version; auxiliary tanks and ASW removed. UH-2C is 2-engine conversion of UH-2A/B. HH-2C used for SAR but is armed; result of 6 production models and 6 kit conversions. 31 HH-2D to be delivered 1970.

IROQUOIS/HUEYCOBRA, H-1 Series Tactical utility/assault support; skid-gear, single rotor turbine engine. Armament: 4 7·62mm guns, 2 2·75" rocket packages, 2 M79 grenade launchers. UH is IROQUOIS; AH is HUEYCOBRA. UH-1B, D loaned by Army. AH-1J has USMC avionics. (43 ordered; first delivery 1969.)

LAMPS To replace DASH. Manned A/W, ASW, AAW, SAR, light support utility. To have 2 engines. Initially, 10 UH-2C have been converted to interim LAMPS capability.

OBSERVATION

Model	Year Ordered/ Delivered	Number Proc.	Crew-Type	Lbs. Gross Weight	Dimensions OAL	Span	OAH	Engine Number	Model	SHP each, or Thrust (#) in Lbs.	Performance Max. Speed/ Range
O-1C	51/51	60	2-L	2,430	25'9"	36'0"	7'9"	1	0-470-2	265	115/300
O-1G	67/67	8	2-L	2,430	25'9"	36'0"	7'4"	1	0-470-11A	265	115/300

BIRD DOG, O-1 Series Both O-1C,G have Continental engines. O-1A obtained from Army; converted to O-1G.

PATROL

Model	Year Ordered/ Delivered	Number Proc.	Crew-Type	Lbs. Gross Weight	Dimensions OAL	Span	OAH	Engine Number	Model	SHP each, or Thrust (#) in Lbs.	Performance Max. Speed/ Range
P-3A	59/62	157	10-L	127,500	116'10"	99'8"	33'8½"	4	T56-A-10W	4,500	460/3,500
P-3B	65/66	123	10-L	135,000	116'10"	99'8"	33'8½"	4	T56-A-14	4,910	475/4,500
P-3C	68/69	48	10-L	135,000	116'10"	99'8"	33'8½"	4	T56-A-14	4,910	475/4,500
P-2E	50/51	360	9-L	79,895	98'8"	104'	29'4"	2	R3350-36W	3,500	346/3,500
P-2H	52/54	154+	10-L	79,895	98'8"	104'	29'4"	2	R3350-32W	3,700	365/3,500

ORION, P-3 Series Replaces P-2 NEPTUNE; developed from ELECTRA. P-3A (#110 on) has Deltic ASW system. WP-3A is for weather reconnaissance. P-3B has BULLPUP missiles. Two converted to EP-3B 1969 for electronic reconnaissance. P-3C has A-NEW avionics. P-3D has no ASW gear. RP-3D is for PROJECT MAGNET.

NEPTUNE, P-2 Series Armed with 16 5" rockets. Two jet pods (J34-WE-34) assist in takeoff. SP-2E modified 1960 to JL/JZ. 10 converted 1960 to DP-2E. SP-2H modified 1960 to JL/JZ. Four SP-2H modified 1967 to AP-2H for low-level, ground reconnaissance/interdiction.

RESEARCH

Model	Year Ordered/ Delivered	Number Proc.	Crew-Type	Lbs. Gross Weight	Dimensions OAL	Span	OAH	Engine Number	Model	SHP each, or Thrust (#) in Lbs.	Performance Max. Speed/ Range
X-25A	66/68	2	1-L	500	11'4"	5'6"*	6'3"	1	4318G*	90	85/300
X-22A	63/68	2	2-L	18,016	39'6"	39'3"	20'8"	4	YT58-GE-8B	1,250	325/500+

X-142A Tilt-wing V/STOL transport. Fleet trials 1966 on *Bennington* (CVS-20). Five purchased 1964 by USAF. Last unit transferred to NASA.

X-25A Rotor diameter is 16'8". Has McCulloch engine. Demonstrates a/c escape-system (gyrocopter). In R&D (1 is manned, 1 is drone).

X-22A Heavily damaged first model replaced by second. Has improve V/STOL handling; hover ceiling is 12,400'. Tri-service tests 1968. Still in R&D.

TRAINER

Model	Year Ordered/ Delivered	Number Proc.	Crew-Type	Lbs. Gross Weight	Dimensions OAL	Span	OAH	Engine Number	Model	SHP each, or Thrust (#) in Lbs.	Performance Max. Speed/ Range
T-39D	61/63	42	5-L	17,760	44'0"	44'6"	16'0"	2	J60-P-3A	3,000#	560/2,500
T-34B	54/55	423	2-L	2,985	25'11"	32'10"	9'7"	1	0-470-4	225	188/750
T-29B	tr/62	12	14-L	43,575	74'8"	91'9"	27'3"	2	R2800-97	2,400	290/
T-28B	52/53	490	2-L	8,038	32'11"	40'7"	12'7"	1	R1820-86A	1,425	346/1,035
T-28C	55/56	299	2-C	8,531	32'11"	40'7"	12'7"	1	R1820-86A	1,425	290/830
T-2A	55/58	217	2-L	11,000	38'9½"	36'0"	14'11"	1	J34-WE-46	3,400#	416/836
T-2B	64/65	97	2-C	13,280	38'3"	38'2"	14'8"	2	J60-P-6	3,000#	485/966
T-2C	64/69	84	2-C	13,820	38'3"	38'2"	14'8"	2	J85-GE-4	2,950#	485/966
T-1A	54/56	149	2-L	16,700	36'7"	43'0"	12'11"	1	J33-A-24A	6,100#	600/900

SABRELINER, T-39D Subsonic radar training. Three VT-39E purchased 7/68. Four additional a/c purchased 1969–70. VT-39E redesignated CT-39E.

MENTOR, T-34B Primary trainer. Continental engine.

FLYING CLASSROOM, T-29B B/N trainer. Transferred from USAF.

TROJAN, T-28 Series Propeller drive, basic trainer; improved USAF T-28A. Six converted 1956 to DT-28B for target a/c control. T-28C modified for carrier use.

BUCKEYE, T-2 Series Carrier-based jet, basic trainer. T-2B is 2-engine version.

SEASTAR, T-1A Carrier-based. Developed from T-33B.

UTILITY

HU-16C	48/49	94	6-A	26,850	62′10″	80′0″	24′3″	2	R1820-76A/B	1,425	225/2,200
U-11A	60/61	22	1-L	4,800	30′2½″	37′2″	10′3½″	2	0-54-A1A	250	215/1,250
U-6A	/64	2	1-L	5,100	30′4″	48′0″	9′0″	1	R985-AN-14B	450	140/470
U-1B	55/56	15	2-L	8,000	41′10″	58′0″	13′0″	1	R1340-AN-3	600	158/830

ALBATROSS, HU-16 HU-16C is SAR amphibian. LU-16C is for USCG polar service. 31 HU-16C rebuilt 1959 to HU-16D. HU-16E is for USCG general purpose SAR.

AZTEC, U-11A CONUS light logistic support. Has Lycoming engine.

BEAVER, U-6A Light utility STOL.

OTTER, U-1B Polar transport STOL; has ski gear.

V/STOL

OV-10A	64/67	114	2-L	13,800	41′7″	40′0″	15′1″	2	T76-G-10/12	715	281/1,400+
AV-8A	69/71	12	1-L	22,400	45′8″	25′3″	11′3″	1	PEGASUS 6	19,200#	.9M/2,000+

BRONCO, OV-10A Tri-service, multipurpose a/c. Tandem, light weight with Garrett AiResearch engines. Has 4 7.62mm guns and centerline station for 20mm gun pod. OV-10B built for West Germany. OV-10C built for Thailand.

AV-8A, (HARRIER) Ordered for USMC. Hovers and makes 360° turn at same time. Has 7 weapon mounts and 30mm gun. Formerly designated AV-6B.

POPULAR NAMES/SERIES/BUILDER

Name	Series	Builder
ACADEME	TC-4C	GR
ALBATROSS	HU-16	GR
AZTEC	U-11	PA
BEAVER	U-6	DH
BIRD DOG	O-1	CE
BRONCO	OV-10	NH
BUCKEYE	T-2	NH
CHICKASAW	H-19	SI
CONSTELLATION	C-121	LO
CORSAIR II	A-7	CV
COUGAR	F-9	GR
CRUSADER	F-8	CV

Name	Series	Builder
DASH	QH-50	GY
FLYING CLASSROOM	T-29	CO
GREYHOUND	C-2	GR
GULFSTREAM I	C-4	GR
GULFSTREAM II	C-11	GR
HAWKEYE	E-2	GR
HERCULES	C-130	LM
HUEYCOBRA	AH-1	BF
INTRUDER	A-6	GR
IROQUOIS	UH-1	BF

continued

Popular Names/Series/Builder—*continued*

Name	Series	Builder
LIFTMASTER	C-118	DO
MENTOR	T-34	BH
NAVIGATOR	C-45J	BH
NEPTUNE	P-2	LO
ORION	P-3	LO
OTTER	U-1	DH
PACKET	C-119	FA
PANTHER	DF-9E	GR
PHANTOM II	F-4	MC
PROVIDER	C-123	FA
SABRELINER	T-39	NA
SAMARITAN	C-131	CO
SEA KING	H-3	SI
SEA KNIGHT	H-46	BV
SEA STALLION	H-53	SI
SEABAT	H-34G	SI
SEAGUARD	H-52	SI
SEAHORSE	H-34D	SI
SEARANGER	TH-57	BF
SEASPRITE	H-2	KA
SEASTAR	T-1	LO
SHOOTING STAR	T-33	LO
SIOUX	H-13	BF
SKYHAWK	A-4	DO
SKYNIGHT	F-10	DO
SKYMASTER	C-54	DO
SKYRAIDER	A-1	DO
SKYRAY	F-6	DO
SKYTRAIN	C-47	DO
SKYTRAIN	C-117	DO
SKYWARRIOR	A-3	DO
TIGER	F-11	GR
TOMCAT	F-14	GR
TRACER	E-1	GR
TRACKER	S-2	GR
TRADER	C-1	GR
TROJAN	T-28	NH
VIGILANTE	RA-5	NH
WARNING STAR	C-121	LO

NEW/OLD AIRCRAFT DESIGNATIONS

New	Old
AEW	
E-1B	WF-2
E-2A	W2F-1
ASW	
S-2A	S2F-1
TS-2A	S2F-1T
S-2B	S2F-1S
S-2C	S2F-2
RS-2C	S2F-2P
S-2D	S2F-3
S-2E	S2F-3S
S-2F	S2F-1S1
ATTACK	
A-3A	A3D-1
EA-3A	A3D-1Q
RA-3A	A3D-1P
A-3B	A3D-2
EA-3B	A3D-2Q
C-47J	R4D-6
EC-47J	R4D-6Q
TC-47K	R4D-7
VC-54N	R5D-1Z
C-54P	R5D-2
VC-54P	R5D-2Z
C-54Q	R5D-3
VC-54Q	R5D-3Z
C-54R	R5D-4R
C-54S	R5D-5
VC-54S	R5D-5Z
C-54T	R5D-5R
C-117D	R4D-8
LC-117D	R4D-8L
VC-117D	R4D-8Z
TC-117D	R4D-8T
C-118B	R6D-1
VC-118B	R6D-1Z
RF-4B	F4H-1P
F-6A	F4D-1
F-8A	F8U-1
DF-8A	F8U-1D
QF-8A	F8U-1KD
RF-8A	F8U-1P
TF-8A	F8U-1T
F-8B	F8U-1E
F-8C	F8U-2
F-8D	F8U-2N
F-8E	F8U-2NE
QF-9G	F9F-6K2
AF-9J	F9F-8B
TF-9J	F9F-8T
F-10B	F3D-2
EF-10B	F3D-2Q
TF-10B	F3D-2T2
F-11A	F11F-1
SH-34J	HSS-1N
CH-46A	HRB-1
CH-46C	HC-1A
QH-50A	DSN-1
QH-50B	DSN-2
QH-50C	DSN-3
OBSERVATION	
O-1C	OE-2
PATROL	
P-2E	P2V-5F
DP-2E	P2V-5FD
SP-2E	P2V-5FS
P-2H	P2V-7
SP-2H	P2V-7S
P-3A	P3V-1
TRAINER	
T-1A	T2V-1
T-2A	T2J-1

RA-3B	A3D-2P
TA-3B	A3D-2T
A-4A	A4D-1
A-4B	A4D-2
A-4C	A4D-2N
A-4E	A4D-5
A-5A	A3J-1
RA-5C	A3J-3
A-6A	A2F-1
EA-6A	A2F-1H
CARGO TRANSPORT	
RC-45J	SNB-5P
UC-45J	SNB-5
C-47H	R4D-5
LC-47H	R4D-5L
SC-47H	R4D-5S
TC-47H	R4D-5R

C-119F	R4Q-2
C-121J	R7V-1
EC-121K	WV-2
EC-121M	WV-2Q
WC-121N	WV-3
HC-130B	SC-130B
C-130F	GV-1U
KC-130F	GV-1
LC-130F	C-130BL
C-131F	R4Y-1
C-131G	R4Y-2
C-1A	TF-1
EC-1A	TF-1Q
FIGHTER	
F-4A	F4H-1F
F-4B	F4H-1

HELICOPTER	
UH-1B	HU-1B
UH-1E	HU-1E
UH-2A	HU2K-1
UH-2B	HU2K-1U
SH-3A	HSS-2
VH-3A	HSS-2Z
TH-13M	HTL-6
TH-13N	HTL-7
UH-13P	HUL-1
HH-13Q	HUL-1G
CH-19E	HRS-3
LH-34D	HUS-1L
UH-34D	HUS-1
VH-34D	HUS-1Z
UH-34E	HUS-1A

T-2B	T2J-2
T-28B	T-28B
T-28C	T-28C
T-29B	T-29B
T-33B	TV-2
T-39D	T3J-1
UTILITY	
U-1B	UC-1
U-6A	L-20A
U-11A	UO-1
HU-16C	UF-1
LU-16C	UF-1L
HU-16D	UF-2
HU-16E	UF-2G
V/STOL	
XV-6A	VZ-12

AIRCRAFT MANUFACTURERS' CODE

Code	Manufacturer
BF	Bell Helicopter, Fort Worth, Texas.
BH	Beech AC Corp., Wichita, Kansas.
BV	Boeing Co. (Vertol), Morton, Pa.
CE	Cessna AC Company, Wichita, Kansas.
CV	Ling Temco Vought, Dallas, Texas.
DH	De Havilland AC, Toronto, Canada.
DO	McDonnell-Douglas, Santa Monica, California.
FA	Fairchild AC Div., Hagerstown, Maryland.
GR	Grumman AC Div., Bethpage, Long Island, N.Y.
GY	Gyrodyne Company, St. James, Long Island, N.Y.
KA	Kaman AC Corp., Bloomfield, Connecticut.
LM	Lockheed AC Corp., Marietta, Ga.
LO	Lockheed AC Corp., Burbank, Cal.
MC	McDonnell-Douglas, St. Louis, Mo.
NA	North American Aviation, Inglewood, California.
NH	North American Aviation, Columbus, Ohio.
PA	Piper AC Corp., Lockhaven, Pa.
SI	Sikorsky Aircraft Division, Stratford, Connecticut.

AIRCRAFT PHASING OUT (FEW REMAIN) OR PHASED OUT

ATTACK: SKYRAIDER (EA-1F, A-1E, NA-1E, NA-1G.

FIGHTER: FURY (F-1), SKYRAY (F-6A), COUGAR (TAF-9J, QF-9G, QF-9J, TF-9J), SKYNIGHT (F-10B, EF-10B, TF-10B), TIGER (F-11A).

HELICOPTER: SIOUX (H13 series), CHICKASAW (H-19 series).

TRAINER: SHOOTING STAR (T-33B).

E-2A HAWKEYE (left) and E-1B TRACER (right). 12–26–68.

Grumman Aircraft

S-2D TRACKER.

Grumman Aircraft

S-2D TRACKER.

Lockheed Aircraft

S-3A (unnamed).

Arthur L. Schoeni, Ling-Temco-Vought

A-7A CORSAIR II.

Grumman Aircraft

A-6A INTRUDER.

North American Rockwell

RA-5C VIGILANTE.

Grumman Aircraft

EA-6A INTRUDER.

Grumman Aircraft

EA-6B INTRUDER. Note four-seat arrangement.

A-4E SKYHAWK.

A-4F SKYHAWK, tailhook down, approaching CVA-31. Note electronics hump aft of cockpit. 10–22–69.

A-4C SKYHAWK. 7–11–64.

McDonnell Douglas

TA-4J SKYHAWK.

A-4B SKYHAWK. Note ROCKEYE I antitank weapon. 2–20–63.

KA-3B SKYWARRIOR refueling an A-4B SKYHAWK. 3–68.

EA-3B SKYWARRIOR refueling from A-4B SKYHAWK. Note ECM pod on EA-3B's rudder. 10–26–67.

RA-3B SKYWARRIOR. 10–2–64.

McDonnell Douglas

TA-3B SKYWARRIOR.

McDonnell Douglas

A-3B SKYWARRIOR.

Grumman Aircraft

F-111B (unnamed), wings swept.

Grumman Aircraft

F-111B (unnamed).

F-14A TOMCAT.

F-14A TOMCAT.

Arthur L. Schoeni, Ling-Temco-Vought

F-8D CRUSADER.

Arthur L. Schoeni, Ling-Temco-Vought.

F-8J CRUSADER.

Arthur L. Schoeni, Ling-Temco-Vought

NTF-8A CRUSADER, formerly designated TF-8A.

F-8E CRUSADER.

Arthur L. Schoeni, Ling-Temco-Vought

RF-8G CRUSADER, remanufactured from RF-8A.

F-4J PHANTOM II armed with SPARROW missiles.

RF-4B PHANTOM II. Note absence of IFR sensor under the nose. 7–9–65.

McDonnell Douglas

F-4B PHANTOM II.

VC-11A GULFSTREAM II.

VC-4A GULFSTREAM I. 5–17–69.

Grumman Aircraft

TC–4C ACADEME modified from GULFSTREAM I.

C-1A TRADER landing on *Essex* (CVS-9). 4–4–61.

Grumman Aircraft

C-2A GREYHOUND.

C-121J SUPER CONSTELLATION. 11–27–65.

Lockheed Aircraft

EC-12IK WARNING STAR (SUPER CONSTELLATION).

Lockheed Aircraft

EC-130E HERCULES used for LORAN calibration.

Lockheed Aircraft

KC-130F HERCULES.

LC-130F HERCULES. Note ski/wheel under nose. 10–15–60.

C-131 F/G SAMARITAN.

C-123 PROVIDER, in old Coast Guard markings.

McDonnell Douglas

C-118B LIFTMASTER.

C-119F PACKET. 12–12–60.

C-117D SKYTRAIN, a super DC-3 after major redesign.

C-54P SKYMASTER. 1/58.

LC-47H SKYTRAIN.

UH-1B IROQUOIS. 1–68.

Beech Aircraft

C-45 NAVIGATOR, basic model (earlier SNB-2 is similar).

Kaman Aerospace

UH-2A/B SEASPRITE.

Kaman Aerospace

UH-2C SEASPRITE. Note two engine mod.

Kaman Aerospace

HH-2C SEASPRITE. Note chin-mounted turret.

Sikorsky Aircraft

SH-3D SEA KING

Sikorsky Aircraft

HH-3F SEA KING.

Sikorsky Aircraft

RH-3A SEA KING, an airborne minesweeper. USS *Thomas J. Gary* (DER-326) is in background.

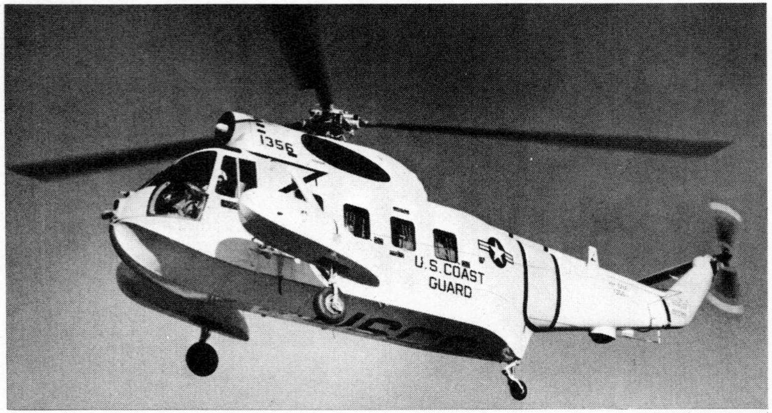

Sikorsky Aircraft

HH-52A SEAGUARD, first amphibious helicopter built with a flying boat-type hull.

Sikorsky Aircraft

SH-34J SEABAT.

UH-46A SEA KNIGHT retrieving an A-4 SKYHAWK.

QH-50 DASH (early version) carrying MK 46 torpedo. 1–65.

Sikorsky Aircraft

CH-53A SEA STALLION.

TH-57A SEARANGER.

SP-2H NEPTUNE. 10–30–65.

Lockheed Aircraft

P-3C ORION.

Bell Aerosystems

X-22A aircraft #2 airborne.

P-3B ORION. Note BULLPUP missiles. 2–13–69.

O-2 BIRD DOG.

XC-142A. This is a composite photo-montage of tri-service research V/STOL transport.

HARRIER V/STOL taking off.

Bensen Aircraft

X-25A Bensen Gyrocopter.

North American Rockwell

T-39D SABRELINER, a radar indoctrination trainer.

North American Aviation

T-28 TROJAN, a land-based basic trainer.

Beech Aircraft

T-34B MENTOR.

North American Aviation

T-28C TROJAN modified for carrier service. Note tailhook.

T-29B FLYING CLASSROOM. 10–28–68.

Lockheed Aircraft

T-1A SEASTAR.

T-2C BUCKEYE. This is the first production model #98.

North American Rockwell

HU-16E ALBATROSS.

U-11A AZTEC. 6–15–61.

U-1B OTTER. 12–65.

U-6A BEAVER. 12/3/66.

The Navy's last attack version of the Douglas SKYRAIDER bows out at Lemoore, California on 4–10–68. VA-25's last A-1H flew against Vietnam targets from *Coral Sea* (CVA-43) and will go to the Naval Air Museum, Pensacola. The ceremony ends 21-plus years of service for this first-line carrier attack plane.

North American Aviation

OV-10A BRONCO.

10. MISSILES AND CONVENTIONAL ORDNANCE

The Department of Defense shifted over to a new missile and rocket identification system on 9–18–62—all hardware already in existence on that date was redesignated. See the last part of this section for an old/new cross-reference list.

Explanation of Missile Letters and Numbers

LAUNCH ENVIRONMENT—a letter indicating the environment from which the vehicle is launched.
MISSION—a letter designating the primary mission of the vehicle.
TYPE VEHICLE—a letter designating the kind of vehicle.
DESIGN NUMBER—a number designating each missile type with the same design.
SERIES SYMBOL—the letter *A* is placed to the right of a new design number. Letters in alphabetical order (except *I* and *O*) denote improvements or modifications on a design.

STATUS PREFIX —a letter indicating that the vehicle is being used for experiments or tests.

Example: TERRIER, RIM-2D

TERRIER is the popular name assigned to that missile family. *R* is the launch environment (ship). *I* is the mission (aerial intercept). *M* is the vehicle type (guided missile). *2* is the design number. *D* is the fourth version of the original design.

Symbols

LAUNCH ENVIRONMENT
- A Air
- B Multiple
- M Mobile
- P Soft pad
- R Ship
- U Underwater

MISSION
- G Surface attack
- I Intercept, aerial
- Q Drone
- T Training
- U Underwater attack

TYPE VEHICLE
- M Guided missile
- N Probe
- R Rocket

STATUS PREFIX
- X Experimental
- Y Prototype
- Z Planning

Abbreviations

- ARM Antiradiation missile
- ER Extended range
- IR Infrared homing
- LPR Liquid propellant rocket
- MR Medium range
- N.A. Not available
- SAR Semiactive homing radar
- SPR Solid propellant rocket

AIR-AIR MISSILES

Number	Name	Manufacturer	Guidance	Type Engine
AIM-7C/D	SPARROW III	Raytheon	SAR	SPR
AIM-7E	SPARROW IIIB	Raytheon	SAR	SPR
AIM-7F	SPARROW MK 38	Raytheon	SAR	SPR
AIM-7G	SPARROW MK 58	Raytheon	SAR	SPR
AIM-9A	SIDEWINDER 1	Philco	IR	SPR
AIM-9B	SIDEWINDER 1A	Philco/G.E.	IR	SPR
AIM-9C	SIDEWINDER 1C	Motorola	SAR	SPR
AIM-9D	SIDEWINDER 1C	Philco	IR	SPR
AIM-54A	PHOENIX	Hughes	Radar Homing	SPR

SPARROW 1 phased out of production; replaced by AIM-7C/D. SPARROW 11 experimental, now deleted. SEA SPARROW data similar to AIM-7E; part of BPMDS.

SIDEWINDER: AIM-9A is SIDEWINDER 1. AIM-9B is 1A (Navy/Air Force). SIDEWINDER 1B was never operational. AIM-9C is SIDEWINDER 1C with SARAH (semiactive radar alternate head). AIM-9D is SIDEWINDER 1C with IRAH (infrared alternate head). AIM-9E is modified AIM-9B for USAF. AIM-9F is modified AIM-9B, German model. AIM-9G is AIM-9D with SEAM (SIDEWINDER expanded acquisition mode). YAIM-9H is AIM-9G with solid state GCG (guidance control group). AIM-9I, not used. AIM-9J is modified AIM-9B for USAF. ZAIM-9K is new GCG (Navy).

PHOENIX AGM-54A for F-111B and F-14A aircraft.

AIR-SURFACE MISSILES

AGM-12B	BULLPUP A	Martin/Maxson	Radio	LPR
AGM-12C	BULLPUP B	Martin	Radio	LPR
ATM-12A	BULLPUP TRAINER	Martin Marietta	N.A.	N.A.
ATM-12B	BULLPUP TRAINER	Maxson	Radio	N.A.
AGM-45A	SHRIKE	Texas Inst.	ARM	SPR
AGM-53A	CONDOR	No. American	TV	LPR
AGM-62A	WALLEYE	Martin/Hughes	TV	none
AGM-78A/B	STANDARD ARM	G.D., Pomona	Passive Homing	SPR

BULLPUP A AGM-12B has nose-mounted control planes, 250# warhead. BULLPUP B AGM-12C has 1,000# warhead. SHRIKE AGM-45A four-section missile senses/homes on enemy radar emissions. CONDOR AGM-53A is a 'launch and leave' missile for A-6 INTRUDER. WALLEYE AGM-62A is a TV-guided glide bomb; homes on enemy operating radar. STANDARD ARM AGM-78A/B is an anti-radar missile. FAT ALBERT is similar to WALLEYE, but heavier and with larger warhead.

SURFACE-AIR MISSILES

RIM-2D	TERRIER	G.D., Pomona	Beam-rider	SPR
RIM-2F	TERRIER	G.D., Pomona	Semiactive homing	SPR
RIM-8A/H	TALOS	Bendix	Semiactive homing	RJ
RIM-24A/C	TARTAR	G.D., Pomona	SAR	SPR
RIM-66A/B	STANDARD MR	G.D., Pomona	Semiactive homing	SPR
RIM-67A/B	STANDARD ER	G.D., Pomona	Semiactive homing	SPR

TERRIER RIM-2 series is employed on CLG-6/8, CGN-9, CVA-63/64,66, and DLG-6/35. TALOS RIM-8 series is employed on CLG-3/5, CGN-9, and CG-10/12. RIM-8H (ARM) is an antiradiation version. TARTAR RIM-24 series is employed on DDG-2/24, 31/36, DEG-1/6, and CG-10/12. STANDARD MR RIM-66 series is to replace TARTAR. STANDARD ER RIM-67 series is to replace TERRIER. ZRIM-85A (planning) is a medium range surface-air missile for use against attack aircraft, air-surface/surface-surface missiles, and surface targets. ZRGM-59A is a landing support weapon; surface-surface.

GROUND-LAUNCHED MISSILES

MIM-23A	HAWK	Raytheon	Semiactive homing	SPR
MIM-43A	REDEYE	G.D., Pomona	Infrared	SPR

HAWK MIM-23A is a USMC low-altitude air defense weapon. REDEYE MIM-43A used by USMC; weapon is shoulder-fired from a bazooka.

SUBMARINE-LAUNCHED MISSILES

Number	Name	Manufacturer	Guidance	Type Engine
UGM-27B/C	POLARIS A2/3	Lockheed	Inertial	SPR
UUM-44A	SUBROC	Goodyear	Inertial	SPR
UGM-73A	POSEIDON	Lockheed	Inertial	SPR

POLARIS UGM-27 series: UGM-27A (A-1) retired from service late 1965; missile portions utilized in missile/space programs; UGM-27B (A-2) being replaced by POSEIDON. SUBROC UUM-44A is a submarine-launched nuclear depth bomb. POSEIDON UGM-73A has 10 nuclear warheads for 10 targets per one missile. Eventually for all SSBN-616 class.

TARGET MISSILES/DRONES

Number	Name	Manufacturer	Guidance	Type Engine
BQM-34A	FIREBEE	Ryan	Radio	Jet
BQM-34E	FIREBEE II	Ryan	Radio	Jet
MQM-36A	(none)	Northrop	Radio	Prop.
AQM-37A	(none)	Beech	Program	LPR
AQM-38B	(none)	Northrop	Radio	SPR
MQM-74A	CHUKAR	Northrop	Radio	Jet

FIREBEE BQM-34A is a swept-wing target missile; also tows targets. AQM-34B/C also in the series. BQM-34E (new) simulates supersonic enemy aircraft; parachute recovery and flotation capability. AQM-37A is a decoy and target; also has limited reconnaissance capability. MQM-39A is a prop-driven drone; not listed in above tables; status uncertain. PQM-56A is produced by Nord Aviation of France; no data available. CHUKAR MQM-74A (new) is a recoverable gunnery drone; ship or shore JATO-launched.

ANTISUBMARINE ROCKETS

Number	Name	Manufacturer	Guidance	Type Engine
RUR-4A	WEAPON ALPHA		(none)	
RUR-5A	ASROC	Honeywell		SPR

WEAPON ALPHA RUR-4A was formerly WEAPON ABLE; phasing out. ASROC RUR-5A can be used as homing torpedo or nuclear depth bomb. Modified ASROC can be fired from MK 10 MOD 7/8 TERRIER launcher and new MK 26 TARTAR launcher.

GROUND LAUNCHED ROCKETS

Number	Name	Manufacturer	Guidance	Type Engine
MGR-1A/B	HONEST JOHN	Douglas	(none)	SPR
MGR-3A	LITTLE JOHN	Emerson	(none)	SPR

Both are unguided artillery rockets.

MISSILE DATA

Number	Name	OAL	Span Fins	Body Diam.	Launch Weight	Range in miles	Max. Speed
AIR TO AIR MISSILES							
AIM-7C/D	SPARROW III	12'0"	3'2"	8"	350	5+	M3
AIM-7E	SPARROW IIIB	12'0"	3'4"	8"	450	12	M2.5
AIM-9A	SIDEWINDER 1	9'2"	1'9"	5"	159	2	M2.5
AIM-9B	SIDEWINDER 1A	9'5"	2'0"	5"	160	2	M2+
AIM-9C/D	SIDEWINDER 1C	9'6"	2'2"	5"	185	10	M2+
AIM-54A	PHOENIX	13'0"	3'0"	1'3"	838	30+	M2+
AIR TO SURFACE MISSILES							
AGM-12B	BULLPUP A	11'0"	3'4"	1'0"	571	6+	M1.8
AGM-12C	BULLPUP B	13'7"	4'0"	1'6"	1,785	8+	M2+
AGM-45A	SHRIKE	10'0"	3'0"	8"	390	8+	N.A.
AGM-53A	CONDOR	N.A.	N.A.	N.A.	N.A.	30+	N.A.
AGM-62A	WALLEYE	11'4"	3'9"	1'9"	1,100	N.A.	N.A.
AGM-78A	STANDARD ARM	15'0"	3'7"	1'1½"	1,350	N.A.	M1+
AGM-78B	STANDARD ARM	14'0"	3'7"	1'1½"	1,300	N.A.	M1+
SURFACE TO AIR MISSILES							
RIM-2D/F	TERRIER	26'6"	5'3"	1'2"	3,070	20+	M2.5
RIM-8E	TALOS	33'6"	9'0"	2'6"	7,700	65+	M2.5+
RIM-8G	TALOS	33'6"	9'0"	2'6"	7,700	65+	M2.5+
RIM-24B/C	TARTAR	14'10"	3'6"	1'1½"	1,300	10+	M2.5+
RIM-66A/B	STANDARD MR	15'0"	3'6"	1'1½"	1,300	12+	M2.5+
RIM 67A/B	STANDARD ER	27'0"	5'2"	1'1½"	3,000	30+	M2.5+
GROUND-LAUNCHED MISSILES							
MIM-23A	HAWK	16'6"	3'11"	1'2"	1,295	22	M2.5
MIM-43A	REDEYE	4'0"	4"	3"	20	N.A.	N.A.
SUBMARINE BASED MISSILES							
UGM-27B	POLARIS A2	31'0"	none	4'6"	30,000	1,725	M5/10
UGM-27C	POLARIS A3	32'0"	none	4'6"	35,000	2,880	M5/10
UUM-44A	SUBROC	20'6"	1'9"	1'9"	4,000	N.A.	N.A.
UGM-73A	POSEIDON	34'0"	none	6'2"	60,000	2,800+	N.A.
TARGET MISSILES/DRONES							
BQM-34A	FIREBEE	22'11"	12'11"	3'10"	2,500	900	M.96
BQM-34E	FIREBEE 2	28'3"	8'11"	2'1"	2,300	805	M1.8
MQM-36A	(none)	13'7"	11'6"	2'7"	327	90	220
AQM-37A	(none)	13'6"	3'4"	1'1"	565	100+	M3+
AQM-38B	(none)	9'8"	5'0"	1'0"	301	30	M1+
MQM-74A	CHUKAR	11'4"	5'7"	1'2"	317	400+	460
ROCKETS							
RUR-4A	WEAPON ALPHA	8'6"	N.A.	1'1"	500	N.A.	N.A.
RUR-5A	ASROC	15'0"	2'6"	1'0"	1,000	N.A.	M1
XAGR-14A	ZAP	8'9"	1'2"	6"	170	N.A.	N.A.
BATTLEFIELD SUPPORT ROCKETS							
MGR-1A	HONEST JOHN	27'3"	9'1"	2'6"	5,820	10	M1.5
MGR-1B	HONEST JOHN	26'0"	4'6"	2'6"	4,719	10+	M1.5
MGR-3A	LITTLE JOHN	14'5"	1'11"	1'1½"	780	10	N.A.

ROCKET SERIES—DESIGN NUMBER AND POPULAR NAMES*

No.	F/S	Name
1	M/A	HONEST JOHN
2	F	GENIE
3	M/A	LITTLE JOHN
4	N	WEAPON ALPHA
5	N	ASROC
6	F	
7	F	
8	F	
9	F	
10	F	
11	F	
12	F	
13	F	
14	N	ZAP

* A–Army. F–Air Force. N–Navy/Marines. M–Marines.

MISSILE SERIES—DESIGN NUMBER AND POPULAR NAMES*

No.	F/S	Name
1	F	MATADOR
2	N	TERRIER
3	A	NIKE AJAX
4	F	FALCON
6	N	REGULUS I
7	N/F	SPARROW
8	N	TALOS
9	N/F	SIDEWINDER
10	F	BOMARC
12	N/F	BULLPUP
13	F	MACE
14	A	NIKE HERCULES
15	N	REGULUS II
16	F	ATLAS
17	F	THOR
20	F	QUAIL
22	A	SS II
23	A/M	HAWK
24	N	TARTAR
25	F	TITAN
26	F	FALCON
27	N	POLARIS
28	F	HOUND DOG
29	A	SERGEANT
30	F	MINUTEMAN
31	A	PERSHING
32	A	ENTAC
33	A/F	(drone)
34	N/F	FIREBEE
35	N/F	(TALOS trainer)
36	N	(drone)
37	N	(drone)
38	N/F	(drone)
39	N/A/F	CARDINAL
41	N	PETREL
42	A/M	REDHEAD/ ROADRUNNER
43	A/M	REDEYE
44	N	SUBROC
45	N/F	SHRIKE
46	N	SEA MAULER
47	F	FALCON
49	A	NIKE ZEUS
50	N	TYPHON LR
51	A	SHILLELAGH
52	A	LANCE
53	N	CONDOR
54	N	PHOENIX
55	N	TYPHON MR
56	N	(drone)
57	A	(drone)
58	A	OVERSEER
59	N	(support)
60	A	KINGFISHER
61	A	CARDINAL
62	N	WALLEYE
63	N	(planning)
64	F	HORNET
65	F	MAVERICK
66	N	STANDARD MR
67	N	STANDARD ER
69	F	SRAM
71	A	TOW
72	A/M	CHAPARRAL
73	N	POSEIDON
74	N	CHUKAR
76	F	(new)
77	A	DRAGON
78	N/F	STANDARD ARM
79	F	(new)
80	F	VIPER
81	F	(new)
82	F	(new)
85	N	(planning)

* A–Army. F–Air Force. N–Navy/Marines. M–Marines.

POPULAR NAMES—MISSILES ROCKETS

Name	Designation
ASROC	RUR-5
BULLPUP	AGM-12
CARDINAL	MQM-39*
CHUKAR	MQM-74
CONDOR	AGM-53
FIREBEE	AQM-34
HAWK	MIM-23
HONEST JOHN	MGR-1
PETREL	AQM-41†
PHOENIX	AIM-54
POLARIS	UGM-27
POSEIDON	UGM-73
REDEYE	MIM-43
REGULUS I	RGM-6†
REGULUS II	RGM-15†
SEA MAULER	RIM-46†
SHRIKE	AGM-45
SIDEWINDER	AIM-9
SPARROW	AIM-7
STANDARD (MR)	RIM-66
STANDARD (ER)	RIM-67
SUBROC	UUM-44
TALOS	RIM-8
TARTAR	RIM-24
TAURUS	RGM-59*
TERRIER	RIM-2
TYPHON (LR)	RIM-50†
TYPHON (MR)	RIM-55†
WALLEYE	AGM-62
WEAPON ALPHA	RUR-4

* Status not known; presume phased out/ cancelled.

† Phased out/cancelled.

NEW/OLD MISSILE DESIGNATIONS

New	Old	New	Old	New	Old	New	Old
RIM-2A	SAM-N-7	AIM-7E	AAM-N-6B	AGM-12B	ASM-N-7A	AQM-37A	KD2B-1
RIM-2B	SAM-N-7	RIM-8A	SAM-N-6B	ATM-12B	ASM-N-7A	AQM-38B	RP-78
RIM-2C	SAM-N-7	RIM-8B	SAM-N-6BW	AGM-12C	ASM-N-7B	MQM-39A	KDB-1
RIM-2D	SAM-N-7	RIM-8C	SAM-N-6B1	RGM-15A	SSM-N-9	XQM-40A	KD6G-2
RIM-2E	SAM-N-7	RIM-8D	SAM-N-6BW1	MQM-15A	KD2U-1	AQM-41A	AUM-N-2
RGM-6A	SSM-N-8	RIM-8E	SAM-N-6C1	MIM-23A	M3	AGM-45A	ASM-N-10
RGM-6B	SSM-N-8A	RIM-8F	SAM-N-6B1-CW	RIM-24A	SAM-N-7	RIM-50A	SAM-N-8
BQM-6C	KDU-1	AIM-9A	AAM-N-7	RIM-24B	SAM-N-7	AGM-53A	ASM-N-11
AIM-7A	AAM-N-2	AIM-9B	AAM-N-7	BQM-34A	Q-2C	AIM-54A	AAM-N-11
AIM-7B	AAM-N-3	AIM-9C	AAM-N-7	AQM-34B	KDA-1	RIM-55A	SAM-N-9
AIM-7C	AAM-N-6	AIM-9D	AAM-N-7	AQM-34C	KDA-4	PQM-56A	CT-41
AIM-7D	AAM-N-6A	ATM-12A	ASM-N-7	MQM-36A	KD2R-5		

CONVENTIONAL ORDNANCE

Guns	Mark/Mod.	Barrel Weight in Pounds	Barrel Length in Inches	Range in Yards	Rounds per Minute per Mount
BARRELS					
16"/50	7/0	239,156	800·0	42,345	—
8"/55	15/	37,500	440·0	30,400	—
8"/55	16/	37,500	440·0	30,400	—
6"/47	16/	11,000	282·0	26,040	—
5"/54	16/	5,600	270·0	25,900	—
5"/54	19/	3,560	270·0	25,900	—
5"/38	12/1	4,000	190·0	17,300	—
3"/50	22/0	1,240	150·0	14,000	—
MOUNTS					
5"/54	42/	—	—	25,900	40
5"/54	45/	—	—	25,900	20
3"/50[1]	33/0	—	—	14,000	50
3"/50[2]	34/0	—	—	14,000	50
40mm[3]	1/16.3 & 4	202	88·6	10,850	140-160
MACHINE GUNS					
20mm	—	26·2	52·5	4,800	850
.50 cal.	M2HB	28·0	45·0	7,000	550

[1] Twin mount. [2] Single mount. [3] Quad mount. There is also a Mark 2 (twin-barrel) mount and a Mark 3 (single-barrel).

AIM-7 SPARROW III, launched by PHANTOM II. 8–13–64.

RIM-7 SEA SPARROW, launched from *Tioga County* (LST-1158) during tests. 10–5–65.

AIM-9 SIDEWINDER family from top to bottom: IA (AIM-9B), IC (AIM-9D), and IC (AIM-9C). 3–19–64.

Hughes Aircraft

AIM-54A PHOENIX.

Martin Marietta

AGM-12C BULLPUP carried by A-4 SKYHAWK.

AGM-62A WALLEYE undergoing aerodynamic tests. 2–7–64.

AGM-45A SHRIKE launched by A-4 SKYHAWK. 10–6–65.

RIM-2 TERRIER on *Kitty Hawk* (CVA-63). 9–24–61.

RIM-24 TARTAR.

RIM-8 TALOS launched from *Galveston* (CLG-3).

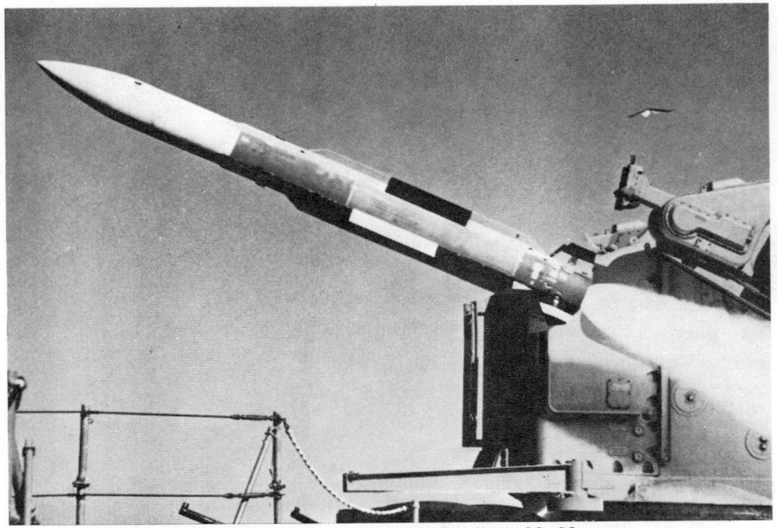

RIM-66 STANDARD launched by *Buchanan* (DDG-14). 1–30–68.

Westinghouse

A-3 POLARIS/C-3 POSEIDON installation details.

A-3 POLARIS fired from underwater. 9–17–64.

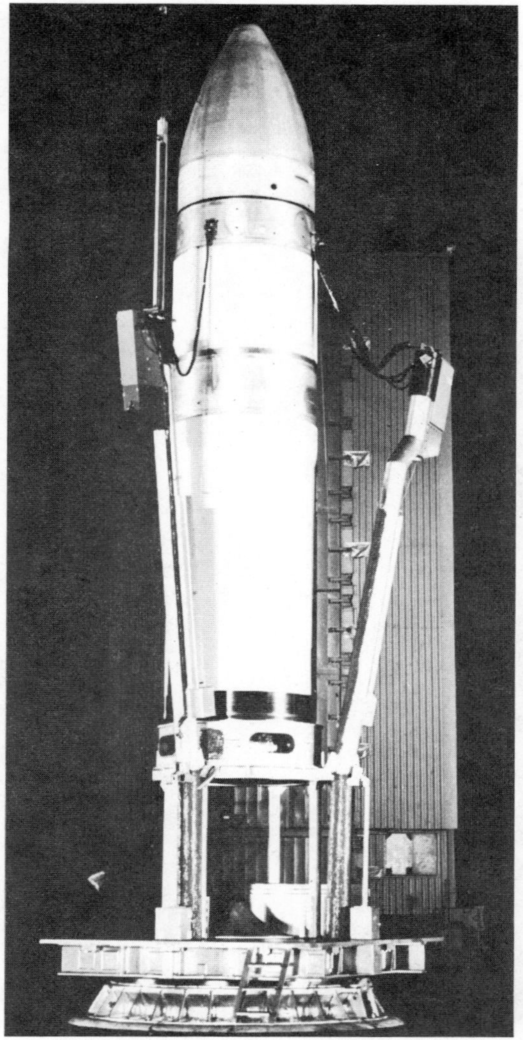

C-3 POSEIDON during prelaunch activities. 8–16–68.

Goodyear Aerospace

UUM-44A SUBROC being loaded aboard *Permit* (SSN-594).

Northrop Ventura

MQM-36A, a propeller-driven target drone.

Arthur L. Schoeni, Ling-Temco-Vought

MQM-15A REGULUS II, a wheeled drone.

Northrop Ventura

MQM-74A CHUKAR.

Ryan

BQM-34A FIREBEE.

Beech Aircraft

AQM-37A mounted on a PHANTOM F-4.

RUR-5A ASROC airborne. 5–18–65.

11. U.S. COAST GUARD

The United States Coast Guard was established by an Act of Congress on 28 January 1915, combining the functions of the Revenue Cutter Service and the Lifesaving Service. On 1 July 1939, the Lighthouse Service was absorbed by the Coast Guard. Originally under Treasury Department control, the Coast Guard, on 1 April 1967, passed on to the newly formed Department of Transportation. In time of national emergency, or when the President so directs, the Coast Guard operates under the operational control of the Navy.

By end FY–1971, the Coast Guard Register listed 310 vessels of various types, sizes, and shapes. A summary of these vessels follows:

High Endurance Cutter (WHEC)	36
Icebreaker (WAGB)	10
Medium Endurance Cutter (WMEC)	22
Patrol Craft, Large (WPB)	26
Patrol Craft, Small (WPB)	53
Harbor Tug, Medium (WYTM)	14
Harbor Tug, Small (WYTL)	15
Oceanographic Cutter (WAGO)	3
Cargo Cutter (WAK)	1
Buoy Tender, Seagoing (WLB)	39
Buoy Tender, Coastal (WLM)	17
Buoy Tender, Inland (WLI)	22
Construction Tender, Inland (WLIC)	10
Buoy Tender, River (WLR)	25
Lightship (WLV)	11
Training Cutter (WIX)	2
Reserve Training Cutter (WTR)	4

The above figures include those vessels under construction. A conventionally powered WAGB is requested under USCG FY–1971 program as part of long-range plan to replace all the "Wind" class icebreakers.

It should be mentioned that, unlike the Navy, the Coast Guard officially refers to all classes by the vessels' length. In conformity with this publication, each class is listed by the name of the ship that has the lowest hull number within the class. In a few cases, the lowest hull number of the class remaining on the Register is used. Because of their inland stations, river buoy tenders (WLR) in text carry the status symbol "IW,A" to signify "inland waters, active;" this is not to be confused with inland waterways.

Class	Number	No. in Class	Displ.	Length Overall	Draft	Beam	Type of Propulsion	Screws/ SHP	Max. Speed (Kts)	Allowance Officers	Enlisted	Armament
Hamilton	WHEC-715	12	3,050	378′	20′	42′	2D(F.M.), 2 P.W. Gas Turbines	2/36,000	29	15	137	1 5″/38, 2 81mm mortars, 4 .50 cal. mg., 2 triple TT (MK.32).
Bibb	WHEC-31	6	2,414	327′	15′	41′	2B(B.W.), G.T.(West.)	2/6,200	19·8	13	131	1 5″/38, 2 81mm mortars, 4 .50 cal. mg.
"Casco"	WHEC-370	6	2,800	311′	14′	41′	4D(F.M.)#38D81/8	2/6,080	19	13	137	1 5″/38, 2 81mm mortars, 4 .50 cal. mg.
Owasco	WHEC-39	12	1,913	255′	17′	43′	2B(F.W.)Turbine Elect.(West.)	1/4,000	18·4	13	127	1 5″/38, 2 81mm mortars, 4 .50 cal. mg.
Glacier	WAGB-4	1	8,449	310′	29′	74′	10D(F.M.), 2 West. EM.	2/21,000	17·6	14	216	4 .50 cal. mg.
Mackinaw	WAGB-83	1	5,252	290′	19′	74′	6D(F.M.), 3 West. EM.	3/10,000	18·7	10	117	Unarmed
"Wind"	WAGB-278	7	6,515	269′	29′	64′	6D(F.M.), 2 West. EM.	2/10,000	16	14	167	4 .50 cal. mg.
Storis	WAGB-38	1	1,925	230′	15′	43′	3D(C.B.), 1 West. EM.	1/1,800	14	10	96	1 3″/50, 2 .50 cal. mg.
Yocona	WMEC-168	1	1,745	213′	15′	41′	2D(C.B.)#GSB-8	2/3,000	15·5	7	65	2 .50 cal. mg.
Reliance	WMEC-615	5	970	211′	10′	34′	2D/ALCO), 2 Solar Gas Turbines	2/5,000	18	7	54	1 3″/50, 2 .50 cal. mg.
Resolute	WMEC-620	11	1,007	211′	10′	34′	2D(ALCO)	2/5,000	18	7	54	1 3″/50, 2 .50 cal. mg.
"Avoyel"	WMEC-150	3	1,731	205′	17′	39′	1D(Cleveland)#12-278A	1/3,000	16·2	7	65	1 3″/50, 2 .50 cal. mg.
Modoc	WMEC-194	2	860	143′	14′	34′	1D(Cleveland)#12-278A	1/1,500	13·5	5	42	2 .50 cal. mg.

"*Cape*" (A)	WPB-95300	12	105	95′	6′	20′	4D(Cummins) # VT12-600M	2/2,324	20	1	13	1 81mm mortar, 1 .50 cal. mg. (# 95300/02, 95304 have only 2 .50 cal. mg.)
"*Cape*" (B)	WPB-95312	8	105	95′	6′	20′	4D(Cummins) # VT12-600M	2/2,324	20	1	13	1 81mm mortar, 1 .50 cal. mg. (# 95314, 18/19 have only 2 .50 cal. mg.)
"*Cape*" (C)	WPB-95321	6	105	95′	6′	20′	4D(Cummins) # VT12-600M	2/2,324	21	1	13	1 81mm mortar, 1 .50 cal. mg. (# 95326, 95328 have only 2 .50 cal. mg.)
"*Point*" (C)	WPB-82302	44	67	83′	6′	18′	2D(Cummins) # VT12-900M	2/1,600	20	0	8	1 81mm mortar, 1 .50 cal. mg. (# 82318, 34/35, 82338/40, 43 have only 2 .50 cal. mg.)
"*Point*" (D)	WPB-82371	9	67	83′	6′	18′	2D(Cummins) # VT12-900M	2/1,600	20	0	8	2 .50 cal. mg.
Manitou	WYTM-60	9	370	110′	11′	27′	Ingersol-Rand Type S	1/1,000	11·2	1	19	Unarmed
Arundel	WYTM-90	4	370	110′	11′	27′	Ingersoll-Rand Type S	1/1,000	11·2	1	19	Unarmed
Messenger	WYTM-85009	1	230	85′	9′	23′	Enterprise DMG-38	1/700	9·5	0	10	Unarmed
Capstan	WYTL-65601	6	72	65′	7′	19′	1D(Caterpiller) # D375-D	1/400	9·8	0	10	Unarmed
Bridle	WYTL-65607	3	72	65′	7′	19′	1D(Waukesha) # LRD-BSM	1/400	9·8	0	10	Unarmed
Hawser	WYTL-65610	3	72	65′	7′	19′	1D(Waukesha) # LRD-BSM	1/400	9·8	0	10	Unarmed
Bitt	WYTL-65613	3	72	65′	7′	19′	1D(Caterpiller) # D379-D	1/400	9·8	0	10	Unarmed
Rockaway	WAGO-377	1	2,800	311′	14′	41′	4D(F.M.) # 38D81/8	2/6,080	19	13	107	2 81mm mortars, 4 .50 cal. mg.
Acushnet	WAGO-167	1	1,745	213′	15′	41′	2D(C.B.) # G8B8 Stand.	2/3,000	15·5	7	57	Unarmed
Evergreen	WAGO-295	1	1,025	180′	13′	37′	2D(C.B.) # GN8-600, 1 EM (West.)	1/1,000	12·8	6	51	2 .50 cal. mg.
Kukui	WAK-186	1	5,636	339′	18′	50′	Nordberg Diesel	1/1,700	11	12	95	Unarmed
Magnolia	WLB-328	1	1,240	189′	13′	38′	Steam Engine	2/1,200	11·3	5	47	Unarmed
Balsam	WLB-62	12	1,025	180′	13′	37′	2D(C.B.) # GN8-600, 1 EM (West.)	1/1,000	12·8	6	47	2 .50 cal. mg. (277, 296, 300 have 1 3″/50 only. 289, 303 are unarmed).
Ironwood	WLB-297	6	1,025	180′	13′	37′	2D(C.B.) # GN8-700, 1 EM (West.)	1/1,200	13	6	47	2 .50 cal. mg. (305 is unarmed)
Basswood	WLB-388	20	1,025	180′	13′	37′	2D(C.B.) # GN8-700, 1 EM (West.)	1/1,200	13	6	47	2 .50 cal. mg. (394, 402 have 1 3″/50 only. 392 398, 404, 406/7 are unarmed)
Juniper	WLM-224	1	794	177′	9′	33′	2D(C.B.) # GN-6	2/900	10·8	4	34	Unarmed
Fir	WLM-212	3	989	175′	12′	34′	2D(F.M.) # 38D8-1/8	2/1,350	12	5	35	Unarmed
Lilac	WLM-227	1	997	173′	12′	34′	Steam Engine	2/1,000	11·5	4	32	Unarmed
Red Wood	WLM-685	5	512	157′	6′	33′	2D(Caterpiller) # D398A	2/1,800	12·8	4	27	Unarmed
White Sumac	WLM-540	7	600	133′	9′	31′	2D(Union) Model 06	2/600	9·8	1	20	Unarmed
"*Tamarack*"	WLI-248	0	400	124′	8′	30′	Diesels	1/520	10			Unarmed
Maple	WLI-234	3	375	122′	8′	28′	2D(G.M.) # 8268	2/800	10	1	19	Unarmed
Cosmos	WLI-293	7	178	100′	5′	24′	2D(Caterpiller) # D353	2/600	10·5	1	14	Unarmed
Azalea	WLI-641	1	200	100′	5′	24′	2D(G.M.)	2/440	9·0	1	13	Unarmed
Buckthorn	WLI-642	1	200	100′	4′	24′	2D(Caterpiller) # 353D	2/600	10·9	1	13	Unarmed
Tern	WLI-80801	1	168	80′	5′	25′	2D(G.M.)	2/450	10	1	19	Unarmed
Clematis	WLI-74286	2	93	74′	4′	19′	2D(G.M.) # 6-71	2/330	8·0	0	9	Unarmed
Elm	WLI-72260	1	78	72′	5′	17′	Diesels	2/330	9·4			Unarmed
Blueberry	WLI-65302	1	45	65′	4′	17′	2D(G.M.) # 6-71	2/330	10·5	0	5	Unarmed

continued

U.S. Coast Guard—*continued*

Class	Number	No. in Class	Displ.	Length Overall	Draft	Beam	Type of Propulsion	Screws/ SHP	Max. Speed (Kts)	Allowance Officers	Enlisted	Armament
Blackberry	WLI-65303	3	68	65′	4′	17′	2D(G.M.)#6-110	1/220	9·0	0	5	Unarmed
Bayberry	WLI-65400	2	68	65′	4′	17′	2D(G.M.)#6-110	2/440	11·3	0	5	Unarmed
Anvil	WLIC-75301	2	145	75′	4′	22′	2D(Caterpiller)#D-353	2/600	10	0	9	Unarmed
Sledge	WLIC-75303	3	145	75′	4′	22′	2D(Caterpiller)#D-353	2/600	10	1	9	Unarmed
Clamp	WLIC-75306	5	145	76′	4′	22′	2D(Waukeska)#F1905-DSIM	2/600	10·2	0	9	Unarmed
Fern	WLR-304	2	315	115′	6′	31′	3D(F.M.)#35F10A	3/960	10·7	1	22	Unarmed
Forsythia	WLR-63	4	280	114′	4′	26′	2D(G.M.)#8-268	2/800	11	1	20	Unarmed
Goldenrod	WLR-213	2	235	104′	4′	24′	2D(G.M.)#8-268A	2/800	11·5	1	16	Unarmed
Lantana	WLR-80310	1	235	80′	6′	30′	3D(Murphy)#ME-650	3/450	10	1	19	Unarmed
Gasconade	WLR-75401	9	145	75′	4′	22′	2D(Caterpiller)#D353	2/600	10·8	0	12	Unarmed
Oleander	WLR-73264	1	90	73′	5′	18′	2D(G.M.) Gray#G71	2/300	12	0	10	Unarmed
Ouachita	WLR-65501	6	139	66′	5′	21′	2D(Waukesha)	2/600	12·5	0	10	Unarmed
Nantucket	WLV-534	1	1,100	149′	16′	32′	1D(C.B.)#GSB-8	1/900	9	1	19	Unarmed
"San Francisco"	WLV-523	3	630	133′	13′	30′	1D(G.M.)#8-268, 1 EM (West.)	1/350	8	1	15	Unarmed
New Orleans	WLV-189	5	600	128′	11′	30′	1D(G.M.)#6-2678	1/600	9	1	15	Unarmed
Boston	WLV-539	1	449	115′	13′	26′	1D(C.B.)#GN-8	1/300	9	1	14	Unarmed
Lake Huron	WLV-526	1	340	97′	10′	24′	Diesel	1/340	10			Unarmed
Eagle	WIX-327	1	1,784	295′	17′	40′	Sail and aux. diesel	1/700	10·5			Unarmed
Cuyahoga	WIX-157	1	290	125′	8′	24′	Diesels	1/800	13·2	1	10	Unarmed
Courier	WTR-410	1	7,500	339′	18′	50′	1D(Nordberg)#82D	1/1,700	11	10	45	Unarmed
Unimak	WTR-379	1	2,800	311′	14′	41′	4D(F.M.)#38D81/8	2/6,080	19	12	79	1 5″/38, 2 81mm mortar 4 .50 cal. mg.
Tanager	WTR-885	1	1,077	221′	14′	32′	2D(G.M.)#12-278A	2/3,474	17·5	6	41	Unarmed
Lamar	WTR-899	1	881	184′	9′	33′	2D(G.M.)#12-278A	2/2,000	15·4			1 3″/50

12 HIGH ENDURANCE CUTTERS, *HAMILTON (378′)* CLASS

Name	Completed	Number	F/S	Name	Completed	Number	F/S	Name	Completed	Number	F/S
Midgett		WHEC-726	AA	*Morgenthau*	2–69	WHEC-722	AA	*Chase*	3–68	WHEC-718	AA
Jarvis		WHEC-725	PA	*Gallatin*	12–68	WHEC-721	AA	*Mellon*	12–67	WHEC-717	PA
Munroe		WHEC-724	AA	*Sherman*	8–68	WHEC-720	AA	*Dallas*	10–67	WHEC-716	AA
Rush	7–69	WHEC-723	PA	*Boutwell*	6–68	WHEC-719	AA	*Hamilton*	2–67	WHEC-715	AA

Authorized as WPGs; to WHECs 5–1–66; 33 projected. Replacing *Casco* class cutters. Have oceanographic facilities, elaborate communications, meteorological data-collecting facilities, clipper bow, helicopter platform and hanger between the 2 side-by-side funnels. Largest USCG/USN ships to be fitted with gas turbine propulsion. All built by Avondale.

6 HIGH ENDURANCE CUTTERS, *BIBB (327')* CLASS

Name	Number	F/S	Name	Number	F/S	Name	Number	F/S
Taney (ex-*Roger B.*)	WHEC-37	PA	*Ingham* (ex-*Samuel D.*)	WHEC-35	AA	*Campbell* (ex-*George W.*)	WHEC-32	AA
Spencer (ex-*John C.*)	WHEC-36	AA	*Duane* (ex-*William J.*)	WHEC-33	AA	*Bibb* (ex-*George M.*)	WHEC-31	AA

Completed 1936–37 as WPGs; to WHEC on 5–1–66. Originally named with full name of Treasury Secretary; first name and middle initial dropped soon after completion. Seventh ship of class, *Hamilton* (ex-*Alexander*) (WPG-34), lost in WW II.

6 HIGH ENDURANCE CUTTERS/WEATHER SHIP, *"CASCO" (311')* CLASS

Gresham (ex AVP-57)	WAGW-387	AA	*Cook Inlet* (ex AVP-36)	WHEC-384	AA	*Chincoteague* (ex AVP-24)	WHEC-375	AA
McCulloch (ex AVP-56)	WHEC-386	AA	*Castle Rock* (ex AVP-35)	WHEC-383	AA	*Abescon* (ex AVP-23)	WHEC-374	AA

Originally completed 1942–44 as AVPs in USN *Barnegat* class (except WHEC-386/7 were completed as *Wachapreague*, AGP-8 and *Willoughby*, AGP-9). Acquired on loan 1947–49 and rated WAVP. WHEC-386/7 loans made permanent shortly after transfer; remainder 10–66. All WAVPs to WHEC on 5–1–66. Originally 18 in class; 8 were disposed of 1967–70 and 2 transferred to Vietnam. WHEC-387 rerated weather ship 1969. Two others serve as WAGO and WTR.

12 HIGH ENDURANCE CUTTERS, *OWASCO (255')* CLASS

Ponchartrain (ex-*Okeechobe*)	WHEC-70	PA	*Klamath*	WHEC-66	PA	*Sebago* (ex-*Wachusett*)	WHEC-42	AA
Mendota	WHEC-69	AA	*Winona*	WHEC-65	PA	*Chatauqua*	WHEC-41	PA
Androscoggin	WHEC-68	AA	*Escanaba* (ex-*Otsego*)	WHEC-64	AA	*Winnebago*	WHEC-40	PA
Minnetonka (ex-*Sunapee*)	WHEC-67	PA	*Wachusett* (ex-*Huron*)	WHEC-44	PA	*Owasco*	WHEC-39	AA

Completed 1945–46 as WPGs; originally 13 in class (*Iroquois*, WPG-43 disposed of 1965).

1 ICEBREAKER, *GLACIER (310')* CLASS

Glacier (ex-USN AGB-4)	WAGB-4	PA

Commissioned in USN 5–27–55 as AGB-4. Struck from NVR, transferred to USCG, and commissioned 6–30–66 as part of plan to consolidate icebreaking under one organization. Has heavily armored bow, helicopter deck aft, and small hangar.

1 ICEBREAKER, *MACKINAW (290')* CLASS

Mackinaw (ex-*Manitowoc*)	WAGB-83	GLA

Built especially for service on the Great Lakes. Commissioned in CG 12–20–44. Has helicopter deck aft. Reclassified from WAG on 5–1–66.

7 ICEBREAKERS, "*WIND*" (269') CLASS

Name	Number	F/S	Name	Number	F/S	Name	Number	F/S
Edisto (ex-USN AGB-2)	WAGB-284	AA				*Eastwind*	WAGB-279	AR*
Burton Island (ex-USN AGB-1)	WAGB-283	PA	*Westwind*	WAGB-281	AA	*Staten Island*		
Northwind	WAGB-282	PA	*Southwind* (ex-USN *Atka*, AGB-3)	WAGB-280	AA	(ex-USN *Northwind*, AGB-5)	WAGB-278	PA

All designed and built as heavy duty icebreakers 1943–47. All have helicopter decks and telescopic hangars. WAGB-278, 280, and 281 served in Russian Navy in 1940s. WAGB-278, 280, 283/284 acquired from USN 1965–66 and struck from NVR. WAGB-279 decommissioned 12–13–69.

1 ICEBREAKER, *STORIS* (230') CLASS

Name	Number	F/S
Storis (ex-*Eskimo*)	WAGB-38	PA

Built in 1942. Serves primarily as search-rescue, supply, and law enforcement vessel at Kodiak, Alaska. Reclassified from WAG 5–1–66. Has helicopter platform aft.

1 MEDIUM ENDURANCE CUTTER, *YOCONA* (213') CLASS

Name	Number	F/S
Yocona (ex-*Wat*)	WMEC-168	PA

Built as USS *Seize* (ARS-26) of USN *Escape* class. Commissioned 11–3–44. Transferred to USCG permanently on loan after WW II. Reconfigured as tug and reclassified WAT. To WMEC in 1968. Sister ship *Acushnet* (WAT-167) was rerated WAGO at the same time.

5 MEDIUM ENDURANCE CUTTERS, *RELIANCE* (210') *A* CLASS

Name	Number	F/S	Name	Number	F/S	Name	Number	F/S
Confidence	WMEC-619	PA	*Vigilant*	WMEC-617	AA	*Reliance*	WMEC-615	AA
Active	WMEC-618	AA	*Diligence*	WMEC-616	AA			

Completed 1964–66; to WMEC 5–1–66. Replaced *Alert* and *Argo* class cutters. Have helicopter deck aft; no hangar and no funnels. Powered by either diesels or gas turbines. Primary duty is search-rescue.

11 MEDIUM ENDURANCE CUTTERS, *RESOLUTE* (210') *B* CLASS

Name	Number	F/S	Name	Number	F/S	Name	Number	F/S
Alert	WMEC-630	AA	*Dependable*	WMEC-626	AA	*Courageous*	WMEC-622	AA
Decisive	WMEC-629	AA	*Venturous*	WMEC-625	PA	*Valiant*	WMEC-621	AA
Durable	WMEC-628	AA	*Dauntless*	WMEC-624	AA	*Resolute*	WMEC-620	PA
Vigorous	WMEC-627	AA	*Steadfast*	WMEC-623	AA			

Completed 1967–69. Same as *A* class above except powered by diesels only.

3 MEDIUM ENDURANCE CUTTERS, "*AVOYEL*" (205′) CLASS

Name	Number	F/S
Tamaroa (ex-USN *Zuni*, ATF-95)	WMEC-166	AA
Cherokee (ex-USN ATF-66)	WMEC-165	AA
Chilula (ex-USN ATF-153)	WMEC-153	AA

Former *Cherokee* class ATFs. Commissioned in USN 1940–45. WMEC-165/66 to USCG 6–29–46; WMEC-153 in 1956; permanently transferred 1969. Original USCG rating was WATF; to WMEC 1968. Sister *Avoyel* (WMEC-150) decommissioned 9–30–69.

2 MEDIUM ENDURANCE CUTTERS, *MODOC* (143′) CLASS

Name	Number	F/S
Comanche (ex-USN ATA-202)	WMEC-202	PA
Modoc (ex-USN ATA-194)	WMEC-194	PA

Former USN *Sotoyomo* class ATAs; commissioned 1944–45. *Modoc* is ex-USS *Bagaduce*. Acquired by USCG 1959; WMEC-202 is permanent while WMEC-194 is on loan from MARAD. Both were rated as WATA to WMEC 1968.

12 PATROL CRAFT, LARGE, "*CAPE*" (95′) *A* CLASS

Name	Number	F/S	Name	Number	F/S
Cape Hedge	WPB-95311	PA	*Cape Hatteras*	WPB-95305	PA
Cape Wash	WPB-95310	PA	*Cape Gull*	WPB-95304	AA
Cape Carter	WPB-95309	PA	*Cape Upright*	WPB-95303	AA
Cape Strait	WPB-95308	AA	*Cape Higgon*	WPB-95302	PA
Cape Current	WPB-95307	AA	*Cape Coral*	WPB-95301	PA
Cape George	WPB-95306	AA	*Cape Small*	WPB-95300	PA

Constructed in 1953. Replace the 83′ wooden boats of WW II. Primary duties are search-rescue and port security.

8 PATROL CRAFT, LARGE, "*CAPE*" (95′) *B* CLASS

Name	Number	F/S	Name	Number	F/S
Cape Starr	WPB-95320	AA	*Cape Fox*	WPB-95316	AA
Cape Romain	WPB-95319	PA	*Cape Fairweather*	WPB-95314	AA
Cape Newagen	WPB-95318	PA	*Cape Morgan*	WPB-95313	AA
Cape Jellison	WPB-95317	PA	*Cape Knox*	WPB-95312	AA

Built in 1955. Similar to *A* and *C* classes.

6 PATROL CRAFT, LARGE, "*CAPE*" (95′) *C* CLASS

Name	Number	F/S	Name	Number	F/S
Cape York	WPB-95332	AA	*Cape Shoalwater*	WPB-95324	AA
Cape Henlopen	WPB-95328	PA	*Cape Horn*	WPB-95322	AA
Cape Corwin	WPB-95326	AA	*Cape Cross*	WPB-95321	AA

Constructed 1958–59. Nine of this class transferred to USN 1968 for further transfer to South Korean Navy (see Section 12).

44 PATROL CRAFT, SMALL, "*POINT*" (82′) *C* CLASS

Name	Number	F/S	Name	Number	F/S
Point Richmond	WPB-82370	PA	*Point Barrow*	WPB-82348	PA
Point Heyer	WPB-82369	PA	*Point Bonita*	WPB-82347	AA
Point Warde	WPB-82368	AA	*Point Arena*	WPB-82346	AA
Point Knoll	WPB-82367	AA	*Point Judith*	WPB-82345	PA
Point Lobos	WPB-82366	AA	*Point Estero*	WPB-82344	AA
Point Turner	WPB-82365	AA	*Point Wells*	WPB-82343	AA
Point Whitehorn	WPB-82364	AA	*Point Baker*	WPB-82342	AA
Point Nowell	WPB-82363	AA	*Point Lookout*	WPB-82341	AA
Point Brown	WPB-82362	AA	*Point Batan*	WPB-82340	AA
Point Charles	WPB-82361	AA	*Point Chico*	WPB-82339	PA
Point Winslow	WPB-82360	PA	*Point Bridge*	WPB-82338	PA
Point Steele	WPB-82359	AA	*Point Divide*	WPB-82337	PA
Point Stuart	WPB-82358	PA	*Point Glass*	WPB-82336	PA
Point Huron	WPB-82357	AA	*Point Countess*	WPB-82335	PA
Point Francis	WPB-82356	AA	*Point Ledge*	WPB-82334	PA
Point Hannon	WPB-82355	AA	*Point Highland*	WPB-82333	AA
Point Evans	WPB-82354	PA	*Point Roberts*	WPB-82332	AA
Point Monroe	WPB-82353	AA	*Point Herron*	WPB-82318	AA
Point Sal	WPB-82352	AA	*Point Thatcher*	WPB-82314	AA
Point Bennett	WPB-82351	PA	*Point Swift*	WPB-82312	AA
Point Franklin	WPB-82350	AA	*Point Verde*	WPB-82311	AA
Point Spencer	WPB-82349	AA	*Point Hope*	WPB-82302	AA

Built 1960–70 for search-rescue and law enforcement. Originally unnamed; named 1–64. 26 transferred to South Vietnam after service with Riverine/Coastal Force. Replaced by new construction. Were 39 in class; 4 added from *A* and 1 from *B* classes.

9 PATROL CRAFT, SMALL, "*POINT*" (82′) *D* CLASS

Name	Number	F/S	Name	Number	F/S
Point Martin	WPB-82379	AA	*Point Carrew*	WPB-82374	PA
Point Jackson	WPB-82378	AA	*Point Camden*	WPB-82373	PA
Point Hobart	WPB-82377	PA	*Point Brower*	WPB-82372	PA
Point Harris	WPB-82376	PA	*Point Barnes*	WPB-82371	AA
Point Doran	WPB-82375	PA			

Repeat construction of *C* class. Less armament.

9 HARBOR TUGS, MEDIUM, *MANITOU* (110′) *A* CLASS

Name	Number	F/S	Name	Number	F/S
Manitou	WYTM-60	AA	*Chinook*	WYTM-96	AA
Kaw	WYTM-61	GLA	*Ojibwa*	WYTM-97	GLA
Apalachee	WYTM-71	AA	*Snohomish*	WYTM-98	AA
Yankton	WYTM-72	AA	*Sauk*	WYTM-99	AA
Mohican	WYTM-73	AA			

Built in 1943.

4 HARBOR TUGS, MEDIUM, *ARUNDEL* (110′) *B* CLASS

Arundel	WYTM-90	GLA
Mahoning	WYTM-91	AA
Naugatuck	WYTM-92	GLA
Raritan	WYTM-93	GLA

Built in 1939.

1 HARBOR TUG, MEDIUM, *MESSENGER* (85′) CLASS

Messenger	WYTM-85009	AA

Built in 1944.

6 HARBOR TUGS, SMALL, *CAPSTAN* (65′) *A* CLASS

Capstan	WYTL-65601	AA
Chock	WYTL-65602	AA
Swivel	WYTL-65603	AA
Tackle	WYTL-65604	AA
Towline	WYTL-65605	AA
Catenary	WYTL-65606	AA

Built 1961–62. Provide towing, assistance, boarding, firefighting, and icebreaking.

3 HARBOR TUGS, SMALL, *BRIDLE* (65′) *B* CLASS

Bridle	WYTL-65607	AA
Pendant	WYTL-65608	AA
Shackle	WYTL-65609	AA

Built 1963.

3 HARBOR TUGS, SMALL, *HAWSER* (65′) *C* CLASS

Hawser	WYTL-65610	AA
Line	WYTL-65611	AA
Wire	WYTL-65612	AA

Built 1963.

3 HARBOR TUGS, SMALL, *BITT* (65′) *D* CLASS

Name	Number	F/S	Name	Number	F/S
Bitt	WYTL-65613	PA			
Bollard	WYTL-65614	PA			
Cleat	WYTL-65615	AA			

Built 1966–67.

1 OCEANOGRAPHIC CUTTER, *ROCKAWAY* (311′) CLASS

Rockaway (ex-WAVP, USN AVP-29)	WAGO-377	AA

Originally USN *Barnegat* class AVP. Commissioned in USN 1–6–43. Acquired on loan from USN in late 1940s as WAVP; rerated WHEC in 1966, later rerated WAGO.

1 OCEANOGRAPHIC CUTTER, *ACUSHNET* (213′) CLASS

Acushnet	WAGO-167	AA

Built as USS *Shackle* (ARS-9); commissioned on 2–5–44. Decommissioned after WW II, transferred to USCG, reconfigured as tug, and classified WAT-167. Rerated WAGO 1968.

1 OCEANOGRAPHIC CUTTER, *EVERGREEN* (180′) CLASS

Evergreen	WAGO-295	AA

Built 1943 as *Balsam* class seagoing buoy tender.

1 CARGO CUTTER, *KUKUI* (339′) CLASS

Kukui	WAK-186	PA

Completed 1945 for USN as *Colquitt* (AK-174) on C1-M-AV1 hull design. Transferred to USCG permanently on 3–11–46 and reclassified WAK-186. Carries supplies to CG stations in Pacific.

2 BUOY TENDERS, SEAGOING, *MAGNOLIA* (189′) CLASS

Magnolia	WLB-328	PA
[Willow]	WLB-332	Sold

Former Army mine planters built in 1942. Acquired and commissioned in USN on 4–7–44 as *Barricade* (ACM-3) and 3–6–45 as *Picket* (ACM-8). Transferred to USCG 1946. To WLB 1–1–65.

12 BUOY TENDERS, SEAGOING, *BALSAM* (180′) *A* CLASS

Balsam	WLB-62	PA	*Clover*	WLB-292	PA
Cactus	WLB-270	PA	*Sorrel*	WLB-296	PA
Cowslip	WLB-277	AA	*Citrus*	WLB-300	PA
Woodbine	WLB-289	GLA	*Conifer*	WLB-301	AA
Gentian	WLB-290	AA	*Madrona*	WLB-302	AA
Laurel	WLB-291	AA	*Tupelo*	WLB-303	PA

Built in 1942–44. WLB-62, 296, and 300 are ice reinforced. WLB-277 has bow thruster. *Cactus* was designated an oceanographic vessel on 4–30–67 (see photo section), but reverted to WLB in 1969.

6 BUOY TENDERS, SEAGOING, *IRONWOOD* (180′) *B* CLASS

Ironwood	WLB-297	PA	*Planetree*	WLB-307	PA
Mesquite	WLB-305	GLA	*Papaw*	WLB-308	AA
Buttonwood	WLB-306	AA	*Sweetgum*	WLB-309	AA

Built 1943–44.

20 BUOY TENDERS, SEAGOING, *BASSWOOD* (180′) *C* CLASS

Basswood	WLB-388	PA	*Redbud*	WLB-398	AA
Bittersweet	WLB-389	PA	*Sagebrush*	WLB-399	AA
Blackhaw	WLB-390	PA	*Salvia*	WLB-400	AA
Blackthorn	WLB-391	AA	*Sassafras*	WLB-401	AA
Bramble	WLB-392	GLA	*Sedge*	WLB-402	PA
Firebush	WLB-393	AA	*Spar*	WLB-403	AA
Hornbeam	WLB-394	AA	*Sundew*	WLB-404	GLA
Iris	WLB-395	AA	*Sweetbrier*	WLB-405	PA
Mallow	WLB-396	PA	*Acacia*	WLB-406	GLA
Mariposa	WLB-397	AA	*Woodbrush*	WLB-407	GLA

Built in 1943–44. WLB-390, 392, 398, and 402/404 are ice-reinforced. WLB-389, 394 have bow thruster. *Redbud* was acquired by USN on 3–25–49 as AG-398. To AKL-398 on 3–31–49. Transferred to MSC on 2–20–52. Employed as cargo ship, icebreaker, and communications ship. Returned to USCG 11–20–70.

1 BUOY TENDER, COASTAL, *JUNIPER* (177′) CLASS

Juniper	WLM-224	AA

Built 1941. Reclassified from WAGL 1–1–65.

3 BUOY TENDERS, COASTAL, *FIR* (175′) CLASS

Fir	WLM-212	PA
Hollyhock	WLM-220	AA
Walnut	WLM-252	PA

Built in 1937–39. Reclassified from WAGL 1–1–65.

1 BUOY TENDER, COASTAL, *LILAC* (173′) CLASS

Lilac	WLM-227	AA

Built 1933. Reclassified from WAGL 1–1–65. Scheduled to decommission 1971.

5 BUOY TENDERS, COASTAL, *RED WOOD* (157′) CLASS

Red Wood	WLM-685	AA	*Red Cedar*	WLM-688	AA
Red Beech	WLM-686	AA	*Red Oak*	WLM-689	AA
Red Birch	WLM-687	PA			

Built in 1964-71. Steering/engine controls from bridge wings and pilot house.

7 BUOY TENDERS, COASTAL, *WHITE SUMAC* (133′) CLASS

White Sumac	WLM-540	AA	*White Heath*	WLM-545	AA
White Bush	WLM-542	PA	*White Lupine*	WLM-546	AA
White Holly	WLM-543	PA	*White Pine*	WLM-547	AA
White Sage	WLM-544	AA			

Built in 1942–44. Former USN YFs. An eighth ship, *White Alder* (WLM-541), was sunk by collision 12–7–68.

1 BUOY TENDER, INLAND, *TAMARACK* (124′) CLASS

[Tamarack]	WLI-248	Sold

Built 1934.

3 BUOY TENDERS, INLAND, *MAPLE* (122′) CLASS

Maple	WLI-234	AA
Narcissus	WLI-238	AA
Zinnia	WLI-255	AA

Built 1939. WLI-238, 255 have greater SHP, speed, and boom capacity than *Maple*.

7 BUOY TENDERS, INLAND, *COSMOS* (100′) *A* CLASS

Name	Number	F/S	Name	Number	F/S
Cosmos	WLI-293	AA	*Smilax*	WLI-315	AA
Barberry	WLI-294	AR*	*Primrose*	WLI-316	AA
Rambler	WLI-298	AA	*Verbena*	WLI-317	AA
Bluebell	WLI-313	PA			

Built 1942–45. *Cosmos* and *Smilax* have construction barges assigned. *Barberry* and *Verbena* have pile drivers installed. WLI-294 decommissioned 9–1–70.

1 BUOY TENDER, INLAND, *AZALEA* (100′) *B* CLASS

Azalea	WLI-641	AA

Built 1958. Has pile driver installed.

1 BUOY TENDER, INLAND, *BUCKTHORN* (100′) *C* CLASS

Buckthorn	WLI-642	GLA

Built 1963. Pilothouse and upper deckhouse constructed of aluminium.

1 BUOY TENDER, INLAND, *TERN* (80′) CLASS

Tern	WLI-80801	AA

Built 1969. Prototype design with first USCG gantry crane installed, under evaluation for year or more.

2 BUOY TENDERS, INLAND, *CLEMATIS* (74′) CLASS

Clematis	WLI-74286	AA
Shadbush	WLI-74287	AA

Built 1944.

1 BUOY TENDER, INLAND, *ELM* (72′) CLASS

Elm	WLI-72260	AR*

Built 1937. Decommissioned 7–30–69.

1 BUOY TENDER, INLAND, *BLUEBERRY* (65302) CLASS

Name	Number	F/S	Name	Number	F/S
Blueberry	WLI-65302	PA			

Built 1942.

3 BUOY TENDERS, INLAND, *BLACKBERRY* (65303) CLASS

Blackberry	WLI-65303	AA
Chokeberry	WLI-65304	AA
Loganberry	WLI-65305	AA

Built 1946.

2 BUOY TENDERS, INLAND, *BAYBERRY* (65400) CLASS

Bayberry	WLI-65400	PA
Elderberry	WLI-65401	PA

Built 1954.

2 CONSTRUCTION TENDERS, INLAND, *ANVIL* (75′) *A* CLASS

Anvil	WLIC-75301	AA
Hammer	WLIC-75302	AA

Built 1962.

3 CONSTRUCTION TENDERS, INLAND, *SLEDGE* (75′) *B* CLASS

Sledge	WLIC-75303	AA
Mallet	WLIC-75304	AA
Vise	WLIC-75305	AA

Built 1962.

5 CONSTRUCTION TENDERS, INLAND, *CLAMP* (75′) *D* CLASS

Clamp	WLIC-75306	AA	*Hatchet*	WLIC-75309	AA
Wedge	WLIC-75307	AA	*Axe*	WLIC-75310	AA
Spike	WLIC-75308	AA			

Built 1964–65.

2 BUOY TENDERS, RIVER, *FERN* (115′) CLASS

Fern	WLR-304	IW,A
Sumac	WLR-311	IW,A

Built 1942–43.

4 BUOY TENDERS, RIVER, *FORSYTHIA* (114′) CLASS

Forsythia	WLR-63	IW,A	*Sycamore*	WLR-268	IW,A
Dogwood	WLR-259	IW,A	*Foxglove*	WLR-285	IW,A

Built 1940–45. *Foxglove* displaces 350 tons, has 6′ draft, engines provide 1200 SHP (three screws), and 8500-mile range. *Dogwood* and *Sycamore* displace 230 tons.

2 BUOY TENDERS, RIVER, *GOLDENROD* (104′) CLASS

Goldenrod	WLR-213	IW,A
Poplar	WLR-241	IW,A

Built 1938–39.

1 BUOY TENDER, RIVER, *LANTANA* (80′) CLASS

Lantana	WLR-80310	IW,A

Built 1943.

9 BUOY TENDERS, RIVER, *GASCONADE* (75′) CLASS

Gasconade	WLR-75401	IW,A	*Kickapoo*	WLR-75406	IW,A
Muskingum	WLR-75402	IW,A	*Kanawha*	WLR-75407	IW,A
Wyaconda	WLR-75403	IW,A	*Patoka*	WLR-75408	IW,A
Chippewa	WLR-75404	IW,A	*Chena*	WLR-75409	Bldg.
Cheyenne	WLR-75405	IW,A			

Built 1964–70.

1 BUOY TENDER, RIVER, *OLEANDER* (73′) CLASS

Oleander	WLR-73264	IW,A

Built 1940.

6 BUOY TENDERS, RIVER, *OUACHITA* (65′) CLASS

Ouachita	WLR-65501	IW,A	*Scioto*	WLR-65504	IW,A
Cimarron	WLR-65502	IW,A	*Osage*	WLR-65505	IW,A
Obion	WLR-65503	IW,A	*Sangamon*	WLR-65506	IW,A

Built 1960–62.

1 LIGHTSHIP, *NANTUCKET* (149′) CLASS

Nantucket	WLV-534	AA

Built 1936.

3 LIGHTSHIPS, *"SAN FRANCISCO"* (133′) CLASS

[San Francisco]	WLV-523	Struck	*Portland*	WLV-536	AA
Five Fathom	WLV-530	AR*	*Delaware*	WLV-538	AA

Built in 1923–30. *Five Fathom* decommissioned 8–31–70. All lightships to be replaced with automated buoys.

5 LIGHTSHIPS, *NEW ORLEANS* (128′) CLASS

New Orleans	WLV-189	AA	*Relief*	WLV-605	PA
Umatilla Reef	WLV-196	PA	*[Blunts Reef]*	WLV-612	Struck
Columbia River	WLV-604	PA	*Relief*	WLV-613	AA

Built 1946–52. WLV-605 is the Pacific station-relief ship while WLV-613 is her Atlantic station counterpart. They relieve the normal station ship for yard period, repairs, etc.

1 LIGHTSHIP, *BOSTON* (115′) CLASS

Boston	WLV-539	AA

Built 1938.

1 LIGHTSHIP, *LAKE HURON* (97′) CLASS

Lake Huron	WLV-526	GLR*

Built 1921. Decommissioned 8–25–70.

1 TRAINING CUTTER, *EAGLE* (295′) CLASS

Name	Number	F/S
Eagle	WIX-327	AA

Built in 1936 by Blohm and Voss, Hamburg, Germany. Was German Navy training ship. Awarded to USN as war prize January 1946. Transferred to USCG July 1946 for use as Coast Guard Academy training vessel. Fully rigged as a bark. Can reach 18 knots with full sail. Fully rigged, has 21,351 square feet of sail.

1 TRAINING CUTTER, *CUYAHOGA* (125′) CLASS

Cuyahoga	WIX-157	AA

Last survivor of the *Alert* class cutters. Completed 1926 as WPC-157. Became training cutter at Yorktown, Va. in late 1950s.

1 RESERVE TRAINING CUTTER, *COURIER* (339′) CLASS

Courier (ex-WAGR, USN AK-176)	WTR-410	AA

Sister ship of *Kukui* (WAK-186). Built on C1-M-AV1 hull design. Completed for the USN in 1945 but never commissioned. Saw mercantile service as SS *Coastal Messenger* until acquired by Coast Guard (from MARAD) in 1951 and commissioned 2–15–52. Served as relay station for "Voice of America" from 9–7–52 until 5–17–64. Decommissioned 8–25–64; recommissioned as training cutter on 7–1–65; communications gear removed.

1 RESERVE TRAINING CUTTER, *UNIMAK* (311′) CLASS

Unimak	WTR-379	AA

Completed as AVP-31 in *Barnegat* class; commissioned in USN 12–31–43. Transferred to Coast Guard in 9/48. Became WAVP-379. To WHEC 5–1–66; to WTR 1969.

1 RESERVE TRAINING CUTTER, *TANAGER* (211′) CLASS

Tanager (ex WTR-385, USN MSF-385)	WTR-885	PA

Commissioned in USN on 7–28–45, as a steel-hulled minesweeper of the *Auk* class. Transferred to USCG 10–4–63 for use as a training cutter. Sweep gear removed and superstructure extended aft to provide extra living compartment. Commissioned as WTR-385 on 7–16–64; later reclassified WTR-885. Transferred to Pacific 1969.

1 RESERVE TRAINING CUTTER, *LAMAR* (184′) CLASS

Name	Number	F/S
Lamar	WTR-899	DPR*

Originally commissioned in USN as PCE-899 on 3–17–45 as a *Marfa* class PCE. Transferred to USCG on 7–29–64. Decommissioned 9–30–69 for disposal.

3 AIR CUSHION VEHICLES (ACV, ex-USN PACV)

Transferred to Coast Guard 10/69 after two operational/evaluation tours by USN in Vietnam. First unit converted by Transportation Technology Inc.; reclassified HOVER 01. Conversion included removal of armament and armor plate; replaced with service communication and search-rescue gear. Two units will undergo year-long evaluation test in San Francisco Bay area. The third unit scheduled to support an Advanced Research Projects Agency project in the Arctic. Data not included in Coast Guard tables; see Riverine tables in Section 4 (PACV). See also Part Four of that section for Navy notes and photos.

COAST GUARD AIRCRAFT IN SERVICE AS OF JANUARY 1971

Number in Service	Model Number	Type
1	VC-11A	Grumman GULFSTREAM II (Administrative transport)
1	VC-4A	Grumman GULFSTREAM I (Administrative transport)
12	HC-130B	Lockheed HERCULES
1	EC-130E	Lockheed HERCULES (No. 1414)
3	HC-130H	Lockheed HERCULES
38	HU-16E	Grumman ALBATROSS (amphibian)
6	C-123B	Fairchild PROVIDER
22	HH-3F	Sikorsky PELICAN (helicopter)
93	HH-52A	Sikorsky SEAGUARD (helicopter)

For data on above aircraft, see Section 9.

USCGC *Boutwell* (WHEC-719). 6–3–68. **Hamilton (378′)** *class.*

USCGC *Duane* (WHEC-33). **Bibb (327′)** *class.*

USCGC *Absecon* (WHEC-374). **"Casco" (311′)** *class.*

USCGC *Wachusett* (WHEC-44). 8–26–68. **Owasco (255′)** *class.*

USCGC *Glacier* (WAGB-4). 2–9–68. **Glacier (310′)** *class.*

USCGC *Mackinaw* (WAGB-83). 3–19–69. **Mackinaw (290′)** *class.*

USCGC *Northwind* (WAGB-282) with an HH-52A reconnaissance helicopter about to land on her deck. 9–69. **"Wind" (269′)** *class.*

USCGC *Storis* (WAGB-38). 4–27–68. **Storis (230′)** *class.*

USCGC *Reliance* (WPC-615). 7–10–64. **Reliance (210′) A** *class.*

USCGC *Cape Carter* (WPB-95309), "A" class. **"Cape" (95′) A** *class.*

USCGC *Tamaroa* (WMEC-1060). **"Avoyel" (205′)** *class.*

USCGC *Cape Starr* (WPB-95320), "B" class. Note differences between "A" and "B" classes in amidships structures around stacks. 8–1–69. **"Cape" (95′) B** *class.*

USCGC *Point Bonita* (WPB-82347), "C" class. 8–5–69. **"Point" (82′) C** *class.*

USCGC *Yankton* (WYTM-72), "A" class. 1–12–69. **Manitou (110′) A** *class.*

USCGC *Messenger* (WYTM-85009. 2–27–68. **Messenger (85′)** *class.*

USCGC *Pendant* (WYTL-65609), "B" class. 5–8–68. **Bridle (65′) B** *class.*

USCGC *Towline* (WYTL-65605), "A" class 2–17–67. **Capstan (65′) A** *class.*

USCGC *Rockaway* (WAGO-377), which replaced cancelled WAGA-701. 6–67. **Rockaway (311′)** *class.*

USCGC *Kukui* (WAK-186). 1–8–70. **Kukui (339′)** *class.*

USCGC *Cactus* (WLB-270), "A" class. Though buoy tenders are normally painted black, she is painted white as an oceanographic vessel. 4–28–69. **Balsam (180′) A** *class.*

USCGC *Spar* (WLB-403), "C" class. 10–3–68. **Basswood (180′) C** *class.*

USCGC *Fir* (WLM-212). 11–3–69. **Fir (175′)** *class.*

USCGC *White Lupine* (WLM-546). 5–26–69. **White Sumac (133′)** *class.*

USCGC *Red Birch* (WLM-687). 11–1–68. **Red Wood (157′)** *class.*

USCGC *Buckthorn* (WLI-642), "C" class. Note location of boom for 360° rotation and centerline spud. 9–23–64. **Buckthorn (100′) C** *class.*

USCGC *Tern* (WLI-80801). Note gantry crane, rails, and adjustable arms. 6–24–69.
Tern (80′) *class.*

USCGC *Five Fathom* (WLV-530). 10–2–63. **"San Francisco" (133′)** *class.*

USCGC *Courier* (WTR-410). **Courier (339′)** *class.*

USCGC *Tanager* (WTR-885). **Tanager (211′)** *class.*

12. FOREIGN TRANSFERS

This is a chronological listing of major vessels transferred to friendly nations under the International Logistics Program (formerly MDAP) since 1–1–65. There are five methods of transfer.

SALE (A)—the recipient buys the vessel and receives the title.

SALE (B)—the recipient contracts with a US firm for construction, pays all fees, and US provides technical assistance.

LOAN— USN retains title; recipient pays operating and maintenance costs.

GRANT AID— recipient receives the ship in lieu of money. US retains title and pays modification, activation, etc., costs.

LEASE—similar to loan except the navy of the recipient nation, rather than the government, makes the request directly. US retains title.

OFF-SHORE PROCUREMENT (OSP)—vessel is built in a foreign yard and US pays half the costs.

All US–or foreign-built vessels for transfer are assigned USN hull numbers for accounting purposes.

Date	Recipient	USN Name/Hull Number	New Name/Hull Number	Mode
3–20–64	Peru	*Bellatrix* (AKA-3)	*Independencia* (AKA-21)	Sale
6–1–64	Greece	LST-325	*Syros* (L-144)	Grant Aid
10–22–64	Denmark	SS-554	*Springeren* (S-329)	Grant Aid
1–65	Columbia	*Tonti* (AOG-76)	*Mamonal* (BT-62)	Grant Aid
1–13–65	Dominican Republic	*Signet* (MSF-302)	*Separacion* (BDM-454)	Sale
1–13–65	Dominican Republic	*Skirmish* (MSF-303)	*Tortugero* (BDM-455)	Sale
1–21–65	Greece	MSC-299	*Aigli* (M-246)	Grant Aid
2–2–65	Spain	*Achernar* (AKA-53)	*Castilla* (TA-21)	Grant Aid
2–12–65	Denmark	PT-821	*Soloven* (P-510)	OSP
2–26–65	Greece	*Scabbardfish* (SS-397)	*Triaina* (S-86)	Loan
3–5–65	Taiwan	MSC-302	*Yung Hsin* (MSC-159)	Grant Aid
4–3–65	Taiwan	*Donald W. Wolf* (APD-129)	*Hwa Shan* (PF-33)	Sale
4–3–65	Taiwan	*Kinzer* (APD-91)	*Yu Shan* (PF-32)	Sale
4–15–65	Taiwan	MSC-300	*Yung Ju* (MSC-160)	Grant Aid
4–22–65	Turkey	PC-1639	*Demirhisar* (P-112)	Grant Aid
6–10–65	Turkey	MSC-311	*Sigacik* (M-265)	Grant Aid
6–12–65	Philippines	*Murrelet* (MSF-372)	*Rizal* (PS-69)	Grant Aid
6–18–65	Burma	*Farmington* (PCE-894)	*Yon Taing Aung* (PCE-41)	Grant Aid
6–24–65	Turkey	PC-1642	*Sivrihisar* (P-115)	Grant Aid
7–1–65	Turkey	PC-1643	*Kochisar* (P-116)	Grant Aid
7–9–65	Thailand	MSC-303	*Bangkeo* (MSC-6)	Grant Aid
7–9–65	Turkey	MSC-312	*Sapanca* (M-266)	Grant Aid
7–17–65	Australia	DDG-25	*Perth* (D-38)	Sale (B)
7–22–65	Taiwan	*Redstart* (MSF-378)	*Wu Sheng* (PCE-66)	Grant Aid
8–14–65	Columbia	*Tollberg* (APD-103)	*Almirante Padilla* (DT-03)	Grant Aid
8–26–65	Thailand	MSC-301	*Tadindeng* (MSC-7)	Grant Aid
9–8–65	Turkey	MSC-304	*Silifke* (M-263)	Grant Aid
9–17–65	Thailand	MSC-313	*Donchedi* (MSC-8)	Grant Aid
11–18–65	Taiwan	*Waxwing* (MSF-389)	*Chu Yung* (PCE-47)	Grant Aid
11–22–65	Taiwan	*Gantner* (APD-42)	*Wen Shan* (PF-34)	Sale
11–22–65	Taiwan	APD-98 (ex-*Truxtun*)	*Fu Shan* (PF-35)	Sale
11–22–65	Taiwan	*Kline* (APD-120)	*Shoa Shan* (PF-37)	Sale

11–65	Ecuador	*Mulberry* (AN-27)	*Orion* (H-101)	Loan
11–30–65	Ecuador	PGM-75	*Quito* (LC-71)	Grant Aid
11–30–65	Ecuador	PGM-76	*Guayaquil* (LC-72)	Grant Aid
12–9–65	Australia	DDG-26	*Hobart* (D-39)	Sale (B)
1–66	Taiwan	*Chickasaw* (ATF-83)	*Ta Tung* (ATF-548)	Sale
1–5–66	Dominican Republic	PGM-77	*Betelgeuse* (GC-102)	Grant Aid
1–19–66	Vietnam	PGM-72	*Thai Binh* (HQ-612)	Grant Aid
1–19–66	Vietnam	PGM-73	*Thi Tu* (HQ-613)	Grant Aid
1–19–66	Vietnam	PGM-74	*Song Tu* (HQ-614)	Grant Aid
2–1–66	Thailand	PGM-71	T-11	Grant Aid
2–11–66	Turkey	MSC-305	*Saros* (M-264)	Grant Aid
2–14–66	France	*Locust* (AN-22)	*Locuste* (A-765)	Sale
2–22–66	Taiwan	*Walter B. Cobb* (APD-106)	None. Sunk enroute.	Sale
3–66	Norway	MSC-103 (ex-Belgian)	*Tana* (M-313)	Grant Aid
3–31–66	Italy	*Besugo* (AGSS-321)	*Francesco Morosini* (S-508)	Loan
3–31–66	Italy	*Capitaine* (AGSS-336)	*Alfredo Cappellini* (S-507)	Loan
5–66	Norway	MSC-104 (ex-Belgian)	*Alta* (M-314)	Grant Aid
5–16–66	Thailand	*Stark County* (LST-1134)	*Pangan* (LST-3)	Loan
5–18–66	Taiwan	MSC-306	*Yung Lo* (MSC-161)	Grant Aid
5–25–66	Denmark	PC-1644	*Peder Skram* (F-352)	Grant Aid
6–1–66	Korea	*Harry L. Corl* (APD-108)	*Ah San* (APD-82)	Grant Aid
6–1–66	Korea	*Julius A. Raven* (APD-110)	*Ung Po* (PG-83)	Grant Aid
6–2–66	Vietnam	PGM-80	*Tay Sa* (HQ-615)	Grant Aid
6–13–66	Taiwan	*Bull* (APD-78)	*Lu Shan* (PF-36)	Sale
7–11–66	Taiwan	*Register* (APD-92)	*Tai Shan* (PF-38)	Sale
7–11–66	Taiwan	*Raymon W. Herndon* (APD-121)	*Heng Shan* (PF-39)	Sale
7–11–66	Vietnam	*Brattleboro* (EPCER-852)	*Ngoc Hoi* (HQ-12)	Grant Aid
7–21–66	Vietnam	PGM-81	*Phu Qui* (HQ-617)	Grant Aid
8–18–66	Uruguay	*Chickadee* (MSF-59)	*Commandante Pedro Campbell* (MSF-1)	Lease
8–29–66	Vietnam	PGM-82	*Hong Sa* (HQ-616)	Grant Aid
9–66	Norway	MSC-151 (ex-Belgian)	*Glomma* (M-317)	Grant Aid
9–19–66	Peru	PGM-78	*Rio Sama* (PC-11)	Grant Aid
9–30–66	Vietnam	PGM-83	*Hon Troc* (HQ-618)	Grant Aid
11–66	Thailand	PGM-79	T-12	Grant Aid
11–15–66	Chile	*Joseph E. Campbell* (APD-49)	*Riqueleme* (APD-28)	Sale
11–15–66	Chile	*Odum* (APD-71)	*Serrano* (APD-26)	Sale
11–15–66	Chile	*Jack C. Robinson* (APD-72)	*Orella* (APD-27)	Sale
11–15–66	Chile	*Daniel T. Griffin* (APD-38)	*Uribe* (APD-29)	Sale
12–2–66	Liberia	PGM-102	*Alert* (102)	Grant Aid
12–8–66	Vietnam	PGM-91	*Tho Chau* (HQ-619)	Grant Aid
12–20–66	Portugal	DE-1039	*Almirante Pereira Da Silva* (F-472)	Grant Aid
1–14–67	Turkey	*Clarence K. Bronson* (DD-668)	*Istanbul* (D-340)	Loan
2–28–67	Turkey	*Van Valkenburg* (DD-656)	*Izmir* (D-341)	Loan
3–31–67	Burma	*Creddock* (MSF-356)	*Yon Gyi Aung* (PCE-42)	Grant Aid
4–67	Korea	PT-812	*Olpemi-I* (PB-1)	Grant Aid
4–67	Korea	*Report* (MSF-289)	*Kojin* (PCE-50)	Grant Aid
5–17–67	Taiwan	*George W. Ingram* (APD-43)	*Kang Shan* (PF-42)	Grant Aid
5–17–67	Taiwan	*Blessman* (APD-48)	*Chung Shan* (PF-43)	Grant Aid
6–1–67	Taiwan	*Kimberly* (DD-521)	*An Yang* (DD-18)	Grant Aid
7–14–67	Ecuador	*Enright* (APD-66)	*25 De Julio* (E-12)	Sale

continued

Foreign Transfers—*continued*

Date	Recipient	USN Name/Hull Number	New Name/Hull Number	Mode
7–23–67	Korea	*Kephart* (APD-61)	*Kyong Buk* (PG-85)	Grant Aid
7–23–67	Korea	*Hayter* (APD-80)	*Chun Nam* (PG-86)	Grant Aid
7–23–67	Korea	*William H. Hobby* (APD-95)	*Chr Ju* (PG-87)	Grant Aid
8–2–67	Brazil	*Lewis Hancock* (DD-675)	*Piaui* (D-31)	Loan
8–7–67	Turkey	MSC-315	*Sariyer* (M-267)	Grant Aid
8–7–67	Turkey	MSI-15	*Foca* (M-500)	Grant Aid
8–15–67	Taiwan	*Steady* (MSF-118)	*Ping Ching* (PCE-70)	Sale
8–19–67	Philippines	*Vigilance* (MSF-324)	*Quezon* (PS-70)	Grant Aid
8–28–67	Thailand	PGM-107	T-13	Grant Aid
8–30–67	Spain	*Cabot* (AVT-3)	*Dedalo* (PH-01)	Loan
9–6–67	France	*Sandlewood* (AN-32)	*Lucoile* (A-777)	Grant Aid
9–14–67	Turkey	PGM-104	AB-21 (P-117)	Grant Aid
9–15–67	Turkey	MSI-16	*Fethiye* (M-501)	Grant Aid
10–27–67	Turkey	MSI-17	*Fatsa* (M-502)	Grant Aid
11–3–67	Iran	PGM-103	*Parvin* (PC-65)	Sale
11–17–67	Korea	*Speed* (MSF-116)	*Sunchon* (PCE-1002)	Grant Aid
11–29–67	Portugal	DE-1042	*Almirante Gago Coutinho* (F-473)	Grant Aid
12–1–67	Turkey	MSI-18	*Finike* (M-503)	Grant Aid
12–10–67	Italy	*St. George* (AV-16)	*Andrea Bafile* (A-5314)	Grant Aid
12–15–67	Germany	*Charles Ausburne* (DD-570)	Z-6 (D-180)	Sale
12–15–67	Philippines	*Booth* (DE-170)	*Datu Kalantiaw* (PS-76)	Loan
12–15–67	Korea	*Dextrous* (MSF-341)	*Koje* (PCE-1003)	Loan
12–15–67	Philippines	PCF-33	PCF-300	Grant Aid
12–15–67	Philippines	PCF-34	PCF-301	Grant Aid
12–15–67	Philippines	PCF-83	PCF-302	Grant Aid
12–15–67	Philippines	PCF-84	PCF-303	Grant Aid
12–15–67	Philippines	PCF-85	PCF-304	Grant Aid
12–15–67	Philippines	PCF-86	PCF-305	Grant Aid
12–16–67	Australia	DDG-27	*Brisbane* (D-41)	Sale (B)
12–27–67	Turkey	PGM-105	AB-22 (P-118)	Grant Aid
1–8–68	Turkey	PGM-106	AB-23 (P-119)	Grant Aid
1–9–68	Philippines	USCGC *Nettle* (WAKL-169)	*Limasawa* (L-47)	Lease
3–68	Philippines	*Altus* (PC-568)	*Nueva Viscaya* (PS-80)	Grant Aid
4–24–68	Turkey	PGM-108	AB-24 (P-120)	Grant Aid
4–27–68	Korea	*Halsey Powell* (DD-686)	*Seoul* (DD-92)	Grant Aid
5–1–68	Norway	*Gardiners Bay* (AVP-39)	*Haakon VII* (A-537)	Sale
5–10–68	Brazil	*Irwin* (DD-794)	*Santa Catarina* (D-32)	Loan
6–10–68	Taiwan	*Yarnall* (DD-541)	*Kun Yang* (DD-19)	Sale
6–20–68	Korea	MSC-316	*Sam Chok* (MSC-528)	Grant Aid
7–2–68	Columbia	*Burke* (APD-65)	*Almirante Brion* (DT-07)	Sale
7–10–68	Taiwan	*Riley* (DE-579)	*Tai Yuan* (DE-27)	Grant Aid
9–6–68	Columbia	*Bassett* (APD-73)	*Almirante Tono* (DT-04)	Grant Aid
9–24–68	Korea	*Cape Providence* (USCG)	PB-6	Grant Aid
9–24–68	Korea	*Cape Rosier* (USCG)	PB-3	Grant Aid
9–24–68	Korea	*Cape Sable* (USCG)	PB-5	Grant Aid
10–1–68	Portugal	*Formoe* (DE-509)	*Diogo Cao* (F-333)	Sale
10–15–68	Uruguay	*Nahant* (AN-83)	*Rou Huracan* (BT-30)	Sale
11–1–68	Portugal	*McCoy Reynolds* (DE-440)	*Corte Real* (F-334)	Sale

11–4–68	Portugal	DE-1046	*Almirante Magalhaes Correia* (F-474)	Grant Aid
11–13–68	Korea	*Cape Falcon* (USCG)	PB-9	Grant Aid
11–13–68	Korea	*Cape Florida* (USCG)	PB-7	Grant Aid
11–13–68	Korea	*Cape Porpoise* (USCG)	PB-8	Grant Aid
11–13–68	Korea	*Cape Trinity* (USCG)	PB-10	Grant Aid
11–15–68	Korea	*Hickox* (DD-673)	*Pusan* (DD-93)	Grant Aid
11–21–68	Greece	MSC-317	*Argo* (M-213)	Grant Aid
11–21–68	Greece	MSC-318	*Aura* (M-214)	Grant Aid
12–2–68	Canada	*Argonaut* (SS-475)	*Rainbow* (SS-75)	Sale
1–15–69	France	*Rosewood* (AN-31)	*Libellule* (A-730)	Sale
2–7–69	Turkey	*Anthedon* (AS-24)	*Donatan* (A-583)	Sale
2–11–69	Iran	PF-105	*Milanian* (F-27)	Grant Aid
2–13–69	Iran	PF-106	*Kahnamuie* (F-28)	Grant Aid
2–17–69	Mexico	*Barber* (LPR-57)	*Coahuila* (B-7)	Sale
2–17–69	Mexico	*Rednour* (APD-102)	*Chihuahua* (B-8)	Sale
2–18–69	Taiwan	*Schmitt* (APD-76)	*Lung Shan* (PF-44)	Sale
2–18–69	Taiwan	*Geronimo* (ATA-207)	*Chiu Lien* (AGS-563)	Sale
3–12–69	Germany	DDG-28	*Lutjens* (D-185)	Sale (B)
3–24–69	Korea	*Cape Darby* (USCG)	PB-11	Grant Aid
3–24–69	Korea	*Cape Kiwana* (USCG)	PB-12	Grant Aid
4–1–69	Korea	*Pasco* (PF-6)(ex-Japanese, for cannibalization)		Unknown
4–1–69	Korea	*Gloucester* (PF-22)(ex-Japanese, for cannibalization)		Unknown
4–4–69	Vietnam	*Coconino County* (LST-603)	*Vung Tau* (HQ-503)	Lease
5–69	Thailand	PGM-113	T-14	Grant Aid
5–16–69	Vietnam	*Point Garnet* (USCG)	*Le Van Nga* (HQ-701)	Grant Aid
5–16–69	Vietnam	*Point League* (USCG)	*Le Phuoc Duc* (HQ-700)	
6–69	Thailand	PGM-114	T-15	Grant Aid
6–5–69	Columbia	*Rockville* (PCER-851)	*San Andreas* (LC-151)	Sale
7–69	Thailand	PGM-115	T-16	Grant Aid
7–2–69	Italy	*Taylor* (DD-468)	*Lanclere* (D-560)	Sale
7–2–69	Italy	*Walker* (DD-517)	*Fante* (D-561)	Sale
7–29–69	Greece	MSC-153 (ex-Belgian)	*Antiopi* (M-205)	Grant Aid
7–29–69	Greece	MSC-169 (ex-Belgian)	*Atlanti* (M-202)	Grant Aid
8–18–69	Thailand	PGM-116	T-17	Grant Aid
9–15–69	Vietnam	*Point Clear* (USCG)	*Huynh Van Duc* (HQ-702)	Grant Aid
9–20–69	Germany	DDG-29	*Molders* (D-186)	Sale (B)
9–26–69	Greece	MSC-154 (ex-Belgian)	*Faeda* (M-206)	Grant Aid
9–26–69	Greece	MSC-170 (ex-Belgian)	*Thalia* (M-210)	Grant Aid
9–26–69	Greece	MSC-171 (ex-Belgian)	*Niovi* (M-254)	Grant Aid
10–1–69	Turkey	*Boyd* (DD-544)	*Iskenderun* (D-343)	Sale
10–1–69	Turkey	*Cogswell* (DD-651)	*Izmit* (D-342)	Sale
10–2–69	Thailand	PGM-117	T-18	Grant Aid
10–30–69	Taiwan	MSC-77 (ex-Belgian)		Grant Aid
10–30–69	Taiwan	MSC-101 (ex-Belgian)		Grant Aid
10–30–69	Taiwan	MSC-63 (ex-Belgian)		Grant Aid
10–30–69	Taiwan	MSC-78 (ex-Belgian)		Grant Aid
10–30–69	Taiwan	MSC-152 (ex-Belgian, for cannibalization)		Grant Aid
10–30–69	Taiwan	MSC-64 (ex-Belgian)		Grant Aid
10–30–69	Taiwan	MSC-65 (ex-Belgian)		Grant Aid
11–10–69	Uruguay	MSC-94 (ex-French)	*Rio Negro* (MS-32)	Grant Aid
11–11–69	Vietnam	*Point Gammon* (USCG)	*Nguyen Dao* (HQ-703)	Grant Aid

continued

Foreign Transfers—*continued*

Date	Recipient	USN Name/Hull Number	New Name/Hull Number	Mode
11–15–69	Turkey	*Preston* (DD-795)	*Icel* (D-344)	Sale
11–17–69	Vietnam	*Point Comfort* (USCG)	*Dao Thuc* (HQ-704)	Grant Aid
11–24–69	Columbia	*Ruchamkin* (LPR-89)	*Cordoba* (DT-15)	Lease
11–26–69	Philippines	*Caddo Parish* (LST-515)	*Bataan* (LT-85)	Grant Aid)
11–26–69	Philippines	*Hickman County* (LST-825)	*Cagayan* (LT-86)	Grant Aid
11–26–69	Philippines	*Madera County* (LST-905)	*Ilicos Norte* (LT-87)	Grant Aid
12–9–69	Taiwan	*Brush* (DD-745)		Sale
12–9–69	Taiwan	*Samuel N. Moore* (DD-747)		Sale
12–9–69	Taiwan	*Bristol* (DD-857)		Sale
12–9–69	Vietnam	*Point Ellis* (USCG)	(HQ-705)	Grant Aid
12–11–69	Vietnam	*Point Hudson* (USCG)	(HQ-707)	Grant Aid
12–11–69	Vietnam	*Point Slocum* (USCG)	(HQ-706)	Grant Aid
1–12–70	Vietnam	*Point White* (USCG)	(HQ-708)	Grant Aid
1–17–70	Italy	*Prichett* (DD-561)	*Geniere* (D-555)	Sale
2–14–70	Vietnam	*Point Glover* (USCG)	*Dao Van Danh* (HQ-711)	Grant Aid
2–14–70	Vietnam	*Point Dume* (USCG)	*Truong Truyen* (HQ-709)	Grant Aid
2–14–70	Vietnam	*Point Arden* (USCG)	*Pham Ngoc Chau* (HQ-710)	Grant Aid
2–21–70	Vietnam	*Point Jefferson* (USCG)	— (HQ-712)	Grant Aid
3– –70	Korea	MSI-93 (ex-Belgian)	SURO-6	Grant Aid
3–12–70	Thailand	*Stone County* (LST-1141)	*Lanta* (LST-4)	Lease
3–16–70	Vietnam	*Point Young* (USCG)	(HQ-714)	Grant Aid
3–16–70	Vietnam	*Point Kennedy* (USCG)	(HQ-713)	Grant Aid
3–24–70	Turkey	MSC-124 (ex-French)	*Seicuk* (M-508)	Grant Aid
3–24–70	Turkey	MSC-142 (ex-French)	*Sey Hau* (M-509)	Grant Aid
3–27–70	Vietnam	*Point Partridge* (USCG)	*Bui Viet Thanh* (HQ-715)	Grant Aid
4–1–70	Vietnam	*Bulloch County* (LST-509)	*Qui Nhon* (HQ-504)	Lease
4–1–70	Vietnam	*Jerome County* (LST-848)	*Nha Trang* (HQ-505)	Lease
4–29–70	Vietnam	*Point Welcome* (USCG)	*Nguyen Han* (HQ-717)	Grant Aid
4–29–70	Vietnam	*Point Caution* (USCG)	*Nguyen An* (HQ-716)	Grant Aid
5–2–70	Germany	DDG-30	*Rommel* (D-187)	Sale (B)
5–12–70	Taiwan	*Haynsworth* (DD-700)		Sale
5–25–70	Argentina	*Gunston Hall* (LSD-5)	*Candido De Lasala* (Q-43)	Sale
5–26–70	Vietnam	*Point Lomas* (USCG)	(HQ-718)	Grant Aid
5–26–70	Vietnam	*Point Banks* (USCG)	(HQ-719)	Grant Aid
6–3–70	Vietnam	*Prowess* (IX-305)	*Ha Hoi* (HQ-13)	Grant Aid
6–3–70	Vietnam	*Amherst* (PCER-853)	*Van Kiep II* (HQ-14)	Grant Aid
6–12–70	Turkey	*Greenlet* (ASR-10)	*Akin* (A-585)	Lease
6–15–70	Vietnam	*Point Grace* (USCG)	*Dam Thoai* (HQ-721)	Grant Aid
6–15–70	Vietnam	*Point Mast* (USCG)	*Ho Dang La* (HQ-720)	Grant Aid
7–14–70	Vietnam	*Point Orient* (USCG)	*Nguyen Kim Hung* (HQ-723)	Grant Aid
7–14–70	Vietnam	*Point Grey* (USCG)	*Nuy Bo* (HQ-722)	Grant Aid
7–15–70	Indonesia	*Clarke County* (LST-601)	*Teluk Saleh* (LST-510)	Lease
7–15–70	Indonesia	*Iredell County* (LST-839)	*Teluk Bome* (LST-511)	Lease
8–2–70	Iran	PGM-122	(PC-67)	Grant Aid
8–6–70	Taiwan	*Ellyson* (DD-454) (ex-Japanese)		Sale
8–6–70	Taiwan	*Macomb* (DD-458) (ex-Japanese, for cannibalization)		Sale
8–10–70	New Zealand	*Charles H. Davis* (AGOR-5)	*Tui* (A-2)	Lease
8–11–70	Taiwan	*English* (DD-696)		Sale

8–15–70	Vietnam	*Point Cypress* (USCG)	(HQ-725)	Grant Aid
8–15–70	Vietnam	*Point Marone* (USCG)	(HQ-724)	Grant Aid
8–19–70	Mexico	*Harrison* (DD-573)		Sale
8–19–70	Mexico	*John Rogers* (DD-574)		Sale
9–4–70	Uraguay	MSO-451 (ex-French)	*Maldonado*	Grant Aid
10–12–70	Vietnam	*Harnett County* (AGP-821)	*My Tho* (HQ-800)	Lease
11–70	Turkey	MSC-131 (ex-Belgian)	*Seyman*	Grant Aid
11–27–70	Turkey	*Razorback* (SS-394)	*Murat Reis* (S-336)	Sale
12–7–70	Greece	MSC-314	*Alkion* (M-211)	Grant Aid
12–7–70	Greece	MSC-319	*Pleias* (M-240)	Grant Aid
12–15–70	Turkey	*Sea Fox* (SS-402)	*Burak Reis* (S-335)	Sale
1–71	Indonesia	*Tidewater* (AD-31)	*Dumai*	Lease
1–1–71	Vietnam	*Yakutat* (WHEC-380)	*Tran Nhat Duat* (HQ-03)	Grant Aid
1–1–71	Vietnam	*Bering Strait* (WHEC-382)	*Tran Quan Khai* (HQ-02)	Grant Aid
1–1–71	Greece	*Fort Mandan* (LSD-21)	*Nafkratoussa*	Lease
1–23–71	Greece	*Frank Knox* (DD-742)	*Themistocles* (D-210)	Sale
2–71	Taiwan	*Ernest G. Small* (DD-838)		Sale
2–13–71	Vietnam	*Camp* (DER-251)	*Tran Hung Dao* (HQ-01)	Grant Aid
3–5–71	Greece	*Page County* (LST-1076)	*Kriti* (L-171)	Lease
3–19–71	Iran	*Zellars* (DD-777)		Sale
3–19–71	Iran	*Gainard* (DD-706)		Sale
3–27–71	Turkey	*Forrest Royal* (DD-872)	*Adatepe* (D-353)	Sale
4–7–71	Indonesia	*Jacana* (MSC-193)	*Palau Alor* (717)	Lease
4–7–71	Indonesia	*Meadowlark* (MSC-196)	*Palau Arauh* (718)	Lease
4–24–71	Vietnam	*Garrett County* (AGP-786)	*Can Tho* (HQ-801)	Lease
5–24–71	Brazil	*Outagamie County* (LST-1073)	*Garcia D'Avila* (G-28)	Lease

13. RECLASSIFIED AND RENAMED SHIPS

This is a chronological listing of vessels that were reclassified and/or underwent a name change since 1–1–65. Certain vessels indicated were not named until after reclassification. These are indicated with the word "unnamed" in the name column. "No name" indicates that the craft is not a commissioned vessel. A dash in the "from" column indicates that the craft bore no previous USN classification.

Date of Change	Name or Number	From	To
3–1–65	no name	YFU-1	YFB-86
3–1–65	no name	YFU-15	LCU-776
3–1–65	no name	YFN-289	YFNX-23
3–1–65	no name	BR-6435	YFRN-1235
3–1–65	no name	BR-6436	YFRN-1236
3–1–65	no name	YR-79	YRR-10
3–22–65	SS-260	*Lapon*	name cancelled
3–22–65	SS-320	*Bergall*	name cancelled
3–22–65	SS-363	*Guitarro*	name cancelled
3–22–65	SS-364	*Hammerhead*	name cancelled
3–22–65	SS-366	*Hawkbill*	name cancelled
3–22–65	SS-381	*Sandlance*	name cancelled
3–22–65	ex-SS *American Flyer*	—	*Flyer* (AG-178)
3–27–65	ex-*Albemarle* (AV-5)	*Albemarle* (AV-5)	*Corpus Christi Bay* (ARVH-1)
4–8–65	AGM-19	*Mission San Fernando*	*Muscle Shoals*
4–8–65	AGM-20	*Mission De Pala*	*Johnstown*
4–8–65	AGM-21	*Mission San Juan*	*Flagstaff*
4–8–65	AGMR-2	*Saipan*	*Arlington*
4–15–65	*Bream*	SS-243	AGSS-243
4–21–65	LSM-161	*Kodiak*	name cancelled
5–15–65	*Tunny*	SSG-282	SS-282
5–22–65	ex-SS *Ethiopia Victory*	—	*Victoria* (AK-281)
8–15–65	*Halibut*	SSGN-587	SSN-587
9–1–65	AGM-19	*Muscle Shoals*	*Vanguard*
9–1–65	AGM-20	*Johnstown*	*Redstone*
9–1–65	AGM-21	*Flagstaff*	*Mercury*
11–1–65	*Virgo*	AKA-20	AE-30
11–1–65	*Chara*	AKA-58	AE-31
12–15–65	*Valcour*	AVP-55	AGF-1
3–1–66	*Prowess*	MSF-280	IX-305
4–1–66	*Spokane*	CLAA-120	AG-191
4–5–66	DEG-6	*Furer*	*Julius A. Furer*
6–1–66	*Orleans Parish*	MSC-6	LST-1069
7–1–66	*Charr*	SS-328	AGSS-328
8–4–66	AGSS-304	*Seahorse*	name cancelled
8–4–66	AGSS-411	*Spadefish*	name cancelled

Date of Change	Name or Number	From	To
9–15–66	*Decatur*	DD-936	DDG-31
10–1–66	*Tunny*	SS-282	APSS-282
10–25–66	AGSS-387	*Pintado*	name cancelled
12–1–66	*Sgt. George D. Keathley*	APC-117	AGS-35
3–15–67	*John Paul Jones*	DD–932	DDG–32
3–15–67	*Parsons*	DD-949	DDG-33
3–15–67	*Somers*	DD-947	DDG-34
3–15–67	*Mitscher*	DL-2	DDG-35
3–15–67	*John S. McCain*	DL-3	DDG-36
4–1–67	*Elk River*	LSMR-501	IX-501
4–1–67	*Chain*	ARS-20	AGOR-17
4–1–67	*Snatch*	ARS-27	AGOR-18
4–1–67	*Asheville*	PGM-84	PG-84
4–1–67	*Gallup*	PGM-85	PG-85
4–1–67	*Antelope*	PGM-86	PG-86
4–1–67	*Ready*	PGM-87	PG-87
4–1–67	*Crockett*	PGM-88	PG-88
4–1–67	*Marathon*	PGM-89	PG-89
4–1–67	*Canon*	PGM-90	PG-90
4–1–67	*Tacoma*	PGM-92	PG-92
4–1–67	*Welch*	PGM-93	PG-93
4–1–67	*Chehalis*	PGM-94	PG-94
4–1–67	unnamed	PGM-95/101	PG-95/101
5–1–67	*Croaker*	SS-246	AGSS-246
5–1–67	*Medregal*	SS-480	AGSS-480
6–1–67	*Banner*	AKL-25	AGER-1
6–1–67	*Pueblo*	AKL-44	AGER-2
6–1–67	*Palm Beach*	AKL-45	AGER-3
6–15–67	*Piper*	SS-409	AGSS-409
9–1–67	no name	YDT-11	YRST-1
9–1–67	no name	YDT-12	YRST-2
9–1–67	no name	YDT-13	YRST-3
9–1–67	ex-German *Ausdauer*	—	YHLC-1
9–1–67	ex-German *Energie*	—	YHLC-2
9–1–67	ex-HMS LC-23	(leased)	YMLC-5
9–1–67	ex-HMS LC-24	(leased)	YMLC-6
9–1–67	ex-HMS LC-26	(leased)	YMLC-7

9–1–67	ex-HMS LC-27	(leased)	YMLC-8
9–1–67	no name	LCU-1348	YLLC-1
9–1–67	no name	YFU-16	YLLC-2
9–1–67	no name	YFU-33	YLLC-3
9–1–67	no name	LCU-1459	YLLC-4
9–1–67	no name	YFU-2	YLLC-5
11–1–67	*Salvager*	ARSD-3	YMLC-3
11–1–67	*Windlass*	ARSD-4	YMLC-4
4–1–68	*Naubec*	AN-84	YRST-4
4–1–68	*Fairview*	EPCER-850	PCER-850
4–1–68	*Rockville*	EPCER-851	PCER-851
4–1–68	*Rexburg*	EPCER-855	PCER-855
4–1–68	*Marysville*	EPCER-857	PCER-857
4–1–68	*Compass Island*	EAG-153	AG-153
4–1–68	*Observation Island*	EAG-154	AG-154
5–1–68	*Boston*	CAG-1	CA-69
5–1–68	*Canberra*	CAG-2	CA-70
5–1–68	*Carp*	SS-338	AGSS-338
5–1–68	*Torsk*	SS-423	AGSS-423
5–16–68	no name	LCU-649	YFU-83
5–16–68	no name	LCU-715	YFU-84
5–16–68	no name	LCU-1373	YFU-85
6–29–68	*Sea Cat*	SS-399	AGSS-399
6–29–68	*Requin*	SS-481	AGSS-481
6–29–68	*Salmon*	SS-573	AGSS-573
6–29–68	*Saluda*	IX-87	YAG-87
7–16–68	DD-441	*Wilkes*	name cancelled
8–30–68	*Grayback*	SSG-574	LPSS-574
10–1–68	*Blue Ridge*	AGC-19	LCC-19
10–1–68	unnamed	AGC-20	LCC-20
10–1–68	*Durham*	AKA-114	LKA-114
10–1–68	*Mobile*	AKA-115	LKA-115
10–1–68	*St. Louis*	AKA-116	LKA-116
10–1–68	unnamed	AKA-117	LKA-117
12–14–68	*Charleston*	AKA-113	LKA-113
1–1–69	*Tunny*	APSS-282	LPSS-282
1–1–69	*Perch*	APSS-313	LPSS-313
1–1–69	*Sealion*	APSS-315	LPSS-315
1–1–69	*Mount McKinley*	AGC-7	LCC-7
1–1–69	*Eldorado*	AGC-11	LCC-11
1–1–69	*Estes*	AGC-12	LCC-12
1–1–69	*Pocono*	AGC-16	LCC-16
1–1–69	*Taconic*	AGC-17	LCC-17
1–1–69	*Thuban*	AKA-19	LKA-19
1–1–69	*Algol*	AKA-54	LKA-54
1–1–69	*Arneb*	AKA-56	LKA-56
1–1–69	*Capricornus*	AKA-57	LKA-57
1–1–69	*Muliphen*	AKA-61	LKA-61
1–1–69	*Wyandot*	AKA-92	AK-283
1–1–69	*Yancey*	AKA-93	LKA-93
1–1–69	*Winston*	AKA-94	LKA-94
1–1–69	*Merrick*	AKA-97	LKA-97
1–1–69	*Rankin*	AKA-103	LKA-103
1–1–69	*Seminole*	AKA-104	LKA-104
1–1–69	*Skagit*	AKA-105	LKA-105
1–1–69	*Union*	AKA-106	LKA-106
1–1–69	*Vermilion*	AKA-107	LKA-107
1–1–69	*Washburn*	AKA-108	LKA-108
1–1–69	*Tulare*	AKA-112	LKA-112
1–1–69	*Butternut*	AN-9	ANL-9
1–1–69	*Cohoes*	AN-78	ANL-78
1–1–69	*Cambria*	APA-36	LPA-36
1–1–69	*Chilton*	APA-38	LPA-38
1–1–69	*Fremont*	APA-44	LPA-44
1–1–69	*Henrico*	APA-45	LPA-45
1–1–69	*Sandoval*	APA-194	LPA-194
1–1–69	*Magoffin*	APA-199	LPA-199
1–1–69	*Talladega*	APA-208	LPA-208
1–1–69	*Montrose*	APA-212	LPA-212
1–1–69	*Mountrail*	APA-213	LPA-213
1–1–69	*Navarro*	APA-215	LPA-215
1–1–69	*Okanogan*	APA-220	LPA-220
1–1–69	*Pickaway*	APA-222	LPA-222
1–1–69	*Bexar*	APA-237	LPA-237
1–1–69	*Paul Revere*	APA-248	LPA-248
1–1–69	*Francis Marion*	APA-249	LPA-249
1–1–69	*Laning*	APD-55	LPR-55
1–1–69	*Barber*	APD-57	LPR-57
1–1–69	*Hollis*	APD-86	LPR-86
1–1–69	*Ruchamkin*	APD-89	LPR-89
1–1–69	*Kirwin*	APD-90	LPR-90
1–1–69	*Ringness*	APD-100	LPR-100
1–1–69	*Knudson*	APD-101	LPR-101
1–1–69	*Beverly W. Reid*	APD-119	LPR-119
1–1–69	*Diachenko*	APD-123	LPR-123
1–1–69	*Horace A. Bass*	APD-124	LPR-124
1–1–69	*Begor*	APD-127	LPR-127
1–1–69	*Cook*	APD-130	LPR-130
1–1–69	*Balduck*	APD-132	LPR-132
1–1–69	*Weiss*	APD-135	LPR-135
1–1–69	*Lexington*	CVS-16	CVT-16
1–1–69	*Kenneth D. Bailey*	DDR-713	DD-713
1–1–69	*Frank Knox*	DDR-742	DD-742
1–1–69	*Goodrich*	DDR-831	DD-831
1–1–69	*Turner*	DDR-834	DD-834
1–1–69	*Ernest G. Small*	DDR-838	DD-838
1–1–69	*Duncan*	DDR-874	DD-874
1–1–69	*Robert H. Smith*	DM-23	MMD-23
1–1–69	*Thomas E. Fraser*	DM-24	MMD-24
1–1–69	*Shannon*	DM-25	MMD-25

continued

Reclassified and Renamed Ships—*continued*

Date of Change	Name or Number	From	To
1–1–69	*Harry F. Bauer*	DM-26	MMD-26
1–1–69	*Adams*	DM-27	MMD-27
1–1–69	*Tolman*	DM-28	MMD-28
1–1–69	*Henry A. Wiley*	DM-29	MMD-29
1–1–69	*Shea*	DM-30	MMD-30
1–1–69	*Lindsey*	DM-32	MMD-32
1–1–69	*Gwin*	DM-33	MMD-33
1–1–69	*Carronade*	IFS-1	LFR-1
1–1–69	*Big Black River*	LSMR-401	LFR-401
1–1–69	*Broadkill River*	LSMR-405	LFR-405
1–1–69	*Clarion River*	LSMR-409	LFR-409
1–1–69	*Des Plaines River*	LSMR-412	LFR-412
1–1–69	*Lamoille River*	LSMR-512	LFR-512
1–1–69	*Laramie River*	LSMR-513	LFR-513
1–1–69	*Owyhee River*	LSMR-515	LFR-515
1–1–69	*Red River*	LSMR-522	LFR-522
1–1–69	*St. Francis River*	LSMR-525	LFR-525
1–1–69	*Smoky Hill River*	LSMR-531	LFR-531
1–1–69	*White River*	LSMR-536	LFR-536
1–1–69	no name	LSM-335	AG-335
1–1–69	*Comet*	LSV-7	AKR-7
1–1–69	*Taurus*	LSV-8	AKR-8
1–1–69	*Sea Lift*	LSV-9	AKR-9
2–69	no name	AKL-17	*New Bedford* (IX-308)
2–1–69	*Runner*	SS-476	AGSS-476
2–27–69	no name	YFU-83	LCU-649
2–27–69	no name	YFU-84	LCU-715
2–27–69	no name	YFU-85	LCU-1373
4–16–69	*Sherburne*	APA-205	AGM-22
5–69	no name	YW-87	IX-309
6–30–69	*Shangri-La*	CVA-38	CVS-38
6–30–69	*Salmon*	AGSS-573	SS-573
6–30–69	*Sablefish*	SS-303	AGSS-303

Date of Change	Name or Number	From	To
6–30–69	*Bugara*	SS-331	AGSS-331
6–30–69	*Carbonero*	SS-337	AGSS-337
6–30–69	*Cusk*	SS-348	AGSS-348
6–30–69	*Sea Owl*	SS-405	AGSS-405
6–30–69	*Irex*	SS-482	AGSS-482
6–30–69	*Spinax*	SS-489	AGSS-489
8–19–69	ex-SS *Marshfield Victory*	—	*Marshfield* (AK-282)
8–29–69	ex-USCG *Brier* (WLI-299)	—	*Brier* (IX-307)
9–1–69	*Trieste II*	—	X-2
9–15–69	*Chopper*	SS-342	AGSS-342
10–1–69	*Bugara*	AGSS-331	SS-331
10–1–69	*Carbonero*	AGSS-337	SS-337
10–1–69	*Medregal*	AGSS-480	SS-480
10–1–69	*Becuna*	SS-319	AGSS-319
10–1–69	*Blenny*	SS-324	AGSS-324
10–1–69	*Atule*	SS-403	AGSS-403
10–1–69	*Tench*	SS-417	AGSS-417
10–21–69	*Ticonderoga*	CVA-14	CVS-14
11–1–69	*Sea Poacher*	SS-406	AGSS-406
12–1–69	*Coastal Crusader*	AGM-16	AGS-36
5–25–70	CVAN-69	*Eisenhower*	*Dwight D. Eisenhower*
6–17–70	no name	LCU-1576	YFU-89
6–17–70	no name	LCU-1582	YFU-90
6–17–70	no name	LCU-1608	YFU-91
6–17–70	no name	ARD-18	ARDM-3
7–1–70	no name	IX-309	YAG-61
9–25–70	*Garrett County*	LST-786	AGP-786
9–25–70	*Harnett County*	LST-821	AGP-821
9–25–70	*Hunterdon County*	LST-838	AGP-838
9–25–70	*S. P. Lee*	T-AGS-31	T-AG-191
12–3–70	YTB-814	*Waxahatchie*	*Waxahachie*
2–26–71	*Benewah*	APB-35	IX-311
3–12–71	*Grand Canyon*	AD-28	AR-28

14. STRIKE LIST

This is a chronological listing of vessels struck from the NVR since 1–1–65. For easier use, the list is divided into 3 parts: commissioned USN ships, noncommissioned USN craft, and USCG vessels.

A. Commissioned U.S.N. Ships

Strike Date	Name and/or Hull Number	Comments
1–1–65	*Signet* (MSF-302)	Sold/Dominican Republic.
1–1–65	*Skirmish* (MSF-303)	Sold/Dominican Republic.
2–1–65	*Earle B. Hall* (APD-107)	Scrapped.
3–1–65	*Donald W. Wolf* (APD-129)	Sold/Taiwan.
3–1–65	*Kinzer* (APD-91)	Sold/Taiwan.
4–1–65	*Ahrens* (DE-575)	Scrapped.
4–1–65	*Bass* (SS-551)	Ex SSK-2. Scrapped.
4–1–65	*Bonita* (SS-552)	Ex SSK-3. Scrapped.
4–1–65	*Flaherty* (DE-135)	Scrapped.
4–1–65	*Fogg* (DE-57)	Scrapped.
4–1–65	*Fresno* (CLAA-121)	Scrapped.
4–1–65	*Frost* (DE-144)	Scrapped.
4–1–65	*Highland Light* (IX-48)	Schoolship for private Institution.
4–1–65	*Investigator* (AGR-9)	Trans./MARAD for layup.
4–1–65	*McDermut* (DD-677)	Scrapped.
4–1–65	*Redstart* (MSF-378)	Sold/Taiwan.
4–1–65	*Skywatcher* (AGR-3)	Trans./MARAD for layup.
4–1–65	*Smalley* (DD-565)	Scrapped.
4–1–65	*Vigil* (AGR-12)	Trans./MARAD for layup.
4–1–65	*Waxwing* (MSF-389)	Sold/Taiwan.
5–1–65	*Caldwell* (DD-605)	Scrapped.
5–1–65	*Daniel A. Joy* (DE-585)	Scrapped.
5–1–65	*Foreman* (DE-633)	Scrapped.
6–1–65	*Durik* (DE-666)	Scrapped.
6–1–65	LSM-161 (ex-*Kodiak*)	Salvage/fire-fighting training hulk, Pearl Harbor.
6–1–65	*Maloy* (EDE-791)	Scrapped.
6–1–65	*Murray* (DD-576)	Scrapped.
7–1–65	*Fowler* (DE-222)	Scrapped.
7–1–65	*Grafton* (PCS-1431)	Sold (mercantile).
7–1–65	*Pillsbury* (DER-133)	Scrapped.
7–1–65	*Scott* (DE-214)	Scrapped.
7–1–65	*Scroggins* (DE-799)	Scrapped.
7–1–65	*Searcher* (AGR-4)	Trans./MARAD for layup; to be scrapped.
7–1–65	*Interpreter* (AGR-14)	Trans./MARAD for layup.
7–1–65	*Yamacraw* (ARC-5)	Ex-USCG. Scrapped.
8–1–65	*Borum* (DE-790)	Scrapped.

continued

Commissioned U.S.N. Ships—*continued*

Strike Date	Name and/or Hull Number	Comments
8–1–65	*Carroll* (DE-171)	Scrapped.
8–1–65	*Harmon* (DE-678)	Scrapped.
8–1–65	*Jupiter* (AVS-8)	Trans./MARAD for layup.
8–1–65	*Micka* (DE-176)	Scrapped.
8–1–65	*Sirius* (AF-60)	Trans./MARAD for layup.
8–15–65	*Potawatomi* (ATF-109)	Grounded/sunk while on lease to Chile.
8–16–65	*Mulberry* (AN-27)	Reinstated on the NVR this date; loaned to Ecuador.
8–20–65	*Bowers* (APD-40)	Sunk in typhoon while on loan to Philippines; raised/scrapped.
9–1–65	*Guardian* (AGR-1)	Trans./MARAD for layup.
9–1–65	*Lookout* (AGR-2)	Trans./MARAD for layup.
9–1–65	*Outpost* (AGR-10)	Trans./MARAD for layup.
9–1–65	*Interceptor* (AGR-8)	Trans./MARAD for layup.
9–1–65	*Interdictor* (AGR-13)	Trans./MARAD for layup.
9–1–65	*Locator* (AGR-6)	Trans./MARAD for layup.
9–1–65	*Picket* (AGR-7)	Trans./MARAD for layup.
9–1–65	*Protector* (AGR-11)	Trans./MARAD for layup.
9–1–65	*Scanner* (AGR-5)	Trans./MARAD for layup.
9–1–65	*Tracer* (AGR-15)	Trans./MARAD for layup.
9–1–65	*Watchman* (AGR-16)	Trans./MARAD for layup.
9–1–65	*Antares* (AKS-33)	Trans./MARAD for layup after being damaged by fire.
9–1–65	*Flint* (CLAA-97)	Scrapped.
11–1–65	*Brough* (DE-148)	Scrapped.
11–1–65	*Edisto* (AGB-2)	Trans./USCG 10–20–65.
11–1–65	*Foss* (DE-59)	Scrapped.
11–1–65	*George A. Johnson* (DE-583)	Grounded enroute breakers; scrapped.
11–1–65	*Sellstrom* (DER-255)	Scrapped.
11–1–65	*Spangenberg* (DE-223)	Scrapped.
11–1–65	*Tingey* (DD-539)	Sunk as target 5–66.
11–1–65	*Weatherford* (EPC-618)	Last steel hull PC in USN; Salvage training hulk until 1–11–68. Sunk as target.
11–1–65	*William T. Powell* (DE-213)	Ex-DER. Scrapped.
11–1–65	*Brattleboro* (EPCER-852)	Trans./South Vietnam.
12–1–65	*Douglas A. Munro* (DE-422)	Sunk as target.
12–1–65	*Ulvert M. Moore* (DE-442)	Sunk as target 7–13–66.
1–1–66	*Lewis* (DE-535)	Sunk as target 4–66.
1–1–66	*Naifeh* (DE-352)	Sunk as target 7–11–66.
1–15–66	APD-98 (ex-*Truxtun*)	Sold/Taiwan.
1–15–66	*Gantner* (APD-42)	Sold/Taiwan.
1–15–66	*Harry L. Corl* (APD-108)	Sold/Korea.
1–15–66	*Julius A. Raven* (APD-110)	Sold/Korea.
1–15–66	*Kline* (APD-120)	Sold/Taiwan.
1–15–66	*Walter B. Cobb* (APD-106)	Sold/Taiwan. Sank 4–21–66 by collision while under tow to Taiwan.
1–20–66	*Locust* (AN-22)	Reinstated on NVR this date for sale to France.
2–1–66	*Jenks* (DE-665)	Scrapped.
3–1–66	*Staten Island* (AGB-5)	Trans./USCG 2–1–66.
4–1–66	*Burdo* (APD-133)	Scrapped.
4–1–66	*Cofer* (APD-62)	Scrapped.
4–1–66	*Corson* (AVP-37)	Sunk as target.
4–1–66	*Edison* (DD-439)	Scrapped.

4–1–66	*Somersworth* (PCER-849)	Sold (mercantile).
4–1–66	*Suisun* (AVP-53)	Sunk as target 10–66.
4–1–66	*Vincennes* (CL-64)	Sunk as target 10–28–69.
4–27–66	AKL-27	Salvage training hulk (1966–71); scrapped.
5–1–66	*Duxbury Bay* (AVP-38)	Scrapped.
5–1–66	*Gregory* (DD-802)	Renamed *Indoctrinator* 5–20–66. Served as moored nonoperable training hulk to 1–8–71. Grounded 3–4–71 while serving as a target.
5–1–66	*Heyliger* (DE-510)	Sunk as target.
5–1–66	*Hubbard* (APD-53)	Scrapped.
5–1–66	*Kendrick* (DD-612)	Sunk as target 3–2–68.
5–1–66	*Martin H. Ray* (DE-338)	Scrapped.
5–1–66	*Maurice J. Manuel* (DE-351)	Sunk as target.
5–1–66	*Straus* (DE-408)	Sunk as target.
5–1–66	*Walsh* (APD-111)	Scrapped.
6–1–66	*Lloyd* (APD-63)	Scrapped.
6–1–66	*Speed* (MSF-116)	Trans./Rep. of Korea.
6–1–66	*Tucson* (CLAA-98)	Experimental hulk (1966–1970); scrapped.
6–15–66	*Bull* (APD-78)	Sold/Taiwan as APD-106 replacement.
7–1–66	*Robert E. Peary* (DE-132)	Scrapped.
7–1–66	*Glacier* (AGB-4)	Trans./USCG 6–30–66.
7–1–66	*Cross* (DE-448)	Scrapped.
7–1–66	*Greenwich Bay* (AVP-41)	Scrapped.
7–1–66	*Haas* (DE-424)	Scrapped.
8–1–66	*Calvert* (APA-32)	Cargo handling training hulk since 1966.
8–1–66	*Colahan* (DD-658)	Sunk as target 12–18–66.
8–1–66	*Scribner* (APD-122)	Scrapped.
9–1–66	*Fessenden* (DER-142)	Sunk as target 12–20–67.
9–1–66	*Raymon W. Herndon* (APD-121)	Sold/Taiwan.
9–1–66	*Register* (APD-92)	Sold/Taiwan.
9–1–66	*Saufley* (EDD-465)	Sunk as target 2–20–68.
11–1–66	*Atka* (AGB-3)	Trans./USCG 10–31–66.
11–1–66	*Bunker Hill* (AVT-9)	Retained for use as electronic test platform since 1965.
11–1–66	*Gadwall* (MSF-362)	Sold (mercantile).
11–1–66	*Revenge* (MSF-110)	Scrapped.
12–1–66	*Currier* (DE-700)	Sunk as target 7–67.
12–1–66	*Daniel T. Griffin* (APD-38)	Sold/Chile.
12–1–66	*General J. C. Breckenridge* (AP-176)	Trans./MARAD for layup.
12–1–66	*General W. A. Mann* (AP-112)	Trans./MARAD for layup.
12–1–66	*General William Mitchell* (AP-114)	Trans./MARAD for layup.
12–1–66	*Harveson* (DER-316)	Sunk as target 10–10–67.
12–1–66	*Hayter* (APD-80)	Trans./Rep. of Korea.
12–1–66	*Jack C. Robinson* (APD-72)	Sold/Chile.
12–1–66	*Odum* (APD-71)	Sold/Chile.
12–1–66	*Joseph E. Campbell* (APD-49)	Sold/Chile.
12–1–66	*Knight* (DD-633)	Ex-DMS. Sunk as target 10–27–67.
12–1–66	*Motive* (MSF-102)	Sunk as target 1–11–67.
12–1–66	*Nuthatch* (MSF-60)	Sunk as target 10–14–67.
12–1–66	*Oracle* (MSF-103)	Sunk as target.
12–1–66	*Peiffer* (DE-588)	Sunk as target 5–67.
12–1–66	*Pheasant* (MSF-61)	Sunk as target.
12–1–66	*Pigeon* (MSF-374)	Scrapped.

continued

Commissioned U.S.N. Ships—*continued*

Strike Date	Name and/or Hull Number	Comments
12–1–66	*Pochard* (MSF-375)	Scrapped.
12–1–66	*Quail* (MSF-377)	Scrapped.
12–1–66	*Token* (MSF-126)	Scrapped.
12–1–66	*Vigilance* (MSF-324)	Trans./Philippines.
12–1–66	*Zeal* (MSF-131)	Sunk as target 1–9–67.
1–1–67	*Burton Island* (AGB-1)	Last Icebreaker in USN. Trans./USCG 12–15–66.
1–31–67	*Mahnomen County* (LST-912)	Grounded/broached at Chu Lai, South Vietnam; salvage unsuccessful; hulk destroyed.
2–20–67	*Greenwood* (DE-679)	Scrapped.
3–1–67	AGSS-304 (ex-*Seahorse*)	Scrapped.
3–1–67	AGSS-387 (ex-*Pintado*)	Scrapped.
3–1–67	*Devilfish* (AGSS-292)	Sunk as target 8–14–68.
3–1–67	*Hackleback* (AGSS-295)	Scrapped.
3–1–67	*Heed* (MSF-100)	Scrapped.
3–1–67	*Inaugral* (MSF-242)	Tourist attraction at St. Louis, Missouri.
3–1–67	*John P. Gray* (APD-74)	Scrapped.
3–1–67	*Pipefish* (AGSS-388)	Scrapped.
3–1–67	*Piranha* (AGSS-389)	Scrapped.
3–1–67	*Rednour* (APD-102)	Sold/Mexico.
3–1–67	*Staff* (MSF-114)	Scrapped.
3–1–67	*Haven* (AH-12)	Trans./MARAD. Converted tc merchant chemical carrier.
3–1–67	*Stalwart* (MSO-493)	Capsized/sank pierside at San Juan, Puerto Rico 6–66 as a result of fire. Raised and scrapped.
3–31–67	*Condor* (MSCO-5)	Returned from loan to Japan this date; sunk as target 8–31–69.
3–31–67	*Firecrest* (MSCO-10)	Returned from loan to Japan this date; sunk as target 8–14–69.
3–31–67	*Heron* (MSCO-18)	Returned from loan to Japan this date; sunk as target 8–15–69.
4–1–67	AGSS-411 (ex-*Spadefish*)	Scrapped.
4–1–67	*Moray* (AGSS-300)	Sunk as target 6–18–70.
4–1–67	*Pavlic* (APD-70)	Scrapped.
4–1–67	*Staunch* (MSF-307)	Scrapped.
4–1–67	*Strength* (MSF-309)	Diving/salvage training hulk Washington, D.C.
4–5–67	*Liddle* (APD-60)	Scrapped.
5–1–67	*Abercrombie* (DE-343)	Sunk as target 1–7–68.
5–1–67	*Bassett* (APD-73)	Trans./Columbia.
5–1–67	*Earle V. Johnson* (DE-702)	Scrapped.
5–1–67	*Kephart* (APD-61)	Trans./Korea.
5–1–67	*Raven* (MSF-55)	Sunk as target 7–30–69.
5–1–67	*Schmitt* (APD-76)	Sold/Taiwan.
5–1–67	*Scurry* (MSF-304)	Diving/salvage training hulk.
5–1–67	*Tumult* (MSF-127)	Scrapped.
6–1–67	*Tarawa* (AVT-12)	Ex-CVS. Scrapped.
6–24–67	*Shearwater* (AG-177)	Trans./US Army this date.
6–30–67	*Cero* (AGSS-225)	Scrapped.
6–30–67	*Dentuda* (AGSS-335)	Scrapped.
6–30–67	*Guavina* (AOSS-362)	Only AOSS in USN. Sunk as target 11–67.
6–30–67	*Loggerhead* (AGSS-374)	Conning tower memorialized; hull scrapped.
6–30–67	*Manta* (AGSS-299)	Sunk as target 7–16–69.
6–30–67	*Trepang* (AGSS-412)	Sunk as target 9–16–69.
7–1–67	*Cecil J. Doyle* (DE-368)	Sunk as target.
7–1–67	*Lovelace* (DE-198)	Sunk as target 4–25–68.

7–1–67	*Neuendorf* (DE-200)	Sunk as target 11–30–67.
7–1–67	*Royono* (IX-235)	Sold (mercantile).
7–1–67	*Williams* (DE-372)	Sunk as target 6–29–68.
7–15–67	*Beaufort* (PCS-1387)	Sunk as target.
8–1–67	*Traw* (DE-350)	Sunk as target 8–17–68.
9–1–67	SS-259 (ex-*Jack*)	Returned from loan to Greece; sunk as target.
9–1–67	*Thaddeus Parker* (DE-369)	Scrapped.
10–1–67	*Graylag* (MSF-364)	Sold (mercantile).
10–1–67	*Strategy* (MSF-308)	Scrapped.
11–1–67	*Hazard* (MSF-240)	Memorial at Omaha, Nebraska.
11–1–67	*George Clymer* (APA-27)	Scrapped.
11–1–67	*Jaccard* (DE-355)	Sunk as target 10–4–68.
12–1–67	*Charles Auburne* (DD-570)	Was on loan to Germany. Sold to Germany for scrap.
12–1–67	*Lindenwald* (LSD-6)	Scrapped.
12–1–67	*Muskallung E.* (SS-262)	Sunk as target 7–9–68.
1–1–68	*Jesse Rutherford* (DE-347)	Sunk as target 12–8–68.
1–1–68	*Robert Brazier* (DE-345)	Sunk as target 1–9–69.
2–1–68	*Steady* (MSF-118)	Sold/Taiwan.
2–20–68	*Littlehales* (AGSC-15)	Last Coastal Survey Ship in USN. Sunk as target 4–3–69.
3–1–68	*Bache* (DD-470)	Grounded 2–6–68 off Rhodes, Greece; scrapped.
3–1–68	*Nelson* (DD-623)	Scrapped.
3–1–68	*Welles* (DD-628)	Scrapped.
4–1–68	*Billfish* (AGSS-286)	Scrapped.
4–1–68	*Freedom* (IX-43)	Sold (mercantile).
4–15–68	*Crevalle* (AGSS-291)	Used in nondestructive tests; scrapped.
4–19–68	*Hake* (AGSS-256)	Salvage/training hulk.
5–1–68	*Archerfish* (AGSS-311)	Sunk as target 10–16–68.
5–1–68	*Chatterer* (MSCO-40)	Returned from loan to Japan this date; scrapped.
5–1–68	*Fairview* (PCER-850)	Sold (mercantile).
5–1–68	*Pelican* (MSCO-32)	Returned from loan to Japan this date; scrapped.
5–1–68	*Swallow* (MSCO-36)	Returned from loan to Japan this date; scrapped.
5–1–68	*Gardiners Bay* (AVP-39)	Sold/Norway where she had been on loan.
5–1–68	*Halford* (DD-480)	Scrapped.
5–1–68	*Harrison* (DD-573)	Sold/Mexico.
5–1–68	*John Rogers* (DD-574)	Sold/Mexico.
5–1–68	*Izard* (DD-589)	Scrapped.
5–1–68	*John D. Henley* (DD-553)	Scrapped.
5–1–68	*Paul Hamilton* (DD-590)	Scrapped.
5–1–68	*Wiley* (DD-597)	Scrapped.
5–1–68	*Young* (DD-580)	Sunk as target 4–16–70.
6–1–68	*Bailey* (DD-492)	Sunk as target.
6–1–68	*Buckley* (DE-51)	Ex-DER. Scrapped.
6–1–68	*Burke* (APD-65)	Sold/Columbia.
6–1–68	*Charles F. Hughes* (DD-428)	Sunk as target 3–26–69.
6–1–68	*Edsall* (DE-129)	Scrapped.
6–1–68	*Kalk* (DD-611)	Sunk as target 3–20–69.
6–1–68	*Madison* (DD-425)	Sunk as target 10–14–69.
6–1–68	*Neal A. Scott* (DE-769)	Scrapped.
6–1–68	*Raby* (DE-698)	Ex-DEC. Scrapped.
6–1–68	*Robert I. Paine* (DE-578)	Ex-DER. Scrapped.
6–1–68	*Stevenson* (DD-645)	Scrapped.

continued

Commissioned U.S.N. Ships—*continued*

Strike Date	Name and/or Hull Number	Comments
6–30–68	*Bivin* (DE-536)	Sunk as target 7–17–69.
6–30–68	*Cabrilla* (AGSS-288)	Memorial at Galveston, Tex. (10–68 to 1–71); replaced and scrapped.
6–30–68	*Charles J. Kimmel* (DE-584)	Sunk as target 11–13–69.
6–30–68	*Day* (DE-225)	Sunk as target 3–69.
6–30–68	*Drum* (AGSS-228)	Memorial at Mobile, Ala. with *Alabama*.
6–30–68	*Eugene E. Elmore* (DE-686)	Scrapped.
6–30–68	*Grady* (DE-445)	Scrapped.
6–30–68	*Jack Miller* (DE-410)	Scrapped.
6–30–68	*James E. Craig* (DE-201)	Sunk as target 2–69.
6–30–68	*Lenawee* (APA-195)	Trans./MARAD for layup.
6–30–68	*Metivier* (DE-582)	Scrapped.
6–30–68	*Paddle* (SS-263)	Returned from loan to Brazil; scrapped.
6–30–68	*Presley* (DE-371)	Scrapped.
6–30–68	*Redfish* (AGSS-395)	Sunk as target 2–6–69.
6–30–68	*Renville* (APA-227)	Trans./MARAD for layup.
6–30–68	*Reuben James* (DE-153)	Ex-DER. Test hulk (1968–1971). Sunk as target 3–1–71.
6–30–68	*Richard M. Rowell* (DE-403)	Scrapped.
6–30–68	*Richard S. Bull* (DE-402)	Sunk as target 6–24–69.
6–30–68	*Richey* (DE-385)	Sunk as target 7–69.
6–30–68	*Scorpion* (SSN-589)	Announced as overdue; presumed lost in ATL 5–27–68. Officially declared lost 6–6–68.
6–30–68	*Sheldrake* (AGS-19)	Ex-MSF. Scrapped.
6–30–68	*Thomason* (DE-203)	Scrapped.
6–30–68	*Walter C. Wann* (DE-412)	Scrapped.
6–30–68	*Weeden* (DE-797)	Scrapped.
7–3–68*	*Henrico* (LPA-45)	Transferred MARAD, permanently for layup.
7–31–68	*Manning* (DE-199)	Scrapped.
7–31–68	*Mervine* (DD-489)	Ex-DMS. Scrapped.
7–31–68	*Niblack* (DD-424)	Test hulk 7–31–68 to 9–1–71. Scrapped.
9–1–68	*Burleson* (IX-67)	Ex-APA. Scrapped.
9–17–68	*Witek* (EDD-848)	Sunk as target 6–4–69.
9–23–68	*Albert T. Harris* (DE-447)	Sunk as target 4–9–69.
9–23–68	*Alvin C. Cockrill* (DE-366)	Sunk as target 9–19–69.
9–23–68	*Lowe* (DER-325)	Scrapped.
9–23–68	*Brister* (DER-327)	Scrapped.
9–23–68	*Koiner* (DER-331)	Scrapped.
9–23–68	*Charles E. Brannon* (DE-446)	Scrapped.
9–23–68	*Darby* (DE-218)	Sunk as target 5–24–70.
9–23–68	*Howard D. Crow* (DE-252)	Scrapped.
9–23–68	*Loeser* (DE-680)	Sunk as target.
9–23–68	*McGinty* (DE-365)	Scrapped.
9–23–68	*Newell* (DER-322)	Scrapped.
9–23–68	*Roberts* (DE-749)	Sunk as target.
9–23–68	*Snowden* (DE-246)	Sunk as target 6–27–69.
9–23–68	*Tills* (DE-748)	Sunk as target 4–3–69.
9–23–68	*Walton* (DE-361)	Sunk as target 8–7–69.
10–1–68	*Barton* (DD-722)	Sunk as target 10–8–69.
10–1–68	*Plover* (MSCO-33)	Scrapped.
10–1–68	*Bayfield* (APA-33)	Scrapped.

10–1–68	*Beale* (DD-471)	Sunk as target 6–24–69.
10–1–68	*Formoe* (DE-509)	Sold to Portugal 11–68, where she had been on loan, for scrapping.
10–1–68	*Fulmar* (MSCO-47)	Sold.
10–1–68	*Linnet* (MSCO-24)	Sold.
10–1–68	*Lorikeet* (MSCO-49)	Sold.
10–1–68	*Mattabesset* (AOG-52)	Scrapped.
10–1–68	*Nahant* (AN-83)	Sold/Uruguay.
10–1–68	*Pandemus* (ARL-18)	Sunk as target.
10–1–68	*Philip* (DD-498)	Sunk as target.
10–1–68	*Bellatrix* (AF-62)	Scrapped.
10–1–68	*Cimarron* (AO-22)	Scrapped.
10–1–68	*Cavalier* (APA-37)	Scrapped.
10–1–68	*Reedbird* (MSCO-51)	Sold.
10–1–68	*Siskin* (MSCO-58)	Sold.
10–1–68	*Turkey* (MSCO-56)	Sold.
10–1–68	*Sproston* (DD-577)	Scrapped.
10–1–68	*Sterlet* (SS-392)	Sunk as target 1–31–69.
11–1–68	*Epping Forest* (MSC-7)	Ex-LSD. Scrapped.
11–1–68	*Mathews* (AKA-96)	Scrapped.
11–1–68	*McCoy Reynolds* (DE-440)	Sold to Portugal 11–68, where she had been on loan, for scrapping.
11–1–68	*Monrovia* (APA-31)	Scrapped.
11–1–68	*Oglethorpe* (AKA-100)	Scrapped.
11–1–68	*Telfair* (APA-210)	Scrapped.
11–27–68	*Barber* (LPR-57)	Sold/Mexico.
12–1–68	*Castor* (AKS-1)	Scrapped.
12–1–68	*Uvalde* (AKA-88)	Scrapped.
12–1–68	*Rockbridge* (APA-228)	Scrapped.
12–2–68	*Argonaut* (SS-475)	Sold/Canada.
12–2–68	*Grouper* (AGSS-214)	Ex-SSK. Scrapped.
12–2–68	*Sea Cat* (AGSS-399)	Sunk as target.
12–2–68	*Sea Dog* (AGSS-401)	Used in tests; scrapped.
12–2–68	*Sennet* (SS-408)	Sunk as target.
12–14–68	*Allegheny* (ATA-179)	Donated to private foundation as research vessel.
12–21–68	*Rockville* (PCER-851)	Sold/Columbia.
12–31–68	*Alcor* (AK-259)	Scrapped.
1–1–69	*Pollux* (AKS-4)	Scrapped.
1–1–69	*Targeteer* (YV-3)	Ex-LSMR. Scrapped.
2–1–69	*Peregrine* (AG-176)	Ex-MSF. Scrapped.
5–1–69	*Towhee* (AGS-28)	Ex-MSF. Scrapped.
6–1–69	*Avoyel* (ATF-150)	On loan to Coast Guard. Trans. permanently this date.
6–1–69	*Bryant* (DD-665)	Sunk as target 8–24–69.
6–1–69	*Chilula* (ATF-153)	On loan to Coast Guard. Trans. permanently this date.
6–1–69	*Leyte* (AVT-10)	Ex-CVS. Scrapped.
6–1–69	USNS LST-600 (T-LST-600)	Grounded 12–23–68 off Okinawa during storm; scrapped, after salvage.
6–1–69	*San Pablo* (AGS-30)	Ex-AVP. Scrapped.
6–1–69	*Wampanoag* (ATA-202)	On loan to Coast Guard. Trans. permanently this date.
6–2–69	*Haverfield* (DER-393)	Scrapped.
6–15–69	*Osprey* (MSCO-28)	Returned from loan to Japan; scrapped.
6–15–69	*Vandalia* (PC-1175)	Sunk 1969 while on loan to Taiwan.
6–25–69*	*Taurus* (AKR-8)	Ex-AK, LSD. Scrapped.

*Transferred MARAD this date; strike date not available.

continued

Commissioned U.S.N. Ships—*continued*

Strike Date	Name and/or Hull Number	Comments
6–28–69	*Bluegill* (AGSS-242)	Ex-SSK. Salvage/training hulk.
6–28–69	*Bream* (AGSS-243)	Ex-SSK. Sunk as target 11–8–69.
6–28–69	*Raton* (AGSS-270)	Sunk as target.
6–30–69*	*Aldebaran* (AF-10)	Trans./MARAD permanently for layup.
6–30–69*	*Arcadia* (AD-23)	Trans./MARAD permanently for layup.
6–30–69*	*Kankakee* (AO-39)	Trans./MARAD permanently for layup.
6–30–69	*Silversides* (AGSS-236)	Memorial.
6–30–69	*Tweedy* (DE-532)	Sunk as target 5–70.
6–30–69	*Tunny* (LPSS-282)	Ex-SS, SSG, SS. Sunk as target 6–19–70.
7–1–69	*Frank E. Evans* (DD-754)	Cut in two by collision with HMAS *Melbourne* 6–3–69; bow sank immediately; stern used as target 10–10–69.
7–1–69	*Shasta* (AE-6)	Scrapped.
7–1–69	*Skagit* (LKA-105)	Scrapped.
7–2–69	*Cony* (DD-508)	Sunk as target 4–70.
7–2–69	*Eaton* (DD-510)	Sunk as target 3–27–70
7–2–69	*Jenkins* (DD-447)	FRAM II. Scrapped.
7–2–69	*Taylor* (DD-468)	Sold/Italy.
7–2–69	*Walker* (DD-517)	Sold/Italy.
7–2–69	*Wilhoite* (DER-397)	Sunk as target.
7–12–69	*Vammen* (DE-644)	Sunk as target 2–18–71.
7–12–69	*Whitehurst* (DE-634)	Sunk as target.
7–18–69	*Waller* (DD-466)	Sunk as target 6–17–70.
7–18–69	*Butternut* (ANL-9)	See 10–28–69 entry.
7–19–69	*Marshall* (DD-676)	Scrapped.
7–31–69	*Burrfish* (SS-312)	Ex-SSR. Returned from loan to Canada; sunk as target.
8–1–69	*Fletcher* (DD-445)	Scrapped.
8–1–69	*Tanner* (AGS-15)	Scrapped.
8–8–69	*DeLong* (DE-684)	Sunk as target 2–19–70.
8–31–69*	*Frontier* (AD-25)	Trans./MARAD permanently for layup.
9–2–69	*Salamonie* (AO-26)	Scrapped.
9–13–69	*Rock* (AGSS-274)	Ex-SSR. Sunk as target.
9–13–69	*Bashaw* (AGSS-241)	Ex-SSK. Sunk as target.
9–21–69	*Black* (DD-666)	Scrapped.
9–24–69	*Cusk* (AGSS-348)	Ex-SSG. Scrapped.
9–26–69	*Turner* (DD-834)	Ex-DDR. Scrapped.
10–1–69	*Boyd* (DD-544)	Sold/Turkey.
10–1–69	*Cogswell* (DD-651)	Sold/Turkey.
10–1–69	*Wedderburn* (DD-684)	Sunk as target.
10–9–69	USNS *Richfield* (T-AGM-4)	Trans./MARAD for layup.
10–9–69	USNS *Rose Knot* (T-AGM-14)	Trans./MARAD for layup.
10–9–69	USNS *Coastal Sentry* (T-AGM-15)	Scrapped.
10–9–69	USNS *Timber Hitch* (T-AGM-17)	Trans./MARAD for layup.
10–9–69	USNS *Sampan Hitch* (T-AGM-18)	Trans./MARAD; to be scrapped.
10–9–69	USNS *General Daniel I. Sultan* (T-AP-120)	Trans./MARAD for layup.
10–9–69	USNS *General Hugh J. Gaffey* (T-AP-121)	Trans./MARAD for layup.
10–9–69	USNS *General Edwin D. Patrick* (T-AP-124)	Trans./MARAD for layup.
10–9–69	USNS *General R. M. Blatchford* (T-AP-153)	Trans./MARAD for layup; converted into merchant containership.
10–9–69	USNS *General Leroy Eltinge* (T-AP-154)	Trans./MARAD for layup; converted into merchant containership.
10–11–69	*Spinax* (AGSS-489)	Ex-SSR. Scrapped.

10–17–69	*Harry E. Hubbard* (DD-748)	Scrapped.
10–22–69	*Gyatt* (DD-712)	Ex-DDG. Sunk as target 6–11–70.
10–24–69	*Samuel N. Moore* (DD-747)	Sold/Taiwan.
10–27–69	*Brush* (DD-745)	Sold/Taiwan.
10–28–69	*Butternut* (ANL-9)	Reinstated on NVR this date as YAG-60.
10–31–69	*Alstede* (AF-48)	Scrapped.
10–31–69	*Carter Hall* (LSD-3)	Scrapped.
10–31–69	*Oak Hill* (LSD-7)	Scrapped.
11–1–69	*Sablefish* (AGSS-303)	Scrapped.
11–1–69	*Astoria* (CL-90)	Scrapped.
11–1–69	*Batfish* (AGSS-310)	Memorial at Muskogee, Okla.
11–1–69	*Endicott* (DD-495)	Ex-DMS. Scrapped.
11–1–69	*Gleaves* (DD-423)	Scrapped.
11–1–69	*George* (DE-697)	Scrapped.
11–1–69	*Jobb* (DE-707)	Scrapped.
11–1–69	*Lough* (DE-586)	Scrapped.
11–1–69	*Otter* (DE-210)	Sunk as target 7–6–70.
11–1–69	*Macon* (CA-132)	Sunk as target.
11–1–69	*Rudderow* (DE-224)	Scrapped.
11–2–69	*Montrose* (LPA-212)	Scrapped.
11–3–69	*Munsee* (ATF-107)	Scrapped.
11–7–69*	USNS *Pvt. Jose E. Valdez* (T-AG-169)	Trans./MARAD permanently for layup.
11–8–69	*Parche* (AGSS-384)	Conning tower memorial at Pearl Harbor, Hawaii; hull scrapped.
11–10–69	*Radford* (DD-446)	FRAM II. Scrapped.
11–12–69	*Belle Grove* (LSD-2)	Scrapped.
11–14–69	*Banner* (AGER-1)	Ex-AKL. Scrapped.
11–14–69	*Hyman* (DD-732)	Scrapped.
11–14–69	*Ruff* (MSCO-54)	Last of its type on NVR; sold.
11–15–69	*Preston* (DD-795)	Sold/Turkey.
11–15–69	*Sea Owl* (AGSS-405)	Scrapped.
11–15–69	*Conway* (DD-507)	Sunk as target 6–26–70.
11–15–69	*Cook* (LPR-130)	Ex-APD. Scrapped.
11–17–69	*Irex* (AGSS-482)	Possible memorial.
11–20–69	*Sunnadin* (ATA-197)	Sold.
11–21–69	*Bristol* (DD-857)	Sold/Taiwan.
11–25–69	*Ashland* (LSD-1)	Scrapped.
12–1–69	*Earle* (DD-635)	Ex-DMS. Scrapped.
12–1–69	*H. R. Kenyon* (DE-683)	Scrapped.
12–1–69	*Philippine Sea* (AVT-11)	Ex-CVS. Scrapped.
12–1–69	*Lake Champlain* (CVS-39)	Last axial deck CVA/CVS on list; scrapped.
12–1–69	*Boxer* (LPH-4)	Ex-CVS. Scrapped.
12–1–69	*Paul G. Baker* (DE-642)	Scrapped.
12–1–69	*Palm Beach* (AGER-3)	Ex-AKL. Scrapped.
12–2–69	*Mount Baker* (AE-4)	Trans./MARAD; to be scrapped.
12–19–69	*Maury* (AGS-16)	Ex-AKA. Trans./MARAD; to be scrapped.
12–19–69	*Oxford* (AGTR-1)	Scrapped.
12–19–69	*Georgetown* (AGTR-2)	Scrapped.
12–19–69	*Jamestown* (AGTR-3)	Scrapped.
12–19–69	*Kaskaskia* (AO-27)	Scrapped.

* Transferred MARAD this date; strike date not available.

continued

Commissioned U.S.N. Ships—*continued*

Strike Date	Name and/or Hull Number	Comments
12–19–69	*Graffias* (AF-29)	Trans./MARAD; to be scrapped.
12–30–69	*Cavalla* (AGSS-244)	Memorial at Galveston, Tex.
1–2–70	*Serrano* (AGS-24)	Ex ATF-112. Scrapped.
1–2–70	*Hopewell* (DD-681)	Scrapped.
1–10–70	*Prichett* (DD-561)	Sold/Italy.
1–15–70	*Valley Forge* (LPH-8)	Ex CVS-45. Scrapped.
1–15–70	*Tallahatchee County* (AVB-2)	Ex LST-1154. Last of its type on NVR; scrapped.
1–16–70	*Belmont* (AGTR-4)	Scrapped.
1–20–70	*Ingersoll* (DD-652)	Sunk as target.
1–30–70	*Nicholas* (DD-449)	FRAM II. Scrapped.
1–30–70	*O'Bannon* (DD-450	Scrapped.
1–30–70	*Coates* (DE-685)	Sunk as target.
1–30–70	*J. Douglas Blackwood* (DE-219)	Sunk as target.
1–30–70	*Princeton* (LPH-5)	Ex CVS-37. Scrapped.
1–30–70	*Haynsworth* (DD-700)	Sold/Taiwan.
2–1–70	*Avenge* (MSO-423)	Damaged by fire 10–6–69; scrapped.
2–1–70	*Macomb* (DD-458)	Returned from loan to Japan 12–3–69; Sold/Taiwan.
2–1–70	*Ellyson* (DD-454)	Returned from loan to Japan 12–3–69; Sold/Taiwan.
2–13–70	*Soley* (DD-707)	Damaged by grounding while NRT; sunk as target 9–18–70.
2–14–70	*Renshaw* (DD-499)	Last of ASW *Fletchers*; scrapped.
2–20–70	SS-366 (ex-*Hawkbill*)	Returned from loan to Netherlands this date; sold to Netherlands 4–70 for scrapping.
3–1–70	*Fargo* (CL-106)	Scrapped.
3–2–70	*Rexburg* (PCER-855)	Scrapped.
3–16–70*	*Summit County* (LST-1146)	Trans./MARAD permanently for layup.
3–17–70	*Elokomin* (AO-55)	Scrapped.
3–24–70*	USNS *General Simon B. Buckner* (T-AP-123)	Trans./MARAD permanently for layup.
4–1–70	*Atlanta* (IX-304)	Ex-CL. Sunk by scuttling 10–1–70.
4–1–70	*Albatross* (MSC-289)	Scrapped.
4–1–70	*Gannet* (MSC-290)	Scrapped.
4–1–70*	USNS *Coastal Crusader* (T-AGS-36)	Ex-AGM. Trans./MARAD permanently for layup.
4–7–70*	USNS *General William Weigel* (T-AP-119)	Trans./MARAD permanently for layup.
4–15–70	*Rehoboth* (AGS-50)	Ex-AVP. Scrapped.
4–16–70*	USNS *General Nelson M. Walker* (T-AP-125)	Trans./MARAD permanently for layup.
4–17–70	*St. Francis River* (LFR-525)	Ex-LSMR. Scrapped.
4–23–70*	USNS *General William H. Gordon* (T-AP-117)	Trans./MARAD permanently for layup.
4–28–70	USNS *Sgt. Joseph E. Muller* (T-AG-171)	Trans./MARAD for disposal.
4–28–70	USNS *Mercury* (T-AGM-21)	Trans./MARAD; retrans./Matson, 6–23–70.
4–28–70	USNS *Sgt. Curtis F. Shoup* (T-AG-175)	Trans./MARAD for disposal.
4–28–70	USNS *Range Tracker* (T-AGM-1)	Trans./MARAD for disposal.
4–28–70	USNS *Laurentia* (T-AF-44)	Trans./MARAD for disposal.
4–28–70	USNS *Sgt. Jonah E. Kelley* (T-APC-116)	Trans./MARAD for layup.
4–28–70	USNS *Mission San Rafael* (T-AO-130)	Trans./MARAD for disposal.
5–1–70*	USNS *General John Pope* (T-AP-110)	Trans./MARAD permanently for layup.
5–1–70	*Alexander J. Luke* (DE-577)	Ex-DER. Sunk as target 10–22–70.
5–1–70	*Snatch* (AGOR-18)	Ex ARS-27. Scrapped.
5–1–70	*Abatan* (AW-4)	Ex-AO. Water storage hulk, Guantanamo.
5–8–70	*Clarion River* (LFR-409)	Ex-LSMR. Scrapped.
5–15–70	*English* (DD-696)	Sold/Taiwan.

5–15–70	*Cabezon* (AGSS-334)	Possible memorial.
5–22–70	*White River* (LFR-536)	Ex-LSMR. Scrapped.
5–25–70	*Gunston Hall* (LSD-5)	Sold/Argentina.
5–26–70*	USNS *General Alexander M. Patch* (T-AP-122)	Trans./MARAD permanently for layup.
6–1–70	*John C. Butler* (DE-339)	Sunk as target.
6–1–70	*Ericsson* (DD-440)	Sunk as target.
6–1–70	*Monterey* (AVT-2)	Ex CVL-26. Scrapped.
6–1–70	*San Jacinto* (AVT-5)	Ex CVL-30. Scrapped.
6–1–70	*Siboney* (AKV-12)	Ex CVE-112. Scrapped.
6–1–70	*Tinian* (AKV-23)	Ex CVE-123. Scrapped.
6–1–70	*Tillman* (DD-641)	Scrapped.
6–1–70	*Amycus* (ARL-2)	Ex-LST. Scrapped.
6–1–70	*Liberty* (AGTR-5)	Scrapped.
6–1–70	*Cronin* (DE-704)	Ex-DEC. Sunk as target.
6–1–70	*Joseph E. Connolly* (DE-450)	Sunk as target.
6–1–70	USNS *Chesterfield County* (T-LST-551)	Scrapped.
6–3–70	*Amherst* (PCER-853)	Trans./Vietnam.
6–3–70	*Prowess* (IX-305)	Ex-MSF. Trans./Vietnam.
6–8–70*	USNS *General Maurice Rose* (T-AP-126)	Trans./MARAD permanently for layup.
6–30–70*	USNS *General William O. Darby* (T-AP-127)	Trans./MARAD permanently for layup.
6–30–70	*Penguin* (ASR-12)	Scrapped.
7–1–70	*Parle* (DE-708)	Last active WW II DE on NVR. Sunk as target 10–27–70.
7–1–70	*Cobia* (AGSS-245)	Memorial at Manitowoc, Wisc.
7–1–70	*Redfin* (AGSS-272)	Scrapped.
7–1–70	*Piper* (AGSS-409)	Scrapped.
7–1–70	*Snohomish County* (LST-1126)	Scrapped.
7–1–70	*Whitehall* (PCE-856)	Ex-PCER. Scrapped.
7–1–70	*Havre* (PCE-877)	Hulk for USN Diving/Salvage Training School.
7–1–70	*Ely* (PCE-880)	Donated (mercantile).
7–1–70	*Portage* (PCE-902)	Scrapped.
7–1–70	*Hollidaysburg* (PCS-1385)	Last PCS on the NVR; scrapped.
7–15–70	*Marysville* (PCER-857)	Last of the PCE/PCER family. Scrapped.
7–16–70*	USNS *Bald Eagle* (T-AF-50)	Trans./MARAD permanently for layup.
8–1–70	*Medregal* (SS-480)	Sunk as target, 8–70.
8–1–70	*Pomodon* (SS-486)	Scrapped.
8–7–70	*Rainier* (AE-5)	Trans./MARAD; to be scrapped.
8–8–70	*Segundo* (SS-398)	Sunk as target.
8–12–70	*Luzerne County* (LST-902)	Scrapped.
8–12–70	*Monmouth County* (LST-1032)	Scrapped.
8–12–70	*John W. Weeks* (DD-701)	Sunk as target 11–19–70.
9–1–70	*Mazama* (AE-9)	Scrapped.
9–11–70	*Fechteler* (DD-870)	First FRAM I to be struck. Sunk as target.
9–14–70	*Cambria* (LPA-36)	Scrapped.
9–15–70*	USNS *Mission Capistrano* (T-AG-162)	Ex-AO. Trans./MARAD; to be scrapped.
9–15–70	*Nields* (DD-616)	Scrapped.
9–15–70	USNS *Mission Santa Cruz* (T-AO-133)	Trans./MARAD; to be scrapped.
9–15–70	*John L. Williamson* (DE-370)	Scrapped.
9–15–70	*Fred T. Berry* (DD-858)	Sunk as target.
9–18–70	*Chemung* (AO-30)	Scrapped.
9–25–70	*Jennings County* (LST-846)	Damaged by fire in Vietnam; scrapped.
9–25–70	*Platte* (AO-24)	Scrapped.

*Transferred MARAD this date; strike date not available.

continued

Commissioned U.S.N. Ships—*continued*

Strike Date	Name and/or Hull Number	Comments
10–1–70	*Sagacity* (MSO-469)	Damaged by grounding 3–70; scrapped.
10–1–70	*Bugara* (SS-331)	Accidently sunk in storm 6–1–71.
10–1–70	*Sea Robin* (SS-407)	Scrapped.
10–1–70	*Neches* (AO-47)	Scrapped.
10–1–70	*Conklin* (DE-439)	Scrapped.
10–1–70	*Lindsey* (MMD-32)	Ex-DM, DD. Scrapped.
10–15–70	*Mattaponi* (AO-41)	Scrapped.
10–15–70	*Henry A. Wiley* (MMD-29)	Ex-DM, DD. Scrapped.
11–1–70	*Murphy* (DD-603)	Scrapped.
11–1–70	*Thomas E. Fraser* (MMD-24)	Ex-DM, DD. Scrapped.
11–1–70	*Terror* (MMF-5)	Ex-MM, CM. Only built-for-purpose minelayer on the NVR. Scrapped.
11–1–70	*Oregon City* (CA-122)	Scrapped.
11–1–70	*Shannon* (MMD-25)	Ex-DM, DD, Scrapped.
11–2–70	*Samuel B. Roberts* (DD-823)	FRAM II. Sunk as target.
11–11–70	*Tolowa* (ATF-116)	Damaged by grounding while on loan to Venezuela, 8–70. Sold to Venezuela for scrapping.
11–13–70	*Ernest G. Small* (DD-838)	Ex-DDR. Sold/Taiwan.
11–20–70	*Catskill* (MCS-1)	Ex-LSV. Scrapped.
11–30–70	*Razorback* (SS-394)	Sold/Turkey.
12–1–70	*Adams* (MMD-27)	Ex-DM, DD. Scrapped.
12–1–70	*Tolman* (MMD-28)	Ex-DM, DD. Scrapped.
12–1–70	*Pasadena* (CL-65)	Scrapped.
12–1–70	*Portsmouth* (CL-102)	Scrapped.
12–1–70	*Roanoke* (CL-145)	Scrapped.
12–1–70	*Vella Gulf* (AKV-11)	Ex CVE-111. Scrapped.
12–1–70	*Mayo* (DD-422)	Scrapped.
12–1–70	*Saidor* (AKV-17)	Ex CVE-117. Scrapped.
12–1–70	*Stanley* (DD-478)	Scrapped.
12–1–70	*Badoeng Strait* (AKV-16)	Ex CVE-116. Scrapped.
12–1–70	*Satterlee* (DD-626)	Ex-DMS. Scrapped.
12–1–70	*Cowie* (DD-632)	Ex-DMS. Scrapped.
12–1–70	*Carbonero* (SS-337)	Ex-AGSS, SS. Sunk as target.
12–1–70	*Stanton* (DE-247)	Scrapped.
12–1–70	*Worcester* (CL-144)	Scrapped.
12–14–70	*Sea Fox* (SS-402)	Sold/Turkey.
12–21–70	USNS T-AG-335	Ex-LSM. Trans./Department of Interior.
12–21–70	USNS T-AKL-31	Trans./Department of Interior.
1–2–71	*Champlin* (DD-601)	Scrapped.
1–2–71	*Marchand* (DE-249)	Scrapped.
1–2–71	*Metcalf* (DD-595)	Scrapped.
1–2–71	*Jacob Jones* (DE-130)	Scrapped.
1–2–71	*Pope* (DE-134)	Scrapped.
1–2–71	*J. R. Y. Blakely* (DE-140)	Scrapped.
1–2–71	*Menges* (DE-320)	Scrapped.
1–2–71	*Mosley* (DE-321)	Scrapped.
1–2–71	*Amsterdam* (CL-101)	Scrapped.
1–2–71	*Pride* (DE-323)	Scrapped.
1–2–71	*Sloat* (DE-245)	Scrapped.
1–2–71	*Dale W. Peterson* (DE-337)	Scrapped.

1–2–71	*J. Richard Ward* (DE-243)	Scrapped.
1–15–71	*O'Reilly* (DE-330)	Scrapped.
1–15–71	*Daniel* (DE-335)	Scrapped.
1–15–71	*Wilkes-Barre* (CL-103)	Last *Cleveland* class CL and light cruiser on NVR. Sunk as target.
1–15–71	*Diodon* (SS-349)	Scrapped.
1–30–71	*Frank Knox* (DD-742)	Ex-DDR. FRAM II. Sold/Greece.
2–1–71	*Notable* (MSO-460)	Scrapped.
2–1–71	*Rival* (MSO-468)	Scrapped.
2–1–71	*Salute* (MSO-470)	Scrapped.
2–1–71	*Valor* (MSO-472)	Scrapped.
2–1–71	*Ability* (MSO-519)	Scrapped.

B. Noncommissioned U.S.N. Craft

Struck	Type/Number	Disposition
1–1–65	YC-593	Sold
1–1–65	YC-793	Sold
1–1–65	YFNB-44	Sold
1–1–65	YRB-7	Sold
1–1–65	YSD-40	Sold
1–18–65	YM-20	Sold
2–1–65	YFU-35	Sold
2–1–65	YFU-43	Sold
2–1–65	YTB-287	Sold
2–1–65	YTM-192	Sold
2–1–65	YTM-258	Sold
2–19–65	YTM-261	Sold
3–1–65	YF-868	Sold
4–1–65	YC-767	Sold
4–1–65	YD-212	Sold
4–1–65	YRB-26	Sold
5–1–65	YTM-263	Sold
5–10–65	YP-584	Reinstated on NVR this date
5–10–65	YP-586	Reinstated on NVR this date
5–10–65	YP-589	Reinstated on NVR this date
5–10–65	YP-590	Reinstated on NVR this date
5–15–65	YC-1388	Scuttled
6–1–65	YFNB-41	Trans./NASA
6–1–65	YTL-427	Trans./Taiwan
6–1–65	YTL-428	Trans./Taiwan
8–1–65	YFN-315	Sold
8–1–65	PTF-1	Sunk as target
8–1–65	PTF-2	Sunk as target
8–1–65	YON-240	Sold
11–1–65	YSR-43	Sold
11–9–65	YC-1453	Sunk at sea
12–1–65	PTF-4	War loss.
1–1–66	YD-67	Sold
1–1–66	YFD-18	Sold
3–1–66	YC-705	Sold
3–1–66	YC-1031	Sold
4–1–66	PTF-9	War loss.
5–1–66	PTF-14	War loss.
5–1–66	YD-197	Sold
6–1–66	YC-1354	Sold
6–1–66	YCV-17	Sold
6–1–66	YD-215	Trans./Army
6–1–66	YGN-76	Sold
7–1–66	PTF-8	War loss.
7–1–66	PTF-15	War loss.
8–1–66	YFN-563	Sold
9–1–66	YC-711	Sold
9–1–66	YF-882	Sold
10–1–66	YC-1384	Sold
10–1–66	PTF-16	War loss.
10–1–66	YF-870	Sold
10–31–66	MSB-54	War loss
11–1–66	YC-733	Sold
11–1–66	YC-1082	Sold
12–1–66	YC-942	Sold
12–1–66	YTL-455	Sold
1–14–67	MSB-14	War loss
2–1–67	YTM-138	Sold
2–15–67	MSB-45	War loss
3–1–67	YC-1032	Sold
4–1–67	YON-162	Sold
5–1–67	YNG-12	Sold
5–1–67	YSR-8	Sold
6–1–67	YTM-373	Sold

continued

Noncommissioned U.S.N. Craft—*continued*

Struck	Type/Number	Disposition
7–1–67	YON-144	Trans./Philippines
8–1–67	YFN-301	Sold
9–1–67	YFND-2	Sold
9–1–67	MSB-49	Scrapped
9–1–67	YRB-8	Trans./Interior Department
10–1–67	YW-102	Sold
2–1–68	MSB-43	Scrapped
2–1–68	YO-175	Trans./Taiwan
5–1–68	YD-175	Sold
5–1–68	YFU-12	War loss
7–1–68	YGN-71	Sold
8–1–68	YFN-297	Sold
9–1–68	YFND-13	Sold
1–1–69	YLLC-4	War loss
2–1–69	YOG-70	Sold
2–1–69	YC-798	Sold
3–1–69	YFD-82	Sold.
4–1–69	YFU-78	War loss
6–1–69	YC-1369	Sold
6–1–69	YC-1421	Sold
7–1–69	YTM-150	Sold
8–1–69	YOS-5	Sold
8–1–69	YFB-84	Sold
8–1–69	APL-17	Sold
8–1–69	AFDL-17	Sold
9–1–69	YTM-347	Sold
9–1–69	YTL-451	Sold
9–1–69	YTL-589	Sold
9–1–69	YOG-69	Sold
10–1–69	YC-1397	Sold
10–1–69	YTL-587	Sold
11–1–69	YD-107	Sold
11–1–69	YC-1428	Sunk as target
11–1–69	YC-1429	Test hulk
12–1–69	YRB-27	Sold
1–1–70	YTL-590	Trans./Vietnam
2–1–70	YO-242	Sold
2–1–70	YTM-730	Sold
2–1–70	YTL-566	Sunk
2–1–70	APL-46	Sold
2–1–70	YTL-446	Sold
2–1–70	YM-24	War loss
2–1–70	YTL-436	Sold
3–1–70	YFU-5	Scuttled
3–1–70	YDT-5	Ex-AMC-type. Temp. retained
4–1–70	YFN-994	Sold
4–1–70	YR-61	Sold
5–1–70	YOG-76	War damage/sold
5–1–70	YFNX-9	Sold
6–1–70	YDT-4	Ex-AMC. Last AMC on NVR. Sold
6–1–70	YFU-7	Damaged heavy seas/scrapped
8–1–70	YOS-14	Sold
9–1–70	YOS-18	Sold
9–1–70	YSR-34	Sold
9–1–70	YRDM-6	Sold
9–1–70	YG-21	Sold
10–1–70	YFU-20	Ex-LCU. Sold
10–1–70	YFU-36	Ex-LCU. Sold
11–1–70	YOGN-121	Sold
11–1–70	YG-52	Sold
11–1–70	YTM-267	Sold
11–1–70	YSD-29	Sold
11–1–70	YSD-49	Sold
12–1–70	YSD-50	Sold
12–1–70	YSD-57	Sold
12–1–70	YOG-71	Trans./Vietnam
12–1–70	YC-773	Hulk retained
12–1–70	YC-1066	Sold

C. Coast Guard Vessels

Date Sold	Name and/or Hull Number	Comments
5–20–65	*Cherry* (WLIC-258)	Sold to Surinam.
5–20–65	*Dahlia* (WLIC-288)	Sold to Surinam.
5–28–65	*Wyaconda* (WAGL-75403)	Sold.
6–1–65	*Iroquois* (WPG-43)	Scrapped.
7–1–65	*Yamacraw* (WARC-333)	Loaned to USN 4–16–59. Scrapped.
10–20–65	WYTL-64303	Sold.
11–29–65	*Hawthorn* (WAGL-215)	Scrapped.

2–2–66	*Nemesis* (WPC-111)	Scrapped.
3–8–66	*Petrel* (WIX-70001)	Sold.
5–9–66	*Nike* (WPC-112)	Scrapped.
5–19–66	*Jasmine* (WLI-261)	Scrapped.
5–19–66	*Frederick Lee* (WSC-139)	Sold.
5–19–66	*Bluebonnet* (WLI-257)	Sold.
5–21–66	Lightship WLV-519	Donated for museum/memorial.
9–8–66	WYTL-64306	Donated.
2–20–67	Lightship WLV-531	Trans./A.I.D.
3–3–67	*Oak* (WLM-239)	Trans./Smithsonian Institution.
6–29–67	*Columbine* (WLI-208)	Sold.
9–5–67	Lightship WLV-537	Donated.
10–13–67	Lightship WLV-506	Donated.
12–2–67	*Coos Bay* (WHEC-376)	Trans./USN this date for use as a target.
1–9–68	*Nettle* (WAK-169)	Trans./Philippines.
4–12–68	*Heather* (WLB-331)	Trans./HEW this date/for further trans. to Seattle Community College.
6–4–68	Lightship WLV-528	Trans./A.I.D. this date for further trans. to Surinam.
7–9–68	*Dexter* (WHEC-385)	Ex-AGC, AVP. Trans./USN this date for use as a target.
7–21–68	*Mackinac* (WHEC-371)	Trans./USN this date for use as a target. Ex-AVP.
8–4–68	Lightship WLV-512	Donated for use as a museum.
8–7–68	Lightship WLV-509	Donated for use as a museum.
8–15–68	*Cape Falcon* (WPB-95330)	Trans. to USN for further trans. to South Korea.
8–16–68	*Cape Sable* (WPB-95334)	Trans. to USN for further trans. to South Korea.
8–16–68	*Cape Trinity* (WPB-95331)	Trans. to USN for further trans. to South Korea.
8–30–68	*Cape Rosier* (WPB-95333)	Trans. to USN for further trans. to South Korea.
8–30–68	*Cape Providence* (WPB-95335)	Trans. to USN for further trans. to South Korea.
9–11–68	*Cape Darby* (WPB-95323)	Trans. to USN for further trans. to South Korea.
9–18–68	*Cape Kiwanda* (WPB-95329)	Trans. to USN for further trans. to South Korea.
9–18–68	*Cape Florida* (WPB-95325)	Trans. to USN for further trans. to South Korea.
9–24–68	*Cape Porpoise* (WPB-95327)	Trans. to USN for further trans. to South Korea.
10–30–68	*Matagorda* (WHEC-373)	Ex-AVP. Trans./USN this date for use as a target. Sunk 10–31–69.
11–15–68	*General Greene* (WMEC-140)	Trans. to Newburyport, Mass. for use as a museum.
11–21–68	Lightship WLV-529	Trans. to Hampton, Va. for use as a museum.
11–25–68	*Calumet* (WYTM-86)	Sold.
11–29–68	*Legare* (WMEC-144)	Sold.
12–6–68	*Wisteria* (WLI-254)	Sold.
12–7–68	*White Alder* (WLM-541)	Sunk this date after being rammed and cut in two by a Nationalist Chinese freighter.
12–16–68	*Aurora* (WMEC-103)	Sold.
1–16–69	*Triton* (WMEC-116)	
1–23–69	*Ewing* (WMEC-137)	Sold.
3–10–69	*Brier* (WLI-299)	Trans./USN this date for service as IX-307.
3–24–69	*Arbutus* (WLM-203)	Sold.
4–9–69	*Cartigan* (WMEC-132)	Sold.
4–16–69	*Tuckahoe* (WYTM-89)	Donated to HEW.
4–28–69	*Hickory* (WLI-219)	Sold.
5–13–69	*Casco* (WHEC-370)	Ex-AVP. Trans./USN this date for use as a target 5–15–69.
6–7–69	Lightship WLV-535	Donated for use as a museum.
7–11–69	Lightship WLV-533	Trans./USN and sold to Uruguay.
8–14–69	*Mistletoe* (WLM-237)	Sold.
9–26–69	*Ariadne* (WMEC-101)	Sold.
10–6–69	*Alert* (WMEC-127)	Sold.

continued

Coast Guard Vessels—*continued*

Date Sold	Name and/or Hull Number	Comments
10–16–69	*Agassiz* (WMEC-126)	Trans./Merchant Marine Academy as a training ship.
11–14–69	*McLane* (WMEC-146)	Sold.
12–12–69	*Cahoone* (WMEC-131)	Sold.
2–24–70	*Kimball* (WMEC-143)	Sold.
5–6–70	*Jonquil* (WLB-330)	Sold.
5–21–70	*Navesink* (WYTM-88)	Sold.
5–22–70	*Linden* (WLI-228)	Sold.
5–22–70	*Humboldt* (WHEC-372)	Ex-AVP. Scrapped.
6–18–70	*Half Moon* (WHEC-378)	Ex-AVP. Scrapped.
7–8–70	*Hudson* (WYTM-87)	Trans. to North Western College.
7–8–70	*Avoyel* (WMEC-150)	Ex-ATF. Trans. to Gulf-Atlantic Oceanographic Lab., Inc. as research ship.
7–16–70	*Yeaton* (WMEC-156)	Sold.
9–70	*Barataria* (WHEC-381)	Ex-AVP. Scrapped.
11–70	*Ivy* (WLB-329)	Ex-ACM. Sold.

15. NAVAL SHIPS IN MARAD RESERVE FLEET

By end-FY 1971, 391 merchant-type naval vessels and vessels of Navy design were laid up in five MARAD reserve fleets. The listing here is alphabetical by type and then consecutive by hull number. An asterisk (*) in the date column is the transfer-to-MARAD date; this is used when no strike date is known. The abbreviation "temp." after a ship's name indicates that the ship is in the temporary custody of MARAD for layup but remains on the Naval Vessel Register. The number "1" indicates that the ship is to be disposed of in the immediate future.

Type Number

AD 3, AE 6, AF 21, AG 7, AGC/LCC 6, AGM 5, AGP 1, AGR 9, AGS 2, AH 2, AK 26, AKA/LKA 19, AKN 3, AKS 6, AKV 2, AN 24, AO 25, AOG 8, AP 26, APA/LPA 121, APC 1, AR 5, ARG 9, ARS 1, ARV 1, AS 1, ATA 17, ATF 13, AV 5, AW 2, LSD 8, LST 2, MCS 4.

Reserve Fleet Abbreviations

Hudson—Hudson River, New York*
Suisun—Suisun Bay, San Francisco, California
Mobile—Mobile, Alabama†
James—James River, Virginia
Texas—Beaumont, Texas
Puget—Puget Sound, Olympia, Wash.†

*Officially disbanded 1–1–71.
†To be disbanded.

Example: R1-M-AV3. R1 = refrigerated cargo ship under 400′ long; M = diesel powered AV3 = 3rd variation ("3") of the 22nd modification ("V") of the original design ("A"). **Notes:** Prefix "E" is emergency (EC2 *Liberty* ships); "V" is VC2 *Victory* ships; "Z" is special conversion of standard designs.

CLASSIFICATION OF VESSELS

Type		Length in Feet at Load Water Line 1	2	3	4
C	Cargo	Under 400	400–450	450–500	500–550
P	Passenger	Under 500	500–600	600–700	700–800
N	Coastal Cargo	Under 200	200–250	250–300	300–350
R	Refrigerated Cargo	Under 400	400–450	450–500	500–550
S	Special (Navy)	Under 200	200–300	300–400	400–500
T	Tanker	Under 450	450–500	500–550	550–600

TYPE POWER—NUMBER PROPELLERS—PASSENGERS

	Single Screw		Twin Screw	
Power	1/12 Passengers	13+ Passengers	1/12 Passengers	13+ Passengers
Steam	S	S1	ST	S2
Motor (Diesel)	M	M1	MT	M2
Turbo-Electric	SE	SE1	SET	SE2

Number	Name	Struck	Type	Fleet
AD-20	*Hamul*	7–1–63	C3	Suisun
AD-23	*Arcadia*	6–30–69*	Mod. C3	James
AD-25	*Frontier*	8–31–69*	Mod. C3	Suisun
AE-3	*Lassen*	7–1–61	C2	Suisun
AE-4	*Mount Baker*	12–2–69	C2	Suisun[1]
AE-5	*Rainier*	8–7–70	C2	Suisun[1]
AE-10	*Sangay*	7–1–60	C1-A	Texas
AE-12	*Wrangell* (temp.)	4–29–71*	C2-S-AJ1	James
AE-13	*Akutan*	7–1–60	Mod. C2	Texas
AF-10	*Aldebaran*	6–30–69*	C2	James
AF-11	*Polaris*	10–10–57	C2	Suisun
AF-28	*Hyades* (temp.)	3–18–69*	C2-S-E1	James
AF-29	*Graffias*	12–19–69	C2-S-E1	Suisun[1]
AF-30	*Adria*	7–1–60	R1-M-AV3	Texas
AF-31	*Arequipa*	9–1–61	R1-M-AV3	Suisun
AF-32	*Corduba*	7–1–60	R1-M-AV3	James[1]
AF-34	*Kerstin*	6–16–50	R1-M-AV3	Suisun
AF-35	*Latona*	4–28–49	R1-M-AV3	Suisun

continued

Naval Ships in MARAD Reserve Fleet—*continued*

Number	Name	Struck	Type	Fleet
AF-36	*Lioba*	7–1–60	R1-M-AV3	James
AF-37	*Malabar*	7–1–60	R1-M-AV3	Texas
AF-39	*Palisana*	6–19–46	R1-M-AV3	Puget
AF-40	*Saturn*	8–15–46	ex-German	James
AF-41	*Athanasia*	1–8–46	R1-M-AV3	Puget
AF-44	*Laurentia*	4–28–70	R1-M-AV3	Suisun[1]
AF-49	*Zelima* (temp.)	6–3–70*	R2-S-BV1	Suisun
AF-50	*Bald Eagle*	7–16–70*	C2-S-B1	James
AF-51	*Blue Jacket*	8–19–70*	C2-S-B1	James[1]
AF-54	*Pictor* (temp.)	8–11–70*	R2-S-BV1	Suisun
AF-55	*Aludra* (temp.)	10–1–69*		
AF-61	*Procyon* (temp.)	2–4–71*	R2-S-BV1	Suisun
AG-68	*Basilan*	5–22–47	EC2-S-C5	Suisun
AG-70	*Zaniah*	5–22–47	EC2-S-C5	Suisun
AG-71	*Baham*	5–22–47	EC2-S-C5	Suisun
AG-162	*Mission Capistrano*	9–15–70*	T2-SE-A2	James[1]
AG-169	*Pvt. Jose E. Valdez*	11–7–69*	C1-M-AV1	James
AG-171	*Sgt. Joseph E. Muller*	4–28–70	C1-M-AV1	James[1]
AG-175	*Sgt. Curtis F. Shoup*	4–28–70	C1-M-AV1	Suisun[1]
AGC-3	*Rocky Mount*	7–1–60	C2-S-AJ1	Suisun
LCC-7	*Mount McKinley* (temp.)	11–23–70*	C2-S-AJ1	Suisun
AGC-8	*Mount Olympus*	6–1–61	C2-S-AJ1	Suisun
LCC-12	*Estes* (temp.)	7–16–70*	C2-S-AJ1	Suisun
AGC-15	*Adirondack*	6–1–61	C2-S-AJ1	James
LCC-17	*Taconic* (temp.)	7–22–70*	C2-S-AJ1	James
AGM-4	*Richfield*	10–9–69	VC2-S-AP2	Suisun
AGM-13	*Sword Knot* (temp.)	4–7–71*	C1-M-AV1	Suisun
AGM-14	*Rose Knot*	10–9–69	C1-M-AV1	Suisun
AGM-17	*Timber Hitch*	10–9–69	C1-M-AV1	James
AGM-18	*Sampan Hitch*	10–9–69	C1-M-AV1	Suisun[1]
AGP-13	*Cyrene*	7–19–46	C1-A	Suisun
AGR-5	*Scanner*	9–1–65	ZEC2-S-C5	Suisun
AGR-6	*Locator*	9–1–65	ZEC2-S-C5	Suisun
AGR-7	*Picket*	9–1–65	ZEC2-S-C5	Suisun
AGR-8	*Intercepter*	9–1–65	ZEC2-S-C5	Suisun
AGR-11	*Protector*	9–1–65	ZEC2-S-C5	James
AGR-13	*Interdictor*	9–1–65	ZEC2-S-C5	Suisun
AGR-14	*Interpreter*	7–1–65	ZEC2-S-C5	Suisun
AGR-15	*Tracer*	9–1–65	ZEC2-S-C5	Suisun
AGR-16	*Watchman*	9–1–65	ZEC2-S-C5	Suisun
AGS-16	*Maury*	12–19–69	S4-SE2-BE1	Suisun[1]
AGS-36	*Coastal Crusader*	4–1–70*	C1-M-AV1	Suisun
AH-7	*Hope*	5–21–46	C1-B	Suisun
AH-14	*Tranquility*	9–1–61	C4-S-B2	James
AK-70	*Crater*	6–23–47	EC2-S-C1	Suisun
AK-71	*G. H. Corliss* (ex-USN *Adhara*)	1–3–46	EC2-S-C1	James
AK-77	*George B. Cortelyou* (ex-USN *Cetus*)	11–21–45*	EC2-S-C1	James
AK-91	*Betsy Ross* (ex-USN *Cor Caroli*)	12–19–45	EC2-S-C1	James

Number	Name	Struck	Type	Fleet
AK-95	*Murzin*	6–23–47	EC2-S-C1	Suisun
AK-99	*Bootes*	8–1–47	EC2-S-C1	Suisun
AK-100	*Juan Bautista De Anza* (ex-USN *Lynx*)	11–16–45	EC2-S-C1	Suisun
AK-102	*Triangulum*	7–17–47	EC2-S-C1	Suisun
AK-104	*Ganymede*	8–1–47	EC2-S-C1	Suisun
AK-110	*Increase A. Lapham* (ex-USN *Alkes*)	3–12–46	EC2-S-C1	James
AK-113	*Andrew Rowan* (ex-USN *Butilicus*)	1–8–46	EC2-S-C1	James
AK-124	*Mary Patten* (ex-USN *Azimech*)	1–3–46	EC2-S-C1	James
AK-126	*Megrez*	8–1–47	EC2-S-C1	Suisun
AK-130	*Warren Stone* (ex-USN *Arkab*)	1–21–46	EC2-S-C1	James
AK-136	*Daniel Boone* (ex-USN *Ara*)	11–26–45	EC2-S-C1	James
AK-138	*Cheleb*	5–23–47	EC2-S-C1	Suisun
AK-139	*James S. Hogg* (ex-USN *Pavo*)	12–19–45	EC2-S-C1	James
AK-156	*Alamosa*	6–19–46	C1-M-AV1	Puget
AK-221	*James H. McClintock* (ex-USN *Kenmore*)	2–25–46	EC2-S-C1	Suisun[1]
AK-222	*Josiah D. Whitney* (ex-*Livingston*)	3–12–46	EC2-S-C1	Suisun[1]
AK-227	*Boulder Victory*	9–57*	VC2-S-AP2	Suisun
AK-228	*Provo Victory*	11–53*	VC2-S-AP2	Suisun
AK-231	*Bedford Victory*	5–52*	VC2-S-AP2	Puget
AK-235	*Red Oak Victory*	7–19–46	VC2-S-AP2	Suisun
AK-236	*Lakewood Victory*	6–5–46	VC2-S-AP2	Suisun
AK-248	*Sgt. George E. Peterson*	3–27–59	C1-M-AV1	Mobile
AKA-2	*Procyon*	4–12–46	C2-T	Suisun
AKA-4	*Electra*	7–1–61	C2-T	Suisun
AKA-12	*Libra*	7–1–60	C2-F	James
AKA-13	*Titania*	7–1–61	C2-F	Suisun
LKA-19	*Thuban* (temp.)	9–30–69*	C2-S-B1	James
AKA-23	*Aurelia*	6–19–46	S4-SE2-BE1	Mobile
AKA-24	*Birgit*	5–21–46	S4-SE2-BE1	Mobile
LKA-54	*Algol* (temp.)	7–23–70*	C2-S-B1	James
AKA-55	*Alshain*	7–1–60	C2-S-B1	Texas
LKA-57	*Capricornus* (temp.)	8–12–70*	C2-S-B1	James
AKA-59	*Diphda*	7–1–61	C2-S-B1	Suisun
AKA-60	*Leo*	7–1–60	C2-S-B1	Suisun
LKA-61	*Muliphen* (temp.)	12–2–70*	C2-S-B1	James
LKA-93	*Yancey* (temp.)	3–18–71*	C2-S-B1	James
LKA-94	*Winston* (temp.)	2–17–70*	C2-S-B1	Suisun
LKA-97	*Merrick* (temp.)	12–15–69*	C2-S-B1	Suisun
AKA-99	*Rolette*	7–1–60	C2-S-B1	Suisun
LKA-106	*Union* (temp.)	8–18–70*	C2-S-AJ3	Suisun
LKA-108	*Washburn* (temp.)	8–19–70*	C2-S-AJ3	Suisun
AKN-2	*Sagittarius*	2–7–46	EC2-S-C1	James
AKN-5	*Zebra*	2–7–46	EC2-S-C1	James
AKN-6	*Galilea*	9–1–61	Navy des.	James
AKS-13	*Hesperia*	3–14–47	EC2-S-C1	Suisun
AKS-14	*Iolanda*	4–24–47	EC2-S-C1	Suisun
AKS-15	*Liguria*	4–23–47	EC2-S-C1	Suisun
AKS-20	*Mercury*	8–1–59	C2-S	Texas

AKS-32	*Altair* (temp.)	5–21–69*	VC2-S-AP3	James
AKS-33	*Antares*	9–1–65	VC2-S-AP3	James
AKV-40	*Card* (temp.)	3–10–70*	C3-S-A1	Puget
AKV-42	*Breton* (temp.)	10–26–70*	C3-S-A1	Puget
AN-6	*Aloe*	9–1–62	Navy des.	Puget
AN-7	*Ash*	9–1–62	Navy des.	Puget
AN-8	*Boxwood*	9–1–62	Navy des.	Suisun
AN-10	*Catalpa*	9–1–62	Navy des.	James
AN-11	*Chestnut*	9–1–62	Navy des.	Suisun
AN-12	*Cinchona*	9–1–62	Navy des.	Suisun
AN-13	*Buckeye*	7–1–63	Navy des.	Suisun
AN-14	*Buckthorn*	7–1–63	Navy des.	Suisun
AN-15	*Ebony*	9–1–62	Navy des.	Suisun
AN-16	*Eucalyptus*	9–1–62	Navy des.	Suisun
AN-19	*Holly*	9–1–62	Navy des.	Puget
AN-20	*Elder*	9–1–62	Navy des.	Puget
AN-24	*Mango*	9–1–62	Navy des.	Suisun
AN-26	*Mimosa*	9–1–62	Navy des.	Puget
AN-28	*Palm*	9–1–62	Navy des.	Puget
AN-29	*Hazel*	9–1–62	Navy des.	James
AN-30	*Redwood*	9–1–62	Navy des.	James
AN-35	*Teak*	9–1–62	Navy des.	Suisun
AN-79	*Etlah*	7–1–63	Navy des.	Suisun
AN-81	*Manayunk*	9–1–62	Navy des.	Puget
AN-85	*Oneota*	7–1–63	Navy des.	Suisun
AN-86	*Passaconaway*	7–1–63	Navy des.	Suisun
AN-87	*Passaic*	7–1–63	Navy des.	Suisun
AN-92	*Yazoo*	7–1–63	Navy des.	James
AO-24	*Platte*	9–25–70	T3-S2-A1	Suisun[1]
AO-25	*Sabine* (temp.)	1–22–70*	T3-S2-A1	James
AO-30	*Chemung*	9–18–70	T3-S2-A1	Suisun[1]
AO-36	*Kennebec* (temp.)	8–17–70*	T2-A mod.	Suisun
AO-37	*Merrimack*	2–1–59	T2-A	Texas
AO-39	*Kankakee*	6–30–69*	T2-A	James
AO-41	*Mattaponi*	10–15–70	T2-A	Suisun[1]
AO-42	*Monongahela*	2–1–59	T2-A	Texas
AO-43	*Tappahannock* (temp.)	10–16–70*	T2-A	Suisun
AO-47	*Neches*	10–1–70	T2-A	Suisun[1]
AO-54	*Chikaskia* (temp.)	9–4–70*	T3-S2-A1	James
AO-69	*Enoree*	2–1–59	T3-S-A1	Texas
AO-72	*Niobrara*	2–1–59	T3-S-A1	Texas
AO-84	*Ocklawaha*	6–9–59	T2-SE-A2	Texas
AO-93	*Soubarissen*	7–1–61	T2-SE-A2	Texas
AO-116	*Mission Loreto*	7–16–59	T2-SE-A2	Suisun
AO-117	*Mission Los Angeles*	8–13–59	T2-SE-A2	James
AO-118	*Mission Purisima*	12–4–57	T2-SE-A2	Suisun
AO-128	*Mission San Luis Rey*	11–19–57	T2-SE-A2	Texas
AO-130	*Mission San Rafael*	4–28–70	T2-SE-A2	Texas[1]
AO-133	*Mission Santa Cruz*	9–15–70	T2-SE-A2	James
AO-137	*Mission Santa Ana*	2–25–58	T2-SE-A2	Suisun
AO-138	*Cedar Creek*	10–14–57	T2-SE-A1	Suisun
AO-139	*Muir Woods*	6–10–59	T2-SE-A1	James
AO-141	*Sappa Creek*	7–1–61	T2-SE-A1	Suisun
AOG-2	*Kern*	4–10–58	Navy des.	Suisun
AOG-4	*Wabash*	5–8–58	Navy des.	Suisun
AOG-5	*Susquehanna*	3–26–59	Navy des.	Suisun
AOG-6	*Agawam*	7–1–60	Navy des.	Puget
AOG-10	*Nemasket*	7–1–60	Navy des.	Puget
AOG-49	*Chestatee*	6–1–63	Navy des.	Puget
AOG-51	*Marquoketa*	3–12–58	Navy des.	Suisun
AOG-68	*Peconic*	11–12–57	T1-M-BT1	Texas
AP-110	*General John Pope*	5–1–70*	P2-S2-R2	Suisun
AP-111	*General A. E. Anderson*	12–11–58	P2-S2-R2	Suisun
AP-112	*General William A. Mann*	12–1–66	P2-S2-R2	James
AP-113	*General H. W. Butner*	7–1–61	P2-S2-R2	James
AP-114	*General William Mitchell*	12–1–66	P2-S2-R2	Suisun
AP-115	*General G. M. Randall*	9–1–62	P2-S2-R2	James
AP-116	*General M. C. Meigs*	10–1–58	P2-S2-R2	Puget
AP-117	*General William Gordon*	4–23–70*	P2-S2-R2	James
AP-119	*General William Weigel*	4–7–70*	P2-S2-R2	Suisun
AP-120	*General Daniel I. Sultan*	10–9–69	P2-SE2-R1	Suisun
AP-121	*General Hugh J. Gaffey*	10–9–69	P2-SE2-R1	Suisun
AP-122	*General Alexander M. Patch*	5–26–70*	P2-SE2-R1	James
AP-123	*General Simon B. Buckner*	3–24–70*	P2-SE2-R1	James
AP-124	*General Edwin D. Patrick*	10–9–69	P2-SE2-R1	Suisun
AP-125	*General Nelson M. Walker*	4–16–70*	P2-SE2-R1	James
AP-126	*General Maurice Rose*	6–8–70*	P2-SE2-R1	James
AP-127	*General William O. Darby*	6–30–70*	P2-SE2-R1	James
AP-176	*General J. C. Breckenridge*	12–1–66	P2-S2-R2	Suisun
AP-180	*David C. Shanks*	7–1–61	C3-IN-P&C	Suisun
AP-181	*Fred C. Ainsworth*	7–1–61	C3-IN-P&C	Suisun
AP-187	*Pvt. J. P. Martinez*	11–8–52	VC2-S-AP2	Puget
AP-188	*Aiken Victory*	2–12–53	VC2-S-AP2	Puget
AP-189	*Lt. Raymond O. Beaudoin*	12–22–52	VC2-S-AP2	Puget
AP-191	*Sgt. H. E. Woodford*	12–4–52	VC2-S-AP2	Puget
AP-192	*Sgt. Sylvester Antolak*	11–8–52	VC2-S-AP2	Puget
AP-197	*Geiger* (temp.)	4–27–71*	P2-S1-DN3	Suisun
APA-18	*President Jackson*	10–1–58	C3-A	Suisun[1]
APA-19	*President Adams*	10–1–58	C3-A	Suisun[1]
APA-20	*President Hayes*	10–1–58	C3-IN-P&C	Suisun[1]
APA-25	*Arthur Middleton*	10–1–58	C3-IN-P&C	James[1]
APA-26	*Samuel Chase*	10–1–58	C3-IN-P&C	James[1]
APA-30	*Thomas Jefferson*	10–1–58	C3-A	Suisun
LPA-44	*Fremont* (temp.)	10–10–69*	C3-S-A2	James
LPA-45	*Henrico*	7–3–68*	C3-S-A2	Puget
APA-59	*Audrain*	8–1–47	S4-SE2-BE1	Suisun
APA-117	*Haskell*	6–19–46	VC2-S-AP5	James
APA-118	*Hendry*	3–20–46	VC2-S-AP5	James
APA-119	*Highlands*	2–26–46	VC2-S-AP5	James
APA-120	*Hinsdale*	5–1–46	VC2-S-AP5	James
APA-121	*Hocking*	5–21–46	VC2-S-AP5	James
APA-122	*Kenton*	4–12–46	VC2-S-AP5	James

continued

Naval Ships in MARAD Reserve Fleet—*continued*

Number	Name	Struck	Type	Fleet
APA-123	*Kittson*	3–20–46	VC2-S-AP5	James
APA-124	*La Grange*	11–23–45	VC2-S-AP5	Suisun
APA-125	*Lanier*	3–20–46	VC2-S-AP5	James
APA-126	*St. Mary's*	2–26–46	VC2-S-AP5	Suisun
APA-127	*Allendale*	3–28–46	VC2-S-AP5	James
APA-128	*Arenac*	10–1–58	VC2-S-AP5	James
APA-129	*Marvin H. McIntyre*	6–19–46	VC2-S-AP5	James
APA-130	*Attala*	3–20–46	VC2-S-AP5	James
APA-131	*Bandera*	5–21–46	VC2-S-AP5	James
APA-132	*Barnwell*	10–1–58	VC2-S-AP5	James
APA-133	*Beckham*	5–8–46	VC2-S-AP5	James
APA-134	*Bland*	5–8–46	VC2-S-AP5	James
APA-135	*Bosque*	3–28–46	VC2-S-AP5	James
APA-136	*Botetourt*	7–2–61	VC2-S-AP5	James
APA-137	*Bowie*	3–28–46	VC2-S-AP5	James
APA-138	*Braxton*	7–19–46	VC2-S-AP5	James
APA-139	*Broadwater*	3–20–46	VC2-S-AP5	James
APA-140	*Brookings*	10–1–58	VC2-S-AP5	James
APA-141	*Buckingham*	3–20–46	VC2-S-AP5	James
APA-142	*Clearfield*	3–20–46	VC2-S-AP5	James
APA-143	*Clermont*	3–20–46	VC2-S-AP5	James
APA-144	*Clinton*	10–1–58	VC2-S-AP5	James
APA-145	*Colbert*	3–12–46	VC2-S-AP5	Suisun
APA-146	*Collingsworth*	3–28–46	VC2-S-AP5	James
APA-147	*Cottle*	3–20–46	VC2-S-AP5	James
APA-148	*Crockett*	10–1–58	VC2-S-AP5	James
APA-149	*Audubon*	3–12–46	VC2-S-AP5	James
APA-150	*Bergen*	5–8–46	VC2-S-AP5	James
APA-151	*La Porte*	4–12–46	VC2-S-AP5	James
APA-152	*Latimer*	7–1–60	VC2-S-AP5	Mobile
APA-153	*Laurens*	5–1–46	VC2-S-AP5	James
APA-154	*Lowndes*	5–1–46	VC2-S-AP5	James
APA-155	*Lycoming*	3–28–46	VC2-S-AP5	James
APA-156	*Mellette*	7–1–60	VC2-S-AP5	James
APA-157	*Napa*	6–19–46	VC2-S-AP5	James
APA-158	*Newberry*	3–12–46	VC2-S-AP5	James
APA-159	*Darke*	5–1–46	VC2-S-AP5	James
APA-160	*Deuel*	12–1–58	VC2-S-AP5	James
APA-161	*Dickens*	6–5–46	VC2-S-AP5	James
APA-162	*Drew*	5–21–46	VC2-S-AP5	James
APA-163	*Eastland*	5–1–46	VC2-S-AP5	James
APA-164	*Edgecombe*	10–1–58	VC2-S-AP5	James
APA-165	*Effingham*	6–5–46	VC2-S-AP5	James
APA-166	*Fond Du Lac*	5–1–46	VC2-S-AP5	James
APA-167	*Freestone*	5–1–46	VC2-S-AP5	James
APA-168	*Gage*	10–1–58	VC2-S-AP5	James
APA-169	*Gallatin*	5–8–46	VC2-S-AP5	James
APA-170	*Gosper*	5–1–46	VC2-S-AP5	James

Number	Name	Struck	Type	Fleet
APA-171	*Granville*	5–21–46	VC2-S-AP5	James
APA-172	*Grimes*	10–1–58	VC2-S-AP5	James
APA-173	*Hyde*	6–5–46	VC2-S-AP5	James
APA-174	*Jerauld*	5–21–46	VC2-S-AP5	James
APA-175	*Karnes*	5–1–46	VC2-S-AP5	James
APA-176	*Kershaw*	10–1–58	VC2-S-AP5	James
APA-177	*Kingsbury*	5–1–46	VC2-S-AP5	James
APA-178	*Lander*	4–17–46	VC2-S-AP5	James
APA-179	*Lauderdale*	5–8–46	VC2-S-AP5	James
APA-180	*Lavaca*	10–1–58	VC2-S-AP5	James
APA-187	*Oconto*	6–19–46	VC2-S-AP5	James
APA-188	*Olmsted*	7–1–60	VC2-S-AP5	James
APA-189	*Oxford*	5–1–46	VC2-S-AP5	James
APA-190	*Pickens*	5–1–46	VC2-S-AP5	James
APA-191	*Pondera*	6–19–46	VC2-S-AP5	James
APA-192	*Rutland*	10–1–58	VC2-S-AP5	James
APA-193	*Sanborn*	7–1–60	VC2-S-AP5	Mobile
LPA-194	*Sandoval* (temp.)	8–20–70*	VC2-S-AP5	James
APA-195	*Lenawee*	6–30–68	VC2-S-AP5	Suisun
APA-196	*Logan*	7–1–60	VC2-S-AP5	Suisun
APA-197	*Lubbock*	10–1–58	VC2-S-AP5	Suisun
APA-198	*McCracken*	10–1–58	VC2-S-AP5	Suisun
LPA-199	*Magoffin* (temp.)	10–31–68*	VC2-S-AP5	Suisun
APA-200	*Marathon*	8–15–46	VC2-S-AP5	Suisun
APA-201	*Menard*	9–1–61	VC2-S-AP5	Suisun
APA-202	*Menifee*	10–1–58	VC2-S-AP5	Suisun
APA-203	*Meriwether*	10–1–58	VC2-S-AP5	Suisun
APA-204	*Sarasota*	7–1–60	VC2-S-AP5	James
APA-206	*Sibley*	10–1–58	VC2-S-AP5	Suisun
APA-207	*Mifflin*	10–1–58	VC2-S-AP5	Suisun
LPA-208	*Talladega* (temp.)	10–20–69*	VC2-S-AP5	Puget
APA-209	*Tazewell*	10–1–58	VC2-S-AP5	Puget
APA-211	*Missoula*	10–1–58	VC2-S-AP5	Suisun
LPA-213	*Mountrail* (temp.)	8–13–70*	VC2-S-AP5	James
APA-214	*Natrona*	10–1–58	VC2-S-AP5	Suisun
LPA-215	*Navarro* (temp.)	8–20–70*	VC2-S-AP5	Suisun
APA-216	*Neshoba*	10–1–58	VC2-S-AP5	Suisun
APA-217	*New Kent*	10–1–58	VC2-S-AP5	Mobile
APA-219	*Okaloosa*	10–1–58	VC2-S-AP5	Mobile
LPA-220	*Okanogan* (temp.)	4–20–70*	VC2-S-AP5	Suisun
APA-221	*Oneida*	10–1–58	VC2-S-AP5	Suisun
LPA-222	*Pickaway* (temp.)	8–26–71*	VC2-S-AP5	Suisun
APA-223	*Pitt*	4–23–47	VC2-S-AP5	Suisun
APA-224	*Randall*	7–1–60	VC2-S-AP5	Mobile
APA-225	*Bingham*	7–3–46	VC2-S-AP5	James
APA-226	*Rawlins*	10–1–58	VC2-S-AP5	James
APA-227	*Renville*	6–30–68	VC2-S-AP5	Suisun
APA-229	*Rockingham*	10–1–58	VC2-S-AP5	Suisun

APA-230	*Rockwall*	12–1–58	VC2-S-AP5	James
APA-231	*Saint Croix*	4–23–47	VC2-S-AP5	Suisun
APA-232	*San Saba*	10–1–58	VC2-S-AP5	Suisun
APA-233	*Sevier*	6–23–47	VC2-S-AP5	Suisun
APA-234	*Bollinger*	8–24–55*	VC2-S-AP5	Suisun
APA-235	*Bottineau*	7–1–61	VC2-S-AP5	James
APA-236	*Bronx*	10–1–58	VC2-S-AP5	Suisun
LPA-237	*Bexar* (temp.)	8–7–70*	VC2-S-AP5	Suisun
APA-238	*Dane*	10–1–58	VC2-S-AP5	Suisun
APA-239	*Glynn*	7–1–60	VC2-S-AP5	James
APC-116	*Sgt. Jonah E. Kelley*	4–28–70	C1-M-AV1	James
AR-17	*Assistance* (ex-HMS)	12–13–46	EC2-S-C1	James
AR-18	*Diligence* (ex-HMS)	2–10–49	EC2-S-C1	Suisun
AR-19	*Xanthus*	9–1–62	EC2-S-C1	James
AR-20	*Laertes*	9–1–62	EC2-S-C1	Suisun
AR-21	*Dionysus*	9–1–61	EC2-S-C1	Texas
ARG-2	*Luzon*	9–1–61	EC2-S-C1	Suisun
ARG-3	*Mindanao*	9–1–62	EC2-S-C1	Texas
ARG-5	*Oahu*	7–1–63	EC2-S-C1	Suisun
ARG-6	*Cebu*	9–1–62	EC2-S-C1	Suisun
ARG-7	*Culebra Island*	9–1–62	EC2-S-C1	Suisun
ARG-8	*Maui*	9–1–62	EC2-S-C1	Suisun
ARG-9	*Mona Island*	9–1–62	EC2-S-C1	James
ARG-10	*Palawan*	7–1–63	EC2-S-C1	Suisun
ARG-11	*Samar*	9–1–62	EC2-S-C1	Suisun
ARS-33	*Clamp*	7–1–63	Navy des.	Suisun
ARV-2	*Webster*	9–1–62	EC2-S-C1	James
AS-25	*Apollo*	7–1–63	C3-S-A2	James
ATA-123	*Iuka*	9–1–62	Navy des.	Puget
ATA-175	*Sonoma*	9–1–62	Navy des.	Puget
ATA-178	*Tunica*	9–1–62	Navy des.	Texas
ATA-182	*Unadilla*	9–1–61	Navy des.	Puget
ATA-183	*Nottaway*	9–1–62	Navy des.	Mobile
ATA-189	*Reindeer*	9–1–62	Navy des.	James
ATA-190	*Samoset* (temp.)	12–3–70*	Navy des.	James
ATA-193	*Stallion* (temp.)	12–3–70*	Navy des.	James
ATA-201	*Challenge*	9–1–62	Navy des.	James
ATA-203	*Navigator*	9–1–62	Navy des.	Mobile
ATA-205	*Sciota*	9–1–62	Navy des.	Puget
ATA-212	*Algorma*	9–1–62	Navy des.	Puget
ATA-213	*Keywadin* (temp.)	12–8–70*	Navy des.	James
ATA-241	unnamed	9–1–62	Ex-Army	Puget
ATA-242	unnamed	9–1–62	Ex-Army	Puget
ATA-243	unnamed	9–1–62	Ex-Army	Puget
ATA-245	*Tuscarora*	9–1–61	Navy des.	James
ATF-69	*Chippewa*	9–1–61	Navy des.	Texas
ATF-71	*Hopi*	7–1–63	Navy des.	James
ATF-82	*Carib*	7–1–63	Navy des.	Suisun
ATF-87	*Moreno*	9–1–61	Navy des.	Texas
ATF-88	*Narragansett*	9–1–61	Navy des.	Texas
ATF-97	*Alsea*	9–1–62	Navy des.	James
ATF-102	*Hidatsa*	7–1–63	Navy des.	Suisun
ATF-104	*Jicarilla*	7–1–63	Navy des.	Suisun
ATF-115	*Tenimo*	9–1–62	Navy des.	Texas
ATF-118	*Wenatchee*	9–1–62	Navy des.	Texas
ATF-148	*Achomawi*	9–1–62	Navy des.	Mobile
ATF-151	*Chawasha*	9–1–62	Navy des.	Suisun
ATF-154	*Chirariko*	9–1–62	Navy des.	Suisun
AV-4	*Curtiss*	7–1–63	Navy des.	Suisun
AV-7	*Currituck*	4–1–71	Navy des.	Suisun
AV-12	*Pine Island*	2–1–71	Navy des.	Puget
AV-13	*Salisbury Sound*	2–1–71	Navy des.	Puget
AV-15	*Hamlin*	7–1–63	Mod. C3	Suisun
AW-2	*Wildcat*	6–10–47	ZET1-S-C3	Puget[1]
AW-3	*Pasig*	7–1–60	T2-SE-A2	Puget
LSD-13	*Casa Grande* (temp.)	10–21–70*	Navy des.	James
LSD-14	*Rushmore* (temp.)	2–10–71*		
LSD-15	*Shadwell* (temp.)	9–9–70*	Navy des.	James
LSD-16	*Cabildo* (temp.)	7–9–70*	Navy des.	Suisun
LSD-18	*Colonial* (temp.)	9–2–70*	Navy des.	Suisun
LSD-20	*Donner* (temp.)	4–27–71*	Navy des.	James
LSD-26	*Tortuga* (temp.)	6–10–70*	Navy des.	Suisun
LSD-27	*Whetstone* (temp.)	7–2–70*	Navy des.	Suisun
LST-602	*Clearwater County* (temp.)	10–17–69*	Navy des.	Puget[1]
LST-1146	*Summit County*	3–16–70*	Navy des.	Suisun
MCS-2	*Ozark* (temp.)	11–17–70*	Navy des.	Suisun
MCS-3	*Osage*	9–1–61	Navy des.	Texas
MCS-4	*Saugus*	7–1–61	Navy des.	Suisun
MCS-5	*Monitor*	9–1–61	Navy des.	Texas

*The Hudson River Reserve Fleet was disbanded 1–1–70. Ships in the Fleet have been scrapped or transferred to the James River Reserve Fleet.

MARAD NOTES: a) On 7 April 1969, *Polaris* (AF-11) was reacquired from MARAD by the Navy for removal of spare parts and other equipment. She was returned to MARAD 25 April 1969. b) *Sonoma* (ATA-175) and *Iuka* (ATA-123) were reacquired by the Navy 29 April 1971. *Sciota* (ATA-205) and *Algorma* (ATA-212) were reacquired from MARAD on 29 March 1971. All were reacquired by the Navy for tow to Suisun Bay by Navy tugboat. Upon delivery, all 4 will be reacquired by MARAD and laid up.
Since the last edition, the following ships, in Maritime custody, but still on the Naval Vessel Register have been scrapped: *Kula Gulf* (AKV-8), *Point Cruz* (AKV-19), *Core* (AKV-41) and *Croatan* (AKV-43). In addition, *Warrick* (AKA-89) and *Whiteside* (AKA-90) were reacquired from MARAD on 20 April and 22 April 1971 respectively and sunk as targets in 5–70.

GLOSSARY OF TERMS AND ABBREVIATIONS

A. Ship and Craft Classifications

AD	Destroyer Tender
ADG	Degaussing Ship
AE	Ammunition Ship
AF	Store Ship
AFDB	Large Auxiliary Floating Dry Dock (non-self-propelled)
AFDL	Small Auxiliary Floating Dry Dock (non-self-propelled)
AFDM	Medium Auxiliary Floating Dry Dock (non-self-propelled)
AFS	Combat Store Ship
AG	Miscellaneous
AGDE	Escort Research Ship
AGEH	Hydrofoil Research Ship
AGER	Environmental Research Ship
AGF	Miscellaneous Command Ship
AGM	Missile Range Instrumentation Ship
AGMR	Major Communications Relay Ship
AGOR	Oceanographic Research Ship
AGP	Patrol Craft Tender
AGS	Surveying Ship
AGSS	Auxiliary Submarine
AGTR	Technical Research Ship
AH	Hospital Ship
AK	Cargo Ship
AKD	Cargo Ship Dock
AKL	Light Cargo Ship
AKR	Vehicle Cargo Ship
AKS	Stores Issue Ship
AKV	Cargo Ship and Aircraft Ferry
ANL	Net Laying Ship
AO	Oiler
AOE	Fast Combat Support Ship
AOG	Gasoline Tanker
AOR	Replenishment Oiler
AP	Transport
APB	Self-Propelled Barracks Ship
APL	Barracks Craft (non-self-propelled)
AR	Repair Ship
ARB	Battle Damage Repair Ship
ARC	Cable Repairing Ship
ARD	Auxiliary Repair Dry Dock (non-self-propelled)
ARDM	Medium Auxiliary Repair Dry Dock (non-self-propelled)
ARG	Internal Combustion Engine Repair Ship
ARL	Landing Craft Repair Ship
ARS	Salvage Ship
ARSD	Salvage Lifting Ship
ARST	Salvage Craft Tender
ARVA	Aircraft Repair Ship (aircraft)
ARVE	Aircraft Repair Ship (engine)
ARVH	Aircraft Repair Ship (helicopter)
AS	Submarine Tender
ASPB	Assault Support Patrol Boat
ASR	Submarine Rescue Ship
ATA	Auxiliary Ocean Tug
ATC	Armored Troop Carrier
ATF	Fleet Ocean Tug
ATS	Salvage and Rescue Ship
AV	Seaplane Tender
AVM	Guided Missile Ship
AVT	Auxiliary Aircraft Transport
AW	Distilling Ship
BB	Battleship
CA	Heavy Cruiser
CC	Command Ship
CCB	Command and Control Boat
CG	Guided Missile Cruiser
CGN	Guided Missile Cruiser (nuclear propulsion)
CL	Light Cruiser
CLG	Guided Missile Light Cruiser
CVA	Attack Aircraft Carrier
CVAN	Attack Aircraft Carrier (nuclear propulsion)
CVS	ASW Support Aircraft Carrier
CVT	Training Aircraft Carrier
DD	Destroyer
DDG	Guided Missile Destroyer
DE	Escort Ship
DEG	Guided Missile Escort Ship
DER	Radar Picket Escort Ship
DL	Frigate
DLG	Guided Missile Frigate

DLGN	Guided Missile Frigate (nuclear propulsion)
FDL	Fast Deployment Logistics Ship
IX	Unclassified Miscellaneous
LCA	Landing Craft, Assualt
LCC (ex-AGC)	Amphibious Command Ship
LCM	Landing Craft, Mechanized
LCPL	Landing Craft, Personnel. Large
LCPR	Landing Craft, Personnel, Ramped
LCU	Landing Craft, Utility
LCVP	Landing Craft, Vehicle, Personnel
LFR (ex-IFS and LSMR)	Inshore Fire Support Ship
LFS	Amphibious Fire Support Ship
LHA	Amphibious Assault Ship (general purpose)
LKA (ex-AKA)	Amphibious Cargo Ship
LPA (ex-APA)	Amphibious Transport
LPD	Amphibious Transport Dock
LPH	Amphibious Assault Ship
LPR (ex-APD)	Amphibious Transport (small)
LPSS (ex-APSS)	Amphibious Transport Submarine
LSD	Dock Landing Ship
LST	Tank Landing Ship
LWT	Amphibious Warping Tug
MCS	Mine Countermeasures Ship
MHA	Minehunter, Auxiliary
MHC	Minehunter, Coastal
MMC	Minelayer, Coastal
MMD (ex-DM)	Minelayer, Fast
MMF	Minelayer, Fleet
MON	Monitor
MSA	Minesweeper, Auxiliary
MSB	Minesweeping Boat
MSC	Minesweeper, Coastal (nonmagnetic)
MSCO	Minesweeper, Coastal (old)
MSD	Minesweeper, Drone
MSF	Minesweeper, Fleet (steel hull)
MSI	Minesweeper, Inshore
MSL	Minesweeping Launch
MSM	Minesweeper, River (Converted LCM-6)
MSO	Minesweeper, Ocean (nonmagnetic)
MSR	Minesweeper, Patrol
MSS	Minesweeper, Special (device)
NR	Submersible Research Vehicle (nuclear propulsion)
PAVC	Patrol Air Cushion Vehicle
PBR	River Patrol Boat
PCE	Patrol Escort
PCER	Patrol Rescue Escort
PCF	Patrol Craft, Inshore
PCH	Patrol Craft (hydrofoil)
PCS	Patrol Craft, Submarine
PG	Patrol Gunboat
PGH	Patrol Gunboat (hydrofoil)
PTF	Fast Patrol Craft
RPC	River Patrol Craft
SS	Submarine
SSBN	Fleet Ballistic Missile Submarine (nuclear propulsion)
SSG	Guided Missile Submarine
SSN	Submarine (nuclear propulsion)
SST	Target and Training Submarine (self-propelled)
WAGB	Icebreaker (Coast Guard)
WAGO	Oceanographic Cutter (Coast Guard)
WAK	Cargo Ship (Coast Guard)
WAT (old designation)	Oceangoing Tug (Coast Guard)
WATA	Oceangoing Tug (Coast Guard)
WHEC (ex-WPG)	High Endurance Cutter (Coast Guard)
WIX	Training Cutter (Coast Guard)
WMEC (ex-WPC)	Medium Endurance Cutter (Coast Guard)
WPB	Patrol Boat (Coast Guard)
WTR	Training Ship (Coast Guard)
X	Submersible Craft (self-propelled)
YAG	Miscellaneous Auxiliary (self-propelled)
YC	Open Lighter (non-self-propelled)
YCF	Car Float (non-self-propelled)
YCV	Aircraft Transportation Lighter (non-self-propelled)
YD	Floating Crane (non-self propelled)
YDT	Diving Tender (non-self-propelled)
YF	Covered Lighter (self-propelled)
YFB	Ferryboat or Launch (self-propelled)
YFD	Yard Floating Dry Dock (non-self-propelled)
YFN	Covered Lighter (non-self-propelled)
YFNB	Large Covered Lighter (non-self-propelled)
YFND	Dry Dock Companion Craft (non-self-propelled)
YFNX	Lighter (special purpose, non-self-propelled)
YFP	Floating Power Barge (non-self-propelled)
YFR	Refrigerated Covered Lighter (self-propelled)
YFRN	Refrigerated Covered Lighter (non-self-propelled)
YFRT	Covered Lighter (range-tender, self-propelled)
YFU	Harbor Utility Craft (self-propelled)
YG	Garbage Lighter (self-propelled)
YGN	Garbage Lighter (non-self-propelled)
YHLC	Salvage Lift Craft, Heavy (non-self-propelled)
YM	Dredge (self-propelled)
YMLC	Salvage Lift Craft, Medium (non-self-propelled)
YLLC	Salvage Lift Craft, Light (self-propelled)
YNG	Gate Craft (non-self-propelled)

continued

Classifications—*continued*

YO	Fuel Oil Barge (self-propelled)
YOG	Gasoline Barge (self-propelled)
YOGN	Gasoline Barge (non-self-propelled)
YON	Fuel Oil Barge (non-self-propelled)
YOS	Oil Storage Barge (non-self-propelled)
YP	Patrol Craft (self-propelled)
YPD	Floating Pile Driver (non-self-propelled)
YR	Floating Workshop (non-self-propelled)
YRB	Repair and Berthing Barge (non-self-propelled)
YRBM	Repair, Berthing, and Messing Barge (non-self-propelled)
YRBM (L)	Repair, Berthing, and Messing Barge (large) (non-self-propelled)
YRDH	Floating Dry Dock Workshop (hull) (non-self-propelled)
YRDM	Floating Dry Dock Workshop (machine) (non-self-propelled)
YRR	Radiological Repair Barge (non-self-propelled)
YRST	Salvage Craft Tender (non-self-propelled)
YSD	Seaplane Wrecking Derrick (self-propelled)
YSR	Sludge Removal Barge (non-self-propelled)
YTB	Large Harbor Tug (self-propelled)
YTL	Small Harbor Tug (self-propelled)
YTM	Medium Harbor Tug (self-propelled)
YV	Drone Aircraft Catapult Control Craft (self-propelled)
YW	Water Barge (self-propelled)
YWN	Water Barge (non-self-propelled)

B. Fleet Status Abbreviations

AA	Active, in commission, Atlantic
AR	In reserve, out of commission, Atlantic (since end of WW II)
AR*	In reserve, out of commission, Atlantic (since end of Korean War)
ASA	Active, in service, Atlantic
ASR*	In reserve, out of service, Atlantic
DAR	Scheduled for disposal, in reserve, out of commission, Atlantic
DPR	Scheduled for disposal, in reserve, out of commission, Pacific
DTAR	Scheduled for disposal, in MSC Atlantic Reserve
DTPR	Scheduled for disposal, in MSC Pacific Reserve
GLA	Active, Great Lakes
MARAD	Transferred to MARAD permanently, but not stricken from NVR (see section 14)
MSC	Assigned to Military Sealift Command (see section 8)
NRT	Assigned to Naval Reserve Training (see section 7)
PA	Active, in commission, Pacific
PR	In reserve, out of commission, Pacific (since end of WW II)
PR*	In reserve, out of commission, Pacific (since end of Korean War)
PSA	Active, in service, Pacific
PSR*	In reserve, out of service, Pacific
SPEC	In special status
Struck	Struck from NVR after completion of manuscript (see section 14)
TAA	Active, MSC, Atlantic
TAR	In reserve, MSC, Atlantic
TFEA	Active, MSC, Far East
TFER	In reserve, MSC, Far East
TPA	Active, MSC, Pacific
TPR	In reserve, MSC, Pacific
TWWR	Active, MSC, World-wide routes

C. Shipbuilders

Alabama	Alabama Dry Dock and Shipbuilding Corporation, Mobile, Ala.
Albina	Albina Engine and Machine Works, Inc., Portland, Ore.
American	American Shipbuilding Company, Toledo, Ohio
Avondale	Avondale Shipyards, Inc., Westwego, La.
Bath Iron	Bath Iron Works Corporation, Bath, Me.
Beth., Baltimore	Bethlehem Steel Corporation, Baltimore, Md.
Beth., Fore River	Bethlehem Steel Corporation, Fore River, Mass.
Beth., Hingham	Bethlehem Steel Corporation, Hingham, Mass.
Beth., Quincy	Bethlehem Steel Corporation, Quincy, Mass.
Beth., San Pedro	Bethlehem Steel Corporation, San Pedro, Cal.
Beth., S.F.	Bethlehem Steel Corporation, San Francisco, Cal.
Beth., Sparrows Pt.	Bethlehem Steel Corporation, Sparrows Point, Md.
Beth., Staten Is.	Bethlehem Steel Corporation, Staten Island, N.Y.
Boeing, Seattle	The Boeing Company, Seattle, Wash.
Boatservice, Norway	Boatservice Ltd. A/S, Mandel, Norway
Boland	Boland Machine Manufacturing Company, New Orleans, La.
Boston Navy	Boston Naval Shipyard, Boston, Mass.
Brooks	Brooks Marine, Lowestoft, England
Brown, Houston	Brown Shipbuilding Company, Houston, Tex.
Charleston Navy	Charleston Naval Shipyard, Charleston, S.C.
Christy	Christy Corporation, Sturgeon Bay, Wisc.
Consol. Steel	Consolidated Steel Corporation, Orange, Tex.
Cramp	Cramp Shipbuilding Company, Philadelphia, Pa.
Defoe	Defoe Shipbuilding Company, Bay City, Mich.

Dillingham	Dillingham Shipyard, Honolulu, Hawaii
Dravo, Neville Is.	Dravo Corporation, Neville Island, Pa.
Electric Boat	Electric Boat Company, Groton, Conn.
Federal	Federal Shipbuilding and Drydock Company, Kearny, N.J.
Gen. Dyn., Groton	General Dynamics Corporation, Electric Boat Division, Groton, Conn.
Gen. Dyn., Quincy	General Dynamics Corporation, Quincy Shipbuilding Division, Quincy, Mass.
Gibbs	Gibbs Corporation, Jacksonville, Fla.
Grumman	Grumman Aircraft, Stuart, Fla.
Gulf, Chickasaw	Gulf Shipbuilding Corporation, Chickasaw, Ala.
Ingalls	Ingalls Shipbuilding Division, Litton Systems Inc., Pascagoula, Miss.
LB Navy	Long Beach Naval Shipyard, Long Beach, Cal.
Lockheed	Lockheed Shipbuilding and Construction Company, Seattle, Wash.
Lockheed, Sunnyvale	Lockheed Missile and Space Company, Sunnyvale, Cal.
Manitowoc	Manitowoc Shipbuilding Company, Manitowoc, Wisc.
Mare Island	Mare Island Naval Shipyard, Vallejo, Cal.
Marinette	Marinette Marine Corporation, Marinette, Wisc.
Marietta	Marietta Manufacturing Company, Marietta, W. Va.
National Steel	National Steel and Shipbuilding Company, San Diego, Cal.
Newport News	Newport News Shipbuilding and Drydock Company, Newport News, Va.
Norfolk Navy	Norfolk Naval Shipyard, Norfolk, Va.
Norfolk SB & DD	Norfolk Shipbuilding and Drydock Company
NW Marine	Northwest Marine Iron Works, Portland, Ore.
NY Navy	New York Naval Shipyard, Brooklyn, N.Y.
NY Shipbuilding	New York Shipbuilding Corporation, Camden, N.J.
Peterson	Peterson Builders, Inc., Sturgeon Bay, Wisc.
Phil. Navy	Philadelphia Naval Shipyard, Philadelphia, Pa.
Portsmouth Navy	Portsmouth Naval Shipyard, Kittery, Me.
PS B & DD	Puget Sound Bridge and Dry Dock Company, Bremerton, Wash.
PS Navy	Puget Sound Naval Shipyard, Seattle, Wash.
Pullman	Pullman Standard Car Manufacturing Company, Chicago, Ill.
Seattle-Tacoma	Seattle-Tacoma Shipbuilding Corporation, Seattle, Wash.
Sewart Seacraft	Teledyne, Inc., Sewart Seacraft Division, Berwick, La.
SF Navy	San Francisco Naval Shipyard, San Francisco, Cal.
Tacoma	Tacoma Boat Building Company, Tacoma, Wash.
Tampa	Tampa Shipbuilding Company, Tampa, Fla.
Todd	Todd Shipyards Corporation
Todd-Pacific	Todd-Pacific Shipyard, Seattle, Wash.
Todd, San Pedro	Todd Shipyards Corporation, San Pedro, Cal.
Todd, Seattle	Todd Shipyards Corporation, Seattle, Wash.
Trumpy	John Trumpy and Sons, Inc., Annapolis, Md.
Upper Clyde, Scot.	Upper Clyde Shipbuilding, Glasgow, Scotland
Western	Western Pipe and Steel Company, Los Angeles, Cal.
Wheeler	Wheeler Shipbuilding Company, Whitestone, N.Y.
Willamette	Willamette Iron and Steel Corporation, Portland, Ore.

D. Engine Manufacturers

A.C.	Allis Chalmers
Alco	American Locomotive Co.
Beth.	Bethlehem Steel Co.
B.S.	Busch-Sulzer
B & W	Babcock and Wilcox Co.
C.B.	Cooper Bessemer
C.E.	Combustion Engineering
C.H.	Cutler-Hammer
CTC	Caterpillar Tractor Co.
DeLaval	DeLaval Turbine Co.
Detroit	Detroit Diesel Co.
Ell.	Elliott Co.
Enterprise	Enterprise Diesel Co.
F.M.	Fairbanks, Morse Co.
F.W.	Foster Wheeler
G.E.	General Electric
G.M.	General Motors
Gen. Mach.	General Machine Co.
Grey	Grey Marine Diesel Co.
Harn.	Harnischfeger Corp.
N.D.	Napier Deltic Co.
N.N.	Newport News Shipbuilding and Dry Dock Co.
Nordberg	Nordberg Diesel Co.
NYS	New York Shipbuilding Corp.
Packard	Packard Diesel Co.
Paxman	Paxman Diesel Co.
Proteus	Bristol Siddeley Marine Proteus Co.
R.R.	Rolls Royce
Skinner	Skinner-Unaflow Co.
West.	Westinghouse
Winton	Winton Diesel Co.

E. Miscellaneous Abbreviations

AA	Antiaircraft
AAW	Anti-air warfare
ASROC	Antisubmarine rocket
ASW	Antisubmarine warfare
B	Boilers
BPDMS	Basic point defense missile system
D	Diesels
DEW	Distant early warning
ECM	Electronic countermeasures
ECCM	Electronic counter-countermeasures
EM	Electric motors
FAST	Fast automatic shuttle transfer system
FRAM I	Fleet rehabilitation and modernization program (extended ship's life 8 years)
FRAM II	Fleet rehabilitation and modernization program (extended ship's life 5 years)
F/S	Fleet status
FY	Fiscal year
GT	Geared turbines
ILP (ex-MDAP)	International logistics program
Mack	Combination mast and smoke stack
MARAD (ex-MARCOMM)	Maritime Administration
MARCOMM	Maritime Commission
MDAP	Military defense assistance pact
MK	Mark
mm	Millimeter
Mod	Modification
NRT	Naval reserve training
NTDS	Naval tactical data system
NVR	Naval Vessel Register
PUFFS	Passive underwater fire control feasibility system
R	Reactors
RS	Reciprocating steam
RAP	Rocket-assisted projectiles
SCB	Ship Characteristics Board
SINS	Ship inertial navigation system
ST	Steam turbines
SUBROC	Submarine rocket
SUBSAFE	Submarine safety program
TACAN	Tactical air navigation
VDS	Variable depth sonar
VTOL	Vertical takeoff and landing

ADDENDA:

Closed 27 September 1971

1. WARSHIPS

B. SURFACE COMBATANTS

Los Angeles (CA-135) had her name cancelled 5–5–71. *Richmond K. Turner* (DLG-20) started her AAW modernization on 5–5–71. *Luce* (DLG-7) recommissioned on 5–22–71 after her AAW modernization for duty with the Atlantic Fleet. First of the DXGs to be built under FY 1975. Approximately 28 units will be built. *McCaffery* (DD-860) is active in the Atlantic Fleet, not in reserve. *Arnold J. Isbell* (DD-869) will replace *Maddox* (DD-731) in 5–72 as Naval Reserve Training Ship at Long Beach. *Johnston* (DD-821) was commissioned on 8–23–46, not 10–10–45. *Ingraham* (DD-694) was sold to Greece on 7–16–71, after being struck, as *Miaoulis* (D-211). *Strong* (DD-758) will replace *Harwood* (DD-861) as Naval Reserve Training Ship at Charleston in 11–71. *Harwood* (DD-861) will be loaned to Turkey. *Miller* (DD-535) had her name changed to *James Miller* on 8–5–71. *Cowell* (DD-547) and *Braine* (DD-630) were both struck on 8–17–71 and sold to Argentina on the same date as *Almirante Storni* (D-24) and *Almirante Domecq Garcia* (D-25) respectively. *Twining* (DD-540) was struck on 8–1–71 and sold to Taiwan on 8–16–71. *Mullany* (DD-528) was struck on 10–6–71 and sold to Taiwan on the same date as *Ching Yang* (DD-9).

C. OCEAN ESCORTS

Brewton (DE-1086) will be assigned to the Atlantic Fleet upon commissioning. *Kirk* (DE-1087) will be assigned to the Pacific Fleet upon commissioning. *Conolly* (DE-1073) had her name changed to *Robert E. Peary* on 5–12–71. DE-1090 has been named *Ainsworth* and DE-1091 has been named *Miller*. *Reasoner* (DE-1063) was commissioned 7–31–71. *Downes* (DE-1071) was commissioned 8–28–71. *Fanning* (DE-1076) was commissioned 7–23–71. *Paul* (DE-1080) was commissioned 8–14–71. *Aylwin* (DE-1081) was commissioned 9–18–71. *Forster* (DER-334) was transferred to Vietnam on 9–25–71 as *Tran Khanh Du* (HQ-04).

E. SUBMARINES

Lewis and Clark is now active in the Pacific Fleet. *James Madison* (SSBN-627) deployed with the first POSEIDON missiles on 3–31–71. SSBN's 655/659 will receive POSEIDON refits under FY 1972 or later. *Casimir Pulaski* (SSBN-633) completed her POSEIDON refit on 4–30–71. Contract for the POSEIDON conversion of *Kamehameha* (SSBN-642) was awarded on 7–12–71 to General Dynamics, Groton. Conversion begun on 7–15–71. Contract for the POSEIDON conversion of *James K. Polk* (SSBN-645) was awarded to Newport News SB & DD Co. on 7–16–71. *George C. Marshall* (SSBN-654) POSEIDON conversion contract was awarded to Puget Sound Naval Shipyard on 8–15–71. Conversion begun 9–15–71. *Patrick Henry* (SSBN-599) was transferred to the Atlantic Fleet 12–2–71. *Redfish* (SSN-680) had her name changed to *William H. Bates* on 6–25–71. Upon commissioning *William H. Bates* and *Batfish* will be assigned to the Atlantic Fleet. *Pintado* (SSN-672) was commissioned 9–11–71. *Sandlance* (SSN-660) was commissioned 9–25–71. *Menhaden* (SS–377) was decommissioned 8–13–71 at San Diego and laid up in reserve. *Cubera* (SS-347) and *Grampus* (SS-523) will be decommissioned in early 1972. *Grampus* will be struck. *Becuna* (AGSS-319), *Blenny* (AGSS-324), *Atule* (AGSS-403), *Sea Poacher* (AGSS-406) and *Tench* (AGSS-417) were reclassified back to SS on 6–30–71. *Catfish* (SS-339) and *Chivo* (SS-341) were struck on 7–1–71 and sold to Argentina on the same date as *Sante Fe* (S-14) and *Santiago Del Estero* (S-13) respectively. The two submarines that previously bore these names, *Lamprey* (SS-372) and *Macabi* (SS-375), were returned to the U.S. Navy, struck, and sold to Argentina for cannibalization and scrapping on 9–1–71. *Ronquil* (SS-396) was struck and sold to Spain 7–1–71 as S-32. *Pomfret* (SS-391) and *Thornback* (SS-418) were loaned to Turkey on 7–1–71 as *Oruc Reis* (S-337) and *Uluc Ali Reis* (S-338) respectively. *Silversides* (AGSS-236), if not memorialized, will be sunk as target.

F. PATROL SHIPS

Benicia (PG-96) was transferred to Korea on 10–15–71 as *Paekku* (PGM-11). She is the first ship less than 10 years old that has been transferred to a foreign country under the International Logistics Program (formerly Military Defense Assistance Pact).

2. AMPHIBIOUS WARFARE SHIPS

Pocono (LCC-16) was decommissioned 9–16–71 at Norfolk. *Rankin* (LKA-103), *Seminole* (LKA-104), and *Vermilion* (LKA-107) were transferred to the temporary custody of MARAD for layup on 8–12–71, 5–20–71, and 7–27–71 respectively. All remain on the Naval Vessel Register and are laid up at Suisun Bay (104) and James River (remainder). *Ponce* (LPD-15) was commissioned 7–10–71. *Arneb* (LKA-56) was decommissioned 8–12–71. She will be disposed of. *Perch* (LPSS-313) was reclassified as IXSS-313 and rerated as a service craft on 6–30–71. *George W. Ingram* (APD-43) and *Blessman* (APD-48) were struck, sold to Taiwan on 1–1–67 and 6–1–67 respectively. *William M. Hobby* (APD-95) was struck, transferred to Korea on 5–1–67. *San Marcos* (LSD-25) was decommissioned on 7–1–71 and loaned to Spain as *Galicia* (TA-31). *Boulder* (LST-1190) was commissioned 6–4–71. *Racine* (LST-1191) was commissioned 7–9–71. *Harlan County* (LST-1196) and *Barnstable County* (LST-1197) will be assigned to the Atlantic Fleet upon commissioning. *Walworth County* (LST-1164) was decommissioned 4–71. *Wexford County* (LST-1168) and *Terrebonne Parish* (LST-1156) will be transferred to Spain on 10–30–71. *Tom Green County* (LST-1159) will be transferred to Spain in 1–72. *Vernon County* (LST-1161) and *Washtenaw County* (LST-1166) will decommission in 1972. *Graham County* (LST-1176) and *Lorain County* (LST-1177) will decommission in 1972. *Park County* (LST-1077) was transferred to Mexico 9–20–71 as *Rio Parnuco. Holmes County* (LST-836) was transferred to Singapore on 7–1–71 as *Endurance* (A-81). LST-572 is operated by MSC as a research ship. LST-488 is operated by MSC as a research ship.

3. MINE WARFARE SHIPS

Harry F. Bauer (MMD-26) and *Gwin* (MMD-33) were struck on 8–15–71 and scrapped. *Hummingbird* (MSC-192) was transferred to Indonesia on 7–12–71 as *Pulau Ampalasha* (720). *Frigate Bird* (MSC-191) was transferred to Indonesia on 8–11–71 as *Pulau Antung* (721). *Falcon* (MSC-190) and *Limpkin* (MSC-195) were transferred to Indonesia on 6–24–71 as *Pulau Aru* (722) and *Pulau Anjer* (719) respectively. *Conflict* (MSO-426), and *Guide* (MSO-447) will decommission in 1972. One of these ships will be transferred to Spain. *Dynamic* (MSO-432), *Pivot* (MSO-463), and *Persistant* (MSO-491) were transferred to Spain on 7–1–71 as *Guadalete* (M-41), *Guadalmednia* (M-42), and *Guadalquivir* (M-43) respectively. *Esteem* (MSO-438) was recommissioned 8–27–71 after undergoing an extensive modernization. Active Pacific Fleet.

4. COMBATANT CRAFT

Flagstaff (PGH-1) was fitted with 1 single 152mm, in lieu of her forward single 40mm, in early 1971 for tests. PTF-3, 5, 6, and 7 were transferred to Vietnam on 1–26–65.

5. AUXILIARY SHIPS

Firedrake (AE-14) and *Paricutin* (AE-18) were transferred to the temporary custody of MARAD, for layup, on 7–21–71 and 7–29–71 respectively. Both remain on the Naval Vessel Register and are laid up at Suisun Bay. *Mauna Loa* (AE-8) was transferred to the temporary custody of MARAD, for layup, on 7–8–71. She remains on the NVR and is berthed at James River. On 8–16–71 while moored in Hong Kong harbor, *Regulus* (AF-57) broke her moorings during a typhoon and ran hard aground. Extensive hull damage resulted. Rated as beyond economical repair, she was struck on 9–10–71 and will be scrapped "where is as is". *Coastal Crusader* (AGS-36) was transferred to the permanent custody of MARAD, for layup, on 4–1–70. She remains on the NVR and is berthed at Suisun Bay. *Sword Knot* (AGM-13), the last active ship of her class, was transferred to the permanent custody of MARAD, on 4–7–71, for layup. She remains on the NVR and is berthed at Suisun Bay. *Hayes* (AGOR-16) was completed on 7–21–71 and transferred to MSC for service. *Hunterdon County* (AGP-838), the last active ship of her class, was transferred to Malaysia on 7–1–71 for further service. *Cod* (AGSS-224), *Angler* (AGSS-240), *Croaker* (AGSS-246), *Rasher* (AGSS-269), *Bowfin* (AGSS-287), *Ling* (AGSS-297), *Lionfish* (AGSS-298), *Roncador* (AGSS-301), *Charr* (AGSS-328), *Carp* (AGSS-338), *Chopper* (AGSS-342), *Pampanito* (AGSS-383), *Torsk* (AGSS-423), *Runner* (AGSS-476) and *Requin* (AGSS-471) were all reclassified to IXSS, with the same hull number, on 6–30–71. This was the first phase of the eventual phase-out of all nonoperational submarine trainers. *Chopper* (IXSS-342) was later struck on 10–1–71. *Mark* (AKL-12) was decommissioned and transferred to Taiwan on 7–1–71. *Brule* (AKL-28), the last active ship of her type, was decommissioned and transferred to Korea on 11–1–71. *Croatan* (AKV-43), *Core* (AKV-41), *Card* (AKV-40), *Point Cruz* (AKV-19) and *Kula Gulf* (AKV-8) were struck from the Naval Vessel Register on 9–15–70 and transferred to MARAD for sale as scrap. *Breton* (AKV-42) was struck on 8–6–71 and scrapped. *Cohoes* (ANL-78) is scheduled for decommissioning. *Amphion* (AR-13) was decommissioned on 10–1–71 and leased to Iran. *Tutuila* (ARG-4), the last active ship of her class, is scheduled for decommissioning and strike. *Askari* (ARL-30) was decommissioned and transferred to Indonesia on 8–31–71 as *Djaja Widjaja. Sphinx* (ARL-24) was decommissioned on 9–30–71 at Bremerton. *Indra* (ARL-37) was decommissioned 4–70. *Satyr* (ARL-23) was decommissioned on 10–15–71. *Krishna* (ARL-38), the last active ship of her class, was decommissioned on 10–30–71 and transferred to the Philippines. *Dixon* (AS-37) was commissioned on 8–7–71 for duty with the Pacific Fleet. She replaced *Nereus* (AS-17) which decommissioned at Mare Island on 10–21–71. *Pelias* (AS-14) was struck on 8–1–71 and transferred to MARAD for disposal. The unnamed (ATA-240) was struck on 8–4–71 and transferred to the Army for cannibalization and scrapping. *Koka* (ATA-185) was decommissioned on 9–1–71 and transferred to the Department of Health, Education, and Welfare for further service in American Samoa. *Wandank* (ATA-204) was decommissioned on 7–1–71 and transferred to the Department of Interior for further service in the Pacific Trust Territories. *Tillamook* (ATA-192) was decommissioned on 7–1–71 (not 7–25–71) and was transferred to the Korean equivalent of the Coast and Geodetic Survey, via the State Department, as *Tan Yung. Kalmia* (ATA-184) was decommissioned and transferred to Columbia on 7–1–71 as *Bahia Utria* (RM-75). *Mahopac* (ATA-196) was decommissioned and transferred to Taiwan on 7–1–71. *Umpaqua* (ATA-209) was decommissioned and transferred to Columbia on 7–1–71 as *Bahia Honda. Utina* (ATF-163) was decommissioned and leased to Venezuela on 9–3–71 as *Felipe Larrazabal. Kiowa* (ATF-72) and *Sioux* (ATF-75) will be decommissioned in 1972 and replaced by *Brunswick* (ATS-3) and *Beaufort* (ATS-2). *Seneca* (ATF-91) was decommissioned on 7–1–71. *Arikara* (ATF-98) was decommissioned on 7–1–71 and transferred to Chile as *Aldea* (ATF-63). Upon commissioning, *Ortolan* (ASR-22) will be assigned to the Pacific Fleet. *Namakagon* (AOG-53), formerly on loan to New Zealand, was returned to the U.S. Navy on 6–29–71 and leased to Taiwan on the same date.

6. SERVICE CRAFT

ARCO (ARD-29) may be leased to Iran. On 1 June 1971, the following service craft were instated on the Naval Vessel Register: *Alvin* became *Alvin* (DSV-2), *Turtle* became *Turtle* (DSV-3), *Sea Cliff* became *Sea Cliff* (DSV-4), and *Nemo* became *Nemo* (DSV-5). On the same date, the four craft were placed in service. On 1 June 1971, *Trieste II* (X-2) was reclassified DSV-1. A new construction DSV has been dropped. On 1 June 1971, LCU-1488, 1491, and 1609 were reclassified YFU-94/96. Army Craft BD-6631 was instated on the NVR, and placed in service, as YD-232. In Part B of this section in the text, make the following changes to the totals in the summary of minor service craft: delete 1 ARD, 1 YAG, 4 YC, add 2 YD, 2 YDT, delete 3 YF, *Suitland* (YF-336) is now *Suitland* (YDT-15), add 12 YFD, delete 4 YFN, 1 YFNB, 1 YFND, add 1 YFP, 1 YFRT, 3 YFU, delete 3 YLLC, delete YM remarks (add in its place YM-36 is named *Schweizer*), add 4 YM, delete 2

YNG, 1 YOG, 1 YOGN, 1 YPD, add 1 YR, delete 1 YRB, 1 YRBM, 1 YSD, add 1 YTB (increase total under construction to 18), delete 4 YTL and 2 YTM. In the "Names of Large Harbor Tugs (YTB) and Medium Harbor Tugs (YTM)" table, delete the following names and hull numbers: *Osceola* (YTM-129), *Conchardee* (YTM-412), and *Makah* (YTM-772). To the YTB section, add the hull numbers YTB-816/827. None is yet named.

7. NAVAL RESERVE TRAINING SHIPS

Delete *Chopper* (AGSS-342). She was not replaced.

8. MILITARY SEALIFT COMMAND

USNS *Wilkes* (T-AGS-33) was assigned to MSC Atlantic for duty.

10. MISSILES

ZAGM-84A is HARPOON, an anti-ship missile capable of launch from ships or aircraft. The missile is being developed by McDonnell Douglas.

11. U.S. COAST GUARD

A new icebreaker, numbered WAGB-10, is to be built by Lockheed SB & Construction Co. She will be the world's most powerful icebreaker. A class of 4 is projected to replace the 7 *"Wind"* class breakers. This ship will displace 12,000 tons, have a length of 400 feet, and have a shaft horsepower of 60,000. *Westwind* (WAGB-281) was placed "in commission, special" on 9–15–71 as a result of heavy damage suffered from an unknown cause. She will be laid up at Curtis Bay, with a skeleton crew of 40 men, until FY 1973 when funds will become available for her repair. *Edisto* (WAGB-284) had her homeport changed from Boston to Milwaukee on 12–1–71. *Tamarack* (WLI-248) was sold for scrapping on 8–2–71. *Willow* (WLB-332) was sold for scrapping on 7–28–71.

12. FOREIGN TRANSFERS

St. George (AV-16) was sold to Italy on 12–10–68 as *Andrea Bafile* (A-5314). *Macomb* (DD-458) has been named *Hsuen Yang* (DD-16), replacing the ex-USS *Rodman* (DD-456) which had previously borne the name. *Rodman* and *Ellyson* (DD-454) will be scrapped. The Mexican name of *Harrison* (DD-573) is *Cuitlahuac*. The Mexican name of *John Rogers* (DD-574) is *Cuantemoc*. Both will be used as gunboats. The Iranian names of *Gainard* (DD-706) and *Zellars* (DD-777) are *Babr* (DD-2) and *Palang* (DD-3) respectively. *Windsor* (ARD-22) was transferred to Taiwan on 6–1–71.

13. RECLASSIFIED AND RENAMED SHIPS

The following service craft have been reclassified or instated on the Naval Vessel Register and placed in service. On 1 April 1971, YF-294 was reclassified YDT-14, *Suitland* (YF-336) was reclassified *Suitland* (YDT-15), YF-852 was reclassified YFRT-523, YFN-1162 was reclassified YFP-13, LCU-1620 and 1625 were reclassified YFU-92/93, several barges lashed together for sonar tests were instated on the Naval Vessel Register as IX-310 and placed in service, and ex-Army craft BD-3031 was instated on the NVR as YD-231.

14. STRIKE LIST

The following ships, not already mentioned in the text or the preceding sections of the Addenda, were struck from the Naval Vessel Register on the indicated dates:

A. COMMISSIONED USN SHIPS

Poole (DE-151) was struck on 1–2–71. *Baltimore* (CA-68) was struck on 2–15–71. *Fall River* (CA-131) was struck on 2–19–71. *Mingo* (SS-261) was returned from loan to Japan and struck 2–20–71. *Gainard* (DD-706) was struck on 2–26–71. *Swanson* (DD-443) and ex-*Wilkes* (DD-441) were struck on 3–1–71. *Zellars* (DD-777) was struck on 3–19–71. *Albert W. Grant* (DD-649) was struck on 4–14–71. *Bennion* (DD-662) was struck on 4–15–71. *Gherardi* (DD-637), *Farenholt* (DD-491), *Grayson* (DD-435), *Frankford* (DD-497), *Boyle* (DD-600), *Meade* (DD-602), *Bancroft* (DD-598), *Kearny* (DD-432), and *Hambleton* (DD-455) were all struck on 6–1–71. *Halfbeak* (SS-352), *Catfish* (SS-339), *Chivo* (SS-341), *Ronquil* (SS-396), *Sabalo* (SS-302), *Woolsey* (DD-437), *Fitch* (DD-462), *Carmick* (DD-493), *Parker* (DD-604), *Coghlan* (DD-606), *Frazier* (DD-607), *Gansevoort* (DD-608), *Gillespie* (DD-609), *Hobby* (DD-610), *Laub* (DD-613), *MacKenzie* (DD-614), *McLanahan* (DD-615), *Ordronaux* (DD-617), *Edwards* (DD-619), *Jeffers* (DD-621), *Thompson* (DD-627), *Herndon* (DD-638), *Stockton* (DD-646) and *Thorn* (DD-647) were all struck on 7–1–71. *Icefish* (SS-367) was returned from loan to the Netherlands and struck on 7–15–71. *Lamprey* (SS-372) and *Macabi* (SS-375) were returned from loan to Argentina and struck on 9–1–71. *Merrill* (DE-392) was struck 4–2–71.

Robert H. Smith (MMD-23) was struck on 2–26–71. *Harry F. Bauer* (MMD-26), and *Gwin* (MMD-33) were struck on 8–15–71.

Pine Island (AV-12) and *Salisbury Sound* (AV-13) were struck on 2–1–71. *Virgo* (AE-30) was struck on 2–18–71. *Currituck* (AV-7), *Chandeleur* (AV-10), *Cape Gloucester* (AKV-9), *Commencement Bay* (AKV-37), and *Rendova* (AKV-14) were struck on 4–1–71. *Taurus* (AKR-8) was struck on 6–22–71 (2 years after she was scrapped). *Rabaul* (AKV-21), the last of her type on the NVR, was struck 9–1–71.

B. NON-COMMISSIONED USN CRAFT

Granville S. Hall (YAG-40) was struck on 5–1–71. YSR-10, YTM-538, YFB-65, and YFB-66 were struck on 1–1–71. YD-227 was struck on 4–1–71. YO-70, YFP-1 were struck on 5–1–71. YFU-63, YSD-76, YTM-128, 275 were struck on 6–1–71. YAG-60 (ex-*Butternut* ANL-9), YG-31, ARD-10, and YM-12 were struck on 7–1–71. YTL-456, 452, 586, 457, YRBM-17, YOG-131, YLLC-1, 3, 5 were struck on 7–15–71. YFU-47, YNG-16, YFU-8, YSD-44, YNG-4, YPD-44 were struck on 8–1–71. YTM-412, YFND-10, YRB-6, YFD-15 were struck on 9–1–71. YFN-1185, 995, YTM-772, YC-790, YC-808 were struck on 10–1–71.

15. NAVAL SHIPS IN THE MARAD RESERVE FLEET

As of the closing of the Addenda there were 381 former navy vessels in the Maritime Reserve Fleet.

On 1 September 1971, the following ships were transferred from the temporary to the permanent custody of MARAD: *Hyades* (AF-28), *Altair* (AKS-32), *Thuban* (LKA-19), *Fremont* (LPA-44), *Sabine* (AO-25), *Algol* (LKA-54), *Bald Eagle* (AF-50), *Blue Jacket* (AF-51), *Taconic* (LCC-17), *Sandoval* (LPA-194), *Mountrail* (LPA-213), *Capricornus* (LKA-57), *Shadwell* (LSD-15), *Rushmore* (LSD-14), *Casa Grande* (LSD-13), *Ozark* (MCS-2), *Keywadin* (ATA-213), *Stallion* (ATA-190), *Samoset* (ATA-193), *Whetstone* (LSD-27), *Estes* (LCC-12), *Pickaway* (LPA-222), *Navarro* (LPA-215), *Kennebec* (AO-36), *Union* (LKA-107), *Washburn* (LKA-108), *Colonial* (LSD-18), *Tappahannock* (AO-43), *Mount McKinley* (LCC-7), *Pvt. Jose E. Valdez* (AG-169), *Mauna Loa* (AE-8). *Mission Capistrano* (AG-162), *Zelima* (AF-49), *Tortuga* (LSD-26) and *Muliphen* (LKA-61). All of the preceding vessels still remain on the Naval Vessel Register.

Add the following vessels to the MARAD list: *Virgo* (AE-30), having been struck on 2–18–71, was transferred to MARAD for disposal and is temporarily berthed at Suisun Bay. *Cambria* (LPA-36), having been struck on 9–14–70, was transferred to MARAD and laid up at James River. *Catskill* (MCS-1), having been struck on 11–20–70, was transferred to MARAD and laid up at Suisun Bay.

Delete the following vessels from the MARAD list: *Card* (AKV-40), *Breton* (AKV-42), *Aloe* (AN-6), *Ash* (AN-7), *Palm* (AN-28), *Platte* (AO-24), *Chemung* (AO-30), *Mission San Rafael* (AO-130), *Mission Santa Cruz* (AO-133), unnamed (ATA-241), unnamed (ATA-242), unnamed (ATA-243), and *Pawnee* (ATF-74).

INDEX

(Hull numbers in parentheses indicates former classification)

(Hull numbers in parentheses indicates former classification)

(Hull numbers in parentheses indicates former classification)

(Hull numbers in parentheses indicates former classification)

(Hull numbers in parentheses indicates former classification)

Designed by Edward Martin Wilson.

Composed in seven-point Univers with two points of leading by
Tinker N. A. Corporation, New York, New York.

Printed offset on fifty-pound Banta Pigmented Offset and bound in twelve-point
Carolina Coated Cover by the George Banta Company, Menasha, Wisconsin.